Hinduism

A SHORT HISTORY

OTHER BOOKS IN THIS SERIES:

Buddhism: A Short Introduction, Klaus K. Klostermaier, ISBN 1–85168–186–8
Buddhism: A Short History, Edward Conze, ISBN 1–85168–221–X
Hinduism: A Short Introduction, Klaus K. Klostermaier, ISBN 1–85168–220–1
Hindu Writings: A Short Introduction to the Major Sources, Klaus K. Klostermaier, ISBN 1–85168–230–9
Islam: A Short History, William Montgomery Watt, ISBN 1–85168–205–8
A Short Introduction to Islamic Philosophy, Theology and Mysticism, Majid Fakhry, ISBN 1–85168–134–5
Muhammad: A Short Biography, Martin Forward, ISBN 1–85168–131–0
Jesus Christ: A Short Biography, Martin Forward, ISBN 1–85168–172–8
Judaism: A Short History, Lavinia and Dan Cohn-Sherbok, ISBN 1–85168–206–6
Judaism: A Short Introduction, Lavinia and Dan Cohn-Sherbok, ISBN 1–85168–207–4
A Short Reader in Judaism, Lavinia and Dan Cohn-Sherbok, ISBN 1–85168–112–4
A Short Introduction to the Old Testament Prophets, E. W. Heaton, ISBN 1–85168–114–0
Sufism: A Short Introduction, William C. Chittick, ISBN 1–85168–211–2
The Bahá'í Faith: A Short History, Peter Smith, ISBN 1–85168–208–2
The Bahá'í Faith: A Short Introduction, Moojan Momen, ISBN 1–85168–209–0

RELATED TITLES PUBLISHED BY ONEWORLD:

A Concise Encyclopedia of Hinduism, Klaus K. Klostermaier, ISBN 1–85168–175–2
The Bhagavad Gita: A Verse Translation, Geoffrey Parrinder, ISBN 1–85168–117–5
Hindu and Muslim Mysticism, R. C. Zaehner, ISBN 1–85168–046–2

Hinduism

A SHORT HISTORY

Klaus K. Klostermaier

ONEWORLD
OXFORD

HINDUISM: A SHORT HISTORY

Oneworld Publications
(Sales and Editorial)
185 Banbury Road
Oxford OX2 7AR
England
http://www.oneworld-publications.com

Oneworld Publications
(US Marketing Office)
160 N. Washington St.
4th Floor, Boston
MA 02114
USA

A CIP record for this title is available
from the British Library and the Library of Congress

ISBN 1–85168–213–9

Cover design by Design Deluxe
Typeset by LaserScript Limited, Mitcham, Surrey
Printed and bound in England by Clays Ltd, St Ives plc

CONTENTS

PREFACE

Hinduism: A Short History is the second in a series that comprises *Hinduism: A Short Introduction* (Oneworld, 1998) and *Hindu Writings: A Short Introduction to the Major Sources* (to be published later this year).

A History of Hinduism, with all the controversy that surrounds the very term "Hinduism," and in the absence of a commonly agreed upon periodization of the intellectual development of India, is necessarily an interpretative construct, built on many assumptions. Chapter 1, The Introduction, lays out alternative schemata underlying such an undertaking and also gives a short survey of the sources upon which it rests. Chapter 2, a short history of two prominent Hindu centers – Mathurā and Vārāṇasī – mirrors like a microcosm the vicissitues of Hinduism over several thousands of years. Chapter 3 tells the controversial story of the beginnings of Hinduism. This is followed by a short history of the Vedic Indra religion. One chapter each is then devoted to the parallel histories of Vaiṣṇavism, Śaivism and Śāktism, the three major branches of "mainstream Hinduism," followed by a chapter on the Smārtas, the non-sectarian orthodox Hindus. Chapter 9 deals with the history of Hindu philosophy, which was always intimately connected with Hindu religion. The last chapter is devoted to Modern Hinduism, covering the new movements of the nineteenth and twentieth centuries; it also discusses the present situation and future prospects of Hinduism. A fairly extensive Glossary offers translations and explanations of Sanskrit terms used. The Select Bibliography documents the literature referred to, and offers suggestions for further reading in the history of Hinduism.

The book is intended for the non-specialist reader. However, ample documentation has been provided with numerous references both to original sources and to scholarly literature, which will enable the serious student to follow up the issues mentioned. Hindu source literature available in original languages and in translations, as well as secondary literature on Hinduism, in a great number of modern languages, has become extremely vast. Rich resources for the study of each and every aspect of the history of Hinduism mentioned in this book are available today to continue reading for an entire lifetime.

Gratitude is due to all the scholars whose work has been made use of, as acknowleged. Special thanks to Harold Coward (University of Victoria) for numerous detailed suggestions for improvement of the typescript. My thanks also extend to the friendly and efficient staff of Oneworld Publications, Oxford, for their unfailing courtesy and cooperation.

Klaus K. Klostermaier
Winnipeg, August 1, 1999

1 INTRODUCTION

WHAT IS HINDUISM?

Hinduism is unlike any of the other major historic religions. It does not claim an identifiable human founder or a specific origin in history – some Hindus derive their tradition from a primeval revelation of the Supreme, others consider it the beginningless *sanātana dharma*, the eternal law that governs everything, independently of any divine or human agent – nor has it ever rejected a parent tradition from which it separated as a rebel child, as all others have done. Hindus had not found it necessary to define "the essentials of Hinduism" or prove it different from other religions until challenged by break-away spiritual movements like Buddhism or invaders from outside, who wanted to impose their own religions, such as Islam and Christianity.

Traditional Hinduism has preserved surprisingly much of the character of autochthonous native traditions, maintaining the holistic, all-embracing approach typical of these: there is no hard and fast distinction between the sacred and the secular, no strict separation of religious ritual from essential daily activities, no real difference or tension between religion and culture.

The various branches of what became known as "Hinduism" do not have a common creed and they do not demand from their followers any declaration of a "Hindu" faith. Until recently one could not become a Hindu unless one was born into a Hindu family; and one could not cease to be a Hindu if one was born a Hindu. As far as one's membership in the Hindu community was concerned, it did not matter what one thought or believed as long as one participated in the traditional rituals, which were also part and parcel of traditional Indian culture. On the other hand, many of the *saṃpradāyas*, specific worship traditions within Hinduism, draw very close and narrow boundaries: those who wish to be members must obey a very strict regimen with regard to diet, life-style, reading, and worship; they must not accept the teachings of any other *saṃpradāya*, or read books or listen to sermons from them.

Left to itself the large and old Hindu civilization quietly appropriated whatever was brought into it from the outside, absorbed it, transformed it, and made it part of its own. That process of assimilation was disturbed in a major way first by the massive onslaught of Islamic conquerors from the tenth century C.E. onwards. The Muslims came to conquer India and to covert the native "idolaters" to their own religion. The rigid monotheism of Islam, the exclusivity claim of Mohammed's revelation, the rejection of the caste system proved irreconcilable with the native religio-cultural traditions of India.

While Islam could claim partial successes – for over half a millennium most of India was under Muslim rule and a third of the population accepted Islam[1] – it generated a resistance among Hindus who began to realize an identity of their own based on their native "Hindu" traditions. Not by accident was it that from the eleventh century onwards *nibandhas* were composed – encyclopedic works that collected Hindu legal traditions, information about Hindu holy places, Hindu rituals, and customs of all *saṃpradāyas*. Hindus became aware of Hinduism as distinct from Islam. Islamic hostility toward "idolatry" further served to underscore the differences between Hindu traditions and other religions.

The second major disturbance was created by Western European powers from the sixteenth century C.E. onwards. While the main interest of the Portuguese, the Dutch, the Danish, the French and the English – all of whom established colonies in India – was trade, they were soon persuaded by the ecclesiastical powers of their homebases that they also had a duty to spread their Christian faith among the heathen.

Notwithstanding the presence of significant groups of indigenous Christians, who had lived for centuries peacefully side by side with their Hindu neighbors,[2] the European Churchmen of various denominations considered India a mission field to be harvested for their sectarian Western Christian Churches. By demanding from the citizens of Goa, the first European colony on Indian soil, either to convert to the Catholic Church or to emigrate, the Portuguese established a hard and fast line between Christianity and Hinduism, and also made sure that future relations between the two religions were based on hostility and exclusivity. Like Islam, Christianity became a foreign invader and remained a foreign religio-cultural presence in India. It also provoked a reaction and a resistance among Hindus that became quite articulate from the end of the nineteenth century onwards.[3]

The term "Hinduism" has recently been problematized in western scholarly literature. "Hindutva," the Indian-languages equivalent,[4] identified with a cultural political program promoted by right-wing Hindu political parties and extremist Hindu organizations, is viewed with suspicion and apprehension by many non-Hindus. Some question the appropriateness of the very word "Hinduism," which, they say, is an "orientalist construct" invented by western colonial interest. All agree that the term "Hindu" was imposed on the Indians by outsiders. However, the designation "Hindū" has meanwhile been adopted by Indians themselves, who identify their religion as "Hinduism" over against Islam or Christianity.[5] Others deny historic validity to the very notion of "Hinduism" prior to nineteenth century "Neo-Hinduism," which arose as a reaction to Christianity, the religion of the foreign colonizers.

The global designation "Hinduism" is apt to disguise the great diversity of Indian religious traditions. Till very recently "Hindus" defined their religious identities by using specific appellations like Vaiṣṇava, Śaiva, Śākta, Smārta etc., and several modern movements like the Ramakrishna Mission and the International Society for Krishna Consciousness emphatically denied being "Hindu," so as not to be identified with other branches of Hinduism that hold beliefs contrary to their own.

THE MEANING OF "HISTORY"

There is an uncanny resemblance between the original Greek word *historia* and the Sanskrit term for history, *itihāsa*, meaning both story and history (in the modern sense), tale, narrative, as well as the event narrated and told. Herodotus, commonly called the "Father of History" in the West, offers in his *Historiae* a great variety of reports about events observed by himself, about customs of other peoples, about tales and traditions whose authority he was not able to vouchsafe. By comparison Indian *itihāsa*, as reflected in the Epics and the Purāṇas, also consists of a rich store of historical events and legends, of myths and of moral lessons inextricably interwoven in order to tell a story, not to document "facts."

History writing in a more narrow sense is not unknown to India: the Buddhists chronicled the progress of their missions,[6] and the famous *Rājataraṅgiṇī* documents several centuries of Kashmir's history. The Upaniṣads maintained lists of *guru-paraṃparās*, containing scores of genealogies of teacher–disciple successions. But they give no dates and no references that allow precise dating by comparison with historic figures or events elsewhere. The Purāṇas contain many lists of dynasties and attempts have been made to identify these names and to relate them to datable rulers outside India and to historic events.[7] There are *Digvijayas*, records of the encounters of great teachers with their opponents, temple-chronicles, like the *Koil Olugu*, that faithfully describes the history of Śrīraṅgam, and undoubtedly there are still many undiscovered manuscripts with historical information on many persons and places in India.

However, history in the modern sense, a chronological write-up of past events, the recording of "facts, nothing but facts," was never popular with Hindus.[8] They were seeking meaning in their religious texts, not résumés of past events. Mahatma Gandhi once said, when doubts about the historicity of the person of Jesus were expressed, that even if it should be proven that Jesus never lived, the Sermon on the Mount would still be true for him.

Until recently Hindus had found it rather unnecessary to prove the historicity of *avatāras* like Rāma and Kṛṣṇa. Should endeavors of recent Hindu scholarship to find such proof be successful, that would probably not change anything for those who had always considered Rāma and Kṛṣṇa manifestations of the divine, their teaching a revelation, and their myths profoundly symbolically meaningful. It might, however, fuel competition between Hinduism and Christianity, pitting a historical Rāma and Kṛṣṇa against a historical Christ, and possibly worshipers of the one against worshipers of the other in an attempt to prove one to be the "only true god."

On a philosophical level, Hindus always made a distinction between appearance and reality, rating the waking consciousness, in which we note "facts," lower in comparison to other states of awareness, in which we note "ideas." Hinduism is a state of mind rather than an assembly of facts or a chronological sequence of events. The re-interpretations of scriptural texts, which Hindu *ācāryas* have undertaken throughout the ages, and the freedom with which contemporary Hindu teachers modify traditional teachings and modernize ancient symbolisms, should caution us not to expect much enlightenment concerning the essentials of Hinduism from a "history of Hinduism" in the modern sense.

Most Hindus believe that the series of events which we call "history" repeats itself endlessly in a never-ending cycle. It is quite significant that some major Hindu schools of thought identify this self-repeating factual world (*saṃsāra*) with *māyā* (deception), or *avidyā* (ignorance). A kind of "higher ignorance" can well be assumed to be the basis of a "history" that is content with documenting appearances and describing surface events.

One of the favorite images in South Indian Vaiṣṇava temples shows Viṣṇu resting on *śeṣa*, the coiled up world-snake representing eternity. The philosophy associated with this image opens up a new horizon for the philosophy of history; there is not only one human history and one universe, there are – in succession – many universes and many histories rolled up underneath the deity! What would be the meaning of these, in their totality, and what would be the purpose of the many universes?

A HISTORY OF HINDUISM?

In the light of the foregoing, it appears that history in the modern sense may not be the best approach to understand Hinduism. That point can also be proven by examining attempts to write histories of Hinduism. A history of Hinduism does not work as a history of Christianity or even a history of Buddhism works for understanding the content of these traditions. In Hinduism the momentous event of a foundation at one point in time, the initial splash in the water, from which concentric circles expand to cover an ever-wider part of the total surface, is absent. The waves that carried Hinduism to a great many shores are not connected to a central historic fact nor to a common historic movement.

The idea of a "History of Hinduism," short or long, is almost a contradiction in terms. Hindus call their tradition *sanātana dharma*, the eternal law, and everything of religious importance is termed *anādi*, beginningless. Hinduism has never consciously given up anything of its large heritage that accumulated over the centuries. It appropriated many ideas and practices from many quarters, brought forth many creative minds, developed a large number of traditions that differ from each other in many respects but which collectively form what became known as "Hinduism."

Given all the discussion about "Hinduism" and the fact that the word "Hindu" has become a loaded term in today's India as well as in Indological writing, a clarification may be appropriate before setting out to introduce the reader to this short history of Hinduism. The term Hinduism has been fully accepted by today's "Hindus" and is hardly replaceable by any other designation to describe the religious culture of the majority of the inhabitants of India. The acceptance of the term Hindu by the adherents of this tradition makes it advisable to apply it when dealing with their beliefs and customs. While an extension of the term Hinduism to the earliest sources of the Hindu tradition is clearly an extrapolation, it appears justifiable. There are, after all, historical parallels that have been accepted unquestioningly by scholars and the general public alike.[9]

There is little justification for the divisions found in much western scholarly writing between "Vedism," "Brahmanism," and "Hinduism." If the term "Hinduism" is found problematic in connection with the Vedas and the Brāhmaṇas, which certainly do not use the term, it is equally problematic in its application to the Epics and the Purāṇas, who do not use it either. Inversely, today's Hindus call their living religious traditions "vedic," defining "Hinduism" as *vaidika dharma*, and making acceptance of the Veda as scripture the criterion of "orthodoxy." It would hardly find the approval of those who are critical of the term "Hinduism" to replace it by "Vedic Religion."

In this book "Hinduism" is used as an umbrella designation for all traditions that declare allegiance to the Veda, however tenuous the actual connection with that body of writing might be, and however old or recent the particular branch might be. While speaking of "Hinduism," without qualifying the term each time by a hundred caveats, it will also be made quite clear that Hinduism is not one homogeneous "religion" (in the biblical sense) but a "family of religions," a vast and heterogenous tradition without a common leader, a common center or a common body of teachings.[10]

Hinduism has continually been developing new expressions. It has aptly been compared to a Banyan tree that constantly sends forth new shoots that develop into trunks from which other roots originate to form other trunks, and so forth. The Banyan tree simile not only illustrates the diversity but also the interconnectedness of the countless forms under which "Hinduism" appears. While Hinduism may be lacking a definable doctrinal unity or uniformity in worship and ritual, it surely has a distinct shape of its own when set over against Islam or Christianity.

PROBLEMS IN CONSTRUCTING A HISTORIC SCHEMA OF HINDUISM

In the absence of a general common denominator and of an authoritative institution it is impossible to construct a schema for a history of Hinduism that provides a clear and commonly accepted periodization. While there certainly has been development, and innovation is not unknown to Hinduism, the situation was always complex and not amenable to being fitted into "time lines," suggesting a progressive movement from a point A in the remote past via a point B in recent history to a point C today.

India has been called a "living museum" and Hinduism is as good an example to demonstrate the truth of this statement as any other facet of Indian culture. Side by side with naked Hindu *sādhus* practicing archaic forms of penance and living a life of utter contempt for comfort and hygiene, there are jet-set Hindu gurus who move among millionaires and surround themselves with every luxury imaginable. One still can see Vedic altars being built in today's India and observe Vedic sacrifices being offered accompanied by the muttering of Vedic hymns – rites and compositions that may be six thousand or more years old. One can also see temples built in a futuristic style where worshipers offer obeisance to images of still living teachers accompanied by rock music and the latest in electronic sounds. There are Hindus who find their faith best expressed in the theology of medieval masters, and there are Hindus who have rejected everything from the past for the sake of a complete reinterpretation of traditional beliefs.

The periodization offered in the following pages must be taken with more than just a grain of salt. Although Western scholars, since the early nineteenth century, have labored hard to stick labels with historic dates on the written sources of Hinduism, many of these dates are far from established (the dates given by the experts often vary by thousands of years!) and even when and where they are certain, they may be of limited relevance to a history of Hinduism as a whole.

Accepting, hypothetically, the claim made by many Hindus that Hinduism is "vedic," i.e. based on the collections of books called Veda, we could postulate an initial period of "Vedic religion" that represents the "beginnings" of Hinduism. Apart from the questionable nature of this assumption – there is a counterclaim established by tradition and supported by some scholars, that the Purāṇas are older than the Vedas, and "mainstream Hinduism" alive in Vaiṣṇavism, Śaivism, Śāktism, and others contains a large heritage of un-vedic and possibly pre-Vedic beliefs and practices – the problem about dating the "Vedic period" has given rise to one of the most enduring and most hotly conducted scholarly debates of our time, summarized in chapter 3 of this book.

In the so-called post-Vedic period, the development of Hinduism proper, instead of one, there is a multitude of fairly exclusive, frequently intertwining traditions, whose history is difficult to trace, because of many local variants of each. Things are made more complicated through the appropriation of particular philosophical schools by specific religious traditions, the formation of parallel teaching lines, and the emergence of new sects.

ATTEMPTING A PERIODIZATION OF INDIAN HISTORY

In Joseph E. Schwartzberg's *A Historical Atlas of South Asia*[11] the following periodization of the history of India, and within it, the history of Hinduism, is given:

I. Prehistory, comprising everything from the early Stone Age to the Indus Civilization ("Harappan Era").
II. The Vedic Age.
III. The Age of the Epics (Rāmāyaṇa and Mahābhārata).
IV. The Pre-Mauryan Age.
V. The Mauryas.
VI. The Post-Mauryan Period.
VII. The Imperial Guptas and the Classical Age.
VIII. Kingdoms and Regional Cultures of the 8th through the 12th Centuries.
IX. The Period of the Delhi Sultanate.
X. The Mughal Period.
XI. The Contest for Power and the Establishment of British Supremacy 1707–1857 [The only period with precise years given for events and persons mentioned].
XII. Imperial India and the growth of National Identity, comprising also the "Indian Renaissance" and Hindu Reform Movements.
XIII. Post-Independence India.

Jan Gonda, until his death in 1997, was for many decades the acknowledged doyen of European Indology and a prolific writer on many aspects of Hinduism. He contributed two volumes on Hinduism for a comprehensive series on "The Religions of Mankind."[12] His major divisions are as follows:

I. Veda and Older Hinduism
   1. Vedic (and Brāhmaṇic) Hinduism
   2. Epic (and Purāṇic) Hinduism
II. Younger Hinduism
   1. Major Phases of Post-epic Hinduism
   2. Vaiṣṇavism
   3. Śaivism
   4. Hinduism in the 19th and 20th Centuries

In his Chronology he provides the following dates for the key periods:

2600–1600 B.C.E. Indus-Civilisation.
From 1200 B.C.E. Āryan immigration to India: Development of Vedas.
From 600 B.C.E. The Oldest Upaniṣads.
*c.*200 B.C.E. The Bhagavadgītā.
From 4th century B.C.E. to 2nd century C.E. Development of Rāmāyaṇa.
From 4th century B.C.E. to 4th century C.E. Development of Mahābhārata.
From the 2nd to the 6th century C.E. Expansion of Hinduism into Southeast Asia.
320 C.E. to 6th century C.E. the Gupta Dynasty.
3rd to 5th centuries C.E. Origin of *Viṣṇu Purāṇa*.
7th century C.E. Flowering of Vedānta.
8th century C.E. Origin of Saṃhitā literature; Pāñcarātra.
After 7th century C.E. Development of *bhakti* Movements.
7th to 9th centuries C.E. Period of Brahmanic Reconstruction.

With great reluctance I am offering my own very tentative periodization of the "History of Hinduism." Most Western experts will probably object to the first half – its rationale will be provided in the text itself.

I. Beginnings of the Vedic ritual and textual tradition: possibly as early as 6000 B.C.E. in Northwest India (Saptasindhu), superseding and incorporating earlier local (village) cults.
II. Consolidation and expansion of Vedic tradition, formation of the "Canon" of the *Ṛgveda* and emergence of ritual specialists: *c.*4000 B.C.E.

III. Full flowering of Vedic religion in the Panjab and adjacent areas: *c.*3000 B.C.E. This would also include the so-called "Indus civilization."

IV. Major natural cataclysms and desiccation of Sindh and adjacent areas followed by migrations from the indus area eastward towards the Gangetic plains: As a result of population pressure building up in the Yamunā-Ganges doab the Mahābhārata war was precipitated *c.*1900 B.C.E. Gradual acceptance of Śaivism and Vaiṣṇavism.

V. Internal Disputes and Development of Many Mutually Incompatible ("heterodox") Traditions: while most of these, like the Ajīvikas, have died out, some survived: Jainism (re-organization in the seventh century B.C.E. of an older independent ascetic movement) and Buddhism (originating in the sixth century B.C.E.). For several centuries (300 B.C.E. to 300 C.E.) non-Hindu traditions were dominant in India, and from there expanded into neighbouring countries.

VI. Restoration of Hinduism under the Guptas: from the late fourth century C.E. to the sixth century. Anti-Buddhist and anti-Jain polemics and development of orthodox (non-theistic) Hindu theologies (Mīmāṃsā and Vedānta) as well as of mainstream (theistic) *saṃpradāyas* (Vaiṣṇavism, Śaivism, later also Śāktism). Foundation of Hindu kingdoms in the countries of South East Asia (Indonesia, Kampuchea, Vietnam, Thailand, Myanmar, Philippines).

VII. Repression of Hinduism under Muslim Rule: from *c.*1200 C.E. till about 1800 C.E. Disappearance of Hinduism from public life, cultivation of personal piety (bhakti) and private ritual (Tantra).

VIII. Emergence of new Hindu kingdoms in Muslim-dominated India: Vijayanagara (1336–1565) and Mahārāṣṭra (eighteenth century).

IX. Rising of reformers of Hinduism under British (Christian) influence: nineteenth and early twentieth centuries. Development of a distinct Hindu identity and a Hindu consciousness.

X. Partition of India (1947): formation of a theocratic Indian Muslim State (Pakistan) and a secular Indian democratic state (Bhārat). Efforts by Hindu nationalist political parties to "hinduize" Bhārat and transform it into a Hindu rāṣṭra.

BASIC HINDU SOURCE LITERATURE

The total mass of writings considered Hindu Scriptures, i.e. books that are religiously authoritative and believed inspired by a superhuman agency, far exceeds any scriptural tradition of any other religion. While much of it is accepted as divinely revealed only by believers in particular communities, there is a large corpus of books that form the basis of the "Vedic tradition" and that (at least nominally) is accepted by all Hindus as "sacred." Although writing down of sacred texts was apparently forbidden for a long time, the collection of such texts, the memorization and their recitation, was central to ancient Indian traditions.

Śruti *and* Smṛti

The authoritative Hindu religious literature is divided into two main categories: *śruti* (literally: "that which has been heard") and *smṛti* (literally: "that which has been remembered"). *Śruti* has the connotation of "revelation," "truth" in an unquestionable sense, norm of belief and practice. *Smṛti* bases its authority on the standing of the writer to which it is attributed, authoritative only to the extent to which it conforms to *śruti*. It offers a certain freedom of choice between conflicting opinions, allows interpretation that is more than the mere establishing of the one correct meaning of words and sentences.

Śruti is identical with the Veda (literally "knowledge") in its wider sense, which comprises:

(a) the Veda in the narrower sense, i.e. the four *saṃhitās* (literally "collections")
Ṛg-Veda (Veda of hymns, or verses)
Sāma-Veda (Veda of melodies)
Yajur-Veda (Veda of rituals)
Atharva-Veda (Veda of incantations and spells)

(b) the *Brāhmaṇas*, large texts explanatory of the rituals, associated with each of the four *saṃhitās* as follows:
Ṛg-Veda: (1) *Aitareya (Āśvalāyaṇa)*
(2) *Kauśītakī (Sāṁkhāyana)*

Yajur-Veda: (1) *Taittirīya*
(2) *Śathapatha*

Sāma-Veda: Eight, of which the most important are
(1) *Prauḍha (Pañcaviṃśa)*
(2) *Tāṇḍya*
(3) *Ṣadviṃśa*

Atharva-Veda: *Gopatha*

(c) *Āraṇyakas*, literally "forest treatises," i.e. teachings no longer relating to sacrifice and ritual, namely:
(1) *Bṛhad*
(2) *Taittirīya*
(3) *Aitareya*
(4) *Kauśītakī*

(d) *Upaniṣads*, also called "Vedānta," "end of the Veda," mystical utterances designed to teach the means for liberation from rebirth and all suffering. There is a very large number of these, of whom 108 are usually enumerated as "genuine." The so-called "Major Upaniṣads," commented upon by classical authors, are about ten to twelve.[13] There is a large number of so-called "sectarian Upaniṣads," compendia of Vaiṣṇava, Śaiva, and Śākta teachings and practices, and others.[14]

Smṛti or "Tradition" comprises a very large number of heterogeneous works, classified as follows:

(a) *Smṛtis*, Codes of Law, often introduced by creation narratives and concluded by advice on how to reach salvation. They are fairly numerous, but some have acquired an authority that stands out, such as *Manu-Smṛti*, attributed to Manu, the forefather of all humans now living, *Yājñavalkya-Smṛti*, attributed to an important Vedic sage, *Viṣṇu-Smṛti*, and many others.

(b) *Itihāsa*, "history," comprising the two ancient Indian epics
Rāmāyaṇa
Mahābhārata (including *Bhagavadgītā*)

(c) *Purāṇas*, "old books," texts that provide information about the creation of the universe, about genealogies of patriarchs and kings, rules of life and mythologies of the major deities they are dealing with. They are subdivided into 18 *Mahā-Purāṇas*, "Great Purāṇas," classified according to the deity they are devoted to, and a large number of *Upa-Purāṇas*, "Lesser Purāṇas."

1. The *Mahā-Purāṇas* comprise:
   6 Vaiṣṇava (*sāttvika*) Purāṇas:
   Viṣṇu-Purāṇa
   Nāradīya-Purāṇa
   Bhāgavata-Purāṇa
   Garuḍa-Purāṇa
   Padma-Purāṇa
   Varāha-Purāṇa
   6 Śaiva (*tāmasa*) Purāṇas:
   Matsya-Purāṇa
   Kūrma-Purāṇa
   Liṅga-Purāṇa
   Śiva-Purāṇa
   Skanda-Purāṇa
   Agni-Purāṇa
   6 Brahma (*rājasa*) Purāṇas:
   Brahmā-Purāṇa
   Brahmāṇḍa-Purāṇa
   Brahmavaivarta-Purāṇa
   Mārkaṇḍeya-Purāṇa
   Bhaviṣya-Purāṇa
   Vāmana-Purāṇa
2. *Upa-Purāṇas*, of which there are a large number.
   The ascription to either category is not undisputed. Thus e.g. the Śāktas consider the *(Mahā)-Devī Bhāgavata Purāṇa* a "Mahā-Purāṇa," while others classify it as a "Upa-Purāṇa."

   In general, the members of a particular *saṃpradāya* would consider the Purāṇa, that they adopt as theirs, as *śruti*, revelation, with the same authority as that of the Vedas.
3. Numerous *Sthala-Purāṇas*, works that describe the history of a particular holy place (*sthala*), embellishing it with numerous miraculous events associated with the image and its worship.

The Sūtras

At a certain time, when memorizing the increasingly voluminous primary literature apparently became next to impossible, short compendia, *sūtras* (literally "threads"), were composed that presented the essentials of each discipline in a succinct and reliable manner. In the course of time, virtually all subjects of traditional learning received their *sūtras*. Thus we have in the context of religion *Śrauta-Sūtras*, summarizing the rules applying to public sacrifices; *Gṛhya-Sūtras*, providing a summary of domestic rites; *Kalpa-Sūtras*, compendia of other rituals; *Dharma-Sūtras*, manuals of religious and secular law; and *Śulva-Sūtras*, providing elementary geometry and rules of construction for fire-altars and so forth.

When the Veda became difficult to understand owing to the archaic language it used and the distance in time between its composers and its later students, *Vedāṅgas*, books teaching the auxiliary sciences connected with Veda-study, were provided. Thus we have *Śikṣā* (phonetics), *Chandas* (meter), *Vyākaraṇa* (grammar), *Nirukta* (etymology), *Jyotiṣa* (astronomy) and *Kalpa* (ritual).

While training in the Vedas was mandatory for brahmins in order to enable them to fulfill their priestly duties, very often they were also taught secular subjects, termed *Upa-Vedas* (sciences not connected with Veda-study). The traditional subjects were *Āyur-Veda* (medicine), *Gandharva-Veda* (music and dancing), *Dhanur-Veda* (archery), and *Sthāpatya-Veda* (architecture).

Sectarian Scriptures

In addition to the vast body of writing described above, which forms the common heritage of Hinduism, there is an extensive sectarian literature which advocates tenets that are exclusive to certain *saṃpradāyas* and are not shared by other Hindus. Thus there are numerous *Saṃhitās*, sectarian Vaiṣṇava writings; *Āgamas*, sectarian Śaivite works; and *Tantras*, sectarian Śākta books. By the followers of these *saṃpradāyas* these works are considered revealed (*śruti*) and equal in authority to the Veda. While offering some philosophical reflections on the nature of God, world, and living beings from the specific theological perspective which the particular sect advocates, they are mostly concerned with ritual and with regulations of the life of the devotees. Some are manuals of worship as it is performed in major temples. Thus the *Parameśvara Saṃhitā*,[15] to mention just one example, codifies the worship of the great Viṣṇu sanctuary at Śrīraṅgam, the *Somaśambhupaddhatī*[16] details the daily ritual in South Indian Śiva temples.

While the classification of Hindu scriptures is fairly universally accepted, both the relative and the absolute dating are controversial.

With regard to the relative dating, there are Hindu scholars who assume that the Atharvaveda is older than the Ṛgveda[17] and there is a fairly strong Hindu tradition that insists that the Purāṇas are as old as the Vedas, antedating the epics.

With regard to absolute dating the gap between those who accept the Āryan invasion theory and those who do not is enormous. Because the dating has to be seen in this context, no figures will be mentioned here and the reader is advised to compare the sets of dates provided earlier. The estimated age of Epics, Purāṇas, and Tantras will be mentioned when dealing with these writings. There is a tendency among Hindus to consider scriptures "beginningless" (*anādi*) and to take literally the claim of many of them to be direct revelations from the Supreme – again removing them from any meaningful historical process of dating.

Non-Sanskrit religious literature

There is an ancient rivalry between North and South in India that also extends to language and scriptures. While the North insists on the primacy of Sanskrit scriptures and considers Sanskrit the only sacred language proper, the South claims that Tamil is older than Sanskrit and that certain Tamil writings are on an equal footing with Sanskrit *śruti*. This linguistic cum religious issue came to the fore in medieval Tamilnadu: the *ācāryas* of Śrīraṅgam had the Tamil hymns of the Āḷvārs recited in temple-worship, side by side with Sanskrit hymns. One branch of Śrīvaiṣṇavas, the Vadagalais, even placed the Tamil writings above the Sanskritic ones.

With the development of popular *bhakti* movements, which replaced much of traditional Brahminism and its ritual, compositions in the vernaculars of India also became part of religious ritual. The Hindī re-creation of the *Rāmāyaṇa*, Tulsīdāsa's *Rāmcaritmānas* all but eclipsed Vālmīki's Sanskrit original and the inspired poetry of singers in many tongues became the preferred hymns sung by groups of devotees meeting for *bhajan* singing. The religious literature created by hundreds of saint-singers is enormous.[18]

In addition, contemporary leaders and poets add to the volume. For the devotees of a particular guru his or her words are usually inspired and worth recording and repeating. Thus the recorded conversations of saints like Rāmakrishna Paramahaṃsa, Ramaṇa Maharṣi, Ānandamayī Mā, and many others are treated as "Gospels" by their followers and read out in religious gatherings. There is, quite literally, no end to producing ever more religious literature and there is no hope that any single person could read all of it.

NOTES

1. "Indian Islam" did develop some peculiarities that were frowned upon by Islamic authorities elsewhere, and from the sixteenth century onwards there was considerable interest in upper-class Muslim circles in becoming familiar with and even accepting certain aspects of the Hindu tradition. Sufism, as it developed in India, incorporates many Buddhist and Hindu features.
2. The "St. Thomas Christians" in India trace their origins back to a direct disciple of Jesus, whose tomb they believe to be in St. Thome, near Cennai (Madras). They probably originated from a group of Syrian merchants who settled in India in the fourth century. They still use Syriac as liturgical language and until recently their bishops came from the see of Edessa.
3. Richard F. Young, *Resistant Hinduism. Sanskrit Sources on Anti-Christian Polemics in Early Nineteenth-Century India*, Vienna: Indologisches Institut der Universität Wien, 1981
4. The term "Hindu-dharma" occurs for the first time in Sanskrit literature in Chapter 33 of the *Merutantra* (date unknown, but certainly fairly recent, because it refers already to the English foreigners and their capital London).

   A comprehensive encyclopedic description of Hinduism in Hindī authored by Ramdas Gaur and published in Samvat 1995 (1938 C.E.) carried the title *Hindutva*. It was planned to be paralleled by similar volumes on all other major religions.

   Vir Savarkar's seminal 1938 English essay "Essentials of Hindutva" attempts to differentiate between Hindutva as "Hindu culture" shared by all who live in India, and Hinduism, as a religion, which is not shared by all. This is usually the interpretation given today by the advocates of a "Hindu India" and Hindutva.
5. The Indian expression "Hindu-dharma" is used over against "Isāī-dharma," or "Islām-dharma".
6. Tāranātha's *History of Buddhism in India*, Buston's *History of Buddhism*, the *Culavaṃsa* and the *Mahāvaṃsa*, are the best-known examples.
7. Cf. A. D. Pusalker, "Historical Traditions," in *The History and Culture of the Indian People*, vol. I, Bombay, [4]1965, pp. 271–336.
8. Whereas the rulers in most other countries had their court-chroniclers, singing the praises of their masters and immortalising their great deeds, such a custom was curiously absent in ancient India. Possibly the Indian tradition of considering kings as but one element of the state, and not the raison d'être of it, prevented them from having their deeds recorded by a court historian. The Muslims, who ruled India, left voluminous records of their activities.

9. I am following the same logic by which historians of Christianity apply the term "Christians" to the immediate followers of Jesus, while the term "Christianoi" was coined by outsiders at a later time and it took centuries before becoming universally accepted by the "Christians" as self-designation.
10. In this respect Hinduism is not that different from today's Christianity either. While "Christianity" is considered one "religion," all of whose followers are supposed to accept the New Testament as their scripture and Jesus of Nazareth as their saviour, in reality there have been from the very beginning many independent and mutually exclusive "Christian Churches" whose interpretations of the New Testament as well as customs and forms of worship have hardly anything in common. Still, nobody objects to using the term "Christianity" in connection with works on the "History of Christianity."
11. Joseph E. Schwartzberg, *A Historical Atlas of South Asia*, New York–Oxford: Oxford University Press, second impression, with additional material, 1992.
12. *Die Religionen Indiens*, Stuttgart: Kohlhammer, 1960–63.
13. Śaṅkara commented on sixteen.
14. Hundreds of these have been published with English translations by the Adyar Library.
15. So far no translation into a Western language exists of this text, which was published in 1953 at Śrīraṅgam.
16. Sanskrit text with French translation by H. Brunner-Lachaux, published by the Institut Français d'Indologie at Pondicherry in two volumes, 1963 and 1968.
17. Govinda Krishna Pillai, *Vedic History (Set in Chronology)*, Kitabistan: Allahabad, 1959.
18. Some idea of its range can be gained from J. N. Farquhar, *An Outline of the Religious Literature of India*, originally published by Oxford University Press in 1920, Indian reprint 1967 (Delhi: Motilal Banarsidass). Since then much more has been printed and produced.

2 A SHORT HISTORY OF TWO CITIES: A Microcosm of Hinduism

One of the most noteworthy features of Hinduism is its strong linkage to the physical geography of India, its "Holy Land," whose mountains, lakes, rivers and forests, cities and temples are considered seats of particular deities or a physical manifestation of the Divine itself. Local traditions and mythologies that developed around particular places have strongly molded Hindu practice and beliefs. Actually, Hinduism is a mosaic composed of a large number of such local traditions, conjoined with the pan-Indian practices of the major religious orders (*saṃpradāyas*).

In the Purāṇas there is a frequently mentioned list of seven holy cities, places of pilgrimage that possess special sanctity and whose visit conveys release from rebirth. As the old saying goes: "These seven cities provide liberation: Āvantī (Ujjain), Mathurā, Māyā (Haridwār), Kāśī (Vārāṇasī), Kāñcī (Kāñcīpuram), Purī and Dvārakā." While there are, in addition, literally thousands of places of pilgrimage in India to which millions of Hindus flock every year, the seven ancient cities mentioned above – situated either on sacred rivers or on the sea – are especially sought after, and many people are known to retire to them to spend the eve of their lives surrounded by the sacred atmosphere they convey. Since time immemorial these places have attracted the teachers of various schools of Hinduism; and to this very day, these places of pilgrimage are centers of Hindu learning.

Despite the apparently rural character of the Vedas, cities have always played a crucial role in the history of Hinduism. As places of pilgrimage, *tīrthas*, "fords" or "crossings," they became all but indispensable to the religious practice of the Hindus. While some are actually located on rivers, marking shallow spots that could easily be forded, the term *tīrtha* soon acquired a transcendental significance as a place at which emancipation could be found and from which the "other shore" could be reached. In the same way in which the mediation of Brahmins was considered indispensable for obtaining ritual purity, so the mediation of the sacred place, the *tīrtha*, became essential to Hindus desirous of liberation from rebirth.

All these numerous sacred cities have a rich history and an even richer mythology, often set out in *Sthala Purāṇas*.[1] They are eulogized in *Māhātmyas*,[2] "glorifications" of the place, which highlight the important events associated with it. Since it is not possible to go into the history of all the great Hindu *tīrthas*, and not even feasible to deal with the seven ancient holy cities mentioned above (there are many other holy cities which lay claim to equal antiquity and fame), I shall select just two:[3] Mathurā on the Yamunā, of specific importance to Vaiṣṇavas, because of its historico-mythical association with Kṛṣṇa; and Vārāṇasī (or Banaras, also known as Kāśī) on the Gaṅgā, specially sacred to Śaivas, who consider it Śiva's favourite abode. By sketching out the history of these ancient cities we shall get glimpses of the entire history of Hinduism over several thousand years, its ups and downs, as well as an impression of the co-existence of a great number of different traditions and schools of thought within their walls.

MATHURĀ

Situated in the center of the Hindu heartland, the ancient *Madhyadeśa*, in today's Uttar Pradesh, on the river Yamunā, Mathurā, the largest city of the Braj-maṇḍala, has always been associated with the birth, childhood, and youth of Kṛṣṇa. Those Hindu historians who reckon the Mahābhārata war to have taken place in 3002 B.C.E. would set the date for (the historical) Kṛṣṇa at that time too. Others assign a date of *c.*1500 B.C.E. to him.[4] As the received tradition has it, Mathurā even then was an old city, one of the largest in India, filled with magnificent temples and palaces. Kṛṣṇa, fulfilling a prophecy associated with his birth, killed Kaṃsa, the tyrant of Mathurā, and gave freedom to the people of Vraja.[5]

If the historicity of the Kṛṣṇa tradition is still an object of scholarly controversy, resting largely on the testimony of the Epics and Purāṇas,[6] we are on historically firm ground with the records of Buddhist and Jain establishments in Mathurā from the fifth century B.C.E. onwards. According to Buddhist tradition, the Buddha himself visited Mathurā several times during his life-time. The Jainas claim that the Tīrthaṅkaras Parśvanātha and Mahāvīra visited Mathurā. This sounds quite plausible. The teachers of new paths to salvation expected to find their most receptive audiences in the big cities, where thousands of seekers would be congregated. Mathurā's fame as a city of religious learning and a place of pilgrimage was the reason why Buddhist and Jain monks and nuns settled there. Mathurā is also mentioned as an important city and trading center in the writings of ancient Greek travellers, such as Megasthenes and Arrian.[7]

Mathurā became the capital of the Śaka kingdom in the first century B.C.E. and of that of their successors, the Kuśānas, in the first century C.E. The Kuśānas were adherents of Buddhism and under their patronage in the second century C.E. an important school of Buddhist art developed in Mathurā, whose sculptures became renowned all over India (and are now famous all over the world).[8] A Chinese Buddhist pilgrim, Fa-Hsien, who visited the holy places associated with the Buddha's life in India around 400 C.E., still speaks of Mathurā as a Buddhist city, with twenty Buddhist monasteries in which lived more than three thousand monks and nuns.[9] He mentions also six large stūpas, dedicated to Sariputra, Ānanda, and Mudgalaputra as well as to the Tripitaka Abhidharma, Sutta, and Vinaya. Another Chinese Buddhist pilgrim, Hiuen Tsiang, who visited Mathurā about two hundred years later, still reports the existence of twenty Buddhist monasteries, the presence of two thousand monks and nuns and the practice of worshiping at a number of different stūpas. However, he also notes the existence of five large Hindu temples and the reemergence of Brahmanism in Mathurā.[10]

In the following centuries most of the Buddhist and Jain establishments were abandoned and destroyed, and Mathurā became known again as one of the strongholds of Hinduism – filled with large temples and ashrams. Numerous Śiva liṅgas have been found in and around Mathurā as well as images of Sūrya. On the place on which according to an old tradition Kṛṣṇa was born – the prison-house of Kaṃsa – an enormous temple was erected.

No wonder that Mathurā became a prime target for the Muslim marauders that were advancing from the north-west from the tenth century onwards. Mahmud of Ghazni raided Mathurā in 1017 C.E. His own chronicler described it as "a very large city full of magnificent temples."[11] Strangely, it had been left undefended and so "the Sultan's army plundered the whole city and set fire to the temples. They took immense booty, and by the Sultan's order they broke up a golden image which was 98,300 miṣkals in weight; and there was also found a sapphire weighing 450 miṣkals."

Hurtful as the raid certainly had been, it did not inflict permanent damage. Alberuni, a Muslim scholar and traveller, visiting Mathurā a few decades after the event, describes it as "a holy place crowded with brahmins."[12] During the next century the whole of North India came under the domination of the Muslim invaders who later established their capital at Agra, about 50 kilometers south of Mathurā. While the Muslims systematically razed Hindu temples and built mosques over them, Hindus succeeded even under Muslim rule to build new temples in Mathurā. An inscription dated 1150 C.E. records the erection of a Viṣṇu temple "brilliantly white and touching the clouds" at the site of Kṛṣṇa's putative birthplace.[13] It did not stay in place, however, for long, and was destroyed by the fierce and fanatical Sikander Lodi (ruled 1488–1517).

When Akbar "the Great" (ruled 1556–1605) granted permission to Hindus to rebuild their temples, the Kṛṣṇa-janma-bhūmi temple was restored to some semblance of its old magnificence. In the middle of the seventeenth century several European travelers visited Mathurā and described the temple. François Bernier only mentions "an ancient and magnificent pagan temple" in Mathurā, whereas Jean Baptiste Tavernier, a French physician, describes it at great length: "The temple is of such a vast size that, though in a hollow, one can see it five or six *kos* off, the building being very lofty and very magnificent." It was built of the same red sandstone, of which the Fort in Agra and Delhi's "Red Fort" are made. The temple itself was set on an octagonal sandstone plinth which "has round about it two bands of many kinds of animals, but particularly monkeys, in relief." It had two narrow staircases leading to the main entrance and to the choir. The temple occupied only half of the platform; the other half formed a large empty place. "Like other temples, it is in form of a cross, and has a great dome in the middle with two rather smaller [domes] at the end. Outside, the buidling is covered from top to bottom with figures of animals, such as rams, monkeys, and elephants, carved in stone: and all round there are nothing but niches occupied by different monsters." While finding it "shocking to have before one's eyes such a host of monstrosities," Tavernier admired the architecture of the temple. He also was shown the temple-deity,[14] a statue made of black marble, accompanied by two smaller figures in white marble. The figures were dressed in embroidered robes and covered with pearls and precious stones. Inside the temple Tavernier also saw the processional chariot used to take the deity on outings.[15]

In 1669 the fanatical Moghul ruler Aurangzeb (ruled 1658–80) ordered the destruction of the temple. It was razed to the ground and a huge mosque was built in its place, which is still there today. As his chronicler notes in the *Ma-Asiri 'Alamgiri*: "In the month of Ramazan, 1080 A.H. (December 1669) in the thirteenth of his reign, this justice loving monarch, the constant enemy of tyrants, commanded the destruction of the Hindu temple of Mathurā known by the name of Dehra Keśu Rai, and soon that stronghold of falsehood was levelled with the ground. On the same spot was laid, at great expense, the foundation of a vast mosque." After briefly describing the background to the history of the building he continues: "The richly jewelled idols taken from the pagan temples were transferred to Agra, and there placed beneath the steps leading to the Nawab Begam Sahib's mosque, in order that they might ever be pressed under foot by true believers. Mathurā changed its name to Islāmābad and was thus called in all official documents, as well as by the people."[16]

When, after Aurangzeb's death, the Mughal empire declined rapidly, Braj became part of the sphere of influence of Rājput kings, who partially restored the Hindu holy places. Sawai Jai Singh, whose name is associated with some major buildings, actively supported and reformed Hindu religious life and kept in touch with Hindu religious leaders of the area.

The time of tribulations for the residents of Braj, however, had not ended. In 1757 Ahmad Shah Abdali, an adventurer from Aghanistan, who attempted to install himself as ruler in Delhi, in the wake of a campaign in North India, also overran Mathurā and Vrindāban and caused the worst massacre these places had ever seen. Abdali offered every one of his soldiers five rupees for every head of a Hindu – thousands were slaughtered and beheaded and their houses burnt to the ground.[17]

With the establishment of Mahratta supremacy over Braj later in the eighteenth century, Mathurā began to revive and new temples were built. The British, who took over by 1830, established a cantonment in Mathurā and appointed a District Magistrate. One magistrate, Frederick

Growse, took an active interest in the history and culture of Braj and became instrumental in restoring many ancient Hindu temples.[18]

Under British rule Mathurā regained some of its ancient character as a place of Hindu pilgrimage and learning. Many new temples were built, the ghāts were revived, and Hindu scholars began to settle and teach there again. Mathurā was sufficiently famous by the middle of the nineteenth century to attract the later Swami Dāyānanda, who under the tutelage of Virajānanda Saraswatī, one of its pandits, established the Ārya Samāj, an iconoclastic Hindu reform movement that gained great importance in the Hindu *jāgaran* of the twentieth century. Several million pilgrims visit Mathurā every year, and in spite of the visible presence of Islām – there is a mosque in the very center of Mathurā and there is, of course, the large mosque built on the Kṛṣṇa-janma-bhūmi, which has been targeted by RSS (Rāṣṭrīya Svayamsevak Sangh) activists – Mathurā has again become a major Hindu center. Its numerous large temples are always crowded at the time of worship and its many festivities attract large crowds from distant places as well. Mathurā is the seat of many Hindu centers of study and it also is the home of one of the major archeological museums of India, which houses many treasures found in and around Mathurā over the past century.

For many pilgrims, however, Mathurā (with over a million inhabitants today) is only a transit station for Vrindāban, a small town of about 50,000 permanent residents, *c.*15 km northeast of Mathurā. For Kṛṣṇa devotees Vrindāban is the religious center of the Braj Maṇḍala. In traditional Kṛṣṇa lore Vrindāban[19] is described as the place of Kṛṣṇa's *līlā*, his plays with the *gopīs*, the exemplary devotees. While for most of its history Mathurā was the more important place of pilgrimage, since the sixteenth century Vrindāban became the focus of major temple building and scholarly religious activities. This had much to do with the arrival of representatives of new religious movements such as Gauḍīya Vaiṣṇavism and the Puṣṭimārga, but also with a change in the nature of pilgrimage. Mathurā, as the traditional saying quoted above indicates, was sought by pilgrims in pursuit of liberation. Vrindāban is visited in search of religious experience: the visualization of Kṛṣṇa and the participation in his love games.

Today's Vrindāban is largely the creation of the immediate disciples of Caitanya "Mahāprabhu" (1486–1533), the founder of Gauḍīya Vaiṣṇavism. Being intoxicated with love for Kṛṣṇa,[20] he eagerly sought to relive the scenes so vividly described in the *Bhāgavata-Purāṇa* and traveled with his companions from his native Bengal to the Braj Maṇḍala. He commissioned the highly educated Rūpa and Sanātana Goswāmi in 1517 to live and work in Vrindāban. Rūpa Goswāmi authored the celebrated *Bhakti-rasāmṛta-sindhu*, arguably the most important theological work of the Gauḍīya Vaiṣṇavas, and he also founded the Govinda Deva temple, one of the landmarks in Vrindāban. Sanātana Goswami, his nephew, established the Madanmohan temple. Caitanya sent some more of his immediate disciples to Vrindāban – collectively they came to be known as the "Six Vrindāban Goswāmis" and they enjoyed high prestige among Gauḍīya Vaiṣṇavas. Among them was Gopāla Bhaṭṭa, author of the *Hari-bhakti-vilāsa*, a work detailing the Gauḍīya Vaiṣṇava ritual of worship, and founder of the Rādhāraman temple. Rāgunātha Dāsa, author of the *Vraja-vilāsa-stava*, which gives a description of the holy places of Braj, established Rādhākuṇḍ which became the center for the Bengali Gauḍīya Vaiṣṇavas in Vrindāban. Jīva Goswāmi, the author of the immense theological summa *Ṣat-sandarbha* established the Rādhā Dāmodar temple. In the eighteenth century such famous Gauḍīya Vaiṣṇava scholars as Kṛṣṇadāsa Kavirāja, Viśvanātha Cakravarti, and Baladeva Vidyābhūṣana settled in Vrindāban, enriching both the religious and the cultural life of Braj. It was one of the endeavors of these men not only to work out the theology of Gauḍīya Vaiṣṇavism, but also to teach and educate the masses. For this purpose they wrote a great number of plays, reenacting scenes from the *Bhāgavatam*, and also staging an Indian version of the medieval mystery plays, where allegories of the drama of salvation were played out by personifications of virtues and vices.

Vrindāban was chosen as home also by famous members of other sects. Thus Hit Harivaṁś, the founder of the Rādhāvallabha Sampradāya, and Swāmī Haridās, a gifted poet and singer of the Kṛṣṇa *līlā*, settled in Vrindāban and developed institutions of their own. Since all these scholarly theological luminaries also actively promoted new forms of worship and festivities, Vrindāban soon overflowed with dramatic religious performances and celebrations attended by rapturous crowds.

In the eighteenth century it became fashionable for Rājput nobles to build villas in Vrindāban. Noble ladies retired there to spend their lives participating in temple worship and composing religious lyrics. Wealthy business people had the ghats and temples repaired and expanded in the nineteenth century and Vrindāban turned into one of the busiest places of pilgrimage in the whole of India. In our own time many new foundations were established by Marwaris, new temples and pilgrim shelters were built and the small town is visited every year by some three million people from outside. Vrindāban has also become a center for politically active Hinduism: some of the prominent custodians of temples are also leaders in RSS and VHP (Viśva Hindū Pariṣad). Several modern educational institutions have opened there as well. Some of these are concerned with preserving and exploring the local heritage, such as the Vrindāban Research Institute, and the Śrī Caitanya Prema Samsthāna which is undertaking a major international project of conservation and reconstruction of the Govinda Deva temple. The latter, under its scholarly director Srivatsa Goswami, organized in 1994 an international conference dealing with Braj – the holy land of Kṛṣṇa.[21]

In the 1950s Swami Bon Maharaj, a member of the Neo Caitanyite Gauḍīya Mission, began to develop a Vaiṣṇava Viśva-vidyālaya (Vaiṣṇava University) on a large plot of open land, inspired by the great theological colleges he had seen in the United States. He had to scale down his venture because of lack of local support, but he succeeded in getting his Institute of Oriental Philosophy affiliated with Agra University as a recognized Post-Graduate Research Centre.

The International Society for Krishna Consciousness (ISKCON, better known as "Hare-Krishna Movement") established a major center there too: its large and beautiful Kṛṣṇa Balarāma Maṇḍir has become one of the major attractions of Vrindāban. It is also the site of the *samādhi* (burial) of Swami Bhaktivedanta, the founder of ISKCON, who had lived for many years in Vrindāban before moving to the United States. ISKCON also opened a large boarding school attached to the temple and many married members have settled in its vicinity.

To complete the picture of Mathurā and Vrindāban: both places also have Śiva temples besides temples in which the Goddess receives worship, Muslim mosques, and Sikh gurdwaras. Mathurā also possesses two Christian Churches. Besides Mathurā and Vrindāban, a large number of other places in Braj-Maṇḍala, Kṛṣṇa's territory, are frequented by many pilgrims. There is not sufficient space to describe in detail famous places like Govardhana, Gokula, Mahābana and others, already mentioned in the *Bhāgavatam*. All of them have great significance for Kṛṣṇa *bhaktas*. They are on the path of the great Braj pilgrimage that is undertaken every year by a number of intrepid Kṛṣṇa devotees, lasting approximately three weeks.[22]

In spite of all historic tribulations, devastations and inner dissensions, Hinduism in Braj is as alive as ever, and neither a modern nor a postmodern critique of religion in general, or of Hinduism in particular, has dampened the spirits of the Brajvasis or the pilgrims from outside. If anything, the influx of pilgrims has become larger during the past decades, the number of people wishing to spend the rest of their lives in Vrindāban has increased, and the foundation of new ashrams and new temples moves ahead at an unprecedented pace. Hundreds of thousands of people still come with the expectation to have a vision of Kṛṣṇa and Rādhā, to experience the mystery of passionate love for God, to receive blessings and even to witness miracles of all sorts, about which the locals talk. The very dust of the streets of Vrindāban has been sanctified by the feet of Kṛṣṇa, the gopīs and the devotees and there is a widespread belief that it can cure leprosy, when one rolls in it, as one can see many individuals doing.

VĀRĀṆASĪ

Vārāṇasī, anglicized "Benares/Banaras," also called "Kāśī" (the effulgent) or "Avimukta" (the never forsaken), has probably received over the ages more eulogies than any other city in the world. From the most ancient to the most recent writers, praise has been heaped on this "Holy City," which is so unlike any other.[23] P. V. Kane, writing in 1953 said: "There is hardly any city in the world that can claim greater antiquity, greater continuity and greater popular veneration than Banaras. Banaras has been a holy city for at least thirty centuries. No city in India arouses the religious emotions of Hindus as much as Kāśī does. To the Hindu mind it represents great and unbroken traditions of religious sanctity and learning. It is a miniature of Hindu life through the ages in all its great complexities and contradictions."[24]

Vārāṇasī, the "place between Vārāṇa and Asī" (two small rivers that flow into the Ganges, one forming the northern boundary of the city, the other the southern) has not only been the Hindus' most holy city, but has also found, throughout the last few hundred years, its Western admirers. Diana Eck expresses her admiration thus: "From its commanding position on the River Ganges, Banaras has witnessed the entire history of Indian civilization as it evolved in North India. From the ancient Āryan Kingdoms and their rivalries, through the golden Mauryan and Gupta empires, to the thousand years of Muslim and then British domination, the historical currents of the times have passed through Banaras."[25]

The area now occupied by the city of Vārāṇasī was not the original site of the famous Kāśī of ancient records. The old city was largely situated in Rājghāt, a plateau on the northern edge of present Vārāṇasī. Archeological excavations of the site have yielded evidence of settlements going back to *c*.800 B.C.E. From then on the place was continually occupied.[26]

As the capital of the Kāśis, mentioned in early Indian literature, from the Ṛgveda[27] to the Mahābhārata, in Buddhist and Jaina sources, it must have played a dominant role in the Gangetic plains. There are still wide gaps in the archeological evidence for the history of Vārāṇasi – we cannot match archeological finds and artefacts with the glowing descriptions of the great city of Banares as found in ancient Buddhist documents, which hail it "the chief city of all of India."

From early on the kingdom of Kāśī lived in rivalry with the neighboring kingdom of Kośala – the latter eventually prevailed and Benares became part of Kośala. Kośala in turn was challenged by the more powerful neighboring kingdom of Magadha, which eventually absorbed both Kāśī and Kośala. While the primary goal of these conquerors was presumably the wealth and the strategic importance of the place, Kāśī retained and even strengthened its reputation as a place of traditional learning and became a center not only for Vedic and Upaniṣadic studies, but also for Buddhism and Jainism. Later on it was a matter of prestige for every sect and school to have a presence in Kāśī.

Buddha is reported to have spent several rainy seasons in Vārāṇasī. Nearby Sarnāth, the place at which the Buddha had set the wheel of the dharma in motion, adorned by a *stūpa* in Aśoka's time, remained for fifteen hundred years an important Buddhist center – till it was destroyed by the Muslim general Qutb-ud-din-Aibak. The Jains maintain that two of their twenty-four Tīrthāṅkaras were born in Banaras and they consider it one of their holy places as well. A Jain temple stands even now in Banaras. Vārāṇasī was famous in ancient India for its āśramas, its temples and its places of learning. The famous grammarian Patañjali (second century C.E.) taught there and Śaṅkara (eighth century C.E.), the great reformer of Hindu monasticism, began his work here. Also Rāmānuja (eleventh century C.E.), the foremost Śrīvaiṣṇava *ācārya*, did not fail to visit Vārāṇasī and established a center there, despite the fact that by then Vārāṇasī had become Śiva's own holy place. Also followers of Madhva, of Gorakhnātha, and of Basava settled in Banaras.

During the rule of the Guptas (fourth to sixth centuries C.E.), who initiated a Hindu renaissance, Śaivism became the predominent religion in Vārāṇasī, but the other religions continued to flourish. Under the successors of the Guptas, Vārāṇasī became a stronghold of brahminical Hinduism. However, it was still a place for Buddhist pilgrims to visit, as the testimony of Hiuen Tsiang proves, who described what he saw in the early seventh century: "There are about thirty *sanghārāmas* and 3000 priests. They study the Little Vehicle according to the Sammatīya school. There are a hundred or so Deva temples with about 10,000 sectaries. They honor principally Maheśvara. Some cut their hair off, others tie their hair in a knot, and go naked without clothes; they cover their bodies with ashes, and by the practice of all sorts of austerities they seek to escape from birth and death." Hiuen Tsiang also describes a brass-statue of Śiva, about 30 meters high: "Its appearance is grave and majestic, and appears as though really living."[28] An eighth-century pilgrim by name of Pantha established a Goddess temple, furnishing it with a terrifying image of Caṇḍī.

Vārāṇasī's "Golden Period" lasted for about a century and was abruptly terminated by a Muslim invasion. Under the Gāhadavālas, who came to power in 1094, Banaras became the capital of a prosperous kingdom, whose rulers saw themselves as protectors of the Hindu sacred places. King Govindacandra made large donations to the temples in the city and generously supported Hindu learning. He appointed Lakṣmīdhāra, a learned brahmin, as his chief minister. Lakṣmīdhāra was the author of the famous *Kṛtya-kalpa-tāru*, a kind of encyclopedia of medieval Hinduism in fourteen volumes. He also compiled all available information on over three hundred and fifty temples of Kāśī. At the time of writing this work, the Muslim armies, coming from the north-west, had already conquered large parts of northern India. After the King of Banaras, Rayacandra (a Muslim historian calls him "the chief of idolatry and perdition"[29]) had been killed, the Muslim general Qutb-ud-din Aibak sacked and looted Banaras in 1194. He destroyed nearly a thousand temples and built mosques on top of many. Muslim historians report that 1,400 camel loads of gold and silver were carried away as loot from Banaras.

Undaunted, however, the Hindus began rebuilding and a century later Banaras shone again with the golden pinnacles of its temples. In the early decades of the fourteenth century they were again destroyed – only to be rebuilt again. In 1376 Firoz Shah ordered the destruction of Hindu temples and the building of large mosques in their places. In 1496 Sikander Lodi had all the remaining Hindu temples in Banaras destroyed and renamed the city Mohammadābad. A century later, however, under the more enlightened rule of Akbar, two large new temples were built: the Viśveśvara (Śiva) and the Biṇḍu Mādhava (Viṣṇu) mandirs.

With Aurangzeb's accession to the throne the short phase of toleration ended. In 1659 he ordered the demolition of the temple of Krittivaseśvara and the construction of a large mosque on its site. In 1669 he also had the new Viśveśvara and Biṇḍu Mādhava temples destroyed and mosques built in their place. Astonishingly enough Hindu life and learning continued even under these adverse conditions. Not only did the pandits continue to teach their disciples, one of the greatest Hindu poets, Tulasīdāsa, the author of the famous *Rām-carit-mānas* lived and worked there during this time too.

Hindu life and learning was given a boost through the immigration of six Mahārāṣṭrian brahmins with their families. One of them, Nārāyaṇa Bhaṭṭa, organized the reconstruction of the Viśvanātha temple and also composed a work – the famous *Tri-sthāli-setu* in praise of Banaras, Gāya, and Prayāga. Also during this time, new Hindu religious orders such as the Rāmānandis and the Gorakhpanthis established themselves in Banaras.

With the death of Aurangzeb in 1708 the power of the Muslim rulers in Delhi declined and in 1738 Vārāṇasī came under the rule of Mahārāja Balwant Singh, a Hindu. The city and the temples were rebuilt, largely with the assistance and support of Rājput and Mahrātta nobility. In the second half of the eighteenth century the British gained increasing influence. In fact, Banaras was the first major city outside Bengal which came under the control of the British East India Company. The Company built some major roads through the center of Banaras and it also gave support to Christian missions. Several missionary societies started schools and built churches and hospitals from 1816 onwards. Great expectations were connected with a conversion of this center of Hinduism to Christianity. These hopes were not fulfilled and Banaras regained more and more its position as the leading centre of Hinduism.

In 1791 the Banaras Sanskrit College was founded, which became an important training center for Hindu pandits. In 1906 the groundstone was laid for Benares Hindu University, whose first Vice Chancellor, Paṇḍit Madan Mohan Malavīya, also became the founder of the first nationalist Hindu Party, the Hindū Mahāsabhā. While Benares Hindu

University today is perhaps better known for the excellence of its Faculty of Engineering than for its Hindu theologians, it has developed into a center for Hindu studies in many different branches. It is also the home for a Department for Astrology/Astronomy (*Jyotiṣi*) and produces a widely used *Pañcāṅg*, the astrological/astronomical almanack required by Hindus for the calculation of auspicious/inauspicious times.

Today Banaras is again the destination of millions of pilgrims every year, the home of many Hindu academic and cultural institutions, and the location of important publishers of traditional Hindu literature as well as modern studies. Every major traditional Hindu order has its Banaras branch, and most contemporary religious celebrities such as Ānandamayī Mā and Sathya Sāī Bābā have centers there as well. Banaras has attracted numerous famous ascetics and yogis, such as Tailaṅga Swami and Chote Paramahamsa, reputed to have lived respectively, 270 and 300 years.[30] Great scholars from other parts of India, such as Mahāmahopadhyāya Paṇḍit Gopināth Kavirāj, settled in Vārāṇasī, adding to the fame of the city as a place of higher Hindu learning.

Foreigners too, have felt the peculiar attraction of Banaras even in the twentieth century, in spite of the progress of modernization and industrialization around the city. E. B. Havell, who revived Indian painting and founded an Indian school of art was charmed by Vārāṇasī, which he found "one of the most extraordinary cities of the East."[31] Count Hermann Keyserling devoted a large part of his Indian Travel Diary to Banaras. In it he wrote: "Benares is holy. Europe, grown superficial, hardly understands such truths any more." And: "I feel nearer here than I have ever done so to the heart of the world; here I feel every day as if soon, perhaps even today, I would receive the grace of supreme revelation." And later, returning from the banks of the Ganges: "The atmosphere of devotion which hangs above the river is improbable in its strength: stronger than in any church that I have ever visited. Every would-be Christian priest would do well to sacrifice a year of his theological studies in order to spend this time on the Ganges: here he would discover what piety means. For in Europe all that exists is its remote reflection."[32]

The history and the present condition of life in Mathurā and Banaras provide a glimpse into the history of Hinduism as a whole, and reflect Hinduism as it is lived in many places in today's India. Apart from the excitement that the activities of millions of pilgrims generate who visit the many holy spots in these places, there is an ongoing flurry of celebrations and festivities organized by the many different sects and schools of Hinduism that are resident there. The year has not enough days to accommodate the large number of feast days in the Hindu calendar. There has been no diminishing of the fervor with which Hindus engage in worship, no lessening of the hopes and expectations connected with temple visits. Hinduism may be the most ancient of the religions on earth – it is also ever young and full of exuberant life.

NOTES

1. A *Sthala Purāna* contains the largely legendary history of a temple replete with tales of miraculous events connected with it.
2. Most of the *Māhātmyas* are found in Purāṇas. Often they were printed separately in places to which they refer. There are also digests, like Mitra Miśra's eighteenth-century *Viramitrodaya*, which has a section called *Tīrthaprakāśa* – a collection of such Māhātmyas from various sources.
3. While both the places chosen for this presentation are in Northern India, one could equally easily describe holy cities from South India such as Madurai or Kāñcīpuram, Tirupati, or Śrīraṅgam. My choice was largely influenced by the greater accessibility of sources in languages known to me and by my personal familiarity with the places.
4. Thus S. R. Rao, the excavator of Dvārakā, Kṛṣṇa's legendary capital city, mentioned in the *Mahābhārata*. See S. R. Rao, *The Lost City of Dvārakā*, Delhi, 1999.
5. "The oldest finds in Mathurā Museum are paleoliths dating from about fifty thousand B.C., and the earliest fragments of pottery are Painted Grey Ware dating from about 800 B.C." A. W. Entwistle, *Braj. Centre of Krishna Pilgrimage*. Groningen: Egbert Forsten, 1987, p. 110.
6. The association of Kṛṣṇa-worship with Mathurā does have definite historical confirmation. The ancient Greek writers about India, who had visited the country as ambassadors, report about the worship of "Heracles" in Mathurā; one of them set up a stele in his honor.
7. Arrian (second century C.E.), in his *Indike* summarized the reports of Megasthenes (fourth century B.C.E.) who was Greek ambassador to the court of the Mauryas. He refers to Mathurā as "Methura," the capital city of the Surasenoi, who were worshipers of Herakles. Translation of the *Indike* by J. W. McCrindle (London: Truebner, 1877).
8. The oldest sculptures found in Mathurā (and elsewhere) dating from the third century B.C.E. are so-called Yakṣas and Yakṣīs, tutelary local gods and goddesses of groves and trees, as well as Nāgas, personified snakes, whose worship seems to antedate that of the major Hindu deities and who seem to have been partly merged with them at a later date.
9. That Vedic religion continued to be present in Mathurā as well is attested to by a sacrificial pillar, which was found on the banks of the Yamunā opposite the Swāmi Ghāt, commemorating a Vedic ritual celebrated in 102 C.E. Entwistle, *Braj*, p. 116.
10. The full text (in translation) is quoted in F. Growse, *Mathurā*, p. 109f.

11. Elliot and Dowson, *The History of India as Told by its Own Historians*, vol. II, p. 460f.
12. E. Sachau, *Alberuni's India*. Delhi: S. Chand, 1964 (reprint) II, 147f.
13. Entwistle, *Braj*, p. 123.
14. Tavernier calls it the "Rām-Rām", but in all likelihood it was a Kṛṣṇa figure accompanied by Rādhā and Bālarāma. Rāmā is always presented in white colour, whereas Kṛṣṇa is "black" by definition. Tavernier may have been misguided by the habit of the people of Mathurā to use "Rām-Rām" as greeting.
15. The full text of Tavernier's description is found in F. S. Growse, *Mathurā: A District Memoir* (pp. 128ff.), originally published in 1882, reprinted in 1979 by Asian Educational Services, New Delhi. F. S. Growse was District Magistrate in Mathurā from 1871 to 1877 and described in his "Memoir" his area of work with great sympathy and knowledge. He was responsible for much restoration and conservation work on temples in Mathurā and Vrindāban.
16. Elliot-Dowson, *The History of India . . .* , vol. VII, p. 184f.
17. Entwistle, *Braj*, p. 107f., offers vivid descriptions by contemporaries of this gruesome slaughter.
18. F. S. Growse is the author of one of the most important modern sources for the history of Mathurā: *Mathurā: A District Memoir*, originally published in 1882.
19. Vṛṇḍā is a name for the Tulasī tree, which apparently grew abundantly in the area.The correct Sanskrit spelling for the place is Vṛndāvana, the spelling adopted here – Vrindāban – is the one most frequently used in the place itself. Other variations are Brindaban, Brindabon, Vrindavan.
20. His followers even saw him as an incarnation of Rādhā and Kṛṣṇa.
21. The *Journal of Vaiṣṇava Studies* devoted its Winter 1994 (Vol. 3, No. 1) issues to this conference and printed several of the presentations made.
22. A very vivid and informative description is given in David L. Haberman, *Journey through the Twelve Forests: An Encounter with Krishna*. New York–Oxford: Oxford University Press, 1994.
23. There are a number of *Māhātmyas* of Vārāṇasī in Sanskrit. Besides there is a huge work, the so-called *Kāśī-kaṇḍa* of the *Skāṇḍa Purāṇa*, probably from the fourteenth century, which describes and praises in detail numerous specific holy spots in Banaras.
24. P. V. Kane, *History of Dharmaśāstra*, vol. IV, p. 618, Pune: Bhandarkar Oriental Research Institute, 1953.
25. Diana L. Eck, *Banaras: City of Light*. New York: A. Knopf, 1982, p. 43.
26. See A. K. Narain and T. N. Roy, *Excavations at Rājghāt, 1957–58; 1960–1965*, Varanasi: Banaras Hindu University, 1976.
27. K. S. Sukul, author of *Vārāṇasī Down the Ages* (Patna, 1974) thinks that the Kāśis were a non-āryan people who were subdued by the Vedic āryans.
28. S. Beal, trans. *Si-yu-ki: Buddhist Records of the Western World*. London: Truebner & Co., 1894, II, 44–45.
29. Hasan Nizami, *Taju-l Ma-asir* in Elliot-Dowson, *The History of India as Told by Its Own Historians*, vol. II, p. 223.

30. See Sukul, *Vārāṇasī Down the Ages*, pp. 217–222.
31. E. B. Havell, *Benares, The Sacred city. Sketches of Hindu Life and Religion*. London: Thacker & Co., 2nd ed., 1905, Preface.
32. Count Hermann A. Keyserling, *Indian Travel Diary of a Philosopher*, trans. J. Holroyd-Reece, Mumbay and New Delhi: Bharatiya Vidya Bhavan/Kapur Surya Foundation, second edition 1999. Count Keyserling undertook his Indian travels between 1911 and 1914. Benares occupies 88 pages in the 251-page work! The quotes are on pp. 130, 133, 135.

3 THE BEGINNINGS OF HINDUISM: A Controversy

In most textbooks the beginning of Hinduism is identified with the invasion of India by the Āryans, dated *c.*1500 B.C.E., and their composition of the hymns of the *Ṛgveda*, dated between 1400 and 1200 B.C.E. What the same textbooks do not mention is that the so-called Āryan invasion theory is based on pure speculation, and that there is absolutely no archeological or literary evidence for it. The Āryan invasion of India was the invention of some European scholars of the late nineteenth century and it was resisted as unfounded by others from the very beginning.[1] In the light of recent archeological finds it has become less and less tenable. Nevertheless, the Āryan invasion is still defended and forms part of the standard histories of Hinduism. In the following the arguments pro and con will be presented, and it is left to the reader to judge the merits of the case.

THE ĀRYAN INVASION THEORY

Indian scholars frequently refer to the "Āryan invasion theory" as "colonial-missionary," implying that it was the brain-child of conquerors of foreign colonies who could not but imagine that all elements of higher culture in India must have come from outside that backward country, and who likewise assumed that a religion could only spread in a larger population through a politically supported missionary effort.

There is no doubt that nineteenth-century European attempts to explain the presence of Hindus in India had much to do with the commonly held biblical belief that humankind originated from one pair,

Adam and Eve, who were believed to have been created directly by God in 4005 B.C.E., and that all people on earth descended from one of the sons of Noah, the only human to survive the Great Flood (dated 2350 B.C.E.). The major problem seemed to be to connect peoples *not* mentioned in Chapter Ten of Genesis, "The Peopling of the Earth," with one of the biblical genealogical lists.

Abbé Dubois (1770–1848), spent many years in India (1792–1823), during which he collected a large amount of interesting material concerning the customs and traditions of the Hindus. His (French) manuscript was purchased by the British East India Company and appeared in an English translation under the title *Hindu Manners, Customs and Ceremonies* in 1897 with a Prefatory Note by the Right Hon. F. Max Müller.[2] Abbé Dubois, loath "to oppose [his] conjectures to [the Indians'] absurd fables" categorically stated: "It is practically admitted that India was inhabited very soon after the Deluge, which made a desert of the whole world. The fact that it was so close to the plains of Sennaar, where Noah's descendants remained stationary so long, as well as its good climate and the fertility of the country, soon led to its settlement." Rejecting other scholars' opinions which linked the Indians to Egyptian or Arabic origins, he ventured to suggest them "to be descendants not of Shem, as many argue, but of Japhet."[3] He explains: "According to my theory they reached India from the north, and I should place the first abode of their ancestors in the neighbourhood of the Caucasus".[4] The reasons he provides to substantiate his theory are utterly unconvincing – but he goes on to build the rest of his migration theory (not yet an "Āryan" migration theory) on this shaky foundation.

Max Müller (1823–1903), who was largely responsible for the "Āryan invasion theory" and the "old chronology," was too close in spirit and time to this kind of thinking not to have adopted it fairly unquestioningly. In his Prefatory Note he praises the work of Abbé Dubois as a "trustworthy authority ... which will always retain its value."

When the affinity between many European languages and Sanskrit became a commonly accepted notion, scholars almost automatically concluded that the Sanskrit-speaking ancestors of the present-day Indians had to be found somewhere halfway between India and the western borders of Europe – Northern Germany, Scandinavia, Southern Russia, the Pamir – from which they invaded the Punjab.[5] (It is also worth noting that the early arm-chair scholars who conceived these grandiose migration theories had no actual knowledge of the terrain their "Āryan invaders" were supposed to have traversed, the passes they were supposed to have crossed, or the various climates they were believed to have been living in.) Assuming that the Vedic Indians were semi-nomadic warriors and cattle-breeders, it fitted the picture, when Mohenjo Daro and Harappa were discovered, to assume also that these were the cities the Āryan invaders destroyed under the leadership of their god Indra, the "city-destroyer," and that the dark-skinned indigenous people were the ones on whom they imposed their religion and their caste system.

Western scholars decided to apply their own methodologies and, in the absence of reliable evidence, postulated a time frame for Indian history on the basis of conjecture. Considering the traditional dates for the life of Gautama, the Buddha, as fairly well established in the sixth century B.C.E., supposedly pre-Buddhist Indian records were placed in a sequence that seemed plausible to philologists. Accepting on linguistic grounds the traditional claims that the *Ṛgveda* was the oldest Indian literary document, Max Müller, allowing a timespan of 200 years each for the formation of every class of Vedic literature, and assuming that the Vedic period had come to an end by the time of the Buddha, established the following sequence that was widely accepted:

- *Ṛgveda c.*1200 B.C.E.
- *Yajurveda*, *Sāmaveda*, *Atharvaveda*, *c.*1000 B.C.E.
- *Brāhmaṇas*, *c.*800 B.C.E.
- *Āraṇyakas*, *Upaniṣads*, *c.*600 B.C.E.

Max Müller himself conceded the purely conjectural nature of the Vedic chronology, and in his last work, *The Six Systems of Indian Philosophy*, published shortly before his death, he admitted: "Whatever may be the date of the Vedic hymns, whether 1500 or 15,000 B.C., they have their own unique place and stand by themselves in the literature of the world."[6] There were, already in Max Müller's time, Western scholars, such as Moriz Winternitz and Indians like Bal Gangadhar Tilak, who disagreed with his chronology and postulated a much earlier date for the *Ṛgveda*.

Indian scholars had pointed out that there was no reference in the Veda of a migration from outside India, that all the geographical features mentioned in the *Ṛgveda* were those of northwestern India, and that there was no archeological evidence whatsoever for the Āryan invasion theory. On the other hand, there were references to constellations in

Vedic works whose time frame could be reestablished by commonly accepted astronomical calculations. The dates arrived at, however, 4500 B.C.E. for one observation in the *Ṛgveda*, 3200 B.C.E. for a date in the *Śatapatha Brāhmana*, seemed far too remote to be acceptable, especially if one assumed – as many nineteenth-century scholars did, that the world was only about 6000 years old and that the flood had taken place only 4500 years ago.

DEBUNKING THE ĀRYAN INVASION THEORY

Many contemporary Indian scholars, admittedly motivated not only by academic interests, vehemently reject what they call the "colonial-missionary Āryan invasion theory." They accuse its originators of superimposing – for a reason – the purpose and process of the colonial conquest of India by the Western powers in modern times onto the beginnings of Indian civilization: as the Europeans came to India as bearers of a supposedly superior civilization and a higher religion, so the original Āryans were assumed to have invaded a country that they subjected and on which they imposed their culture and their religion.

A recent major work[7] offers "seventeen arguments: why the Āryan invasion never happened." It may be worthwhile to summarize and analyze these briefly:

1. The Āryan invasion model is based on linguistic conjectures which are unjustified (and wrong). Languages develop much more slowly than assumed by nineteenth-century scholars. Speakers of Indo-European languages may have lived in Anatolia as early as 7000 B.C.E.
2. The supposed large-scale migrations of Āryan people in the second millennium B.C. first into Western Asia and then into northern India (by 1500 B.C.) cannot be maintained in view of the fact that the Hittites were in Anatolia already by 2200 B.C.E. and the Kassites and Mitanni had kings and dynasties by 1600 B.C.E.
3. There is no memory of an invasion or of large-scale migration in the records of Ancient India – neither in the Vedas, in Buddhist or Jain writings, nor in Tamil literature. The fauna and flora, the geography and the climate described in the *Ṛgveda*, are those of northern India.
4. There is a striking cultural continuity between the archeological artefacts of the Indus-Saraswatī civilization and subsequent Indian

society and culture: a continuity of religious ideas, arts, crafts, architecture, and system of weights and measures.

5. The archeological finds of Mehrgarh of *c.*6500 B.C.E. (copper, cattle, barley) reveal a culture similar to that of the Vedic Indians. Contrary to former interpretations, the *Ṛgveda* shows not a nomadic but an urban culture (*puruṣa*, "man," "person," is derived from *pur vāsa* = town-dweller).[8]
6. The Āryan invasion theory was based on the assumption that a nomadic people in possession of horses and chariots defeated an urban civilization that did not know horses, and that horses are depicted only from the middle of the second millennium onwards. Meanwhile archeological evidence for horses has been found in Harappan and pre-Harappan sites; drawings of horses have been found in paleolithic caves in India; drawings of riders on horses dated *c.*4300 B.C.E. have been found in Ukraina. Horse-drawn war chariots are not typical for nomadic breeders but for urban civilizations.
7. The racial diversity found in skeletons in the cities of the Indus civilization is the same as in today's India; there is no evidence of the coming of a new race.
8. The *Ṛgveda* describes a river system in North India that is pre-1900 B.C.E. in the case of the Saraswatī river and pre-2600 B.C.E. in the case of the Drishadvati river. Vedic literature shows a population shift from the Saraswatī (*Ṛgveda*) to the Ganges (Brāhmaṇas and Purāṇas), also evidenced by archeological finds.
9. The astronomical references in the *Ṛgveda* are based on a Pleiades-Kṛttika (Taurean) calendar of *c.*2500 B.C.E. Vedic astronomy and mathematics were well-developed sciences (again, these are not features of a nomadic people).
10. The Indus cities were not destroyed by invaders but deserted by their inhabitants because of desertification of the area. Strabo (*Geography* XV.1.19) reports that Aristobulos had seen thousands of villages and towns deserted because the Indus had changed its course.
11. The battles described in the *Ṛgveda* were not fought between invaders and natives but between people belonging to the same culture.
12. Excavations in Dwārakā have led to the discovery of a site larger than Mohenjodaro, dated *c.*1500 B.C., with architectural structures, use of iron, and a script halfway between Harappan and Brāhmī. Dwārakā has been associated with Krishna and the end of the Vedic period.

13. There is a continuity in the morphology of scripts: Harappan – Brahmi – Devanāgarī.
14. Vedic *ayas*, formerly translated as "iron," probably meant copper or bronze. Iron was found in India before 1500 B.C.E. in Kashmir and Dwārakā.
15. The Purāṇic dynastic lists, with over 120 kings in one Vedic dynasty alone, fit well into the "new chronology." They date back to the third millennium B.C.E. Greek accounts tell of Indian royal lists going back to the seventh millennium B.C.E.
16. The *Ṛgveda* itself shows an advanced and sophisticated culture, the product of a long development, "a civilisation that could not have been delivered to India on horseback" (*In Search of the Cradle*, p. 160).
17. Painted Gray Ware culture in the western Gangetic plains, dated *c.*1100 B.C.E., has been found connected to (earlier) Black and Red Ware.

As already remarked, there is no hint in the Veda of a migration of the people that considered it its own sacred tradition. It would be strange indeed if the Vedic Indians had lost all recollection of such a momentous event in supposedly relatively recent times – much more recent, for instance, than the migration of Abraham and his people, which is well attested and frequently referred to in the Bible. In addition, as has been established recently through satellite photography and geological investigations, the Saraswatī, the mightiest river known to the Ṛgvedic Indians, along whose banks they established numerous major settlements, had dried out completely by 1900 B.C.E. – four centuries before the Āryans were supposed to have invaded India. One can hardly argue for the establishment of Āryan villages along a dry river bed.

When the first remnants of the ruins of the so-called Indus civilization came to light in the early part of the twentieth century, the proponents of the Āryan invasion theory believed they had found the missing archeological evidence: here were the "mighty forts" and the "great cities" which the war-like Indra of the *Ṛgveda* was said to have conquered and destroyed. It then emerged that nobody had destroyed these cities and no evidence of wars of conquest came to light: floods and droughts had made it impossible to sustain large populations in the area, and the people of Mohenjo Daro, Harappa and other places had migrated to more hospitable areas. Ongoing archeological research has not only extended the area of the Indus civilization but has also shown a transition of its later phases to the Gangetic culture. Archeo-geographers have established that a drought lasting two to three hundred years devastated a wide belt of land from Anatolia through Mesopotamia to northern India around 2300 B.C.E. to 2000 B.C.E.

Based on this type of evidence and extrapolating from the Vedic texts, a new story of the origins of Hinduism emerges which reflects the self-consciousness of Hindus and which attempts to replace the "colonial-missionary Āryan invasion theory" by a vision of "India as the Cradle of Civilisation." This new theory considers the Indus civilization as a late Vedic phenomenon and pushes the (inner-Indian) beginnings of the Vedic age back by several thousands of years. One of the reasons for considering the Indus civilization "Vedic" is the evidence of town planning and architectural design, which required a fairly advanced algebraic geometry – of the type preserved in the Vedic *Śulvasūtras*. The widely respected historian of mathematics, A. Seidenberg, concluded, after studying the geometry used in building the Egyptian pyramids and the Mesopotamian citadels, that it reflected a derivative geometry – that is, a geometry derived from the Vedic *Śulva-sūtras*. If that is so, then the knowledge ("Veda") on which the construction of Harappa and Mohenjo Daro is based cannot be later than that civilization itself.[9]

While the *Ṛgveda* has always been held to be the oldest literary document of India and was considered to have preserved the oldest form of Sanskrit, Indians have not taken it to be the source for their early history. For them, *Itihāsa-Purāṇa* served that purpose. The language of these works is more recent than that of the Vedas and the time of their final redaction is much later than the fixation of the Vedic canon. However, they contain detailed information about ancient events and personalities that form part of Indian history. The Ancients, like Herodotus, the father of Greek historiography, did not separate story from history. Nor did they question their sources but tended to juxtapose various information without critically sifting it. Thus we cannot read *Itihāsa-Purāṇa* as the equivalent of a modern textbook of Indian history but rather as a storybook containing information with interpretation, facts and fiction. Indians, however, always took genealogies seriously and we can presume that the puranic lists of dynasties, like the lists of *guru-paramparās* in the *Upaniṣads*, relate the names of real rulers in the correct sequence. On these assumptions we can tentatively reconstruct Indian history to a time around 4500 B.C.E.

A key element in the revision of Ancient Indian History was the recent discovery of Mehrgarh, a settlement in the Hindukush area, which was continuously inhabited for several thousand years from *c.*7000 B.C.E. onwards. This discovery has extended Indian history for several thousands of years before the fairly well datable Indus civilisation.[10]

NEW CHRONOLOGIES

Pulling together archeological evidence as it is available today, the American anthropologist James G. Schaffer developed the following chronology of early Indian civilisation:[11]

1. Early food-producing era (*c.*6500–5000 B.C.E.): no pottery.
2. Regionalization era (5000–2600 B.C.E.): distinct regional styles of pottery and other artifacts.
3. Integration era (2600–1900 B.C.E.): cultural homogeneity and emergence of urban centers like Mohenjo Daro and Harappa.
4. Localization era (1900–1300 B.C.E.); blending of patterns from the integration era with regional ceramic styles.

The Indian archeologist S. P. Gupta proposed the following cultural sequencing:

1. Pre-ceramic Neolithic (8000–6000 B.C.E.)
2. Ceramic Neolithic (6000–5000 B.C.E.)
3. Chalcolithic (5000–3000 B.C.E.)
4. Early Bronze Age (3000–1900 B.C.E.)
5. Late Bronze Age (1900–1200 B.C.E.)
6. Early Iron Age (1200–800 B.C.E.)
7. Late Iron cultures

According to these specialists, there is no break in the cultural development of north-western India from 8000 B.C.E. onwards; similarly there is no indication of a major change, such as a large-scale invasion of another population with a different culture.

N. S. Rajaraman's[12] "New Chronology" of Ancient India, which identifies names of kings and peoples mentioned in the Vedas and Purāṇas, looks somewhat like this:

- 4500 B.C.E.: Mandhātri's victory over the Drohyus, alluded to in the Purāṇas.

- 4000 B.C.E.: Composition of the *Ṛgveda* (excepting books 1 and 10).
- 3700 B.C.E.: Battle of Ten Kings (referred to in the *Ṛgveda*). Beginning of Purāṇic dynastic lists: Agastya, the messenger of Vedic religion in the Dravida country. Vasiṣṭha, his younger brother, author of Vedic works Rāma and *Rāmāyaṇa*.
- 3600 B.C.E.: *Yajur-*, *Sāma-*, *Atharvaveda*: Completion of Vedic Canon.
- 3100 B.C.E.: Age of Kṛṣṇa and Vyāsa. Mahābhārata War. Early *Mahābhārata*.
- 3000 B.C.E.: *Śatapathabrāhmaṇa*, *Śulvasūtras*, *Yajñavālkyasūtra*, Pāṇinī, author of the *Aṣṭādhyayī*, Yāska, author of the *Nirukta*.
- 2900 B.C.: Rise of the civilizations of Ancient Egypt, Mesopotamia and the Indus-Saraswatī doab.[13]
- 2200 B.C.E.: Beginning of large-scale drought: Decline of Harappa.
- 2000 B.C.E.: End of Vedic age.
- 1900 B.C.E.: Saraswatī completely dried out: End of Harappa.

Texts like the *Ṛgveda*, the *Śatapathabrāhmaṇa* and others contain references to eclipses as well as to sidereal markers of the beginning of seasons which allow us, by backward calculation, to determine the time of their composition. Experts assure us that to falsify these dates would have been impossible before the computer age.

OLD VS. NEW, OR SCIENTISTS VS. PHILOLOGISTS?

We are thus left with two widely differing versions of Ancient Indian history, with two radically divergent sets of chronology, and with a great deal of polemic from both sides. Those who defend the Āryan invasion theory and the chronology associated with it accuse the proponents of the "New Chronology" of indulging in Hindu chauvinism. The latter suspect the former of entertaining "colonial-missionary" prejudices and denying originality to the indigenous Indians. The new element that has entered the debate are scientific investigations. While the older theory relied exclusively on philological arguments, the new theory includes astronomical, geological, mathematical, and archeological evidence.[14] On the whole the "New Chronology" seems to rest on better foundations.

Civilizations, both ancient and contemporary, comprise more than literature. Traditionally trained philologists – i.e. grammarians – are generally not able to understand technical language and the scientific information contained in the texts they study. Consider today's scientific literature. It abounds with Greek and Latin technical terms, and contains an abundance of formulae composed of Greek and Hebrew letters. If scholars with only a background in the classical languages were to read such works, they might be able to come up with some acceptable translations of technical terms into modern English but they would hardly be able to make sense of most of what they read, and they certainly would not be able to extract the information which the authors of these works wished to convey through their formulas to people trained in their specialties.

The situation is not too different with regard to ancient Indian texts. The admission of some of the top scholars (like Geldner, who in his translation of the *Ṛgveda* – deemed the best so far – declares many passages "darker than the darkest oracle," or Gonda, who considered the *Ṛgveda* basically untranslatable) of being unable to make sense of a great many texts – and the refusal of most to go beyond a grammatical and etymological analysis of the texts – indicates a deeper problem. The Ancient Indians were not only poets and litterateurs, but they also had their practical sciences and their technical skills, their secrets and their conventions, which are not self-evident to someone who does not share their world. Some progress has been made in deciphering technical Indian medical and astronomical literature of a later age, in reading architectural and arts-related materials. However, much of the technical meaning of the oldest Vedic literature still eludes us.

THE *ṚGVEDA* – A CODE?

The computer scientist/Indologist Subhash Kak believes he has rediscovered the "Vedic Code" on the strength of which he extracts from the structure as well as the words and sentences of the *Ṛgveda* considerable astronomical information which its authors supposedly embedded in it.[15] The assumption of such encoded scientific knowledge would make it understandable why there was such insistence on the preservation of every letter of the text in precisely the sequence the original author had set down. One can take certain liberties with a story, or even a poem, changing words, transposing lines, adding explanatory matter, shortening it, if necessary – and still communicate the intentions and ideas of the author. However, one has to remember and reproduce a scientific formula in precisely the same way it has been set down by the scientist, or it would make no sense at all. While the scientific community can arbitrarily adopt certain letter equivalents for physical units or processes, once it has agreed on their use, one must obey the conventions for the sake of meaningful communication.

Even a non-specialist reader of ancient Indian literature will notice the effort to link macrocosm and microcosm, astronomical and physiological processes, to find correspondences between the various realms of beings, and to order the universe by establishing broad classifications. Vedic sacrifices – the central act of Vedic culture – were to be offered on precisely built geometrically constructed altars and to be performed at astronomically exactly established times. It sounds plausible to expect a correlation between the numbers of bricks prescribed for a particular altar and the distances between stars observed whose movement determined the time of the offerings to be made. Subhash Kak has advanced a great deal of fascinating detail in that connection in his essays on the "Astronomy of the Vedic Altar." He believes that while the Vedic Indians possessed extensive astronomical knowledge which they encoded in the text of the *Ṛgveda*, the code was lost in later times and the Vedic tradition interrupted.

INDIA, THE CRADLE OF CIVILIZATION?

Based on the early dating of the *Ṛgveda* (*c.*4000 B.C.E.), and on the strength of the argument that Vedic astronomy and geometry predates that of the other known ancient civilizations, some scholars, like N. S. Rajaram, Georg Feuerstein, Subhash Kak and David Frawley, have made the daring suggestion that India was the "cradle of civilization."[16] They link the recently discovered early European civilization (which predates Ancient Sumeria and Ancient Egypt by over a millennium) to waves of populations moving out or driven out from north-west India. Later migrations, caused either by climatic changes or by military events, would have brought the Hittites to Western Asia, the Iranians to Afghanistan and Iran, and many others to other parts of Eurasia. Such a scenario would require a complete rewriting of Ancient World History – especially if we add the claims, apparently substantiated by some material evidence, that Vedic Indians had established trade links with Central America and Eastern Africa before 2500 B.C.E. No wonder that the "New Chronology" arouses not only scholarly controversy but emotional excitement as well. Much more hard evidence will be required to fully establish it, and many claims may have to be withdrawn. But there is no doubt that the "old chronology" has been discredited and that much surprise is in store for students not only of Ancient India, but of the Ancient World as a whole.

A CROWN WITNESS FOR THE NEW CHRONOLOGY?

A beautifully sculpted bronze head found near Delhi, named "Vasiṣtha's Head"[17] by a collector, was dated through radio-carbon testing to around 3700 B.C.E. – the time when, according to Hicks and Anderson, the Battle of the Ten Kings took place (Vasiṣtha is mentioned in the *Ṛgveda* as the advisor to King Sudās). A further factor speaking for the "Vedic" character of the Indus civilization is the occurrence of (Vedic) altars in many sites. Fairly important also is the absence of a memory of a migration from outside India in all of ancient Indian literature: the Veda, the Brāhmaṇas, the Epics and the Purāṇas. Granting that the Vedic Saṃhitās were ritual manuals rather than historic records, further progress in revising Ancient Indian history could be expected from a study of *Itihāsa-Purāṇa*, rather than from an analysis of the *Ṛgveda*. In combination with the evaluation of the ever-growing amount of artifacts from the region and a comparison with the findings of the students of early European history, a reinterpretation of the Epics and the older Purāṇas should bring about a more adequate understanding of Vedic India and the history of civilization in South Asia than is available at present.

NOTES

1. One of the prominent Indian scholars who quite early rejected the Āryan invasion theory was Aurobindo Ghose. In *The Secret of the Veda*, written between 1914 and 1916, he points out that the text of the Veda has no reference to any such invasion.
2. Abbé Dubois, *Hindu Manners, Customs and Ceremonies*, third ed., Oxford: Clarendon Press, 1906 (reprint 1959).
3. In 1767 James Parsons had published a long work entitled *The Remains of Japhet, being historical enquiries into the affinity and origins of the European languages*, using samples from over a dozen languages extending from Irish to Bengali.
4. Dubois, *Hindu Manners*, p. 101.
5. The argument was entirely linguistic-speculative; wild contradictory assertions were made from the same linguistic basis by various authors. Among them there was neither agreement on methodology nor on the interpretation of "linguistic facts."
6. Max Müller, *The Six Systems of Indian Philosophy*, p. 35.

7. G. Feuerstein, S. Kak, and D. Frawley, *In Search of the Cradle of Civilization*. Wheaton, Ill.: Quest Books, 1996.
8. Could one also suggest that *Purāṇa*, usually translated "Ancient (Books)" contains a reference to *pur* = city , embodying the "city-traditions" ?
9. A. Seidenberg, "The Geometry of the Vedic Rituals," in *Agni: The Vedic Ritual of the Fire Altar*, vol. II, ed. Frits Staal. Berkeley: Asian Humanities Press, 1983, pp. 95–126.
10. Philip von Zabern (ed.), *Vergessene Städte am Indus: Frühe Kulturen in Pakistan vom 8. bis zum 2. Jahrtausend v. Chr.* Mainz am Rhein: Verlag Philip von Zabern, 1987.
11. The same sequence is also given in a table on "General Chronology of South Asia" on p. 24 of J. M. Kenoyer, *Indus Valley Civilization* (Karachi: American Institute of Pakistan Studies, Oxford University Press, 1998) setting a "Mesolithic transition" period 10,000–6500 B.C.E. between a South Asian "Epi-Paleolithic" and the "Indus Valley Transition."
12. N. S. Rajaram, "The Puzzle of Origins: New Researches in History of Mathematics and Ancient Ecology," *Manthan*, Oct. 1994–March 1995, pp. 150–171.
13. A remark on "Chronology" by J. M. Kenoyer in *Indus Valley Civilization* may be pertinent: "In general the formation of large urban centers such as Mohenjo Daro and Harappa, located in the core areas of the Indus Valley, can be dated from around 2600 to 1900 B.C.E. In speaking of cultures, however, 700 years is an extremely long time, spanning nearly 30 generations. Many important changes in social organization, politics, language and even religion took place during the lives of these cities. We know that in Mesopotamia and Egypt many kingdoms rose and fell within a period of even 100 years, and along with changes in politics there was often a change in the religious order" (p. 25).
14. As Walter S. Fairservis has said: "One of the most complex, important and indeed vexing problems confronting South Asian archeologists today is the relationship of early Vedic culture(s), as described in the *Ṛgveda*, to archeological remains." "The Harappan Civilization and the Ṛgveda," in M. Witzel (ed.), *Inside the Texts – Beyond the Texts*, Cambridge 1997, pp. 61–68. At the end of his article Fairservis lists a number of cultural traits attested in the Ṛgveda and paralleled in Harappan cultural remains. He also insists that "rather than there being a gap between the later 3rd Millennium remains and those of the 2nd Millennium, suggestive of the demise of the earlier and the sudden appearance of the later, in fact some artifactual material is contemporaneous and thus a continuity existed" (p. 61).
15. Subhash Kak, *The Astronomical Code of the Rigveda*. New Delhi: Aditya Prakashan, 1994.
16. *In Search of the Cradle of Civilization*. Wheaton, Ill.: Quest Books, 1995.
17. A photograph and discussion of its age is to be found in G. Feuerstein et al., *In Search . . .* , p. 71.

4 A SHORT HISTORY OF VEDIC RELIGION

THE *ṚGVEDA* AND ITS INTERPRETERS

Although there exist considerable divergences among scholars as regards the age of the hymns of the *Ṛgveda*, as shown before, there has never been any serious doubt that they represent the oldest accessible stratum of Hindu literature. Despite their great antiquity they are still accepted as the basic scripture of the *Sanātana Dharma* and thus are probably the oldest religious text still used by a living religion.

The text of the *Ṛgveda* was preserved by oral tradition over thousands of years and the hymns before us are essentially the same as those recited thousands of years ago at the great *vaidic yajñas*. Especially with regard to content the tradition has been most scrupulous. As A. A. Macdonell wrote: "Excepting simple mistakes of tradition in the first period and more due to grammatical theories in the second period, the old text of the *Ṛgveda* shows itself to have been preserved from a very remote antiquity with marvellous accuracy even in the smallest details."[1]

The practical importance of the Vedic hymns is still very great. Thus S. N. Dasgupta writes:

> Even at this day all the obligatory duties of the Hindus at birth, marriage, death, etc. are performed according to the old Vedic ritual. The prayers that a Brahmin now says three times a day are the same selections of Vedic verses as were used as prayer verses two or three thousand years ago. A little insight into the life of an ordinary Hindu of the present day will show that the system of image worship is one that has been grafted upon his life, the regular obligatory duties of which are ordered according to the

> old Vedic rites. Thus an orthodox Brahmin can dispense with image worship, if he likes, but not so with his daily Vedic prayers or other obligatory ceremonies. Even at this day there are persons who bestow immense sums of money for the performance and teaching of Vedic sacrifices and rituals. Most of the Sanskṛt literatures that flourished after the Vedas base upon them their own validity and appeal to them as authority. Systems of Hindu philosophy not only owe their allegiance to the Vedas but the adherents of each of them would often quarrel with others and maintain its superiority by trying to prove that it and it alone was the faithful follower of the Vedas and represented correctly their views. The laws which regulate the social, legal, domestic and religious customs and rites of the Hindus, even to the present day, are said to be mere systematized memories of old Vedic teachings and are held obligatory on their authority.[2]

Through various devices – the most important being the constitution of an official *Pāda* text – and aids for memorizing the hymns, a very high degree of faithfulness in the transmission of the canonical text was achieved.[3]

With regard to the meaning of the hymns, however, there have been, from very early times, different views. Vedic interpretation is one of the most difficult and fascinating branches of Indological studies.[4]

Shrimat Anirvan suggests that from the very beginning there were two schools of Vedic interpretation: one exoteric, ritualistic, and naturalistic; the other esoteric, spiritualistic, and mystical.[5] Though the earliest Vedic interpretation in the *Brāhmaṇas* is "nothing but a simple paraphrase set in a ritual context, not only inadequate but in some cases misleading,"[6] Yāska in his *Nirukta* (fifth century B.C.E.) refers to a mystical interpretation parallel to the ritualistic one. So he comments on *Ṛgveda* X, 71, 5: "It speaks of the meaning as being the flower and the fruit of the Word. Exoterically, knowledge of the rituals and of the gods are respectively the flower and the fruit; but esoterically, the knowledge of the gods and of the Self are the fruit of the Word."[7]

The *Nirukta* is generally concerned only with part of the Vedic hymns and restricts itself mainly to explanations of difficult and obsolete Vedic words. Yāska is the last of these interpreters and provides a summary of the scholarship of his predecessors. He explicitly mentions several other early Vedic interpreters with whom he is not always in agreement. One of these, a certain Kautsa, declared in his time already that Vedic interpretation was hopeless, since the hymns were obscure, unmeaning, and mutually contradictory.[8]

The history of Indian religious orthodoxy is, in a way, a history of Vedic interpretation. The ritualistic, naturalistic, and pragmatic interpretation of the Vedas was perfected in Pūrva-Mīmāṃsā; the mystical, spiritual, and philosophical interpretation was taken up by the Upaniṣads and developed into Uttara-Mīmāṃsā or Vedānta.

About 2000 years after Yāska there arose the great medieval commentator Sāyaṇa, whose school gave the last extant complete interpretation of the *Vedas* and the *Brāhmaṇas* in a systematic way. There was a time when Vedic scholars thought that Sāyaṇa had established simply a school of interpretation of his own, but the discovery in recent times of the works of several pre-Sāyaṇa commentators made it certain "that Sāyaṇa has been following a continuous tradition of Vedic exegesis beginning from the time of Yāska."[9] Sāyaṇa established the meaning of the hymns by referring them to the ceremonies and rites that made use of them.

A new chapter in Vedic interpretation opened with the beginning of Western Indology. The interest of European scholars in the Veda was sparked by the prevalent historical bent of mind. Questions of "origins" were discussed in all branches of learning and scholars were busy collecting evidence for the development of human culture. Max Müller, who devoted the best part of his life to the editing of the text of the *Ṛgveda* and to the study of its content wrote: "the Veda would never have engaged the serious attention of a large class of scholars, if this ancient literary relic had not been found to shed the most unexpected light on the darkest periods in the history of the most prominent nations of antiquity."[10] Since Sāyaṇa's commentary was universally accepted by orthodox Brahmins and since it was the only known complete commentary which helped to give meaning to dark and difficult passages, early European Vedic scholarship relied upon it. With regard to the nature of the Vedic gods, Sāyaṇa's interpretation and the then prevailing evolutionist outlook combined to stamp them as "personifications of the powers and phenomena of nature."[11]

A critical attitude toward Sāyaṇa developed when comparative philology in the middle of the nineteenth century discovered that a number of the etymologies offered by the old commentators were incorrect. Outstanding, among others, was R. Roth, who together with O. Boethlingk compiled the famous *St. Petersburg Dictionary* in which Vedic words were interpreted by comparing the context of all the places in which a given word occurred.[12] Whereas Sāyaṇa had given different meanings for the same word in different contexts, Roth tried to establish the one original meaning. Roth's method agreed with the established standards of scientific philology which could look back to several centuries of critical study of classical Latin, Greek, and Hebrew texts. Under his inspiration many scholars took up the task of editing and translating the Vedas.[13] R. T. H. Griffith, who made use of some of these translations, remarks in his own version that "many hymns are dark as the darkest oracle."[14] K. F. Geldner, in the admittedly best translation of the entire *Ṛgveda* into a modern European language, concedes at many places that the meaning of a certain word or the translation of a certain phrase is doubtful, dark, or conjectural.[15]

European interest in the Veda awakened also Indian Vedic scholars. Some accepted the naturalistic interpretations, going even further than Western Indologists by giving the Veda a peculiar metereological, or bio-neurological, or physical interpretation;[16] others reacted sharply against these interpretations.

Dayānanda Saraswati and his followers in the Ārya Samāj became the founders of a new school of Vedic interpretation.[17] The Veda was considered the absolute culmination of religious and scientific thought; in the mystico-scientific interpretations of this school the Veda is supposed to contain all modern scientific discoveries, technical inventions, philosophical insights, and mystical perfection. Some scholars associated with the Ārya Samāj go so far as to accuse Western Indologists of mischievously underplaying the age and importance of the Veda, of arrogantly neglecting the Veda's own testimony regarding its divine origin, and of failing to understand its real meaning.[18] Others, like V. S. Agrawala, made studies of the symbolism contained in certain Vedic hymns and thus contributed to a deeper understanding of the complexity of Vedic religion.[19]

Aurobindo Ghose and his school took a different approach. Doubtlessly inspired by the prevailing trend in Western psychology, Aurobindo came to the following conclusion with regard to the Veda: "The *ṛṣis* arranged the substance of their thought in a system of parallelisms by which the same deities were at once internal and external powers of universal Nature, and they managed its expression through a system of double values by which the same language served for their worship in both aspects. But the psychological sense predominates and is more pervading, close-knit and coherent than the physical. The Veda is primarily intended to serve for spiritual enlightenment and self-culture."[20] Aurobindo's criticism of the naturalist-evolutionist type of Western Veda interpretation seems harsh, but justified: "Comparative mythology is the creation of Hellenists interpreting un-Hellenic data from a standpoint which is itself founded on a misunderstanding of the Greek mind."[21]

Modern Western Indology has moved closer toward traditional Indian ideas.[22] A deeper study of history, language, and religion has convinced most that the old commentators, though not perfect from every point of view, are indispensable guides for the correct understanding of the hymns, and that they preserved much of an uninterrupted tradition. Nineteenth-century rationalism, evolutionism, scientism, and historicism has largely been overcome and the study of religions has led to a new understanding of the meaning of myth and symbols.[23]

R. N. Dandekar's view is the most appealing: the Ṛgvedic gods, he contends, are created for the myths and not the myths for the gods. Mythology is primary and the gods secondary, that is, the Vedic *ṛṣis* had a message which they conveyed in images for which they created the concrete figures of the gods. Thus it becomes understandable that Vedic mythology is essentially evolutionary. The character of a certain god in a certain environment undergoes a change with a change of the environment. Much more important than the changing figure of a specific god was the basic underlying potency of which the individual gods were mere expressions and manifestations. The Vedic counterpart of this *mana* power is the *asura*: the essential character of the Vedic gods is that they are *asuras*. This power is shared by all beings: by moving and unmoving ones, by plants, animals, men, and gods. The anthropomorphism of the Vedic gods is highly variable, and there is neither a fixed hierarchy nor, strictly speaking, a "pantheon" of Vedic gods in the sense in which there is a Greek or Roman pantheon. Seeing Vedic religion from this new perspective makes it much easier to understand the development of the Upaniṣads and later Indian religions.[24]

Agni, "Fire," is for the Vedic *ṛṣi* not simply the chemical process of carbonization of organic matter which a modern, scientifically trained person would connect with the word "fire"; there is also a transcendent aspect in it, a hint at something beyond the material reality investigated by chemistry. *Agni* is a *deva* – not a "personification of a natural phenomenon," but the manifestation of a transcendent power. The physical reality of fire is so obvious and so necessary that the Vedic *kavi* (seer-poet) does not think of denying it or spiritualizing it away. The *kavi* is more than a mere observer of natural phenomena registered by the senses – he is "inspired" to feel and express the mystery behind all concrete reality.

THE VEDIC INDRA RELIGION[25]

Indra is the *deva* to whom most of the hymns of the *Ṛgveda* are addressed. A wealth of epithets is given to him to express his importance and describe his nature.[26] But no single trait figures more prominently than his being *vṛtrahan*,[27] the slayer of *vṛtra*. As R. N. Dandekar points out, "Vedic mythology is essentially an 'evolutionary' mythology. At different stages in the evolution of the Vedic mythological thought it has been dominated by different gods and the Indra-dominated mythology represents but a late stage in the course of that evolution." The Ṛgvedic Indra shows three different components: Indra as cosmic power; Indra as a warlike leader of the Āryans; Indra as ancient mythical dragon-killing hero. "Most of the descriptions of Indra are centred round the war with, and subsequent victory over, Vṛtra. This is by far the most outstanding event in Indra's career. A proper understanding of this point would, therefore, serve as an adequate starting point for a critical study of Indra's personality and character."[28]

The Indra-Vṛtra Myth

Ko vṛtraḥ? asks Yāska.[29] Who is Vṛtra? He knows already of a twofold interpretation. The Aitihāsikas consider Vṛtra, the son of Tvaṣṭṛ, to be a demon. The Nairuktās see in him a cloud. Thus we have from early times a mythico-historical and a naturalistic-rationalistic interpretation, not only of Vṛtra, but also of the Indra-Vṛtra myth. According to the first interpretation, the Indra-Vṛtra battle is a fight between god and demon. According to the latter, it is the description of a thunderstorm. These two interpretations have been followed variously by subsequent interpreters. Sāyaṇa interprets Vṛtra as the cloud which holds back the water. But he mentions an interpretation, which he does not accept, that Vṛtra is the "coverer" who holds back from humans the objects of their desire and their aspirations.[30]

R. N. Dandekar attributes the personification of both Vṛtra and Vṛtrahan to the temperament of the warlike Āryan tribes.

> Corresponding to this deification of the human Indra, there took place the demonization of the human Vṛtra. At this later stage of the Ṛgvedic mythology the historical human Vṛtras were collectively transformed into

> the one "demon" who prominently opposed Indra, the great god. And still later, when naturalistic elements came to be superimposed upon Indra's original personality as the result of which Indra came to be regarded as the rain-god, there was a corresponding naturalistic transformation of Vṛtra's personality so that he came to be looked upon as the cloud-demon.

In a note he adds that "it would thus be clear that Vṛtra originally represented neither the cloud, as suggested by the Nairuktas, nor the demon-son of Tvaṣṭṛ, as suggested by the Aitihāsikas."[31]

With the identification of Indra with the hero of the ancient universal dragon-myth, the growth of the personality of the Ṛgvedic Indra had found its fulfillment.[32]

The titles given to Indra – *maghavān*, *mahāvīra*, *deva*, *eka*, *rāja*, etc. – are essential attributes of the High God. The same titles are given to the Saviour God in later times.

Vṛtra is not one of many enemies, not one of many natural phenomena, but he is the sum total of evils. Not only he, but also his mother, the source of all evils, is destroyed by the saving god and the "cows" and the "waters" – words which have again a wealth of meaning in the Vedic religious context – are set free. Śrī Aurobindo sees in the "cows" the key to the meaning of the whole *Ṛgveda*: "cows" stands for truth. Even if we accept a less spiritualistic interpretation, "cows" and "waters" stand here definitely for something which was of vital importance for the Vedic people and Indra is credited with having helped them to obtain it.[33]

Vedic religion was dominated by a belief in supernatural powers, good and bad, to which every phenomenon was ascribed. The feeling of fear and uneasiness in certain situations in which no clearly visible agent was perceptible was ascribed to the influence of demons – the relief from danger and fear was the work of a god. Throughout the history of Indian religions it was always only the Supreme God who was able to defeat the king of the demons. Later reinterpretations of the Indra-Vṛtra myth, in which Indra had first to obtain Viṣṇu's, Śiva's, or Devī's own power in order to be able to slay Vṛtra, prove quite conclusively that the Indra who, without aid, was able to slay Vṛtra together with his mother was the Supreme God saving the world from evil.

Historical events seem to be alluded to in *Ṛgveda* I, 51, 5ff., where Indra is praised for having broken down Pipru's forts, for helping Rjiśvān, saving Kutsa, and for having "mighty Arbuda trodden down under foot."

Similarly in *Ṛgveda* I, 53, 8ff. we read of Indra striking down Karañja and Parṇaya, of his destroying the hundred forts of Vaṅgṛda, of his "overthrowing the twice ten Kings of men with sixty thousand nine-and ninety followers, who came in arms to fight with friendless Suśravas." Indra is praised for having protected Suśravas and Turvayāna, and "making Kutsa, Atithigva, Ayu subject unto this king, the young, the mighty."

In *Yajurveda* and *Atharvaveda*, "the prayerbook of the simple folk, haunted by ghosts,"[34] representing a tradition as old as that of the *Ṛgveda*, the exorcism of demons plays a very important role. Demons do not have fixed abodes; they inhabit caves, crossroads, desolate places.[35] The *Ṛgveda* mentions many groups of demons: Rakṣasās, Yatus, Piśācās, Ārātris, Druḥs. "They are spirits which possess men, kidnap children, spread disease, cause earthquakes and lunar eclipses and evil dreams."[36] It also mentions many individual demons, apart from Vṛtra: Arbuda, Śuṣṇa, Śaṃbara, Pipru, Dhuni-Chumuri, Uraṇa, Varcin, Namuci, Makha. Battling demons is a task for gods, not for men; defeating the supreme demon is a feat which can be accomplished only by the highest god. Indeed, it is through this act of vanquishing the arch-enemy that he gains supremacy over all.

"They call him Indra, Mitra, Varuṇa, Agni and he is heavenly winged Garutmān. To what is One, sages give many a title . . ."[37] It is said that he does not age, that he had been of age as soon as he was born, that he is always young, mighty, and powerful, that he is the son of *ojas*. Omniscience and omnipresence are attributed to him. Above all, he is the slayer of Vṛtra, the serpent from the depth, the great demon. That is the feat which made him what he is: the Supreme Saviour. Thus *Vṛtrahan* is not only a title; it is his essence. The one who slays *Vṛtra*, who covered heaven and earth, is "Lord of Heaven and Earth" – he is Indra. "Vṛtra he quelled and gave men room and freedom."[38]

Early Interpretations of the myth

VEDĀṄGAS

Yāska in his *Nirukta* refers to two interpretations of Vṛtra. He himself prefers the naturalistic one: Vṛtra is a cloud – Indra pierces the clouds and lets the waters flow. But he also often refers to Indra as the destroyer of demons. More interesting for our purpose is the *Bṛhaddevatā* ascribed to Śaunaka; this text belongs to the class of *Anukramāṇis* or "Vedic

Indices," in which for the first time a certain system of Vedic theology is attempted. A certain sacerdotal influence is visible as well as an attempt to establish a hierarchy of gods. Apart from the list of gods, the *Bṛhaddevatā* offers myths in short forms.

The most interesting portion in the *Bṛhaddevatā*, however, is its explanation of the nature of Indra. It declares the sun as identical with Prajāpati, the imperishable Brahman, the source of all being. Everything is just a particle of this One. "Because taking up fluids with his rays, accompanied by Vāyu, he rains upon the world, he is termed Indra."[39] Indra is one of the names of the High God. In the system of gods of the *Bṛhaddevatā*, Indra is the name for the manifestation of God in the middle sphere.

In every fight between the Divine and the Demon, between good and bad, between right and unjust, something of the Indra-Vṛtra battle is contained; every saviour is an "Indra" in whatever form he may appear. And in every evil there is a "Vṛtra"; evil appearing in many forms is vanquished by Indra-God in many forms.[40]

BRĀHMAṆAS

As a rule, the Vedic interpretation of the Brāhmaṇas is not very inspiring.[41] But certain quite typical features occur. Thus the *Śatapatha Brāhmaṇa* reinterprets the Vedic salvation myth in such a way that the god who performs the saving deed appears less important than the ritual sacrifice in whose service the Brāhmaṇa was composed. Indra is still considered to be the strongest and most powerful god, the chief of gods, identical with sun and fire. But quite revealingly the *Śatapatha Brāhmaṇa* says that he is born from *yajña* (sacrifice) and *vāk* (sacred word), produced by *ṛk* (hymn) and *sāman* (tune). Indra's greatness is derived from his activity as the great sacrificer, not from his Vṛtra-slaying, which is but a result of sacrificial power. His victory is not due to his prowess and natural strength but to the performance of Vājapeya. The salvific element is not god but *yajña*; it is no longer necessary to pray to Indra for protection. Indra himself depends on the sacrifice, performed by the Brahmans. The motives for the fights among gods and demons are usually to win a share in the sacrifice. This is the highest reward – which Indra wins.

The *Śatapatha Brāhmaṇa* combines with the Vṛtra-slaying another story about the killing of Tvaṣṭṛ's three-headed son Viśvarūpa. With Soma poured into fire, Tvaṣṭṛ produces Vṛtra "Indra-enemy." Vṛtra "became possessed of Agni and Soma, of all sciences, all glory, all nourishment, all prosperity, since it grew while rolling onward, it became Vṛtra; since he sprang forth footless, therefore he was a serpent. Danu and Danāyu received him like mother and father whence they call him Dānava."[42]

A *mantra* is supposed to have an infallible effect. Because of a wrong accent however, Vṛtra, instead of being invincible and defeating Indra, became the victim of Indra's wrath. Vṛtra's downfall is not due to Indra's *vajra* but to a transfer of Agni-Soma from Vṛtra to Indra "accompanied by all the gods, all the sciences, all glory, all nourishment, all prosperity."

UPANIṢADS

In the Upaniṣads Indra is reinterpreted in accord with the teaching of Vedāntic spirituality. Thus the *Kauśītaki Upaniṣad* has a long chapter in which knowledge of Indra is described as the greatest possible boon to men. Indra reveals himself as the slayer of the three-headed son of Tvaṣṭṛ, the deliverer of the Arunmukhas to the wild dogs, the one who transfixed the people of Prahlāda in the sky, the Paulomas in the atmosphere, the Kālakāñjas on earth. It is noteworthy that there is no mention of the Vṛtra-fight. For the Upaniṣads "Indra is Truth."[43] Indra is to be worshiped as *prāṇa* (breath), as *prajñātma* (the self made as wisdom), as *ayus* (life), as *amṛta* (nectar of immortality). To those who "reverence him as life, as immortality, a full term in this world, immortality, indestructibility in the heavenly world" is offered.[44]

The Upaniṣads are fond of curious etymologies of Indra: in all of them Indra is ultimately identified with *ātman* and *brahman*. The *Bṛhadāraṇyaka Upaniṣad* quotes an old etymology: "Indha (the kindler) by name is this person here in the right eye. Him, who is Indha, people call 'Indra' cryptically, for the gods are fond of the cryptic, as it were, and dislike the evident."[45] The *Chāndogya Upaniṣad* (II, 22, 3) says: "All vowels are embodiments of Indra." And the *Aitareya Upaniṣad* (I, 3, 13ff.): "I have seen it (*idam adarśa*) said he. Therefore his name is *idam-dra*. Idamdra, verily is his name. Him who is Idam-dra they call 'Indra' cryptically, for the gods are fond of the cryptic, as it were."

The profound change which took place in the attitude toward the Vedic gods is best expressed by an episode narrated in the *Chāndogya Upaniṣad*. Prajāpati acts as *guru* to Indra in order to impart *brahmavidyā* to him.[46] Indra's position with regard to the "new salvation" is in no way better than the position of any human or, for that purpose, of even the *asuras*. His is only a temporary advantage. His entire realm is transitory and therefore not interesting for the seeker of immortality. If he does not acquire Brahman knowledge, he will lose his Indrahood one day and be reborn as a lower being. Any mortal can win *brahmavidyā* but not even to the Lord of the Gods is it given by nature.

Indra is still called *Vṛtrahan*, but Vṛtra is never mentioned and salvation is not connected with this deed of Indra. It is, however, interesting to see that in the Upaniṣads Indra is always on the side of the Brahmanknower, never on the side of *avidyā* (which is connected with *asuras*), so that it can be said: he who has *brahmavidyā* has also Indra. Madhva, the only one among the major Vedāntins to write a commentary on the *Ṛgveda*, provides a philosophical explanation of the episode. According to him Vṛtra represents the concentrated essence of ignorance (*ajñāna*), figuratively described as cloud, serpent, or mountain. Indra is the Supreme Being who slays the demon of ignorance, with his weapon of *vajra*, true knowledge, and confers lasting benefit on the cows (individual selves) which have been imprisoned by the power of ignorance.[47]

ITIHĀSA AND PURĀṆA

Most scholars today attribute to *Itihāsa-Purāṇa* considerable importance as a source for Indian religion, independent from the Veda, and parallel to the *Ṛgveda* which is seen as an anthology in which "mythical episodes are referred to in an allusive way" and which constitutes only "remnants of an immense literature of legend which must have existed in an oral form long before."[48] The *Itihāsa-Purāṇa* in many cases preserves the entire myth, whereas the *Ṛgveda* contains only an allusion to the myth.

The existence of Purāṇas from the *Sūtra*-period onwards is certain; there are early references to *Purāṇas* as sources of law. The *Bṛhadāraṇyaka Upaniṣad* mentions *Itihāsa-Purāṇa* among the subjects of study of learned men. Internal evidence from the *Ṛgveda* also justifies the assumption that besides the highly formal hymns used in the official Vedic liturgy there existed popular forms of narratives, oral for many centuries and constantly growing. Several attempts have been made to reconstruct the "Original *Purāṇa Saṃhitā*," which "existed long before the Christian era."[49] Usually the *Vāyu Purāṇa* is considered to be closest to the "Original Purāṇa."[50] Though the actual shape of the Purāṇas and Epics as they are known to us is recent,[51] they preserve materials and myths that might actually be as old as, or even older than, the *Ṛgveda*.[52] Very often the myths have been reinterpreted in the Purāṇas to fit into a sectarian context, but generally the old narrative can be recognized and reconstructed.

The Indra-Vṛtra battle is dealt with in *Itihāsa-Purāṇa* in amazing detail; often the same work has several accounts of it. That may be one more argument for our thesis that the Indra-Vṛtra fight constitutes the great Vedic salvation myth which was so popular that the later Hindu sects could not afford to leave it out but had to reinterpret it to show the superiority of their own accepted god over Indra, the hero of the story.

Indra-Vṛtra in the Rāmāyaṇa

The *Rāmāyaṇa* presupposes the story of the Indra-Vṛtra battle as well known and uses it as a point of reference when describing fierce battles. Thus we find, as in the *Ṛgveda*, only allusions to the drama. The beginning of Indra's reign is placed at the time of the victory which the Devas won over the Dānavas after their fight for *amṛta*, the draught of immortality. There is a reference to "the blessings which the gods, overjoyed poured forth when Vṛtra was destroyed by Indra of the thousand eyes."[53] Several times Vṛtra's fall is mentioned when the poet describes the destruction of a particularly dangerous enemy. The *Rāmāyaṇa* connects the day of Vṛtra's death with the journey of Jaṭāyu and all the vultures to the Sun; as a result their wings were scorched.

Indra-Vṛtra in the Mahābhārata

Unlike the *Rāmāyaṇa*, the *Mahābhārata* deals at great length with the Indra-Vṛtra myth. In the *Mahābhārata* there are five versions of the myth with very significant differences.

FIRST VERSION

The first time the decisive Indra-Vṛtra battle is narrated by Ṛṣi Lomaśa in the *Āraṇyaparvan*; the whole story figures in the Kṛta-Yuga. Vṛtra was the leader of the Kal(ak)eyas, warrior tribes (Dānavas) of great prowess who fought Indra with the *devas*. The *devas* approached Brahmā to get his support in destroying Vṛtra. Brahmā sends them to Ṛṣi Dadhica, to ask him, "for the good of the three worlds: 'give us thy bones.'"[54] The Ṛṣi does as requested, discarding his body. Out of the bones Tvaṣṭṛ forms the terrible *vajra*. Armed with this bone-weapon Indra approaches Vṛtra who at that time occupied the entire earth and heaven. The first encounter is short and disastrous for the *devas*: all the gods, with Indra at their head, have to flee to Viṣṇu. Viṣṇu and all the other gods transfer part of their own energy to Indra. When Indra approaches Vṛtra again, he roars so terribly that Indra is frightened. Then Indra throws his *vajra* again against Vṛtra. Indra, fearing he might not have killed Vṛtra, takes refuge in a lake. The gods are then able to kill off the minor *Dānavas*. Some of the *Dānavas* escape into the depth of the sea, where they plot the destruction of the three worlds. They arrive at the conclusion that the best way to ruin the world is to destroy *saṃnyāsa*, the institution of the life of a "renouncer."

SECOND VERSION

A second Indra-Vṛtra tradition is preserved in the *Udyogaparvan*: Tvaṣṭṛ, the Lord of creatures and foremost of celestials, is engaged in *tapasya* (austerities). Out of dislike for Indra he has created a three-headed son, who was supposed to occupy the throne of Indra. "He read the Vedas with one mouth, drank wine with another, and looked with the third as if he would absorb the whole world!"[55] He is a staunch *tapasvī* (ascetic), and Indra becomes afraid lest he might lose his position. Indra first tries to entice him with the help of *apsaras*. The attempt fails and Indra kills him with his *vajra*. Here the author mentions that Indra contracts the sin of Brāhmaṇa-murder. Indra is afraid the *asura* will come back to life because his eyes are still looking at him. So he asks a carpenter to cut off the three heads. The carpenter argues with Indra but at last is persuaded to do it. Out from the several heads fly a great number of birds.

Tvaṣṭṛ, enraged, creates Vṛtra for the sole purpose of killing Indra. Vṛtra is mighty and powerful like a mountain. In their first encounter Vṛtra remains victorious and swallows Indra. The gods create Jṛmbika to kill Vṛtra. But when Vṛtra yawns, Indra comes out again. The second meeting, too, proves Vṛtra to be superior and Indra flees. The *devas* consult with the *ṛṣis* how to kill Vṛtra. Indra says: "This whole indestructible universe has been pervaded by Vṛtra. There is nothing that can be equal to the task of opposing him. I was capable of yore, but now I am incapable. I believe him to be unapproachable. Powerful and stouthearted, possessing immeasurable strength in fight he would be able to swallow up all the three worlds with the gods, the *asuras* and men . . ."[56] The only solution, again, is to approach Viṣṇu. The *deva*s praise Viṣṇu as *trivikrama* and the one who secured *amṛta* for the gods, as the one who has destroyed *asuras* in battles, who has bound Bali and raised Indra to the throne of heaven. Viṣṇu adivses them to make peace with Vṛtra as a preliminary means for overthrowing him. Viṣṇu himself would enter Indra's *vajra*. The *devas* and *ṛṣis* follow Viṣṇu's advice and offer to Vṛtra "eternal friendship with Indra, happiness and a permanent abode in Indra's regions." Vṛtra, at first suspicious, accepts peace after the *devas* have assured him that Indra would not kill him "by what is dry or wet, stone or wood, weapon or missile, by day or by night." But Indra remains bent on killing Vṛtra. One evening, at dusk ("not by day or by night") he sees the *asura* near the sea when a mass of froth is coming in ("neither wet nor dry"). Combining it with his *vajra* in which Viṣṇu's own energy dwells, he kills Vṛtra with froth. "And when Vṛtra was killed the cardinal points were free from gloom; and there also blew a pleasant breeze, and all beings were much pleased." Indra is again the Lord of the world, which is relieved from all evil.

This account makes much of the sin of Brahmanicide which Indra was supposed to have incurred by killing the three-headed demon and of the "sin of falsehood" incurred by treacherously killing Vṛtra. Indra grows sad: "And he betook himself to the confines of the worlds, and became bereft of his senses and consciousness. And overpowered by his own sins, he could not be recognized. And he lay concealed in water, just like a writhing snake. And when the Lord of celestials oppressed with the dread of Brahmanicide had vanished from sight, the earth looked as if a tempest had passed over it. And it became treeless, and its woods withered; and the course of rivers was interrupted; and the reservoirs lost all their waters; and there was distress among animals on account of cessation of rains. And the deities and all the great *ṛṣis* were in exceeding fear; and the world had no king and was overtaken by disasters. Then the deities and the divine saints in heaven, separated from the chief of the gods, became terrified, and wondered who was to be their king. And nobody had any inclination to act as the king of the gods."[57]

THIRD VERSION

In the *Śāntiparvan* we find two separate and different accounts of the Vṛtra-Indra battle. In the first[58] Vṛtra himself speaks as a *jñāni*, comparing his present condition as devotee of Viṣṇu with his former days when he had practiced severe self-mortification and had tried to defeat Indra. The frame of the story is rather complex: Vṛtra, the great ascetic, has earned a vision of Viṣṇu. It certainly is a problem to explain how such a great saint could be vanquished by Indra. Vṛtra himself explains that, instructed about the way of salvation through Viṣṇu, he had accepted death and thus attained the highest abode. The narration of the battle itself seems strangely unconnected with the introduction. First Vṛtra seems to win a victory over Indra by his physical strength, then by *māyā*. Indra retreats, but through Yoga he dispels Vṛtra's tricks. Bṛhaspati appeals to Mahādeva (Śiva) to destroy Vṛtra. Śiva enters Vṛtra as a fierce fever. Viṣṇu enters the thunderbolt of Indra. The *ṛṣis*, led by Bṛhaspati and Vasiṣṭha, implore Indra to kill Vṛtra, transferring to him their own powers. The effect of the Śiva-fever is disastrous – it weakens Vṛtra to such an extent that Indra can easily kill him with his *vajra*. When Indra enters Viṣṇu's realm, the sin of Brāhmaṇa-murder issues out from Vṛtra in the form of an ugly old woman, persecuting Indra. She seizes him and Indra is deprived of all his energies. Indra then lives for a long time in a lotus stalk. Brahman argues with Brahmanicide to set Indra free. Brahmanicide subsequently is divided into four portions assigned to plants, young women, water, and fire.[59] Thus Indra becomes again pure.

FOURTH VERSION

The other version of the Vṛtra-Indra story in *Śāntiparvan* follows closely the first version.[60] There are some significant minor differences. The first slain by Indra's *vajra* is not Vṛtra but Viśvarūpa, out of whose lifeless body comes Vṛtra. The story of the fight is not narrated: Vṛtra's death is simply reported. The main emphasis in this version seems to lie in showing how Indra could get rid of his sin of Brahman-murder. Indra practices Yoga; through the *siddhi* (secret power) of *aṇimā* (diminution) he is able to enter the fibers of a lotus stalk in Mānasasarovara.

The consequence of the disappearance of Indra is chaos. "The universe became lordless. The attributes of *rajas* and *tamas* assailed the *devas*. The *mantras* uttered by the great *ṛṣis* lost all efficacy. *Rākṣasas* appeared everywhere. The Vedas were about to disappear. The inhabitants of all the worlds, being destitute of a king, lost their strength and began to fall an easy prey to *Rākṣasas* and other evil beings."

Nahuṣa is elected to become king in Indra's place – his infatuation for Saci, Indra's wife, is the cause of his downfall. Asked by the *devas* to restore Indra to his previous position, Viṣṇu replies: "Let Śakra perform a horse-sacrifice in honour of Viṣṇu. He will then be restored to his former position." The *devas* first cannot find Indra in Mānasasarovara; then Śacī goes and succeeds. Bṛhaspati arranges for the sacrifice, "substituting a black antelope for a good steed every way fit to be offered up in sacrifice." Indra "continued to rule in heaven, cleansed of the sin of

Brahmanicide which was divided into four portions and ordained to reside in woman, fire, trees, and kine."[61]

FIFTH VERSION

A fifth version is narrated in *Aśvamedhaparvan*.[62] Pṛthivī, (earth) encompassed by Vṛtra, loses her proper qualities and begins to omit bad odours. Indra hurls his *vajra* at Vṛtra and hurts him. Vṛtra successively enters the waters, *jyotis* (light), *vāyu* (air), *akāśa* (ether), and destroys their proper qualities. Indra persecutes him incessantly. Finally Vṛtra enters Indra's body, robbing him of his senses. In his own body Indra slays Vṛtra by means of his *vajra*.

Indra-Vṛtra in the Purāṇas

The Purāṇas in their present form serve primarily the purpose to corroborate the claims of the various sects that Viṣṇu, Śiva, or Devī, respectively, are the highest deity and Supreme Being. In the Purāṇas the gods become very concrete figures, with distinct personalities and definite features. Thus the Indra of the *Purāṇas* is far more stereotyped than that of the *Ṛgveda*, far more plastic and understandable. He is throughout the chief of the *devas*, the king of a sensual heaven – an important figure in the three worlds but not God Supreme. He is not connected with the ultimate aim of man as seen by the Purāṇas. Despite Indra's devaluation, the ancient myth of his battle with Vṛtra figures prominently in some of the Purāṇas – and though his victory is ultimately credited to the intervention of Viṣṇu, Śiva, or Devi, the story still bears unmistakably the character of a salvation myth.

TRANSFORMATION OF THE MYTH

In those Purāṇas which are usually considered the oldest, namely, the *Vāyu*,[63] *Viṣṇu*,[64] and *Matsya*,[65] we find only short references to the Indra-Vṛtra battle. In the others, various battles of Indra with demons like Kālanemi, Bali, Jambha, Namuci, Paka, and so forth figure more prominently than that with Vṛtra. Especially the story of Indra's fight with Bali seems to have attracted greater interest in later times. But most of them at least mention it. A few deal with it at great length. In order to show the typical transformations of this myth at the hands of the puranic authors we summarize the versions given in one major Vaiṣṇava-Purāṇa, Śaiva-Purāṇa, and Śākta-Purāṇa.

BHĀGAVATA PURĀṆA

The *Bhāgavata Purāṇa* is considered the most authoritative scripture by many Vaiṣṇavas. Though among the more recent ones in its present literary form, it does, no doubt, preserve ancient traditions.[66] Its main purpose is to show Kṛṣṇa as *svayam bhagavān*, as the manifestation of the Supreme Lord Viṣṇu. In a typically sectarian narrative it tells us about Kṛṣṇa's defiance of Indra at Govardhāna[67] – implying that Indra has lost his practical importance and that Kṛṣṇa is now the Lord. Nevertheless, the same Purāṇa narrates at extraordinary length the Indra-Vṛtra story, giving it a sectarian twist, but repeating also many elements of the ancient Vedic myth. The text tries to show that it was all Indra's fault that there was any such battle at all, and only Viṣṇu rescued Indra, who foolishly precipitated the near catastrophe for all the three worlds.

Indra had offended Bṛhaspati, the divine preceptor, whereupon Bṛhaspati deserted the gods. The *asuras* then immediately took up arms against the *devas*. The badly beaten *devas* approached Brahmā for help. Brahmā advised the gods to ask Viśvarūpa, "son of Tvaṣṭṛ, a Brahmin, a *tapasvī*, self-controlled,"[68] to become their *guru*. Viśvarūpa accepted. "Viśvarūpa snatched by means of a prayer addressed to Lord Viṣṇu the fortune of the *asuras* and restored it to the great Indra. Viśvarūpa, nobleminded, taught to Indra the prayer protected by which that mighty god with a thousand eyes was able to conquer the demon hosts."[69] The *Bhāgavata Purāṇa* then describes the *Nārāyaṇa Kavaca*, the great protective prayer, which as such has nothing to do with the Indra-Vṛtra story. But the ultimate victory of Indra is attributed to this "Viṣṇu-armour."

Viśvarūpa had three heads: with one he drank Soma, with the second he drank liquor, and with the third he ate food. He faithfully performed the sacrifices to the gods "since the gods were his fathers." But he secretly offered a share to the *asuras* "for he had his sympathies with the *asuras* because of the affection his mother (Rācanā) bore to them."[70] Indra becomes angry at Viśvarūpa's offering sacrifices to the *asuras*, and cuts off his heads. The first head turns into a Chataka bird, the second into a sparrow, and the third into a partridge. Indra accepts the sin of Brahmanicide, which remains with him for a year, and then divides it into four parts among the earth, water, trees, and women, together with a boon.

Tvaṣṭṛ, whose son had been killed, pours oblations into the sacred fire in order to obtain another son who would kill Indra. "Now from the offering rose a demon of terrible aspect who looked like Death appearing at the time of universal dissolution for the destruction of the worlds. He rapidly grew to the extent of an arrow's throw on every side from day to day, presented the appearance of a burnt hill, and possessed the glow of a mass of evening clouds. With a beard and moustache and hair red as heated copper and eyes as fierce as the midday sun, he danced as if holding the vault of heaven on the end of his brilliant trident, gave a loud roar, and shook the earth with his feet. Terribly afraid, all creatures ran to and fro, as they saw him respiring again and again with his extensive gaping mouth, containing fearful teeth, and deep as a cavern, which seemed to imbibe the firmament, lick the stars with the tongue, and devour the three worlds. That sinful and ferocious demon was rightly named Vṛtra, inasmuch as these worlds were enveloped by that darkness appearing in the form of Tvaṣṭṛ's offspring. Rushing against him with their troops, the generals of the gods assailed him, each with his hosts of celestial missiles and weapons; he, however, swallowed them all."[71]

The humiliated gods this time approach Viṣṇu, addressing him with a long prayer. Viṣṇu, pleased, advises the gods to go to Dadhyanc (Dadhica), the original possessor of the *Nārāyaṇa Kavaca*, and ask his body from him. Out of its limbs the divine artisan Viśvakarman should make a weapon "by means of which and strengthened with my power you will be able to sever the head of Vṛtra. When he is slain you will regain your glory." He concludes: "Enemies can never destroy those who are devoted to me." The *Bhāgavata Purāṇa* locates the Indra-Vṛtra battle on the banks of the Narbadā at the beginning of the *Tretā yuga* "during the very first round of the four *yugas*." Two formidable armies meet: the *asuras* make no impression on the *devas* and thus they flee, leaving Vṛtra alone. Vṛtra appears self-composed, calm, and virtuous, following the rules of scripture, preaching Yoga to his fellow-*asuras* and Viṣṇubhakti to Indra. He curses Indra as a Brahman-murderer and killer of his *guru*, and he prays to Viṣṇu to be reborn as a servant of his servants. Vṛtra and Indra begin to fight.

Vṛtra is clearly superior to Indra and several times Indra is almost slain. It is only Viṣṇu's boon which preserves Indra. Vṛtra swallows Indra. Indra comes out, ripping open Vṛtra's belly, lopping off his arms and his head. But Vṛtra's death at the hands of Indra appears as willed by Vṛtra himself, whose soul entered and merged into Viṣṇu in a resplendent form. "Though revolving quickly, and cutting on all sides, the thunderbolt felled the neck of Vṛtra in as many days as are taken by the northward and southward marches of heavenly bodies at the time appointed for the death of the demon. At that time drums sounded with a loud noise, and *Gandharvas* and *Siddhas* along with hosts of eminent sages, joyously showered flowers on him, glorifying him with sacred hymns celebrating the prowess of the slayer of Vṛtra."[72]

After the Vedic reminiscence the *Bhāgavatam* relapses into its brahmanical bias: Indra is again guilty of Brāhmaṇa murder; though the *devas* are relieved and happy, Indra must be sad. The sin pursues him "in human form, resembling a Pariah-woman suffering from consumption, clad in blood-stained clothes, her limbs trembling due to old age, throwing about her grey hair crying 'stop, stop' and befouling the road with her breath that stinks like fish."[73] Indra hides in the fibers of a lotus stalk in Mānasasarovara for a thousand years, during which time Nahuṣa rules in his stead. Indra's sin is "neutralized through meditation on Śri Hari" and he returns to heaven. "The sin, that had been deprived of its force by Śri Rudra, could not assail him, protected by Goddess Lakṣmī." The Brahmins then prepare a horse-sacrifice in honor of Lord Viṣṇu and thus they exterminate the sin of Vṛtra-killing. Though the author of the *Bhāgavata Purāṇa* narrates the entire myth it is something of an embarrassment for him. He cannot connect it with his ideas of Viṣṇu's salvation and thus it loses much of its original power; although occasionally, in passages that appear like old quotations, the salvation myth comes through.

SKANDA PURĀṆA

Among the *Śaiva Purāṇas* it is only the *Skanda Purāṇa* that narrates the story at length.[74] It is told by Ṛṣi Lomaṣa, when asked how Indra could become king without the help of a *guru*. Viśvarūpa had been Indra's *purohita*. He had three heads: with the first he performed sacrifices for the *pitṛs*, with the second for the *devas* and with the third for the *asuras*. The *devas* accused him of giving the sacrifice that was due to them, to the *asuras*. Indra cuts off his heads with a hundred *vajras*. Now Indra is guilty of Brāhmaṇa-murder. An interpolation tells us that the only means to atone for a *mahāpāpa* (mortal sin) is *kīrtaṇa* (singing the name of the Lord). *Brahmahatyā* runs after Indra as a red, smoking monster. Indra hides in the water for three hundred years of the gods. There is chaos in the three worlds and the whole earth is chastised because of Indra's sin. Indra's *brahmahatyā* is taken from him, and divided into four parts, and

Indra is reinstated as king. Viśvakarman now creates Vṛtra through his *tapas*. Brahma tells the gods that Vṛtra can only be killed through a weapon made from the bones of Dadhici. Dadhici agrees to give up his body. The description of the Indra-Vṛtra battle is brief; Indra immediately kills Vṛtra. The *Purāṇa* remarks that it was only *Śivaliṅgapūjā* which provided Indra with the strength to kill Vṛtra.

DEVĪ-BHĀGAVATAM

The *Devī-Bhāgavatam* is considered by most scholars to be a *Upapurāṇa*.[75] But even so it enjoys great authority among Śāktas. It also narrates the Indra-Vṛtra episode at some length. Its frame is noteworthy: the *ṛṣis* ask Sūta to tell them about Vṛtra. They have already heard something – in a few *ślokas* they narrate the original story.[76] The *Devī-Bhāgavatam* now brings an extended and embellished version. Suta refers to King Janamejaya who had "before" asked the same question, and he narrates what Janameya had been told. First Viśvarūpa is described as a pious *yogi* – but his origin already is connected with his father's hatred for Indra. Indra, worried that Viśvarūpa might try to usurp his place, sends *āpsaras* to tempt him. When this proves a failure he comes on his elephant Airāvata and kills Viśvarūpa with his *vajra*. The *munis* lament his death and call Indra a "great sinner." Indra asks a carpenter to cut off his heads. Only when Indra offers him as a reward a share in the sacrifice, the head of every animal, does he do as he is told. Thousands of birds come out from the severed heads. Tvaṣṭṛ succeeds in producing Vṛtra from *homa*-fire on the eighth day. He gives him various weapons with which he defeats Indra. Vṛtra is described as a model ascetic, practicing *tapas*, bathing in holy rivers, giving food and drink to Brahman-guests. Brahmā grants him the boon not to be wounded by any weapon. In the next battle between *devas* and *asuras*, Vṛtra remains victorious. The beaten *devas* first approach Śiva. Śiva sends all to Viṣṇu who is *chalajñā*, "a knower of tricks and ruses". Viṣṇu advises cunning; he dispatches Gandharvas to seduce Vṛtra and promises to enter Indra's *vajra*. The *devas* are told to pretend friendship with Vṛtra. Then Viṣṇu sends all to Devī. He admits that he himself was able to kill the demons in former times only through her help. The gods approach Devi and praise her, and Devī appears in a beautiful form. Indra finally succeeds in killing Vṛtra at dusk with his *vajra* covered with froth.[77]

If we remove those elements which can be clearly seen as sectarian additions, we get from the various sources a fairly complete idea of a powerful ancient salvation story which anticipates in several of its elements later salvation myths. Names change; the basic issue of salvation remains. Viṣṇu, Śiva, and Devī are the names of the Supreme God in later times; they still battle with demons who endanger the three worlds. The concretization of the figures of Indra and Vṛtra leads to rather absurd final stages: Indra becomes one of the *lokapālas*, a door-keeper of the new High God, and Vṛtra becomes a devotee of the new High God.[78] Modern *bhaktas*, finally, venerate him as a saint.[79] The *Vāyu Purāṇa* tells us that from his mouth thousands of sons issued during his battle with Indra; all of them became followers of Mahendra.[80] The *Matsya Purāṇa* mentions a Vṛtraghātaka as the ninth of twelve *avatāras* of Viṣṇu.[81]

Indra Worship and Iconography

Indra, together with Agni, is the most prominent deity of the *Ṛgveda*, invoked in more than a quarter of the hymns, and asked to help and save people. He is "unrivalled." We do not know anything definite about specific Indra-festivals in Vedic times. Some scholars see evidence that the Indra-Vṛtra war was dramatically performed in honor of Indra at the occasion of an annual Indra festival.[82] There are some references from as late as the seventh or eighth century C.E. which mention some sort of Indra festival in South India.[83] In Nepal, even today, an Indra-*yātrā* is said to be in vogue.[84] J. Gonda thinks that Indra had also been the "genius of generation and agriculture" and that fertility rites had been performed in his honor.[85] Even today some tribes in India in times of drought torture dogs so that Indra may hear their lament and send rain. It is not impossible that the great Vedic salvation myth of the Indra-Vṛtra battle was originally performed in a way similar to the Rāma-Ravaṇa battle re-enacted nowadays at the time of Dassehra. Iconography does not yield anything of interest in connection with the Indra-Vṛtra myth. Most scholars agree that Vedic worship was un-iconic. There are a few scattered verses which might be interpreted as description of Indra images – one hymn is supposed to refer to the selling or lending out of an Indra image[86] – but the evidence is not strong.

There are some early Indra representations on coins, but none of them shows the Vṛtra-battle.[87] On some Indo-Greek coins Indra appears as a personified *vajra*. At an early time the Greeks identified Indra with Zeus, their own High God, and the representations are almost identical. Under the supposition that the figures on coins were copied from then existing cult images one could assume that there had been Indra cult images during the Indo-Greek period. Indra had been the tutelary deity of ancient Śvetavatalāya or Indrapura in the neighborhood of Kapiśa. Some representations show his elephant Airāvata. But at the time, when classical Indian sculpture was developing toward its first golden period, Indra had ceased to be the High God of India, and classical and medieval art knows him only as a lesser divinity, one of the eight *dikpālas*, the guardian deity of the Eastern quarter.

Varāhamīhira's *Bṛhatsaṃhitā* (sixth century C.E.) contains a chapter in which the construction, origin, and use of the Indra-*dhvaja* (banner) is described, without mentioning whether an Indra image was used: "The elephant of Mahendra is white and has four tusks. He has a thunderbolt in his hand and has as his cognizance the third eye placed horizontally on his forehead."[88] The *Aṃśumadbhedāgama* (eighth century C.E.) says that the color of the Indra image should be dark, with two eyes and two arms, with handsome features, adorned with *kirita* (crown), *kuṇḍalas* (earrings), *hara* (necklace), *keyura* (bracelets), dressed in a red garment, carrying in his right hand a *śakti* (missile), in his left an *aṅkuśa* (goad). He should be accompanied by Indrāṇi, standing on his left.[89] Fine panels exist in which Indra is represented in his paradise, Indra on his elephant, and Indra as *lokapāla*, but there is no known representation of the Indra-Vṛtra battle.

PŪRVA MĪMĀṂSĀ: ORTHODOX VEDIC EXEGESIS

Vedic philosophy in the most orthodox sense is represented by Pūrva Mīmāṃsā. Its basic text are the *Mīmāṃsā-Sūtras* ascribed to Jaimini (*c.*600 B.C.E.), and commented upon by many later scholars, the most famous of whom was Śābara (second century B.C.E.), author of the *Śābara-bhāṣya*, who was the major source for later scholars.[90] Among the greatest of later scholars are Kumārila Bhaṭṭa (seventh century C.E.), author of the celebrated *Śloka-vārtika*, the *Tantra-vārtika*, and the *Tup-ṭīka*; commentaries on parts of the *Jaimini-sūtras* and the *Śābara-bhāṣya*, and Prabhākara Miśra (seventh century C.E.), author of the *Bṛhatī*.

The polymath Maṇḍana Miśra (eighth century C.E.) was considered a great Mīmāṃsaka in his youth. After succumbing to Śaṅkara in a philosophical debate he became an Advaitin. As a Mīmāṃsaka he wrote works such as *Vidhi-viveka*, *Bhāvana-viveka* and *Vibhrama-viveka*. The tenth-century scholar Parthasārathi Miśra is considered the most important Mīmāṃsā writer after Kumārila Bhaṭṭa and Prabhākara, and the author of several standard works, such as the *Nyāya-ratna-māla* and the *Tantra-ratna*. He is best known as the author of the much studied *Śāstra-dīpika*. Throughout the centuries Mīmāṃsā, due to its practical importance both for the performance of ritual and for jurisprudence, was cultivated by many great scholars, some of whom were primarily heads of religious schools such as Vedānta Deśika (thirteenth century C.E.) and Madhva (fourteenth century C.E.) or Appayya Dīkṣita (eighteenth century C.E.). Leaving out many important names[91] from the intervening centuries, this short list of eminent Mīmāṃsā scholars is concluded with the name of Gaṅgānātha Jhā (1871–1941), who as the occupant of various important academic positions revitalized the study of Mīmāṃsā, and translated many major works into English.

The sole aim of Mīmāṃsā is to ascertain the exact meaning of Vedic *dharma*: "*Dharma* is that which is indicated by means of the Veda as conducive to the highest good."[92] The Mimāṃsākas take it for granted that the performance of sacrifices is the means to attain the highest good and that the Veda is the instrument for this. "The purpose of the Veda lying in the enjoining of actions, those parts of the Veda which do not serve that purpose are useless; in these therefore the Veda is declared to be non-eternal."[93]

The very use of *karma* as synonymous with *yajña* shows how much at the time of the *Mīmāṃsā-Sūtras* the sacrifice was in vogue as the most prominent religious action. Though most of the great Vedic *yajñas* in the classical sense are no longer performed, the importance of *Pūrva Mīmāṃsā* is still great even today and the principles of Vedic exegesis developed by the Mīmāṃsakas, and their epistemology, are accepted even by many of those who otherwise disagree with their doctrines. Here we are only concerned with Pūrva Mīmāṃsā statements regarding the sacrifice as a means of salvation, a topic central to the interest of the Mīmāṃsakas which constitutes the pivot of their classical works.[94]

In a consistent further development of an objectivation of salvation, classical Mimāṃsā does not admit the existence of any God as creator and destroyer of the universe. The Mīmāṃsakas even formulate arguments which positively disprove the existence of a creator god.[95] The world, according to their views, had always been in existence; there was never any *sṛṣṭsi* (creation) and there will never be a *pralaya* (end of the world). Therefore the only real agent procuring salvation is the impersonal sacrifice, or rather its essence, *apūrva*.[96] "Sacrifice," therefore, is the only topic that is of real interest. The question of the eternity of the Veda[97] – of the means to its correct understanding, of the validity of human knowledge – have to be treated as preliminary to the topic of sacrifice.[98] Pūrva Mīmāṃsā restricts the meaning of "Veda" or scripture to "*mantras* and *brāhmaṇas.*" It also respects *Smṛti* and custom, but for obtaining the "highest fruit" only the Veda is valid.[99]

The Mīmāṃsakas emphasize that "desire for heaven" is the basic presupposition for performing a sacrifice, whose end is to obtain heaven. By that criterion several categories of living beings are excluded from the role of sacrificer; therefore they are not qualified for this role.[100] Deities, too, are excluded, because apart from themselves there are no other deities to whom they could offer sacrifices and there cannot be an offering to oneself.[101] Also the Vedic *ṛṣis*, like Bhṛgu, are not qualified, because they cannot belong to the *gotras* named under "Bhṛgu and so on."[102] Women and *śūdras* are categorically excluded from the performance of sacrifices.[103] Those who have not enough wealth and those who suffer from a physical disability are also not entitled to perform sacrifices conducive to heaven.[104]

The Mīmāṃsakas deal elaborately with various classes of sacrifices. Here it may suffice just to point out the "fruit." Since one of the qualifications of a sacrificer is his desire for heaven, heaven is the highest fruit of sacrifice. The Mīmāṃsakas are equally clear about the fact that heaven cannot be obtained on earth but only after death.[105] To explain the infallible efficacy of the sacrifice they developed the ingenious theory of *apūrva.*[106] Since the act of the sacrifice itself is transitory, it has to create a permanent effect, and this is called *apūrva. Apūrva* is different according to different sacrifices and consequently one of the most important questions is to which particular word in the Vedic injunction the *apūrva* is related. It is considered related to the verb, because the verb (*kriyā*) is expressive of something yet to be accomplished.

The *Mīmāṃsā-Sūtras* are very brief in describing the state to be obtained through sacrifice: heaven. Their authors were probably convinced that one cannot know much about it. The very principles which they establish lead to the conclusion that those passages in the Vedas which describe heaven (because they do not enjoin certain acts) cannot be taken as authoritative. There is one short *sūtra* which says: "That one result would be 'heaven', as that is equally desirable for all."[107] And a short notice by the commentator: "Why so? Because heaven is happiness and everyone seeks for happiness."[108] The *Mīmāṃsā-Sūtras* do not treat the topic *mokṣa*. Nor does Śābara. Prabhākara and Kumārila Bhaṭṭa, however, probably under the influence of Vedānta, deal with *mokṣa*. Śābara had declared that the views about heaven as exposed in *Mahābhārata* and *Purāṇas* can be neglected, since these books are composed by men. Vedic descriptions, too, are mere *arthavāda*, without authority.[109] Both later Mīmāṃsaka schools agree, however, in saying that *mokṣa* consists in not having to assume a body again after death.[110] According to Kumārila Bhaṭṭa, anyone desiring *mokṣa* should perform only prescribed rituals without desiring rewards.[111]

Similarly, for Prabhākara *mokṣa* consists in the disappearance of all merits and demerits, and the cessation of rebirth. Kumārila Bhaṭṭa discusses the role of *jñāna* and *karma* in the process of liberation. Commenting on the text "the fire of knowledge destroys all *karmas*" he maintains that it is only the gross manifestation of *karma* that is referred to as destroyed, not the potency of *karma*. Therefore it cannot be totally uprooted by means of *jñāna*, because the potency of *karma* is not opposed to *jñāna*.

Knowledge can only prevent the formation of new *karma* but cannot destroy its potentiality. Therefore knowledge cannot be the cause of liberation.[112] *Karmas* already acquired have to be borne out. Knowledge is only an auxiliary to *karma* insofar as it makes the performance of *nitya* (prescribed) and *naimittika* (optional) rituals possible without desire for their fruit.[113] In late Pūrva Mīmāṃsā, so it appears, the depersonalization and objectivation of human salvation has come to its logical extreme: "They raise *yajña* to the position of God," says P. V. Kane, "and their dogmas about *yajña* seem to be based upon a sort of commercial or business-like system."[114]

THE CONTINUITY OF VEDIC RELIGION

Worship of Indra, the great god of the *Ṛgveda*, was over the centuries replaced by the worship of Viṣṇu, Śiva and Devī, as the references from the Purāṇas demonstrated. Vedic *yajña* was largely superseded by *pūjā*, the worship of images in homes and temples, at which flowers and fruits, and not animals and soma, are the main offerings. Among intellectuals, the orthodox Vedic exegesis of the Mīmāṃsakas has been pushed from center-stage by the speculative philosophies of Vedānta. However, it would be wrong to conclude that Vedic religion is a thing of the past only.

All Hindus claim that their religion is "vedic" and that they follow the *vaidika dharma*. Vedic, in the traditional Hindu understanding, means much more than the hymns of the *Ṛgveda* and the mythology associated with it. It denotes a way of life, inherited from ancestors, and a specific understanding of the world that is an essential element of all of Hinduism. While Vedic *yajñas* are no longer the main feature of Hindu religious celebrations, they are still performed at many occasions and there has been a noticeable increase in such sacrifices during the last few decades. Also Hindu Vedic scholarship has grown in the recent past and has struck out along new paths.

While purāṇic temple-worship dominates everyday Hindu religiosity, Vedic rites are still performed at the important life-cycle rituals of birth, marriage, and death. At these occasions Vedic hymns in their original language are recited and ceremonies that may reach back thousands of years are re-enacted. Vedic religion is much more than a distant memory of times long past; it is an integral element of contemporary Hinduism that has not ceased to shape the lives and thoughts of Hindus.

Aurobindo Ghose, by giving a new, spiritual interpretation to key words in the Veda, opened up a new understanding of Vedic hymns that has inspired a whole generation. Thus he identified the word "cow," so frequently occurring in the *Ṛgveda*, as "truth" and "light"; he designated Indra as the "Giver of Light" – a universal and timeless figure. "The principle, which Indra represents, is Mind-Power, released from the limits and obscurations of the nervous consciousness," he explains, and "this Light is, in its entire greatness free from limitation, a continent of felicity; this Power is that which befriends the human's soul and carries it safe through the battle, to the end of its march, to the summit of its aspiration."[115]

A rather more down to earth revival of Vedic religion has been accomplished by Upāsanī Bābā Mahārāj, the founder of the Upāsanī Kānya Kumārī Sthān, a Hindu religious order for women who function as Vedic priestesses. When he began educating young women in Sanskrit and training them to perform Vedic homa rituals, there was tremendous opposition from the orthodox brahmins. To make his point, he confined himself to a bamboo cage for fifteen months "for the liberation of his devotees." Women aspirants to priesthood kept joining and when he died in 1941 one of them, Satī Godāvarī Mātājī became the head of the ashram. The ashram, situated in Sakori (Maharastra) in 1992 housed 48 members who had taken the vows of physical purity, celibacy, and daily worship. The women are trained to perform Vedic *śrauta* rituals as well as other ceremonies.[116] Apart from this organization, recently numerous women have been trained as *purohitas* - some of them because of a shortage of male priests, others because of a complaint from the public that the men were performing the rituals too sloppily and carelessly.

NOTES

1. A. A. Macdonell, *A History of Sanskrit Literature*, p. 47. This opinion has been confirmed in the most recent work on the subject. See J. Gonda, *Vedic Literature*, pp. 40ff. See also L. Renou, *Les écoles vediques et la formation du Veda*.
2. S. N. Dasgupta, *HIPh*, vol. I, pp. 10ff.
3. According to tradition Vyāsa arranged the *Saṃhitā* text, Śakalya the *Pāda* text.
4. G. V. Devasthali, "Various schools of Vedic interpretation," in Chinmulgund and Mirashi, *Review*, pp. 31ff.
5. Shrimat Anirvan, "Vedic Exegesis," *CHI*, vol. I, pp. 311–332.
6. Ibid.
7. P. Lakshman Sarup (ed. and trans.), *The Nighantu and the Nirukta*, 2 vols., 1926–67, *Nirukta*, I, 20.
8. A. A. Macdonell, *A History of Sanskrit Literature*, p. 60.
9. Shrimat Anirvan, "Vedic Exegesis."
10. F. Max Müller, *Ṛgveda Saṃhitā*, Preface to the third volume of the first edition, 1st Indian Edition, Varanasi, 1966, p. xli.
11. That is the view of the *magnum opus* of this school, Macdonell's *Vedic Mythology*, Strasbourg, 1897.
12. Boethlingk-Roth, *Sanskrit-Wörterbuch*, 7 vols., St. Petersburg, 1852–1875 (reprint, Graz, 1964).
13. K. Aufrecht brought out a romanized text edition of the *Ṛgveda* in two volumes, Bonn, 1877 (reprint 1955); A. Weber edited the *Yajurveda* (Berlin–London, 1852); T. Benfrey edited the *Sāmaveda* (Leipzig, 1848), Roth and Whitney the *Atharvaveda* (Berlin, 1856). Complete translations of the *Ṛgveda* into European languages were made by H. H. Wilson, M. Williams, R. T. H. Griffith, H. Grassmann, A. Ludwig, and H. F. Geldner. It was also due to Roth's *Zur Litteratur und Geschichte des Weda* (Stuttgart, 1846) that interest in scholarly research into the *Ṛgveda* was aroused in Europe.
14. R. T. H. Griffith, *The Hymns of the Ṛgveda*, vol. I, Preface, p. xiv.
15. K. F. Geldner, *Der Ṛgveda*, 3 vols., Lanman Harvard Oriental series, 1951ff. Cf. also L. Renou, *Études vediques et panineénnes*, vols. 1–17, Paris, 1955–69.
16. Bergaigne had already thought that the mythology of the Vedic Āryans was closely connected with their sacrificial cult which appeared to him to be an imitation of celestial phenomena, distinguishing male and female elements (sun–dawn; lightning–cloud, etc.). Cf. his *Vedic Religion*, vol. II, 1ff. The most important among the new interpreters

is L. B. G. Tilak. Cf. his *The Arctic Home in the Vedas* with the subtitle "Being also a new key to the interpretation of many Vedic texts and legends," Poona, 1903.

17. Cf. Devi Chand, *The Yajur Veda* (English translation), Hoshiarpur: Vedic Research Institute, 1959; Introduction, and the new Ṛgveda edition by Visva Bandhu in eight volumes, Hoshiarpur, 1963–66.
18. Cf. Swami Samarpananand Saraswati, *Maṇi-Sūtra*, Calcutta, n.d., which is supposed to "answer the calculated mischief done by some Western Vaidic scholars and their local protégés to the prestige and inviolability of the Vedas."
19. Vasudeva S. Agrawala, *Sparks from the Vedic Fire*.
20. Sri Aurobindo Ghose, *On the Veda*, pp. 34ff.
21. Ibid., p. 29.
22. See J. Gonda, *Die Religionen Indiens*, vol. I, pp. 55ff. Also some of the contributions in M. Witzel (ed.), *Inside the Texts: Beyond the Texts. New Approaches to the Study of the Vedas*. Harvard Oriental Series, Opera Minor Vol. 2, Columbia, Mo.: South Asia Books, 1997.
23. Cf. J. Gonda, *Vedic Literature*, Wiesbaden, 1975.
24. R. N. Dandekar, *God in Hindu Thought*, Poona, 1968. Publications of the Centre of Advanced Study in Sanskrit Class A, No. 21, University of Poona.
25. See Renate Söhnen, "Rise and Decline of the Indra Religion in the Veda," in M. Witzel, (ed.), *Inside the Texts* ... (1997), pp. 235–243.
26. The etymology of Indra is not clear as yet. A. A. Macdonell, *Sanskrit Literature*, p. 44, derives it from *indu*: drop; J. Gonda, *Die Religionen Indiens*, I, p. 60, from *intoi*: drängend (pushing); R.N. Dandekar, "Vṛtrahā Indra," derives it from *indu*, which he brings in connection with the meaning "virile power." S. S. Sastri, "Vṛṣakapi," *Bhāratīya Vidyā* X (1949), p. 195: "The word Indra is more appropriately derived from *In, Inva* (to rule) (cf. *Nirukta* X, 8, *Br.* IV, 2, 2), and connected with *Ina* (sun, Lord) and Invakas or Ilvalas (stars near the head of Mṛgasirśa) than from Indu." Indra has been declared to be the sun-god (Hillebrandt), the rain-god (Oldenberg), a god of universal character (Roth), and god of fertility as well as battles (Hopkins). About a quarter of the hymns of the *Ṛgveda Saṃhitā* are addressed to Indra, not counting those hymns where he is invoked under different names. Some of the most common epithets which are often used as his proper names are: *vajrabahu, vajrin, śakra, rathestha, somapā, śatakratu, maghavan, apsujit, purbidh, hari, sacipati, gopati.*
27. R. N. Dandekar, "Indra Vrtrahā," reprinted in *Vedic Mythological Tracts*. Delhi, 1979, p. 141.
28. R. N. Dandekar, "Indra Vrtrahā." V. M. Apte, "Vedic Religion," in R. C. Majumdar (general ed.), *HCIP*, vol. I, pp. 375ff.: "The true character of Indra can be understood by ascertaining that of Vṛtra, his opponent ..."
29. Yāska, *Nirukta* II, 16.
30. The *Nirukta* has three different derivations of Vṛtra which are all accepted: from root *vṛ-* to cover, root *vṛt-* to roll, and root *vṛdh-* to grow. Cf. Sāyaṇa on *RV* I, 32.

31. R. N. Dandekar, "Vṛtrahā Indra," p. 175.
32. Ibid. D. D. Kosambi, *An Introduction to the Study of Indian History*, pp. 70ff., sees in the Indra-Vṛtra myth an expression of the historical conquest of the Indus Valley by the Āryans. Vṛtra is an artificial irrigation dam, destroyed by the Āryans, who thereby took away the basis of agriculture. He quotes *RV* II, 15, 8 *rināg rodhamṣi kṛtrimāni* (*rodhas* = dam). Indra is praised for restoring to its natural course the river Vibali which had flooded land along its banks.
33. R. Söhnen in "Rise and Decline of the Indra Religion in the Veda" says: "Assuming the epithet *Vṛtrahan* he absorbed the principle of 'victory' and became the national god of the Indo-Āryan invaders who certainly wanted to break the 'resistance' of the *dāsas* or *dāsyus*."
34. V. M. Apte, *HCIP*, vol. I, p. 236.
35. Ajoy Lahiri, "Indian and Babylonian Demonology – a comparative study," in *Vishveshvaranand Indological Journal*, vol. IV, 2 (Sept. 1966), pp. 186–197.
36. Ibid. Cf., *RV* VII, 104, 20ff.
37. *Ṛgveda* I, 164, 45.
38. Ibid., X, 104, 10.
39. Ibid., I, 68.
40. Thus also Namuci can be called a *vṛtra*: *Ṛgveda* VIII, 14, 13; V, 30, 7. The same saving functions are attributed to Dyaus-Prithvi, to Rudra, Sun, Bṛhaspati.
41. R. Söhnen believes that the authors of the Brāhmaṇas "were not at all especially fond of Indra, but rather liked to degrade him in favour of the sacrifice and its mysterious and magical powers." In M. Witzel (ed.), *Inside the Texts* . . ., p. 238.
42. Ibid., 8ff.
43. Ibid.
44. Ibid.
45. The quote is from *Śatapatha Brāhmaṇa* VI, 1, 1, 2.
46. *Chāndogya Upaniṣad* VIII, 7, 1ff.
47. B. N. K. Sharma, *Madhva's Teachings in His Own Words*, pp. 160ff.
48. L. Renou, *Vedic India*, 9.
49. V. S. Agrawala, "Original Purāṇa Saṃhitā," in *Purāṇa* VIII/2 (1966), pp. 232ff.
50. Agrawala considers (R)Lomaharṣana to have been the original teacher of the *Purāṇa*, who taught it to six pupils. Thus the *Mūla-saṃhitā* was rendered into six *Para-saṃhitās* of 4000–6000 *ślokas* with essentially the same contents: *sarga*, *pratisarga*, *manvantara* and *vamśa*. The *caturpāda* scheme is the original form – it is preserved in *Vāyu-* and *Brahmāṇḍa-Purāṇa*. From the existing *Vāyu-Purāṇa* one may recover the *Mūla-saṃhitā* by eliminating the approximately eighty spurious (interpolated) chapters.
51. According to R. C. Hazra, *Studies in the Purāṇic Records*, there have been two stages in the formation of the *Purāṇas*: from the third to the fifth century A.D. those matters were added to the "original *Purāṇa*" which formed the subject-matter of early *Smṛtis* (Yajñavalkya and

Manu). From the sixth century onwards new topics were added: gifts, glorification of holy places, *vrata*, *pūjā*, consecration of images, sacrifices, astrology, and so forth, which form the bulk of Purāṇic lore. The oldest and most original parts of the Purāṇas appear to be their mythology.

52. A. D. Pusalker, "Purāṇic Studies," in Chinmulgund and Mirashi (eds.), *Review*, pp. 689–773, writes: "In his *Origin and Character of Purāṇa Literature*, B. C. Mazumdar states that *Purāṇa* as a branch of sacred literature did exist in the Vedic days; that it was recognized as the fifth Veda when the Atharva Veda was recognized as the fourth division of the Veda; that for each Vedic school a separate *Purāṇa* was organized such as *Agni* for *Ṛgveda*, *Vāyu* for *Yajurveda*, and *Sūrya* for *Sāmaveda*; and that the modern *Purāṇa* received only a little additional matter by way of accretion from the fifth century onwards, though the modern *Purāṇas* differ radically from the Vedic *Purāṇas*." Several scholars are of the opinion that the *Purāṇas* grew out of the narrations during certain festivals, especially the *Aśvamedha*. Manu, for example, enjoins listening to the *Purāṇa* during the *śrāddha* ceremony. See also "Purāṇas and their Authority in Religious Matters," in *Kalyāṇa Kalpatāru*, August 1952.
53. *Mahābhārata*, II, 22, 13.
54. Ibid., III, 98, 9.
55. Ibid., 9, 4ff.
56. Ibid., V. 10, 1ff.
57. Ibid., V, 10, 47.
58. Ibid., XII, 270, 16ff.
59. Ibid., XII, 273, 39ff.
60. Ibid., XII, 329, 19ff. (one of the few prose portions of the *Mahābhārata*; a so-called *Pāñcarātra Adhyāya*).
61. Ibid., XII, 329, 41.
62. Ibid., XIV, 11.
63. The *Vāyu Purāṇa* is usually regarded as the oldest: "It has preserved much of its ancient, if not original materials, and as such can be rightly called the earliest of the extant Puranic works." R. C. Hazra, "The Purāṇas," *CHI*, vol. II, p. 253. Also A. D. Pusalkar, "Puranic Studies," in Chinmulgund and Mirashi (eds.), *Review*, pp. 735ff., "Researches in Vāyu-Purāṇa."
64. "The *Viṣṇu Purāṇa* is an early work, composed most probably in the last quarter of the third or the first quarter of the fourth century A.D. . . . it has preserved the best text, additions and alterations having been made in it much less freely than in the other *Purāṇas* . . . it is a rich store of interesting myths and legends." R. C. Hazra, ibid., pp. 257ff. Cf. A. D. Pusalker, ibid., p. 735: V. R. Ramacandra Diksitar assigns the *Viṣṇu Purāṇa* to the sixth or seventh century B.C.E.
65. The *Matsya Purāṇa* is "a conglomeration of chapters taken at different times from various sources, especially the *Vāyu Purāṇa* and the *Viṣṇudharmottara* . . . either in the last quarter of the third or the first quarter of the fourth century A.D." R. C. Hazra, ibid., p. 258. Cf. A. D. Pusalkar, ibid., p. 743.

66. A. D. Pusalker, "Purāṇic Studies,", p. 736. R. C. Hazra, *The Purāṇa*, p. 258: "the most popular of the extant Purāṇic works, deserves special attention." Its date of composition is between the sixth and tenth centuries C.E. but possibly it contains sections of an earlier *Bhāgavata*.
67. *Bhāgavata Purāṇa*, X, 24, also *Harivaṃśa* II (Viṣṇuparvan) 18ff. But Indra is introduced as a friend of new-born Kṛṣṇa: *Bhāgavata Purāṇa* X, 3, 50. The rainbow is Indra's bow: X, 20, 18. Indra and the birth of Maruts: VI, 18. In IX, 7, 17 Indra appears to Rohita in a forest. IX, 6, 13ff.: in a battle between gods and demons Indra assumes the form of a bull.
68. Ibid., VI, 7, 25.
69. Ibid., VI, 7, 40 and 8, 42, where it is said: "Indra having learnt this prayer from Viśvarūpa completely and decidedly conquered the demons in battle and enjoyed the sovereignty of the three worlds."
70. Ibid., VI, 9, 3.
71. Ibid., VI, 9, 12–19.
72. Ibid., VI, 12, 33ff.
73. Ibid., VI, 13, 12ff. Verses 1–11 seem to introduce a new narration.
74. *Skanda Purāṇa*, Maheśvarakhaṇḍa-Kedarakhaṇḍa, 15ff.
75. The *Devī-Bhāgavata* itself claims to be a *Mahāpurāṇa*, the real *Bhāgavata* mentioned in the lists of the eighteen *Purāṇas*. Cf. A. D. Pusalkar, "Purāṇic Studies," p. 738. R. C. Hazra, "The Upapurāṇas," *CHI*, II, p. 281, assigns the *Devī-Bhāgavata* to the eleventh or twelfth century C.E. "Its author was a Smārta Śākta Brāhmaṇa of Bengal who lived for a long time in Benares and then wrote this work for infusing Śākta ideas into the members of different sects."
76. *Devī-Bhagavata*, VI, 1, 3–12.
77. Ibid., VI, 6.
78. According to the *Bhāgavata Purāṇa* the demon Bali, who had been defeated by Viṣṇu's Vāmana *avatāra*, becomes Indra in the Savarni Manvantara (VIII, 22, 31ff.). In the Purāṇas the Brahmans, however, are far more important than the gods. The great battles between demons and gods, upon which according to Vedic belief the fate and well-being of humankind depended, have hardly any importance with regard to salvation. A significant story is told in *Bhāgavata Purāṇa* IX, 17, 12ff. Raji, a king of the solar dynasty, defeats the *asuras* and re-enthrones Indra in heaven. Indra "placed himself in his hands, afraid as he was of Prahrāda and other enemies. At the death of their father the sons of Raji did not return heaven to the great Indra, even though he asked for it, and fully appropriated the sacrificial offerings."
79. Vṛtra is worshiped as a saint by Viṣṇu-*bhaktas*. Cf. "Vṛtrāsura" in *Kalyāṇ Santāṅk* 12 (1937), pp. 384–386.
80. *Vāyu Purāṇa*, Uttarakhaṇḍa 7, 34ff.
81. *Matsya Purāṇa* 8, 4; 22, 61. According to *Bhāgavata Purāṇa* VI, 38, Citraketu becomes Vṛtra (also Prahrāda) and Hiraṇyakaśipu takes the role of Indra (VII, 4, 12). As an *avatāra* of Visṇu he defeats Prahrāda (III, 5, 55ff.). According to the *Brahmāṇḍa Purāṇa* Indra represents a face of Śiva (II, 23, 9).
82. Cf. J. N. Banerjea, *Development*, pp. 45ff.

83. The *Silappadigaram* (eighth century C.E.) describes the annual Indra festival of Kariappaumpattinam, the capital of the Cholas, which lasted 28 days. Cf. T. A. G. Gopinath Rao, *Elements* II/II, p. 516ff. According to *Bhāgavata Purāṇa* X, 53, 49ff., the temple of Indra in Vidarbha was visited by Rukminī on the day before her marriage: Indra and Indrāṇī were *kula devatās* of Vidarbha.
84. Cf. J. Gonda, *Die Religionen Indiens*, vol. II, p. 79.
85. Ibid., vol. I, pp. 340ff.
86. The verse in question is *Ṛgveda* IV, 24, 10: "Who will buy this my Indra for ten cows? When he has slain the *vṛtras* he may give him back to me" (translation by R. T. H. Griffith).
87. The names Mitra, Varuṇa, Indra, Nasatya are mentioned on the Boghaz Köi inscriptions (fourteenth century B.C.E.). Cf. *HCIP*, vol. II, p. 613.
88. Ibid., chap. 57, 42.
89. T. A. G. Rao, *Elements*, p. 520.
90. An English translation has been published by Ganganatha Jha in three volumes in the Gaekwad Oriental Series.
91. The interested reader may consult the "Critical Bibliography" by Umesh Mishra, appended to Ganganatha Jha (ed.), *Pūrvamīmāṃsā in Its Sources*, Benares Hindu University, 1942, for further names and details.
92. *Mīmāṃsā-Sūtras* I, 1, 2.
93. Ibid., I, 2, 1.
94. Ganganatha Jha, *Pūrvamīmāṃsā in its Sources*, pp. 359ff.
95. *Śābara Bhāṣya* I, 1, 22: "There can be no creator of this relation because no Soul is cognized as such by any of the means of cognition. If there had been such a creator, he could not have been forgotten." Prabhākara in his *Prakāraṇa Pañcikā* offers arguments against the assumption of a God who would be creator and supervisor of the universe. Kumārila Bhaṭṭa holds that the world is beginningless and hence does not have a creator, nor does it need any. There cannot be any omniscient person.
96. P. V. Kane, *HDhS*, vol. V/II, p. 1210.
97. Ganganatha Jha, *Pūrvamīmāṃsā*, p. 178.
98. Ibid., p. 77f.; "The doctrine of the self-validity of knowledge (*svataḥpramāṇya*) forms the cornerstone on which the whole structure of the Mīmāṃsā philosophy is based. Validity means the certitude of truth. The Mīmāṃsā asserts that all knowledge excepting the action of remembering (*smṛti*) or memory is valid in itself, for it itself certifies its own truth and neither depends on any extraneous condition nor on any other knowledge for its validity." S. N. Dasgupta, *HIPh*, vol. I, p. 372.
99. G. Jha, *Pūrvamīmāṃsā*, p. 176.
100. *Mīmāṃsā-Sūtras* VI, 1, 5.
101. *Śābara-Bhāṣya* on *Sūtra* VI, 1, 5. But according to *Śatapatha Brāhmaṇa* V, 1, 1, 2 gods offer sacrifices to one another.
102. Kumārila Bhaṭṭa, *Tupṭīka* on *Sūtra* VI, 1, 5.
103. *Mīmāṃsā-Sūtras* VI, 1, 6ff. 26ff.

104. Ibid., VI, 1, 39ff.
105. P. V. Kane, *HDhS*, vol. V/II, p. 1212: the *svarga* of the Mīmāṃsakas is different from that of the Vedas or *Purāṇas*: *svarga* is unmixed bliss which cannot be acquired while on earth.
106. *Mīmāṃsā-Sūtras* II, 1, 5: "There is *apūrva*, because action is enjoined." Cf. G. Jha, *Pūrvamīmāṃsā*, pp. 256ff.
107. *Mīmāṃsā-Sūtras* IV, 3, 15.
108. *Śābara Bhāṣya* on IV, 3, 15.
109. Ibid., on VI, 1, 1.
110. *Nyāyaratnakāra*: "Liberation must consist in the destruction of the present body and the non-production of the future body." Quoted by G. Jha, *Pūrvamīmāṃsā*, p. 38. Cf. P. V. Kane, *HDhS*, vol. V/II, p. 1216.
111. *Ślokavārttika*, Sambaṇḍhakṣepa Parihāra 108ff.
112. Cf. N.K. Brahma, *Philosophy of Hindu Sādhana*, chap. VI: Karma-Mārga or Path of Action, pp. 91–136.
113. Ibid., p. 94.
114. P. V. Kane, *HDhS*, p. 1217.
115. "Indra, Giver of Light," in *On the Veda*, Aurobindo Ashram: Pondicherry, 1956, pp. 271–279. Quotes on p. 276 and 279.
116. The information is based on an article in *Hinduism Today*, vol. 14, no. 8 (August 1992) which mentions V. L. Manjul from the Bhandarkar Oriental Research Institute in Pune as source.

5 A SHORT HISTORY OF VAIṢṆAVISM

Vaiṣṇavism has a history of millennia. In the course of time it has absorbed many traditions and undergone various developments. It is not easy to trace the components of modern Vaiṣṇavism. As S. K. Chatterji writes: "Viṣṇu is partly Āryan, a form of the Sun-God, and partly at least the deity is of Dravidian affinity, as a sky-god, whose colour was that of the blue sky (Tamil *viṇ* 'sky'; Prākṛt forms of *Viṣṇu* are *viṇhu* or *veṇhu*)."[1] S. Chattopadhyaya calls the Viṣṇu worshiped by today's Vaiṣṇavas "the accumulation of a host of un-Āryan local deities" and sees in the *avatāras* former tribal totems.[2] Vaiṣṇavas themselves, however, insist that their religion is Vedic, and their philosophers usually claim to represent the only true interpretation of the scriptures.

There are several hymns in the *Ṛgveda Saṃhitā* that are addressed to Viṣṇu[3] but there is no evidence of any particular community of Viṣṇu-worshipers. Viṣṇu is considered in early Vedic exegesis one of the names of the sun, and the solar origin of Viṣṇu seems to be corroborated by other facts also.[4] Some *Brāhmaṇa* passages address Viṣṇu as the "most excellent of the gods," the "greatest,"[5] but that does not warrant the assumption that Vaiṣṇavas existed as a particular sect. Viṣṇu attains a certain prominence in the *Upaniṣads* and the *Sūtras* as the "protector of the embryo in the womb" – a function which he also holds in later Vaiṣṇavism.

The *Mahābhārata* mentions Sātvata and Pāñcarātra cults which could be prototypes of later Vaiṣṇava sects, as well as major non-Vedic sources of Vaiṣṇavism: worship of Nārāyaṇa and Vāsudeva-Kṛṣṇa. It seems fairly certain that the basis of the latter was an historical Kṛṣṇa, a hero from the Vṛṣṇi clan of the Yādava tribe residing in and around Mathurā.[6] In later Vedic literature the Vṛṣṇis are frequently mentioned as irreverent towards Brahmins and as dark complexioned.

Pāṇini (sixth century B.C.E.) in his *Aṣṭādhyayī* mentions "*bhakti* to Vāsudeva." Vāsudeva was the object of such devotion at least as early as the fourth century B.C.E., as proved by the statement of Megasthenes that the Sourasenoi (the people in the Mathurā region) held Heracles in special honor: Heracles was the Greek analogue of Vāsudeva-Kṛṣṇa. This hero of the Yādava clan, who became the leader of a religious movement, was deified and styled *Bhāgavat*, a process which was completed by the second century B.C.E.

The pastoral character attributed to Kṛṣṇa has a different source and belongs to a later period. Probably it is due to his identification with the local deities of the Abhiras and other pastoral tribes. The formal and full identification of Kṛṣṇa-Vāsudeva with the supreme God Viṣṇu is an established fact in the *Bhagavadgītā*. The Brāhmins were keen on bringing this powerful religious sect within their orthodox Vedic faith and called it *Vaiṣṇava dharma*. Also the divinization of four other members of the Vṛṣṇi clan (the later *vyūhas* of Viṣṇu) seems to have taken place already by the first century B.C.E.

Vāsudevism spread through the migration of Yādava tribes. We can see some development of it even in the *Mahābhārata*. In its earliest portions there are several disrespectful attributes given to Vāsudeva, showing thereby that he was not considered divine.[7] But the Besnagar inscription testifies to Vāsudeva worship in the second century B.C.E. Inscriptions at Ghoṣundī and Nānaghāt (first century B.C.E.) mention the worship of Saṁkarṣaṇa and Vāsudeva. At the beginning of the Common Era we find representations of Vāsudeva-Viṣṇu on the Viṣṇumitra coin and the Huviśa seal matrix.

The fully developed *vyūha* doctrine is in evidence in the Mora inscription (second century C.E.). It is one of the central tenets of the earlier Pāñcarātra and the later Śri-Vaiṣṇava religion. Bhāgavatism has an interesting relation to some other sects: the Ajivikas seem to have been devotees of Nārāyaṇa. The Jainas include Vāsudeva and Bāladeva among the sixty-three *śalaka-puruṣas* and the Jain Tirthāṇkara Ṛṣabha was considered an *avatāra* of Viṣṇu by some Bhāgavats. "The later conception of the twenty-four forms of Viṣṇu was probably derived from that of the twenty-four Jain Tirthāṇkaras."[8]

Also Buddhism has apparently contributed to the development of Bhāgavatism. There is a close resemblance between the Buddhist worship of the footprints of the Buddha and the Vaiṣṇava worship of *Viṣṇu-pada*. "The full development of the *avatāra-vāda* seems to have been influenced by the Buddhist conception of the former Buddhas, some of whom were worshiped in their own *stūpas* as early as the third century B.C. That a large number of Buddhists were admitted into the fold of the Vaiṣṇavas toward the close of the Hindu period is suggested by the inclusion of Buddha in the list of *Viṣṇu-avatāras*."[9] It seems that the Bhāgavatas or Pāñcarātrins were also largely responsible for the propagation of image worship among the higher sections of the orthodox Hindus.

While the imperial Guptas supported all branches of the Hindu tradition, they seem to have personally favored Vaiṣṇavism. Their coins show the Garuḍa emblem and Samudragupta is known to have been a Vaiṣṇava. The seventh-century author Bāṇa mentions Bhāgavatas.

From the post-Gupta period onward we find numerous images of Viṣṇu and his *avatāras* all over India. Ānanda Giri (ninth century C.E.) mentions in his *Śaṅkara Digvijaya* six different Vaiṣṇava sects: The *Bhaktas* were associated with Vāsudeva, the *Bhāgavatas* with Bhagavat, the *Vaiṣṇavas* with Nārāyaṇa, the *Cakrinas* with Pāñcarātra, the *Vaikhānasas* with Nārāyaṇa; the *Karmahīnas* were without any specific ritual.

Mādhava (fourteenth century C.E.) describes in his *Sarvadarśana Saṅgraha* two different Vaiṣṇava-*darśanas*: *Rāmānuja-darśana* and *Pūrna-prajñā-darśana*. In the later middle ages numerous *bhakti* movements flourished, and several attempts were made to unify all the Vaiṣṇava sects under one authority. In the fourteenth century all the existing Vaiṣṇava orders were affiliated with one of the four major Vaiṣṇava traditions (*catuḥ-sampradāya*), each distinguished by its own version of Vedānta:

1. The Śrīvaiṣṇava saṃpradāya (Viśiṣṭādvaita)
2. The Brahma saṃpradāya (Dvaita)
3. The Kumāra saṃpradāya (Dvaitādvaita)
4. The Rudra saṃpradāya (Śuddhādvaita)

At the Kumbhamelās, which take place every three years, members of all Vaiṣṇava *saṃpradāyas* (as of all other religious orders) congregate and elect a president. At these as well as at the yearly, predominantly Vaiṣṇava, Māghamelās ("gatherings") in Prāyāg, they regulate their internal affairs.[10]

Philosophically Vaiṣṇavism has absorbed almost every type of thought except the extreme *Advaita* of the Śaṅkara school. Though admitting a wide range of philosophical theories to explain the relationship between God and humans, it never accepted complete identity. The most prominent characteristic of Vaiṣṇavism is the development of *bhakti*.

At a comparatively early time the worship of Vāsudeva was combined with that of Śrī. Originally probably an independent deity – the Indian version of the Great Goddess, connected with harvest and fertility – she became associated with Viṣṇu as his consort. Some peculiar developments within Vaiṣṇavism which elevate the position of Śrī even above Viṣṇu bring Vaiṣṇavism into the vicinity of Tantrism and Śāktism.

Vaiṣṇavism today is a vigorous, if diverse, religion and claims the largest number of followers within mainstream Hinduism. Several of its more recent branches have begun mission work in India and abroad.

THE DEVELOPMENT OF VIṢṆU MYTHOLOGY

Viṣṇu in the Vedas

Only five hymns out of the 1,028 contained in the *Ṛgveda* are addressed to Viṣṇu, and only in a few other instances is Viṣṇu mentioned in other hymns.[11] Nevertheless, we are not justified in concluding from this that "Viṣṇu was a minor deity" when the Saṃhitās were composed.[12] The *Ṛgveda* is representative of only a section of the religion of the vedic Indians, containing hymns used at the highly developed and important *Soma* sacrifice performed by Brahmin orthodoxy. It is correct to say that Viṣṇu did not figure prominently at the *Soma* sacrifice, but the attributes given to him allow us to say that he was important.[13] Together with Indra he is invoked as the saviour from Vṛtra and is called "the greatest."[14] He has the very important function of being "supporter" of heaven and earth, providing living-space for all beings.

THE THREE STRIDES OF VIṢṆU

The most popular myth connected with Viṣṇu from the earliest times is his being *trivikrama* – he who with three strides covered the earth and ether and heaven. The *Ṛgveda Saṃhitā* mentions this "mighty deed of Viṣṇu" several times. It deals especially with the "third step," "the highest step," which is beyond the reach of mortals and which is said to be "the well-loved mansion, where men devoted to the gods are happy."[15] There is a salvific element contained in *Viṣṇu trivikrama*: "he stepped forth over the realms of earth for freedom and for life."[16]

It is not difficult to see a connection between the *trivikrama* myth and the course of the Sun. But the "Sun" in the Vedic context is not the astrophysical body explored by modern science – it is a *deva*, producing immortality for the gods, giving life to men, maintaining the world, absolving sinners from their guilt and cleansing them from their sins. The interpretation which the *Śatapatha Brāhmaṇa* gives to the *trivikrama* myth emphasizes its salvific contents: "Viṣṇu is the sacrifice – by striding he obtained for the gods this all-pervading power which now belongs to them."[17] Viṣṇu *trivikrama* is the "saviour of the *devas*" from the *asuras* who had usurped the three worlds. The defeat of the *asuras* by Viṣṇu returns to the *devas* their power. The *Bṛhaddevatā* treats the name Viṣṇu as one of the names of the Sun: "Because the three regions shine with brilliance as his footsteps, Medhātithi pronounced him *Viṣṇu trivikrama*."[18] The same work derives the etymology of Viṣṇu from the root *viṣ-* (following the *Nirukta*) and explains Viṣṇu as "pervasion" applied to the Sun "who is everything and is contained in everything."[19] The title *trivikrama* in connection with Viṣṇu does not occur in the *Upaniṣads*, but the "highest place of Viṣṇu" plays a large role in Upaniṣadic eschatology.[20] Of special importance for later Vaiṣṇavism is the designation given to Viṣṇu as the "all-pervader." The three steps of the Vedic Viṣṇu *trivikrama* are philosophically interpreted as symbolic of Viṣṇu's transcendence.

THE PROTECTOR OF THE UNBORN

Viṣṇu as protector of the embryo and the preparer of the womb is a fairly frequent motif in Vedic literature: *Ṛgveda*, *Atharvaveda*, *Brāhmaṇas*, and *Upaniṣads* testify to the popularity which Viṣṇu enjoyed under this title.[21] In this function he is practically identical with Prajāpati whose attributes and activities are absorbed by Viṣṇu after the Vedic period. Even the *avatāras* of Viṣṇu can be explained, at least partially, as transformations of Prajāpati mentioned in Vedic literature, taken over by Viṣṇu.

The "Hymn to *Ka*"[22] contains most of the essential elements of Vaiṣṇavism without explicitly mentioning Viṣṇu: *Ka* is an interrogative particle; it also means Prajāpati or the Sun, and is a name of *Viṣṇu*.[23]

Viṣṇu is also known in the Veda as Hiraṇyagarbha, "Golden Germ," floating on the primeval waters, from which everything originated. This motif is taken up also by *Atharvaveda*, *Śatapatha Brāhmaṇa*, some *Upaniṣads* and *Purāṇas*.

The concept of Viṣṇu as the one who "enters," and his connection with the seed, seems to stand at the root of the Vedic belief in Viṣṇu as preparer of the womb for conception in fertility rituals and the protector of the embryo in the womb: the idea already occurs in the *Ṛgveda* and the *Atharvaveda*; it is continued in several *Upaniṣads* and also forms part of Purāṇic belief and popular faith. It is not difficult to abstract from this image the philosophical idea of the immanence of God – a concrete and physical immanence, as later Vaiṣṇava *darśanas* explain.

VIṢṆU *PURUṢA*

Very important elements of later Vaiṣṇavism are contained in the Ṛgvedic *puruṣa-sūkta*. Though the hymn itself does not mention him the whole Vaiṣṇava tradition relates it to Viṣṇu – and this is also corroborated by some interpretations in Vedic works. One of the most often used names of Viṣṇu is puruṣottama, "the Supreme Person."

The *Śatapatha Brāhmaṇa* gives an extended version of the *puruṣa* sacrifice,[24] naming the *puruṣa* Viṣṇu, who was the size of a dwarf. The context is a competition between *devas* and *asuras* for the dominion of the earth: Viṣṇu appears again as the deliverer of the *devas* from their enemies. The *asuras* have defeated the *devas* and are masters over the earth. They concede to the *devas* as much land as "this Viṣṇu lies upon." They enclosed him by means of various verse-meters. "By it they obtained this earth." Viṣṇu, it is said, "was tired and hid himself among the roots of plants." The *devas* find him after a prolonged search and praise him: "Pleasant are you and soft to sit upon. Of good soil are you and auspicious, abounding in food and drink."[25]

On several occasions the *Śatapatha Brāhmaṇa* says that "Viṣṇu is the upper half of the sacrifice."[26] The sacrificer becomes himself Viṣṇu, and a *ṛk* or a *yajus* to Viṣṇu is the means to rectify a fault in the sacrifice. In another way too Viṣṇu is connected with the sacrifice: the principal gods performed a sacrifice at Kurukṣetra. Viṣṇu is the first to complete it and thus he becomes the most excellent among the gods. Again a strange myth follows: Viṣṇu, bow in hand, stepped forward with three arrows, resting his head upon the bow. The other gods apparently want to compete for his position but dare not do so directly. Ants offer themselves to do the job after having secured a boon from the gods. The ants gnaw the bowstring. The bow snaps and tears off Viṣṇu's head which becomes the sun in heaven. The body of *Viṣṇu mahāvīra* is divided by the gods and transformed into various accessories for sacrifice.

In another section the same Brāhmaṇa relates that Prajāpati ordered a Puruṣa Nārāyaṇa to offer a sacrifice. Thrice he offers. The concluding passage contains what are again essentially "Vaiṣṇava" ideas:

> All the worlds have I placed within mine own self and mine own self have I placed within all the worlds; all the gods have I placed within mine own self and mine own self have I placed within all the gods; all the Vedas have I placed within mine own self, and mine own self have I placed within the vital airs. For imperishable indeed are worlds, imperishable the gods, imperishable the Vedas, imperishable the vital airs, imperishable is the All: and verily whosoever knows this, passes from the perishable unto the imperishable, conquers recurrent death and attains the full measure of life.[27]

Later Vaiṣṇava systems usually legitimate their doctrines by references to the Upaniṣads, occasionally also to the Vedas. Madhva, for example, insists that whenever the Vedas speak of the "unborn," the "unknowable," the "immanent," the "being in the waters," we have to understand that Viṣṇu is referred to. Applying this principle one could point out many "Viṣṇu-hymns" in the *Ṛgveda Saṃhitā* – hymns which are addressed to deities like Savitṛ, Prajāpati, and others. Similarly a rereading of the Upaniṣads in the light of later Vaiṣṇava Vedānta *darśanas* yields an abundance of Upaniṣadic materials to illustrate basic Vaiṣṇava theology.

The first account of creation given in the *Bṛhadāraṇyaka Upaniṣad*[28] introduces some familiar Vaiṣṇava motives: in the beginning was Hiraṇyagarbha, hunger and death. He created the universe by sacrificing himself. The second creation account in the same Upaniṣad begins with a *puruṣa-ātman* as First Being and creator, transforming itself successively into man and wife, bull and cow, and so forth.[29] Also the concluding metaphysical explanation makes use of a terminology familiar to Vaiṣṇavas: he is the great unborn Soul, a *puruṣa*, the ruler within the heart, the Lord of all, the overlord of all beings, the protector of beings, the separating dam for keeping the worlds apart, the home of the mendicants, unseizable and indestructible, the provider of food. In the *Kaṭha Upaniṣad* the "highest place of Viṣṇu" is mentioned as the ultimate aim of man.[30] The *Maitri Upaniṣad* calls Viṣṇu "the highest *Brahman*," above *Śabda-Brahman*, and Viṣṇu is mentioned as one of the many names of the One.[31] Typical Vaiṣṇava ideas appear in the early

Upaniṣads: the creator entering his creation after creating it[32] and assuming various forms.[33]

There are numerous so-called Vaiṣṇava Upaniṣads which are considerably more recent. They quite openly propound sectarian Vaiṣṇava doctrines: Viṣṇu is the only redeemer, delivering all from distress and bondage, he purifies all and purges them from mental, verbal, and corporeal sins, and he is the object of love for all. The Vaiṣṇava Upaniṣads contain very few references to myths and are rather theoretical and abstract. They also give instructions regarding rituals and ceremonies.

Viṣṇu in the Epics and Purāṇas

Vaiṣṇavism has Vedic roots, but more than the Vedic literature it is the *Āgamas*, the *Epics*, and the *Purāṇas* that are considered the Holy Books and the main source of Vaiṣṇavism proper. The *Āgamas* are largely compendia of doctrine and ritual associated with temple service. The most significant Viṣṇu myths are found in *Itihāsa* and *Purāṇa*.

The *Vālmiki Rāmāyaṇa*, generally considered the oldest epic poem, seems to have originally described Rāma as an ideal human being, and not as divine. Only later, when Kṛṣṇa had been deified and worshiped as an *avatāra* of Viṣṇu, were certain portions interpolated or rewritten so as to make Rāma also an *avatāra* of Viṣṇu.[34] It is the sixteenth century C.E. *Adhyātma Rāmāyaṇa* which "reminds the reader at every turn that Rāma was conscious of his divinity at all times although he continued to behave like an ordinary man, suffering patiently the sorrows that fell to his lot."[35] Tulasidāsa (1486–1533 C.E.) in his *Rāmcaritmānas* already presupposes the belief in the divinity of Rāma.

The *Mahābhārata* in its present form clearly shows itself predominantly Vaiṣṇava-Kṛṣṇaitic. It mentions also Śauras and Śaivas, Gaṇeśas and Śāktas, and relates their mythologies, but overall it favors Vaiṣṇavism. It is also historically the earliest record of Vaiṣṇavism perceived from a Brahmanical point of view and the oldest document for the Pāñcarātra school.

The Viṣṇu mythology of the Purāṇas is partly identical with that of the *Mahābhārata*, and partly it reflects local legends and tribal lore, woven into the great religion of Vaiṣṇavism which accommodated so many disparate elements.[36]

THE VEDIC VIṢṆU IN ITIHĀSA-PURĀṆA

Though the non-Vedic features of Viṣṇu are more prominent in later Vaiṣṇavism, the Vedic Viṣṇu continues his influence in Epics and Purāṇas, thus forming the link between the Vedic religion and later Hinduism. *Viṣṇu trivikrama* is mentioned often but he hardly evokes associations with the Sun. He is identified with the dwarf mentioned in the Brāhmaṇas, but the Purāṇas and Epics say nothing about the dwarf being sacrificed: the *puruṣa* motif has completely vanished. It is now associated with the Vedic battle of Indra and Viṣṇu against Bali, the leader of the victorious *asuras*. The *Mahābhārata* narrates the Bali-Vāmana-Trivikrama episode in an interpolation.[37] Bali, the king of the Daityas, has conquered the whole world and deprived Indra of his reign. He is about to commence an *aśvamedha*. The gods rush to Viṣṇu beseeching him to interfere. Viṣṇu assumes the form of a young ascetic and appears at Bali's sacrifice. Bali offers him a boon, Vāmana chooses "three strides," wins the whole universe and returns it to Indra.

The *Vālmiki Rāmāyana* adds some details[38] which make it appear a later version of this story. The *Viṣṇu Purāṇa*[39] has only a short reference to Vāmana, who is Viṣṇu's *avatāra* in the Vaivasvata *manvantara*, born from Kaśyapa and Aditī, who covered with three strides the whole universe and returned it to Indra. Bali is mentioned several times – once as the "sinless son of Virocana who would be Indra in the seventh Manvantara."

The *Bhāgavata Purāṇa* connects with this complex myth an apparition of the *Viraṭ* form of Viṣṇu; *Viṣṇu-Vāmana* is an *avatāra* born to *Aditi*.[40] He appears at the sacrifice of the world ruler Bali. According to the rules of propriety, Bali asks *Vāmana* to express any wish that he should grant him. Vāmana asks Bali for as much land as he could cover by three strides. Śukrācārya, his *guru*, suspects that something is wrong and tries to warn Bali. Bali does not heed the warning and misfortune strikes: *Vāmana* grows into the Cosmic Being: "With a single stride he measured the earth which belonged to Bali and covered the sky with his person and the quarters with his arms. To him, as he took a second stride, heaven proved of no account, so that indeed not an atom was left for the third. Extending higher and higher the foot of the Cosmic Person presently reached beyond Maharloka and Jñānaloka as well as beyond Tapoloka."[41] *Viṣṇu-Vāmana* as Cosmic Being binds Bali and releases him after a short time. Bali then enters Sutalā. The purpose of the *trivikrama* deed is the same as in the Vedas: to free the world from the rule of the *asuras*, to defeat them, and to reinstate the *devas*. In the Vedas it had been a feat of prowess and valor; in the Epics and Purāṇas it becomes a trick and deception – *māyā*.

A new feature in the purāṇic *trivikrama* story is that it is said to be not the first of Viṣṇu's deeds: it had been preceded by salvific actions in the forms of the *matsya*, *kūrma*, *varāha*, and *nṛsiṇha avatāras*.[42] The Epics and Purāṇas introduce a historical dimension: the Viṣṇu of the Vedas was a cosmic, a-historical being – the Viṣṇu of Epics and Purāṇas is a saviour who enters human history. A typical feature of purānic Viṣṇu mythology is also that the enemies vanquished in battles are not destroyed but only punished for a short time or even given *mukti* by Viṣṇu: as Viṣṇu appears repeatedly as saviour, so the enemy also appears repeatedly in various forms and incarnations.[43]

The Epic still calls Viṣṇu *Upendra* in several places, the younger brother of Indra. But it also makes clear that the younger has grown stronger than the older and wields more power. Indra comes to Viṣṇu with the request to be taught the right religion.[44] Viṣṇu is still called the "slayer of the *asuras*," especially the "slayer of Madhu" – a demon who according to the *Mahābhārata* originated from the dirt of Viṣṇu's own ears.[45] Among the "thousand names of Viṣṇu" are still found his Vedic attributes, but the emphasis is clearly more on the *avatāras* than on the Vedic Viṣṇu himself.

VIṢṆU-NĀRĀYAṆA

Nārāyaṇa – in Vedic literature the name of a *ṛṣi*[46] – is one of the most popular names of Viṣṇu in Epic and Puranic literature. Often mentioned together with Nara, Nara and Nārāyaṇa are variously identified with Kṛṣṇa and Viṣṇu, or with Vāsudeva and Arjuna. Much of Viṣṇu mythology is recounted under the name of Nārāyaṇa.

It is not easy to reconstruct the Nārāyaṇa religion prior to its fusion with Vaiṣṇavism. L. B. Keny[47] connects Nārāyaṇa with Dravidian and ultimately with Indus civilization sources. The connection of Nārāyaṇa with water is given in a *śloka* of the *Mahābhārata*.[48] *Nārā* is connected with Dravidian *nara* / *nira* – water; *ay* in Tamil means "to lie in a place"; *an* is a masculine termination in Dravidian languages. According to B. G. Bhandarkar, Nārāyaṇa has a cosmic significance: it is a name for the waters as the abode of the primeval germ and the resting place of the *nāras*.[49] The identification of Nārāyaṇa with the *paramātman* must have taken place quite early and Nārāyaṇa was worshiped as the Supreme God before Vāsudeva was identified with him.[50]

The famous Nārāyaṇīniya section of the *Śāntiparvan*[51] is the earliest and longest account of the Nārāyaṇa religion. Nārāyaṇa is introduced as one of the four sons of Dharma: the others are Nara, Hari, and Kṛṣṇa. Nārāyaṇa has a "twofold nature." In the first one Nārāyaṇa and Nara undergo severe *tapasya* at Bādarī, where Nārada visits them. But the "original nature" of Nārāyaṇa dwells in the "White Island" (*Śvetadvīpa*) to which Nārada repairs.

Many scholars have attempted to solve the mystery of the *Śveta-dvīpa*,[52] described as lying to the North and inhabited by a god-like race of men who worshiped Nārāyaṇa as "the god of gods." Even if we have to leave the riddle of *Śveta-dvīpa* unsolved we can consider the account given of the kings' devotion as a summary of the tenets of early Vaiṣṇavism.[53] Its main elements are *ahiṃsā*, *bhakti* to Janardana, the omnipresence of God, and the idea that everything by right belongs to him. There is mention of the *Sātvata* and *Pāñcarātra* ritual. Food is offered to Nārāyaṇa. Nārāyaṇa in *Śvetadvīpa* is identified with Hari. Then "the invisible Nārāyaṇa left the *ṛṣis* and proceeded to a place not known to them." The *ṛṣis* are ordered to preach and spread the Nārāyaṇa religion. The whole section dealing with Nārāyaṇa shows so many inconsistencies, repetitions, and interpolations that we must consider it the result of a combination of several separate Nārāyaṇa traditions.

Three times *Śveta-dvīpa* is described. The last description contains a fairly detailed account of all the major points of Vaiṣṇavism. Very important is the description of the Nārāyaṇa revelation. It looks like a combination of features of the Vedic *puruṣa sūkta* and the Viṣṇu of the Purāṇas. In the course of this manifestation of Nārāyaṇa's "original nature" we hear that the denizens of *Śvetadvīpa* are Nārāyaṇa-*bhaktas* and *muktas*. Nārāyaṇa then identifies himself with Puruṣa, Vāsudeva, Śeṣa, Saṁkarṣaṇa, Sanātkumāra, Pradyumna, Aniruddha, Iśāna and Kṣetrajñā, who are, it seems, emanations from Nārāyaṇa and of the same nature. The theology connected with this revelation is a mixture of theistic Sāṁkhya and Advaita Vedānta. The manifestations are declared to be his *māyā* while his real nature remains unknown. Nārāyaṇa is the sum total of all living beings and he is the *jiva*. Hiraṇyagarbha, Brahman, Rudra, Ādityas, and Vasus come from him.

After this account of Nārāyaṇa in the Śvetadvīpa we return with Nārada to Bādarī – and meet again the *ṛṣis* Nara and Nārāyaṇa, who ask

Nārada whether he has seen the supreme being. The Vedic motif of Viṣṇu *madhusūdana* is brought in; but strangely enough it is said that it was Nārāyaṇa as *hāyagriva*, the horse-head incarnation which does not appear in later *avatāra* systems at all, who killed Madhu and Kaiṭabha.

THE *AVATĀRAS* OF VIṢṆU

The *avatāra* doctrine of recent Vaiṣṇavism is the outcome of a long development and the product of the amalgamation of many cults and traditions. The fact that various important sources of Vaiṣṇavism have a varying number of *avatāras* reflects the growth of the *avatāra* doctrine. Sometimes different names are used strictly as synonyms for Viṣṇu, sometimes they are hypostatized and made *avatāras* of Viṣṇu; even the various Vedic epithets of Viṣṇu like Trivikrama, Kalanemighnā, Rāhujit, and so on, appear as separate and individual *avatāras*. Despite the terminological and theological differences in defining the exact nature and relationship of the *avatāras*, there is no doubt that in Vaiṣṇavism, especially in its soteriology, the *avatāras* play a most important role; in later Vaiṣṇavism Viṣṇu as Savior appears almost exclusively in his *avatāras*. The *avatāra* is almost by definition a "savior"[54] and Viṣṇu must, in order to appear as savior, assume an *avatāra*.[55] The standard number of *avatāras* in later Vaiṣṇavism is ten. The *Mahābhārata* mentions in one place four, in another six, and in a third, ten *avatāras*. The *Bhāgavata Purāṇa* mentions in one place sixteen and in another, twenty-two *avatāras*. The largest number is met with in the *Pāñcarātra Āgamas*: the *Ahirbudhnya Saṃhitā* has no less than thirty-nine. The lists in *Mahābhārata*, *Āgamas*, and *Purāṇas* show also that the distinction between various degrees of manifestations – *vyūhas*, *vibhavas*, partial and complete *avatāras*, and so forth – which plays such a great role in the classic Vaiṣṇava theologies, is either absent or still fluid.

While Rāma and Kṛṣṇa, the most popular *avatāras*, will be dealt with at some length later, it is probably sufficient just to mention the other eight without going into much detail. *Matsya-avatāra* defeated the *asuras* who had stolen the Vedas and returned them to the Brahmans. As *Ekaśṛṅga* he saved Manu from the flood! *Kūrma-avatāra* supported the mountain Maṇḍara which was used by the gods to churn out *amṛta* from the milk ocean and gain immortality. *Varāha-avatāra* lifted the earth out from the waters into which she had sunk and thus saved her: then only *sṛṣṭi* – the "furnishing of the earth" and human history – begins. *Nṛsiṇha-avatāra* saved the Viṣṇu-*bhakta* Prahlāda from the persecutor Hiraṇyakaśipu, and at the same time the whole world, usurped by Hiraṇyakaśipu, the *asura*-king, from the demons. In the latter part it follows the old Vedic pattern of Viṣṇu mythology. *Vāmana-avatāra* defeated Bali, the demon-king, and regained the three worlds for the gods who had been exiled. Also the function of cleansing the world from its sins is attributed to him: from his feet arises the Gaṅgā. *Paraśurāma-avatāra* saved the Brahmans by annihilating the Kṣatriyas. *Balarāma-avatāra* is remembered for killing Pralamba and other demons. *Kalki-avatāra* is the only one to come in the future: he is the eschatological manifestation of Viṣṇu as liberator of the world from Kali and all his evil influences.

Besides these some others figure prominently in Vaiṣṇava scriptures and are still worshiped today by smaller groups of devotees.

We have already mentioned *Hāya-griva-avatāra*. The *Mahābhārata* says that "this of all forms, endued with puissance, is celebrated as the most ancient."[56] Ṛṣi Parameṣṭi sees him in the great ocean in the northeast. He originates when Brahmā invokes Viṣṇu to help him retrieve the Vedas from the *asuras* Madhu and Kaiṭabha, who had stolen them. He recites the Vedic *mantras* loudly and correctly so that the *asuras* become frightened and drop the Vedas. Later the two *asuras* return and see Aniruddha sleeping upon the snake. They prepare for battle to recover the Vedas. "It was thus that Nārāyaṇa, having assumed the form equipped with the horse-head slew the two Dānavas Madhu and Kaiṭabha ... Once more, however, he assumed the same form for the cause of making the religion of *pravṛtti* to flow in the universe."

Kapila is very often mentioned in the epic and the Purāṇas as an *avatāra* of Viṣṇu. In the *Mahābhārata* "Kapila is authoritative in all philosophical matters and his name covers every sort of doctrine. He is in fact the only founder of a philosophical system known to the epic."[57] He is the oldest, the supreme seer, identical with Agni, Śiva, Viṣṇu. But already the *Śāntiparvan* contains a Brahmanic attack on Kapila – later orthodox Vedānta will classify him as a heretic. The *Bhāgavata Purāṇa* has a lengthy account of Viṣṇu taking the form of Kapila through Devahuti.[58] According to Brahmā's announcement he comes "to tear up the roots of *karma* through the instrumentality of śāstraic knowledge and realization." The Sāṁkhya system, then, is described as a means to liberation.

A *swan-avatāra* plays an important role in the *Bhāgavatam*. His teaching, however, is but Sāṁkhya-Yoga and nothing else is added.

Dattātreya occurs in the *Mahābhārata* and in several *Purāṇas* as an *avatāra* of Viṣṇu: he grants boons to Arjuna and he teaches the *sādhyas*.

The essence of his teaching is patience, non-violence, and friendliness. Vyāsa, the compiler of the *Mahābhārata* and the *Purāṇas*, is often called an *avatāra* of Viṣṇu and identified with Kṛṣṇa Dvaipāyana and Nārāyaṇa. He teaches a way of salvation and preserves for humankind Viṣṇu's revelations.

Nārada himself is sometimes mentioned as a separate *avatāra*. Pṛthu, the first king on earth, is considered by some an *avatāra*.

Dhanvantari, the physician of the gods, is also counted among the *avatāras* of Viṣṇu. Healing – liberating from disease and pain – is a salvific activity of Viṣṇu.

Ṛṣabha – otherwise known as a heretic, belonging to the Jaina Digambara sect – is considered as an *avatāra* of Viṣṇu in the *Bhāgavata Purāṇa*.[59] The *Mahābhārata* knows several Ṛṣabhas – one is a *nāga* from Dhṛtarāṣṭra's clan who died in Janamejaya's snake sacrifice. Another is a *rākṣasa*. The third one is an old ascetic – probably the Ṛṣabha whom the *Bhāgavata Purāṇa* is referring to. There is also a Ṛṣabha Dānava or Daitya. This latter may reflect the Brahmans' excommunication of the Jaina saint. In the *Bhāgavata Purāṇa* the *Ṛṣabha-avatāra*'s function is "the preservation of *dharma*." He was the father of Bhārata and held up an example of life in all the four *āśramas*. "He taught the ignorant by his own example the duties that had been forgotten." Toward the end of his life he became a wandering ascetic, representing the *unmatta* type of saint. He died by entering voluntarily into a forest fire. "This *avatāra* of the Lord was intended to give a lesson in the art of liberating oneself to those who are steeped in the quality of *rajas*."[60]

Buddha appears in some places as an *avatāra*; also Dhruva, Dadhibhakta, and others, who are worshiped as saints.

In later Vaiṣṇava theology the *vyūhas* are distinguished from the *avatāras* – every *vyūha* is also given a salvific function, which represents part of Viṣṇu's cosmic function. Later sects have their own ideas regarding *avatāras* – very often they worship the *guru* or the *ācārya* of their own school or sect as an *avatāra* of Viṣṇu. This practice is continued even today.

The famous *Nārāyaṇa-kavaca* is one of the most impressive invocations of all the *avatāras* of Viṣṇu: it points out the functions of the various *avatāras* with regard to the salvation of the individual – changing over from the cosmic-historical to the devotional-personal aspect of Viṣṇu worship.[61] Even here, in a fully developed Vaiṣṇava theology, the distinction between an aspect of Viṣṇu, an *avatāra*, a *vyūha*, a saint, a hypostatized deed of Viṣṇu or Kṛṣṇa, the attributes and instruments of Viṣṇu, and so forth, are constantly blurred.

Rāma: Rāma was worshiped locally as a hero and divine king probably long before he came to be considered an *avatāra* of Viṣṇu. Rāma is certainly older than the Vālmīki *Rāmāyaṇa*. But his worship as *avatāra* of Viṣṇu is comparatively late, later than that of Vāsudeva-Kṛṣṇa. Even now the human features of Rāma (and Sītā) seem to be more in the foreground of popular religious consciousness than his divinity. The attempt to systematically interpret the epic Rāma as a manifestation of the Supreme in its various aspects, the *Adhyātma-rāmāyaṇa*, is ascribed to the sixteenth century.

Kṛṣṇa: The most important among the Viṣṇu *avatāras* is doubtless Kṛṣṇa.[62] Many of his worshipers regard him not as an *avatāra* in the usual sense – Viṣṇu accepting a fictitious form and visibly appearing in it[63] – but Viṣṇu as revealing himself in his own proper and eternal form, the Lord himself, *svayam bhagavān*. An extensive literature has grown up around the so-called Kṛṣṇa problem.[64] Kṛṣṇaitic literature does not tire of repeating that Kṛṣṇa is *the* savior, the ultimate and definite salvific manifestation of Viṣṇu for the benefit of all who are becoming his devotees.

Testimony exists that already around 150 B.C.E. there was Kṛṣṇa-Vāsudeva worship in and near Mathurā.[65] The identification of Kṛṣṇa-Vāsudeva and Viṣṇu must be later. A second important element is the cult of a Kṛṣṇa-Govinda. R. G. Bhandarkar thinks that this Govinda was the tribal deity of the Ahīra-Abhīras of the Kṛṣṇa tradition.[66] Though in one of the Vedic hymns Viṣṇu is already called *gopāla*, the Kṛṣṇa-Gopāla or Govinda seems to be a later, non-Vedic element in Vaiṣṇavism. Still later is the worship of the Divine Child Kṛṣṇa, a quite prominent feature of modern Kṛṣṇaism.[67] The last element can be seen in Kṛṣṇa the lover of the Gopīs – considered to have originated under Tantric influence.[68] Possibly it represents the transfer of the features of the old god of love and fertility to Kṛṣṇa.[69] According to A. D. Pusalker the original Kṛṣṇa who stands at the beginning of Kṛṣṇaism was a real man; the mythology is later growth and embellishment.[70]

Kṛṣṇa's miraculous birth and escape from Kaṃsa, his childhood and youth, his teaching of the *Bhagavadgītā* and the manifestation of his "true form," have been celebrated by Vaiṣṇavas for many centuries. So were the various adventures where he killed a number of demons.

The demoness Pūtanā attempts to suckle him with her poisoned breasts but he sucks the life out of her. The demon Śakaṭāsura crushes a heavy cart under which Kṛṣṇa was lying in a cradle, but with a kick Kṛṣṇa topples it and kills Śakaṭāsura. Kṛṣṇa subdues the Kalīya-nāga and gives good water and fresh air to the people of Braja. He introduces a new cult, the worship of Govardhana hill and the cows instead of Indra-worship, and he protects the *gopas* against Indra's fury. He resuscitates dead people and is helpful in many ways through his miraculous powers. He is the object of passionate love, a love which is liberating and salvific. He is the teacher of the way of salvation through *bhakti*.

Not only was Kṛṣṇaism influenced by the identification of Kṛṣṇa with Viṣṇu, but Vaiṣṇavism was transformed and reinterpreted in the light of the Kṛṣṇa mythology and the religion associated with Kṛṣṇa. Bhāgavatism may have brought into Kṛṣṇa worship an element of cosmic religion.[71] But certainly Kṛṣṇa mythology has brought into Bhāgavatism a strongly human element: Kṛṣṇa is not a god enthroned in majesty, difficult to approach for a mortal; he is a sweet child, a naughty boy, a comrade in youthful adventures, an ardent lover of girls and young women.

Śrī: Though there is not even a mention of Śrī, the companion of Viṣṇu, in the early sources, in later Vaiṣṇavism Śrī becomes an integral part of Viṣṇu cult. The cult of Śrī or Lakṣmī is considerably older than her association with Viṣṇu. It seems probable that the association of Śrī with Viṣṇu followed the same pattern as the association of Nārāyaṇa, Kṛṣṇa, and Rama with Viṣṇu. As a matter of fact, about the same time all Brahmanic gods were given wives, whereas earlier there were only unmarried gods and goddesses.

The inseparability of Śrī and Viṣṇu is emphasized throughout: Viṣṇu has on his body a mark called *śrīvatsa*, which represents the presence of Śrī. In his heaven he is enthroned together with Śrī. Śrī also remains within him in *pralaya*, when the whole of creation is absorbed. Śrī is identified with Rādhā[72] in later Vaiṣṇavism, and Caitanya is considered by his followers to be an incarnation of Kṛṣṇa and Rādhā, Viṣṇu and Śrī in one. Some Vaiṣṇava sects believe that all grace of Viṣṇu comes only through Śrī and thus they worship Śrī directly.

Rādhā and Sītā worship are comparatively late – but later still is their identification with Śrī. The main source of the worship of Śrī together with Viṣṇu is the Pāñcarātra tradition, and more directly South Indian Śrī

Vaiṣṇavism.[73] Śrī Vaiṣṇavism draws heavily on the popular *bhakti* religion of the Āḷvārs so that ultimately we can consider Śrī worship as an element of popular religion combined with Brahmanic Vaiṣṇavism.

THE DEVELOPMENT OF VAIṢṆAVA PHILOSOPHY

Vaiṣṇavism is connected not only with an extensive mythology but also with schools that systematize and philosophically develop the teaching of Vaiṣṇavism. The origins of systematic Vaiṣṇava thought can be seen in the Vedas and Upaniṣads: Viṣṇu's omnipresence and omnipotence is expressed in the *trivikrama* myth. His connection with the "seed" and the "womb" is the basis for his immanence. The *Puruṣa-sūkta* is the source for the Vaiṣṇava tenet of God being not only the efficient but also the material cause of the universe. It may even be the origin of the concept of *Viṣṇu-virāṭ*. The transformation of the creator into various beings, the idea of the creator entering his creation after creating it which is found in some *Upaniṣads*, have an underlying philosophy that could be called Vaiṣṇava. *Kaṭha* and *Muṇḍaka Upaniṣad* contain the doctrine of grace as means to salvation, one of the most basic elements of Vaiṣṇava soteriology. The so-called *Vaiṣṇava Upaniṣads* are early compendia of Vaiṣṇavism. They are quoted by the Vaiṣṇava *ācāryas* to prove that their doctrine is based on *śruti*. In these Viṣṇu appears as the only saviour. They teach that the *jīvas* are part of *brahman* and that release means communion. The way to *mukti* is *bhakti*.

According to Rāmānuja all those parts of the Veda which speak of "power," "part," "splendour," "form," "body," and so forth, mean Viṣṇu and Viṣṇu is meant in the Upaniṣads when they mention "the soul of all," the "Highest Brahman," "Highest Light," "Highest Reality," "Highest Self and Being."

Early Sāṁkhya Vaiṣṇavism

Rāmānuja mentions Kapila and Patañjali as exponents of extra-Vedic schools that should be shunned. The *Bhāgavatam*, however, considers Kapila one of the prominent *avatāras* of Viṣṇu and insists upon Yoga as a means for attaining final release. *Mahābhārata* and *Vaiṣṇava Purāṇas* accept Sāṁkhya-Yoga as a system for obtaining salvation. Over against the classical Sāṁkhya, this Vaiṣṇava-Sāṁkhya, however, insists that Viṣṇu is creator of *prakṛti* and giver of *mokṣa*.

The *Śāntiparvan* of the *Mahābhārata* explains the Sāṁkhya-Yoga way of salvation when dealing with *mokṣa*. It does not explicitly refer in this context to Viṣṇu. The *Bhagavadgītā* describes Sāṁkhya-Yoga as a revelation by Kṛṣṇa and as a way to attain to Kṛṣṇa. With remarkable consistency the basic tenets of Sāṁkhya are inculcated as the basis for true Viṣṇu religions.

The *Pāñcarātra Āgamas*, the doctrinal basis for classical Vaiṣṇavism, build their system of salvation upon a Sāṁkhya-Yoga foundation. The *Jayākhya Saṃhitā*, one of the oldest and most important, explains the "second creation" in terms of theistic Sāṁkhya. The *Ahirbudhnya Saṃhitā*, which presents the most detailed account of Pāñcarātra theology, connects the doctrine of Viṣṇu's *vyūhas* and *śaktis* with the Sāṁkhya system of evolution from *puruṣa-prakṛti* to which *kāla* (time) accedes as the inner (third) principle. The spiritual activity of Viṣṇu is the ultimate force of evolution. Though in details the doctrine of the *Ahirbudhnya Saṃhitā* differs significantly from the Sāṁkhya doctrine as explained in Īśvara Kṛṣṇa's *Kārikā*, the tenor is definitely Sāṁkhya: though bondage of the *jiva* is ascribed to Viṣṇu's *krīḍa*, it is also conceived as beginningless – as in Sāṁkhya. And though *mokṣa* is in its ultimate cause again traced back to the mercy and grace of Viṣṇu, who takes pity on the suffering *jīva*, the grace of God moves the seeker for liberation on to the way of Sāṁkhya-Yoga, which is the instrument of *mokṣa*.

The longest and clearest account of Sāṁkhya Vaiṣṇava soteriology is found in the most important Vaiṣṇava scripture: the *Bhāgavata Purāna*.[74] "The *puruṣa* is no other than the *ātman*, who is beginningless, devoid of attributes, existing beyond *prakṛti*, consisting of the three *guṇas* that thought him in her playful mood. Abiding in *prakṛti*, the *puruṣa* fell a prey to her charms, which obscure knowledge." The *puruṣa* is the all-pervading spirit Viṣṇu, and it is out of his own free will that he accepts *prakṛti*. Apart from this basic difference the following account of the evolution of the universe follows strictly classical Sāṁkhya. *Kāla*, by some considered to be an independent third principle, is Viṣṇu; "In this way the Lord himself, who by His own *māyā* abides unaffected within all living beings as the *puruṣa* and outside them as *kāla* [is the twenty-fifth category]." The *Bhāgavatam* combines the evolution of the various principles with the *vyūha* doctrine. The *sákti* element, too, is integrated into the Sāṁkhya evolution.

The whole explanation of Sāṁkhya in the *Bhāgavatam* has as its only purpose to teach liberation, to provide the bound soul with knowledge and insight into reality and thus to enable it to differentiate matter and spirit and attain to its own nature. The *sādhana* described is a curious mixture of everything: Yoga rules, sometimes literally quoted from the *Yogasūtras*, listening to the stories of Viṣṇu and other typical practices of later Vaiṣṇavism, even theistic Vedānta of the type recommended in the *Bhagavadgītā*. The "eightfold yoga" is in fact a detailed explanation of the meditation on the form of the Lord. The description of the form of the Lord occurs often in the *Bhāgavatam* and is the accepted one in Vaiṣṇavism. The yoga consists in the contemplation of every limb and attribute of the Lord, which are allegorized and spiritualized and associated with various aspects of salvation from various evils. The *samādhi* in this *yoga* of contemplation of the Lord's form consists in "the realization of the true being of the devotee" by "conquering the divine *māyā* of the Lord which veils the true character and brings about the bondage of the *jīva*, a part of the Lord."

In the *Bhāgavatam* Kapila is a teacher of the *bhaktimārga* – he distinguishes the *bhaktas* according to their predominant *guṇas* and differentiates five kinds of *mukti*. Kapila himself considers the "Yoga of devotion" and the "Yoga with eight limbs" as two different ways to *mokṣa*, but he emphasizes that "by following either of these two Yogas a man can attain to the supreme person." Kapila identifies the Bhagavān of *bhakti* with the Brahman and Paramātman of Vedānta, the *para* of Yoga and the *pradhāna-puruṣa* of Sāṁkhya with Fate and with Time: all is Viṣṇu.

Kapila is also the exponent of an eschatology: he describes the happenings at the death of people attached to worldly objects, the messengers of death who pull out their *sūkṣma śarīra* and torture them in various hells, and the process of rebirth in animals and men. In this connection Kapila teaches biology: the process of growth of the embryo, the "suffering of the embryo," and the sorrows of each stage of life – all in order to turn the listener away from matter and toward the Lord. Kapila finally teaches the "two ways" of the soul after death which we have already found in the *Upaniṣads*. At this point Kapila proves that Viṣṇu worship is superior to worship of *pitṛs* and *devas* – only those who worship Viṣṇu are emancipated from rebirth. But *bhakti* liberalism breaks through in the final conclusion of Kapila's teaching: all the traditional ways of *karma*, good works, *yoga*, penances, *bhakti*, Veda study, *jñāna* are means "to attain to the same self-effulgent Lord, who is both with attributes and without attributes." Devahutī, the mother of the

Kapila-*avatāra*, reaches *mukti* through the way taught by her son: she practices *tapasya*, fixes her thoughts on her son Kapila, who was no other than Śrī Hari; she loses her body consciousness (her body is transformed into a river) and merges her mind into Vāsudeva.

In contrast with this Kapila-*vidyā* we find in the same *Bhāgavatam* portions which condemn Sāṁkhya-Yoga as being ineffective for *mokṣa*, extolling either pure *bhakti*, Viṣṇu worship, or a theistic Vedānta. Since Sāṁkhya represents probably the oldest among the *darśanas* we may consider the passages which accept Sāṁkhya as a way to *mokṣa* as representing the oldest Vaiṣṇava theology. Also the other Vaiṣṇava Purāṇas explain creation and liberation in terms of Sāṁkhya-Yoga.[75] The decisive difference, however, in all the above-mentioned Vaiṣṇava scriptures, is that the stages of bondage and liberation are connected with an act of free will of the Lord and the final stage is usually conceived as companionship with the Lord.

While in classical Sāṁkhya-Yoga no reference is made to *sṛṣṭi* (creation) and *pralaya* (dissolution of the universe), and to repeated existences of the *jīva*, already the early *Pāñcarātra* literature deals with this topic in connection with liberation according to Sāṁkhya-Yoga: after death the liberated *jīva* joins the Lord in Vaikuṇṭha. When the day of the Lord has expired and *mahāpralaya* has taken place nothing remains but the Waters of Infinity and, floating on them, a leaf from a *banyan* tree and upon this a babe whose name is *śūnya* ("zero"). This babe is Viṣṇu in the sleep of *Yoga*, in whose *kukṣī* (chest) are sleeping all the *jīvas*: in the upper part rest the *muktas* (the released), in the middle the *mukti-yogyas* (those capable of release), near the navel the *nitya-baddhas* (those who will always be in bondage), and in the region of the loins the *tamo-yogyas* (those condemned to live in darkness). In this condition the *jīvas* are called *naras*: as abode of the *naras* Viṣṇu is called Nārāyaṇa. When he creates a new universe, by his will he "obscures" the divine nature of the soul by reducing its original omnipotence, omniscience, and omnipresence so as to make it "little-achieving," "little-knowing," and "atomic." If these three restrictions are taken away by the grace of the Lord, *mukti* is achieved.

The Pāñcarātra Vyūha *Doctrine*

Historically this doctrine may represent the attempt to coordinate the worship of several heroes of the Vṛṣṇi clan and to subordinate it to Viṣṇu worship, but the theology of the *vyūhas* goes far beyond that practical purpose and constitutes one of the most characteristic elements of Vaiṣṇava theology. In the *Mahābhārata*, *vyūha* has mostly the meaning of battle array, a certain formation of troops. But it means also body, or part, and this is probably the meaning which is applied in the *vyūha* theology of Pāñcarātra. In the Nārāyaṇīya section of the *Mahābhārata* we find elements of the *vyūha* doctrine: Nārāyaṇa in the form of Aniruddha is seen and worshiped by Nārada. The *puruṣa* that develops anew after a *pralaya* is called Aniruddha in another place. This is just another name of Viṣṇu – out of his navel a lotus springs from which Brahmā develops, here identified with Hiraṇyagarbha. The *Mahābhārata* mentions the *Sātvata Saṃhitā*, one of the oldest *Pāñcarātra āgamas*. The *vyūha* doctrine is theologically probably an extrapolation from the *puruṣa-sūkta*; explaining the possibility of a physical division of the Supreme Person while its transcendence is maintained.

The *Ahirbudhnya Saṃhitā* has a fully developed *vyūha* theory which in this form became an integral part of Vaiṣṇavism. God has six qualities (*guṇas*): knowledge, power, majesty, strength, energy, self-sufficiency. From every pair of *guṇas* one *vyūha* arises: Saṁkarṣaṇa from knowledge and power; Pradyumna from majesty and strength; Aniruddha from energy and self-suffciency. The two *guṇas* mentioned predominate in the *vyūhas*, but since they are all manifestations of Viṣṇu all of them have the full set of six *guṇas* in some measure. The *vyūhas* emanate from one another. All have a soteriological function: Saṁkarṣaṇa is the deity superintending all the individual souls and separating them from *prakṛti*. Pradyumna superintends the *manas* of all beings and instructs them regarding their religious duties. He is also responsible for the creation of all beings: there are some who from the very beginning are fully dedicated to God and become absolutely attached to him. Aniruddha protects the world and leads men to the attainment of ultimate wisdom. These three *vyūhas* are also called the "pure *avatāras* of Viṣṇu." There are also so-called *sākṣād-avatāras* "directly derived from a part of the Lord just as a lamp is lighted from another." A seeker for liberation should worship these transcendent forms.

From each main *vyūha* three subsidiary *vyūhas* emanate: from Vasudeva arise Keśava, Nārāyaṇa, Mādhava; from Saṁkarṣaṇa arise Govinda, Viṣṇu, Madhusūdana; from Pradyumna arise Trivikrama, Vāmana, Śrīdhara; from Aniruddha arise Hṛṣīkeśa, Padmanābha, Dāmodara. They are considered to be the divinities superintending the twelve months of the year and they serve for meditation. In addition to them there are thirty-nine *vibhava avatāras*.

The whole system – especially if compared with other Pāñcarātra treatises – shows that the theory of the *vyūhas* and *vibhavas* is rather fluid: possibly there had been numerous sects and cults connected with the names of the *vyūhas* and *vibhavas* and it proved difficult to find a satisfactory system.

The purpose of the *vibhava-avatāras* is said to be "to give companionship in mundane form to those saints who cannot live without it, to destroy those who are opposed to the saints and to establish the Vedic religion whose essence is *bhakti* to Viṣṇu."[76]

The fourth form of presence of God is that of the *antaryāmī*, the Inner Controller, the Lord residing in the self through whose impulses a person commits evil deeds and goes to hell, or good deeds and goes to heaven. The yogis can perceive the Lord as *antaryāmī* in their hearts.

The fifth kind of divine presence is that of the *arcāvatāra* in images of various sorts.

The *Ahirbudhnya Saṃhitā* mentions that the Highest Lord is always accompanied by the female principle Śrī conceived as his *śakti*. Some *Pāñcarātra āgamas* mention three consorts of Viṣṇu: Lakṣmī, Bhūmī and Nīlā, sometimes identified with *icchā*, *kriyā* and *sākṣātśakti*. In this connection it is also necessary to explain the peculiar *Pāñcarātra* teaching of a differentiation of *jīvas* with respect to their chances of salvation: some are bound, some have become free in time, some are eternally free. These three groups have numerous subdivisions.

There are two kinds of seekers for liberation: those who aspire for *kaivalya* and those who are desirous of *mokṣa*. The latter are either *bhaktas* or *prapannas*. In their specifications of the means necessary to reach *mokṣa* and their classification of *mumukṣus* the individual sects of Vaiṣṇavism differ considerably. In the following we summarize the teaching of Śrīnivāsadāsa as found in his *Yatīndramatadīpikā*.

At death the liberated individual soul merges with the *paramātman* residing in its heart, enters *suṣumna* and leaves the body through *brahmārandha*. Through the rays of the sun it reaches the world of Agni – passing several stations it pierces the orb of the Sun and reaches *sūrya-loka*. The *devatās* of the higher worlds receive it and guide it on. It reaches the river Virajā, the boundary between Prakṛti and Vaikuṇṭha. Here it shakes off the subtle body and receives a non-material, divine body with four arms and ornaments. Indra and Prajāpati, the doorkeepers of

Vaikuṇṭha, let the *mukta* enter Vaikuṇṭha. The text's description of Vaikuṇṭha shows that within Vaikuṇṭha there is yet progress from bliss to bliss till the ultimate fulfillment comes. The *mukta* beholds the Lord himself on His throne and is received into the lap of the Lord, who asks him: "Who are you?" The released answers: "I am a mode of *Brahman*." The *mukta* receives the blessing of the Lord and thus becomes forever a servant of the Lord.

Vaiṣṇava Vedānta

The *Bhāgavata Purāṇa* considers Kapila one of the *avatāras* of Viṣṇu and his Sāṁkhya system as conducive to salvation, but later Vaiṣṇavism rejects Kapila as a heretic and his system as erroneous. After *c.*1000 C.E. the basic philosophy is no longer Sāṁkhya but Vedānta. Some "Vaiṣṇava" ideas in the *Vedas* and *Upaniṣads* have been pointed out before. But Vaiṣṇava Vedānta again is not a unilinear development of Upaniṣadic ideas. It is an attempt – made at different times by different people in different places – to combine the popular Vaiṣṇava tradition with Vedānta. Possibly the purport of the *Brahmasūtras* is theistic Vedānta, and there is good reason to assume that the now lost gloss on the *Brahmasūtras* by Bodhāyana, to which both Śaṅkara and Rāmānuja refer as their authority, had been theistic and possibly Viṣṇuitic.[77]

Each of the four major constituencies of Vaiṣṇavism mentioned above is distinguished by elaborating its own form of Vedānta: the Śrīvaiṣṇavas developed what became known as *Viśiṣṭa-Advaita*; the Brahma *saṃpradāya*, also called Madhva *saṃprādaya* after its most prominent theologian, developed *Dvaita*; the Kumāra *saṃprādaya*, also called Haṃsa or Nimbārka *saṃpradāya*, advocated *Dvaita-Advaita*; and the Rudra *saṃprādaya*, also known as Vallabha *saṃpradāya*, developed *Śuddha-Advaita*. We shall deal with all these in turn.

ŚRĪVAIṢṆAVISM

Vaiṣṇava Vedānta proper began with the *ācāryas* of Śrīraṅgam who tried to combine the fervor of the popular religious literature of the Āḷvārs[78] with the *jñāna* of Vedānta. South Indian tradition speaks of twelve Āḷvārs ("those who have delved into the deity") who lived from the sixth to the ninth century C.E. They composed fervent songs in honor of Viṣṇu in their native Tamil. Nammāḷvār, the fifth, is considered the greatest: his *Tiruvaimoli* is held to be the *Dramidopaniṣad*, the final wisdom of the Tamils.

The first of the Śrīvaiṣṇava *ācāryas*, Nātha Muni (ninth century C.E.) was the son of Īśvara Muni who was well known as a Pāñcarātra master. He collected the songs of the Āḷvārs, gave the collection (*Prabandham*) the status of revealed scripture in Śrīraṅgam, and succeeded in establishing himself as the highest authority with regard to doctrine. Pāñcarātra ritual and doctrinal tradition, the devotion of the Āḷvārs, the philosophy of Vedānta combined with a strong personal faith in the *guru* became the characteristics of Śrīvaiṣṇavism.

Nātha Muni's successor was Yamunācārya (tenth century C.E.), a scholar who left several systematic works, laying the foundation for Vaiṣṇava Vedānta.[79]

The greatest of the *ācāryas*, however, was Rāmānuja (1017–1137).[80] He was a great organizer and propagator of Śrīvaiṣṇavism as well as a theologian, and he suffered from persecutions by Śaivas: he had to flee from Śrīraṅgam and seek refuge in Melkote, which to this time has remained a strong center of Śrīvaiṣṇavism.

According to his own words his intention was not to build a new system, but to popularize and reformulate Vaiṣṇava Vedānta. Much of his writing consists of polemics against Śaṅkara's Advaita Vedānta which he considers a misinterpretation of the *Vedānta sūtras* and a deviation from tradition. But it is much more than mere polemics; it is a mature statement of the theistic tradition of India, a reunification of the two *Mīmāṃsās* of *karma-kāṇḍa* and *jñāna-kāṇḍa* with the *bhakti* tradition. It represents the attempt to establish Vaiṣṇavism as the leading religion of India with a full-fledged philosophy, ritual, *sādhana* (spiritual practice), and central leadership.[81]

While Rāmānuja's Śrīvaiṣṇavism contains much traditional Viṣṇu mythology and Pāñcarātra ritual and *vyūha* speculation, it makes a definitely new contribution with its doctrine of grace. In his theology the function of Brahman as *rakṣaka*, the redeemer, is central and in his *sādhana* of *prapatti* (self-surrender), faith in God as redeemer, is prominent. The Lord is *rakṣaka*, saviour, and the *jīva rakṣya*, in need of salvation. Human beings are essentially receivers of grace; God is essentially a giver of grace.[82] The very purpose of creation of the world is the salvation of the *jīvas*. Two of the six *guṇas* of *īśvara* are directly concerned with salvation: *saulabhya* (accessibility) and *sauṣilya* (condescension).[83] God comes down from his throne to enter into *saṃsāra* for the sake of assisting the struggling *jīva* to attain salvation: God becomes *sājātīya*, a member of the human race, suffers with the *jīva*, endures pain with the *jīva*, and leads the *jīva* by the hand like a friend or lover or guide. This guidance is effected through the *avatāras* and the *guru*, the "fully trustworthy person" who returns the lost *jīva* to his father. Commenting on the verse of the *Bhagavadgītā* in which the Lord tells Arjuna that he delivers himself to his devotee, Rāmānuja says that as the *jīva* cannot live without the Lord, so the Lord cannot live any longer without the *jīva* who has surrendered to him.[84]

Rāmānuja accepts the triad of separate substances: *īśvara–jīvas–prakṛti* (God–souls–matter). One problem is the clarification of the exact relationship between *īśvara* and *jīva*. Rāmānuja also takes over the Pāñcarātra doctrine of three different categories of *jīvas* with regard to salvation. The original nature of *jīva* is purity and bliss, but due to certain limitations it becomes entangled in *saṃsāra* and unhappy. The Lord resides as the *antaryāmī* in the soul to guide it – the *jīva*, however, is free to follow or to go his own way. "The Lord then, recognizing one who performs good actions as one who obeys his commands, blesses that person with piety, riches, worldly pleasures and final release: while one who trangresses His commands He causes to experience the opposite of all these."[85]

There remains, of course, the crucial problem of the relationship of *karman* and *kṛpā*, justice and grace. The "actor" in the principal sense is *īśvara*: "The inwardly ruling highest Self promotes action insofar as it regards in the case of any action the volitional effect made by the individual soul, and then aids that effort by granting its favour or permission. Action is not possible without permission on the part of the highest Self."[86] *Mukti* is ultimately "given" by the grace of *īśvara* – to Rāmānuja this follows from the *śruti*. Yet the need for some kind of cooperation is evident – after Rāmānuja, Śrīvaiṣṇavism split exactly over this point into two schools, one school insisting on active cooperation and the other on passive acceptance.

Since Viṣṇu is *mukti-dātā*, giver of liberation, the role of a *sādhana* (spiritual practice) is only to prepare the way, to dispose the *jīva* for receiving grace. Rāmānuja's *sādhana* follows closely the *Bhagavadgītā*: *prapatti*, self-surrender, is its essence and it includes *karma*, *jñāna*, and *bhakti*. Rāmānuja always emphasizes that *bhakti* in his understanding includes *karma* and *jñana* – *bhakti* is a particular kind of knowledge; it "eliminates the desire for everything else," and it makes a person fit "to be chosen by the supreme Self." *Bhakti* is non-attachment to sense-objects and attachment to the highest; it is a "realization," a vivid perception. The reason why *bhakti* brings bliss is that the nature of *brahman* is blissful – and knowing *Brahman* means participating in his bliss. The *śruti* says "Brahman is bliss." Brahman itself is joy eternal. "Brahman is *rasa*, attaining his *rasa* the knower becomes blissful."[87]

Mokṣa (liberation) is "given" – it is not an autonomous "self-finding" but requires positive action from the side of God. It is the highest degree of *bhakti*: *īśvara* and *jīva* remain distinct entities – between them the relationship of *bhakti* is maintained. There is also an interpenetration of *īśvara* and *jīva*. The *mukta* enjoys the omniscience and omnipresence of God; the only difference is that the liberated person is not creator. *Mukti* means freedom from egotism, not from individuality. It is desirelessness with regard to everything that is not God, but highest desire for him.

Rāmānuja accepts the traditional purāṇic and Pāñcarātra ideas with regard to the form and body of Viṣṇu, with regard to Vaikuṇṭha as paradise, and so forth. In some places, however, he offers a spiritual interpretation of these. Especially in the *Gadyatraya*, his last poetic works, he develops a spiritualistic concept of *mokṣa*: he specifies *bhakti* as *sáraṇāgati* – taking refuge to the Lord – and explains *mokṣa* as being *kaiṁkārya prāpti*, eternal service. The *Vaikuṇṭha Gadya* expresses his desire to be with God in his highest heaven: "When will I see with these eyes my Lord who is my sole treasure, my father, my mother and my all? When will I touch with these hands those tender, beautiful, lotus-like feet of the Lord, when will I enter into them with all my entire being? When will I enter into that ocean of immortality."[88]

As the name Śrī-Vaiṣṇavism suggests, the consort of Viṣṇu plays an important role also in its soteriology. Following the lead of the *Viṣṇu Purāṇa*, Rāmānuja says: "This Śrī, the Mother of the universe, is eternal and knows no separation from Viṣṇu. Even as Viṣṇu is all-pervading, she is all-pervading. When he becomes a *deva*, she assumes a *devī*-form. When he becomes a man, she too becomes a human being. She makes her form conform to the form of Viṣṇu."[89] Consequently, in the same way in which Viṣṇu is saviour, Śrī also is saviour – both in the transcendental (*para*) form and the *avatāras*. Rāmānuja calls Śrī the "Queen of the World" – later forms of Vaiṣṇavism intensify Śrī worship and put Śrī ahead of Viṣṇu, so that Vaiṣṇavism and Śāktism become indistinguishable.

The same holds true of the role of the *guru* in the process of salvation. Rāmānuja insists on the necessity of a *guru*. He recounts the parable of the young prince who in the course of a boyish play leaves his father's court and loses his way. A good Brahmin brings him up – neither the

Brahmin nor the boy being aware of the boy's princely status. When the boy has reached his sixteenth year, a "fully trustworthy person" tells him who his father is and that he longs to see him. The boy is exceedingly happy and starts on his way to his father, who on his account too takes steps to recover his son.[90] Rāmānuja sees in the "fully trustworthy person" of the parable the true *guru*.

The first among the *gurus* is Śrī, *mediatrix* between God and humans. She is the embodiment of grace and mercy whose endeavors win the forgiveness of God for the *jīva*. The human *guru* should be like her: entirely free from egotism, always desirous of the welfare of others, not swayed by the love of fame or profit.[91]

The role of the *guru* becomes exagggerated in some later Vaiṣṇava systems – the *guru* is formally declared to be God incarnate and for all practical purposes even more important than Viṣṇu himself.

In Śrī Vaiṣṇavism the process of salvation is not a process of only shedding wrong notions and un-doing mis-identifications; it is a positive development of the soul's faculties, and the purpose of earthly life is an education in true *bhakti*. Pillai Lokācārya expresses this aptly: "Even the all-loving Father, the Great *īśvara*, does not force his presence on the soul not yet ripe to receive him. With infinite patience He waits and watches the struggle of the soul in *saṃsāra* since the struggle is necessary for the full development of the faculties of the soul."[92]

The released soul is still conscious of being different from *brahman*, though united with him: it sees its true nature. "This true nature consists in the souls having for their inner self the highest self, while they constitute the body of that self and hence are modes of it."[93]

After Rāmānuja the unity of Vaiṣṇavism was disrupted. Two major schools developed: calling themselves the Tengalais (the "Southerners" with their seat in Śrīraṅgam) and the Vadagalais (the "Northerners" with their seat in Kāñcīpuram). The split was based on linguistic as well as dogmatic grounds. The Vadagalais maintained that the Tamil holy books were as important as Sanskrit scriptures as sources of divine revelation and that humans had to cooperate with God in the process of salvation like the young monkey who has to cling to his mother if he is to be carried away from a fire. The Tengalais gave preference to the Sanskrit scriptures and insisted that a soul has simply to wait for salvation from God like a kitten, which its carried out from a deadly fire by its mother.[94]

The major representative of the Tengalais was Lokācārya Pillai (1205–1310 C.E.), author of important works like the *Mumukṣupadi* and the *Tattva-trayam*. The leader of the Vadagalais was Vedānta Deśika (1269–1370 C.E.), the most prolific Śrīvaiṣṇava author and next in importance only to Rāmānuja. Besides theological treatises such as the *Rahasya-traya-sāra*, he also wrote plays, including the *Saṅkalpa Sūryodaya*. Both factions of Śrī Vaiṣṇavism are flourishing today – each has important centers and recognized teachers. While in agreement on most issues, the split is both theologically and socially relevant.[95]

Some of the major temples in possession of the Śrīvaiṣṇavas, like Tirupati in Andhra Pradesh, and Śrīrangam in Tamilnadu, attract many millions of pilgrims every year, regardless of their sectarian affiliation. They have become major tourist attractions as well – the former situated high atop a mountain ridge, the latter occupying an entire island in the Kauverī river, possibly the largest temple complex on earth.

THE BRAHMA OR MADHVA *SAṂPRADĀYA*

Madhva, also called Ānandatīrtha or Pūrnaprajñā (1238–1317),[96] began monastic life as a disciple of an Advaita guru. In spite of disagreements the teacher offered him the succession to the headship of his *maṭha*. Madhva declined and became the most radical exponent of Dvaita-Vedānta. He insists that God as well as the soul and world are real, and fights Advaita, which he dubs *Māyāvāda*, a system that is fixed on illusion, because of its insistence that only *brahman* is true/real and the world is false/unreal. Madhva's system is characterized by the "five differences": an irreducible difference between *brahman* and the individual souls *(jīvas)*; between *brahman* and inanimate objects *(jaḍa)*; between the *jīvas* amongst each other; between the *jīvas* and *jaḍa*; and between inanimate objects amongst each other. The application of external marks expressing surrender to Viṣṇu was considered indispensable when seeking salvation. Stigmatization, which consists of branding the body with the *cakra* (discus) mark of Viṣṇu, is a means to salvation in itself; those who bear the sign are free from sin and go to Vaikuṇṭha. Accepting one of the names of the Lord as one's own name is also prescribed. So is the "tenfold worship."

In Madhva, Vaiṣṇava sectarianism reaches it apex: "Brahmā, Śiva, and the greatest of the gods decay with the decay of their bodies; greater than these is Hari,[97] undecaying, because his body is for the sustentation of Lakṣmī." Viṣṇu is the only *īśvara*, the source of everything, from whom all knowledge comes, the source of bondage and of liberation.

Madhva considered himself the third *avatāra* of Vāyu, the mediator between God and humankind. The first was Hanuman, the second, Bhīma.

As regards the situation of the *jīva*, Madhva accepts the threefold Pāñcarātra division and subdivides the third category – the *baddhas* or souls in bondage – again into souls destined for liberation, souls destined for eternal *saṃsāra*, and souls destined for eternal hell. The essential characteristic of the *jīva* is its being a "reflection" of God. The God-*jīva* relationship is expressed as *biṃba-pratibiṃba*, image and reflection.[98] In many essential points regarding the nature of, and way to, *mokṣa*, he agrees with Rāmānuja. Bondage is explained as "of the nature of ignorance" and is due ultimately to the will of God and not merely to *Karma*. Bondage, however, is a reality and not a mere illusion. As bondage is caused by God's will, so it can be removed only through God's grace: "Release from bondage is possible only through God's grace. It is bestowed on those who have had a direct vision of God. Such vision is vouchsafed to those who have constantly meditated on him in loving devotion after going through the discipline of sincere study of *śāstras* and cogitation, termed *jijñāsa* which sets one's doubts at rest and clears the ground for meditation."[99]

God takes away the veil which he himself had thrown over the *jīva*, but from the side of the *jīva*, *bhakti* is required: "The firm and unshakable love of God which rises above all other ties of love and affection based upon an adequate knowledge and conviction of his great majesty is called *bhakti*. That alone is the means to *mokṣa*."[100]

Bhakti has stages, according to Madhva, and so has *mokṣa*. *Aparokṣa jñāna*, unmediated highest knowledge, "is a flash-like revelation of the Supreme at the fruition of a long and arduous process of *śravaṇa* (listening), *manana* (reflecting), and *nididhyāsana* (contemplating), in the fullness of absolute self-surrendering devotion to the Lord, as our *biṃba*. Ultimately it is He that must choose to reveal himself, pleased by the hungering love of the soul. The *pratibiṃba* must turn in and see his *biṃba* in himself. That is *aparokṣa*."[101] Madhva knows a final *mokṣa* which is achieved only after the dissolution of the subtle body.[102] *Mokṣa* itself is a state of individual bliss: "*Mokṣa* would not be worth having, if the *ātman* does not survive as a self-luminous entity therein. For the *ātman* is the ultimate goal and target of all desires."[103] Madhva refers to several places in the *Vedas* and *Upaniṣads* to prove that *mokṣa* is a blissful, conscious, individual state. We may rightly doubt whether he correctly interprets some of the *Upaniṣads* which seem to speak clearly about a purely transcendent state devoid of pain and pleasure. Like other Pāñcarātrins he assumes that the *ātman* becomes endowed with a celestial body, for the sake of eternal enjoyment.

In the enjoyment of eternal bliss the souls are dependent on God and they differ from one another in the degree of enjoyment. "There is a natural gradation among the released souls as well as disparity in their *sādhanas*. The difference in the nature and quality of *sādhanas* must necessarily have a relation to the result. The existence of such a gradation in *mokṣa* is established by reason and revelation. How can anyone oppose it?"[104] He explains this further: as vessels of different sizes, the rivers and oceans are all "full" of water according to their respective capacities; so also the *jīvas*' "fullness" of bliss is different according to the capacity of their *sādhana*. Those with little capacity are satisfied with little bliss. Those with greater capacity require more. In spite of the inequalities there is harmony. All causes for jealousy and envy are eradicated.

Thus the *ānanda-tāratāmya*, a gradation in bliss, is the logical consequence of his hierarchical conception of reality, with Viṣṇu's will ordering everything. "The released takes everything with the hand of Hari, sees through the eye of Hari only, with the feet of Hari he walks, and this is the state of the released who has attained *sāyujya mukti*."[105] Those fit for this type of *mukti* can enter into the Supreme Lord and at will issue forth, and again assume either spirit forms or material bodies.

Madhva institutionalized his *saṃpradāya* by appointing his disciples as heads of eight monasteries (Aṣṭamaṭhas) in Udipī. Each of them established a line of ordination which has been maintained to the present time. In turn, each of the heads of one of the eight *maṭhas* is appointed for two years to the headship of the Kṛṣṇamaṭha, the most important one. The change of headship is publicly celebrated and widely announced.

Among the successors to Madhva two have been singled out – together with Madhva they are called the "Tri-muni" or "Muni-traya", the triad of teachers. The first of these is Jāyatīrtha (1365–98 C.E.) who wrote important treatises such as the *Vādāvalī* and became known as a fiery opponent of contemporary Advaita scholars. The second is Vyāsarāya (1478–1539) whose *Nyāyāmṛta* continued to engage Advaita Vedānta in a sustained polemic. He has been called "prince of dialecticians" and is famous as a logician in his own right.

The Madhva *sampradāya* is flourishing today in many places, especially in South India, and is championed by recognized scholars such as B. N. K. Sharma, whose *History of Dvaita Vedānta* enumerates hundreds of exponents of Dvaita through the ages.[106]

THE KUMĀRA OR NIMBĀRKA *SAṂPRADĀYA*

Supposedly founded by the legendary Nārada, the son of Sanāt Kumāra, it is also called Haṃsa *sampradāya*. Its most prominent teacher was Nimbārka (1125–62 C.E.), also known as Nimādiyta or Niyamānanda, a Telugu Brahmin. His system became known as Dvaitādvaita. He is a typical and faithful Pāñcarātrin in most respects; in him the tendency to overemphasize the role of the *guru* is already apparent, a feature that led in later times to gross abuses.[107]

The *sādhana* of *gurūpasatti* (Surrender to the Master) found its most systematic expression in his disciple Sundarabhaṭṭa's *Mantrārtha Rahasya*: it is defined as "renouncing one's own self (*ātmanyāsa*) together with whatever belongs to oneself (*ātmīya*) to the Lord through the *guru*."[108] The formal entering upon this *sādhana* consists in the disciple's expressed choice of the *guru* as the only saviour from mundane existence, from the three pains and the six changes, the five miseries and the three *guṇas* of *prakṛti*, the sole master, husband, and friend. The *guru* expresses his acceptance of the disciple as "his servant, son, wife, and friend," and gives the assurance of salvation.[109]

Though theologically it is clear to Nimbārka and his school that God's grace is the only saving element, the nearness of *guru* and God in this system sometimes makes it difficult to distinguish what exactly is meant by *prapatti*, whether it is surrender to God or to the *guru*.

The attainment of highest fulfillment or *mokṣa* is thus described: "Having seen the Lord who is called Mukuṇḍa or Kṛṣṇa from a distance, the *jīva* bows down to Him uttering with happiness the words, 'Salutations to thy lotus-like Feet,' again and again. Then the Lord Kṛṣṇa casts His look of His lotus-like beautiful face, which is tender with kindness and pity, at the *jīva* and welcomes him in an extremely beautiful speech. Then the *jīva* becomes of the nature of the Lord and is liberated from the fetters of *māyā* and never returns to the worldly path again."[110] There the liberated *jīva* assumes all those qualities which were screened from him during the state of bondage.[111]

Nimbārka's followers are concentrated in the Braj-maṇḍala – living in Braj is one of the conditions of a blessed life – and they stage a splendid feast every year in Vrindāban to celebrate Rādhā's birthday. In their devotional practice they place Rādhā even above Kṛṣṇa as the channel through which Kṛṣṇa's grace is obtained and through whom the devotee can approach Kṛṣṇa.

THE RUDRA OR VALLABHA *SAṂPRADĀYA*

Founded by Viṣṇuswāmin (*c.*1200–1250 C.E.), it is also called Vallabha *saṃpradāya*, after its most prominent teacher Vallabha (1481–1533), a Telugu Brahmin who moved to the Brajmaṇḍala.[112] His variety of Vedānta is called Śuddhādvaita. The school became also known as *puṣṭimārga*, the way of grace.[113] It claims to have several million followers especially in Northern India, and maintains hundreds of vibrant centers of worship. It first became known in the West through the unsavoury "Mahārāja libel case,"[114] and as a result was tainted through unfavorable early-nineteenth-century reports.[115] Recently Indian and Western scholars as well as adherents of the Vallabha *saṃpradāya* have brought out translations of original texts and studies of various aspects of Vallabha's teachings.[116]

Vallabha elevates the *Bhāgavata Purāṇa* to the position of most authoritative scripture; his school considers it to be the only authentic commentary on the *Brahmasūtras*. Equally, the *Bhagavadgītā* is accepted as the word of God, providing an explanation to the Veda. Vallabha wrote commentaries on substantial portions of the *Bhāgavatam* and a systematic work *Tattvadīpa*, which synthesizes the teachings of the *Bhāgavatam*. Vallabha discredits all attempts – especially those of the Advaitins – to use reason and speculation to probe the nature of *brahman*. His is a "revelation-only" theology, a teaching which accepts what appear to be inconsistencies and contradictions in scriptural statements rather than attempting to judge revelation by reason.

It is also a "family-religion." Vallabha himself was a family man and his teaching emphasizes the virtues of family life as means to earn God's grace. "The worship of the Lord requires the services of all members of the family, and all are promised the highest bliss that always results from worship or *seva*. This mode of service makes the whole family free from worldly ties even when leading a householder's life, and their whole life becomes divine."[117]

Vallabha was convinced that in his time the duties of the *varṇāśrama-dharma* could no longer be properly fulfilled and that formal *saṃnyāsa*, far from being a spiritual help, could be spiritually harmful if not undertaken in reponse to the love of the Lord. What was important, however, and what was demanded from each and every member of the *saṃpradāya*, was *ātmanivedana*, self-surrender, and surrender of all one's own to the *guru*. There is no doubt that this teaching led not only to misunderstandings but also to malpractices.

Vallabha understands the *puṣṭimārga* not only to be different from *karmamārga* and *jñānamārga*, but also to be above the *śāstrīya bhaktimārga* of all other schools. *Puṣṭi* is the uncaused grace of God for which the devotee prepares but which he cannot direct or influence. "It is impossible to say for what reason God is pleased to extend his grace; it cannot be for the relief of suffering, for there are many sufferers to whom God does not do so."[118]

On the human side *puṣṭi* means doing things out of pure love and not because an action is enjoined by the Veda, and also not because the intellect recognizes the majesty and exalted nature of God. The *puṣṭimārga* is open to all – also to women and low-caste people, even to *patita* ("fallen," people to whom other schools of Hinduism have no hope of salvation to offer); it is free from Vedic commands and is only interested in establishing a relationship between the soul and its Lord – even if that relationship is one born out of anger and resentment.[119]

Vallabha distinguished between *mokṣa* and *nitya līlā* as the ultimate aim. Without denying the possibility of Vedantic *mokṣa*, which he understands as absorption in *Akṣara Brahman*, he holds that *nitya līlā*, eternal enjoyment of the company of God, is much preferable. "When the Lord desires to favour a particular soul – and be it remembered that in showing His favour He is not guided by any other consideration than His own will – He brings out the soul from Himself, gives it a divine body like His own, and plays with it for all time. In this play, which is called *nitya-līlā*, the Lord, remaining subordinate to the soul, gives it the pleasure of His company, which is generally known as *bhajānanda* (the bliss of devotion) or *svarūpānanda* (the bliss of the Lord Himself) which is referred to in the *Taittirīya Upaniṣad*, the *Bhāgavata*, and other Purāṇas."[120]

The uncaused grace of God and the enjoyment of His company is best exemplified by the *gopīs* of Vṛndāvana, who become the models for the followers of the *puṣṭimārga*. The highest title of God, then, is Gopī-jana-vallabha, the darling of the milkmaids.

Becoming a devotee of Kṛṣṇa is the highest aim of a follower of Vallabha.

> One who thinks of God as all and of oneself as emanating from Him, and who serves Him with love, is a devotee ... the highest devotee leaves everything, the mind filled with Kṛṣṇa alone ... wholly absorbed in the love of God. No one, however, can take the path of *bhakti* except through the grace of God. Karma, being of the nature of God's will, manifests itself as His mercy or anger to the devotee ... the law of Karma is mysterious ... we do not know the manner in which God's will manifests itself; sometimes by His grace He may even save a sinner who may not have to take the punishment due to him.[121]

Vallabha seems to assume that the seed of *bhakti* exists as *preman* (spiritual love) – due to the grace of God – in all human beings. It has to be nurtured and increased by self-surrender, listening to scriptures, and chanting His name. It becomes strong if, while leading a householder's life, one remains absorbed in Kṛṣṇa and performs one's duties with a mind fixed on God. This love of God may develop into such a passion (*vyasana*) that one feels unable to do anything else but sing His praises. *Vyasana* is "the inability to remain without God;" under its influence a householder may leave his home and become a saṃnyāsi.[122] "The firm seed of *bhakti* can never be destroyed; it is through affection for God that other attachments are destroyed and by the development of this affection that one renounces the home. It is only when this affection for God grows into a passion that one attains one's end easily."[123]

Seva, "service", is very central to the *puṣṭimārga*. It is a distinctive feature of Vallabha's *saṃpradāya* in so far as it denotes the worship of the image of Śrī Govardhana-nāthajī alone. All worship rendered to other manifestations of the Lord is called *pūjā*, and directed to the Lord's *vibhūtis* only, not his embodiment as Śrī Nāthajī. The original image, supposed to have been revealed to Vallabha on the hill of Girirāja, is the only full presence of the Lord: Pūrṇa Puruṣottama. It is the embodiment of the twelve *skandhas* (parts) of the *Bhāgavata Purāṇa*, each of which forms one specific limb. The tenth *skandha*, which contains the stories of Kṛṣṇa and the *gopīs*, forms the heart of Śrī Nāthajī.

Hardly anywhere in the history of Indian religions do we find a school of thought which seems to cry out so forcefully "Let God Be God!" Nothing is allowed to infringe on His freedom to be God – neither good nor bad works, neither reason nor speculation. His sovereign freedom is manifested from creation in the beginning to redemption in the end. Those whom He has chosen may achieve a state almost like His own – those whom He does not choose may remain in bondage and transmigration forever. "Among the *jīvas* who are bound there may be some with whom God may be pleased and to whom he may grant the complete power of knowledge; the confusing *māyā* leaves its hold upon such persons; they then remain in a free state in their nature as pure intelligence, but they have not the power to control the affairs of the universe."[124]

The Vallabha *saṃpradāya* is a vigorous religious movement today, with most of its members living in the Braj maṇḍala and in Gujarāt. It became recently known in the West through the American followers of Gurujī Mahārāj, the juvenile, cherubic-looking descendant of one of the original followers of Vallabha.

The Gauḍīya Vaiṣṇava saṃpradāya

While all Vaiṣṇava *saṃpradāyas* are supposed to be subsumed under one of the four main branches described, there is one more recent development, which needs separate treatment. Although nominally linked with the Madhva *saṃpradāya*, Bengal Vaiṣṇavism, especially in the form of the Caitanya movement, shows so many features of its own that it deserves a separate treatment. It also has become known and influential in the West as the "Hare Krishna Movement" and so some more detailed information on this branch of Vaiṣṇavism might be welcomed by Western readers.[125]

Kṛṣṇa Caitanya (1486–1533)[126] is one of the most influential figures in modern Vaiṣṇavism and he represents in a way a new type of it: pure emotionalism, ecstatic love for God – a revivalist movement rather than a new school of religion.

Caitanya embodies a Vaiṣṇavism that is only concerned with feelings and emotions. Caitanya was not its author but perhaps its greatest master as regards its practical realization. Caitanya had studied the *Bhāgavata Purāṇa*, had read the poems of Candīdāsa and Vidyāpati, knew Bilvamaṅgala's *Kṛṣṇa-karṇāmṛta* and Jayadeva's *Gītā-govinda*, and indeed the practice of *kīrtaṇa* was widespread already in his time. He must have met quite a number of those *bhaktas* who travelled the length and breadth of India spreading their message of love for Viṣṇu, Kṛṣṇa, and Rāma, through songs and poems.[127] Caitanya did not write any books: his own writing consists of only eight verses, the *Śiksāṣṭaka*. From these we learn that he considered humility as a requirement for receiving the grace of God. His religion consists in "taking the name" and expresses itself as disinterested *bhakti*, accompanied by signs of highest emotion like tears, choked voice, horripilation, etc., and making very intense the desire for union with God.[128]

The theology of the Caitanya movement was articulated by the six Gosvāmis of Vṛndāvana, Caitanya's disciples, of whom the most important were Rūpa Gosvāmi, Jīva Gosvāmi and the younger Sanātana Gosvāmi. Its basis are the *Bhāgavata Purāṇa* and the *Pāñcarātra Brahma Saṃhitā*, the latter especially with regard to ritual. According to Caitanya Kṛṣṇa alone is the full manifestation of God, and the continued presence of Kṛṣṇa in Braja is the central fact around which the practice of this religion moves.[129] Specifically it is the Kṛṣṇa of Vṛndāvana the great lover, and the Gopīs, the beloved, who perfectly responded to the call of love, who are the main theme of this new type of *bhakti* religion.

Much of the theological literature of Caitanya Vaiṣṇavism consists of commentaries on the *Bhāgavata Purāṇa*. The Caitanyites consider it the only authentic *bhāṣya* to the *Brahma-Sūtras*. In their ontology they largely follow the Pāñcarātra tradition, especially as explained by Madhva and Nimbārka. While they accept the definition of the supreme brahman as *saccidānanda*, they stress the *ānanda* element: "it is pure bliss, self differentiated, the ground of all life and the source of all the *rasas* that give human life its meaning and value."[130] Brahman or Bhagavān is only Viṣṇu or Hari, identical with Kṛṣṇa. Therefore in Kṛṣṇa all attributes are found: he is the repository of all excellent qualities. The purpose of existence of devotee and God is none else but to please and enjoy each other. Kṛṣṇa, through his *cit-śakti*, creates the *jīvas*, through his *māyā-śakti* he creates the universe, and though his *hlādinī-śakti* he enjoys everything. His enjoyment constitutes the bliss of the *bhakta*: "*Hlādinī* is so named because of giving delight to Kṛṣṇa who tastes delight through that power. Kṛṣṇa himself is delight. *Hlādinī* is the cause of the *bhakta*'s delight; the essence of *hlādinī* is called *premā*. Rādhā is the modification of Kṛṣṇa's love, her name is the very essence of the delight-giving power. *Hlādinī* makes Kṛṣṇa taste delight. Through *hlādinī* the *bhaktas* are nursed."[131]

The manifestation of this *hlādinī-śakti* of Kṛṣṇa is the *līlā*, the love play of god and humans, exemplified best in the *rasa-līlā* of Kṛṣṇa and the Gopīs in Vṛndāvana.

One of the great contributions of the Caitanya school to *bhakti* religion is its development and analysis of the stages of *bhakti* and especially its system of *rasa*. The main work is Rūpa Gosvāmi's *Bhakti-*

rasāmṛta-sindhu, "The Ocean of the Nectar of the Feeling of Devotional Love": though deliberately making use of the *rasa* systematics of contemporary poetics, it is original in its application of it to Kṛṣṇa-*bhakti*. Rūpa Gosvāmi (*c.*1460–1540), a direct disciple of Caitanya, wrote the work under Caitanya's instructions. It is considered the most authentic exposition of *bhakti* according to Caitanya. Rūpa Gosvāmi incorporated thousands of quotations from authoritative sources so as to make the work a veritable *summa theologica* of *bhakti*. It analyzes and classifies the various types and stages of *bhakti*. Their psychological bases, the *bhāvas*, and their essences, the *rasas*, are described in an ascending series, culminating in *madhura-bhakti-rasa*.

There is no good quality and no cause of enjoyment that is not found in Kṛṣṇa, and much of Caitanya's *bhakti* religion consists in a contemplation and vivid imagination of all the physical features of Kṛṣṇa at various stages of his life, all details of his deeds as recorded in the Purāṇas. Accordingly, *bhakti* is divided into *vātsalya*, *sākhya*, *dāsa*, and *mādhurya*, corresponding to the contemplation of the features and activities of the infant Kṛṣṇa, the child Kṛṣṇa, the boy Kṛṣṇa, and the young man Kṛṣṇa. External signs of *bhakti* – especially of the higher stages – are dancing, rolling on the ground, singing, shouting, laughing loudly, behaving as if mad, fainting, horripilation, and so forth, as well as trembling, shedding of tears, changing of color, and stammering. The highest love for God is that which the Gopīs had; only to such lovers does Kṛṣṇa appear in his own full form.

This *rati* – highest love for Kṛṣṇa as the beloved – has two complementary phases: *sam-bhoga* (togetherness) and *vi-pralaṃba* (separation). *Rati* is itself a modification of Kṛṣṇa's *hlādinī-śakti*, free from *māyā* and *avidyā* and the *sthāyi-bhāva* (constant mood) of *bhakti-rasa*; once it has appeared it cannot be lost again. Its bliss is the most intense, higher than that of *mokṣa*. Kṛṣṇa alone is the *akhila rasāmṛta-mūrti*, "the complete embodiment of the nectar of all feelings"; he excites different *rasas* (sentiments) in different devotees according to their different emotional dispositions.

In details of the description of the various kinds of devotees, the nature of Kṛṣṇa and the nature of salvation, various authors differ. One of the most authoritative works is Jīva Gosvāmi's *Ṣaṭsandarbha*. It distinguishes two categories of *jīvas*: those who possess through God's grace a *saṃskāra* (inborn inclination) toward Bhagavān do not need any instruction (like Prahlāda); those whose inclination to Bhagavān has been obstructed under the influence of *māyā-śakti* need instruction. This "conversion to Bhagavān" – the necessary first step on the way to salvation – is called *abhideya*. It consists in counteracting the superimposed aversion and produces a *bhakti* whose characteristic is devotional worship of Bhagavān. From it proceeds true knowledge of Bhagavat. The *māyā-śakti* is counteracted by the *hlādinī-śakti* of which an atom also exists in a potential state in the *jīva*.

External worship is extremely important for Caitanyites. One reason for this is the belief in the real physical presence of Kṛṣṇa in the objects of worship. It is also considered a natural activity of a devotee: service of one who is dear brings happiness and nothing can be dearer than the Bhagavān. Service itself, especially *kīrtaṇa* (congregational singing of hymns), brings highest bliss to the devotee. *Bhakti* is not an imposition from the outside, but the realization of the true nature of the soul. The highest type of *bhakti* is *prīti* (liking) or *preman* (love), characterized as *duḥkha nivṛtti* (cessation of suffering) and *sukha prāpti* (attainment of bliss), "the attainment of the *jīva*'s natural state and the relinquishing of its otherwise imposed state."

With regard to the *summum bonum* there seems to be confusion, at least with regard to terminology. On the one hand Vedāntic terms are used; on the other hand every association with Śaṅkara's ideas is shunned. The *Bhāgavata Purāṇa* already required the *bhakta* to give up all desire for *mokṣa* – the essential prerequisite for Śaṅkara – and in the *Caitanya-caritāmṛta* we read: "At the sound of *mokṣa* the *bhakta* feels hatred and fear, he prefers hell to it. At the utterance of the word *bhakti*, the mind is filled with joy."[132] However, Jīva Gosvāmi does use the word *mukti* and even knows a *mukti* during lifetime, besides that after death, which is of the usual five kinds, all of which are permanent, that is, there is no return from them into *saṃsāra*. According to him, *mukti* is attainable through *sākṣātkāra* (bodily vision, viz. of Kṛṣṇa) alone, which is produced by *prīti* only. Its essence is apprehension of the Lord in his paradise: only *prīti* gives certainty to it. "Although the *jīva* never becomes perfectly identical with the Bhagavat the chief characteristic of the *sāyujya mukti* is complete immersion in the divine bliss and consequently the capacity of experiencing the Lord in all his intrinsic energies and supersensuous sports becomes lost in the state of immersion. In this respect the *sāyujya mukti* differs from the other four forms of emancipation in which the separate existence and the consequent opportunity for worship and service of the emancipated being still continue. For this reason the *sāyujya mukti* is regarded as inferior and is never desired by the real *bhakta*."[133]

The condition of the released soul is relayed in colourful pictures of a heavenly existence and the descriptions of Vaikuṇṭha in the *Bhāgavata Purāṇa* are taken literally. The true *Bhakta* receives a celestial body to sport forever with Kṛṣṇa. Usually three heavens are mentioned: Vaikuṇṭha, Goloka, and the celestial Vṛṇḍāvana. The followers of the higher, esoteric *bhakti* alone go to Vṛṇḍāvana; they are the *rāgānuga bhaktas*, who experience the love of the *gopīs* to Kṛṣṇa, a love which is itself grace. The lower or *vaidhi bhakti* is "learned": it has to be acquired by following the rules of the *śāstras*. It has sixty-four elements, among which the most important are society of holy men, *kīrtaṇa* of Kṛṣṇa's name, listening to the recitation of the *Bhāgavata Purāṇa*, dwelling in Vraja, and worship of the *mūrti*. All these topics are dealt with at great length in the writings of the six Gosvāmis. The main emphasis is always laid on the singing of the name: "In the *Kaliyuga* the singing of the name is the great *sādhana*. Through *saṁkīrtaṇa* the sin of the world is destroyed, the heart is purified and practice of all kinds of *bhakti* is initiated."[134]

The authentic ritual of the Caitanyites was codified by Gopala Bhaṭṭa, one of the six Vṛṇḍāvana Gosvāmis, in his *Hari-bhakti-vilāsa* – written, according to tradition, under the direct command of Caitanya himself[135] – containing detailed instructions about the way of life of a *bhakta*.

From the sixteenth century till today Gauḍīya Vaiṣṇavism has been a vigorous movement and a major presence in the Hindu religious scene. It succeeded to establish itself at the height of Mughal domination of India and its first representatives built large and beautiful temples in rediscovered Vṛṇḍāvana. It survived the wrath of Aurangzeb and generated revival and resistance movements in nineteenth-century Bengal. The nineteenth-century Neo-Caitanya movement resulted in the establishment of Gauḍīya maṭhas in most major cities in India. Neo-Caitanya missionaries carried their message to Europe, America and Japan before World War II. In 1965 Swāmi Bhaktivedānta "Prabhupāda" launched ISKCON ("International Society for Krishna Consciousness") in New York, from where it spread rapidly throughout much of the world.

VAIṢṆAVA WORSHIP AND DEVOTION

Vaiṣṇavism as we know it today is intimately connected with image worship.[136] True to the idea of the presence of Viṣṇu in space and time which is so basic for Vaiṣṇavism, representations of Viṣṇu in images and through ritual are not only symbolisms but realities. In continuation of the *vyūha* and *vibhava* theories of the Pāñcarātra system, the *arcāvatāra* form of God is conceived as a further extension of his presence and manifestation.[137] Besides the *mūrtis* that are made by humans representing Viṣṇu with a human-like body, Vaiṣṇavas also worship some natural phenomena as presence of Viṣṇu. Among plants the *tulasī* tree is sacred to Viṣṇu and is worshiped: a tulasī plant is found in almost every Vaiṣṇava home. Among minerals the *śālagrāma* (either in the form of a petrified ammonite or of a round granite pebble from the Gaṇḍakī river in Nepal) is held sacred not only as a substitute for a human-made image but often considered a particularly intense presence of Viṣṇu.[138]

There are descriptions of Bhāgavata shrines of pre-Christian and early post-Christian times, but only a few numismatic representations of Vāsudeva-Viṣṇu are connected with the name of Viṣṇumitra (first century B.C.E.).[139] Mathurā and its surroundings had been the home of Vāsudeva-Kṛṣṇa worship from very ancient times, as the Besnagar inscription testifies.[140] At an early age votive columns in honor of Vāsudeva-Viṣṇu, Pradyumna, and Saṁkarṣaṇa were erected.[141] Quite early too is the representation of the *sudarśaṇa-cakra* of Viṣṇu – in fact in several cases the presence of the *cakra* has been used to identify a figure as Viṣṇu.[142] The wheel is an ancient solar symbol, and thus connects later Viṣṇu images with the Vedic Viṣṇu. The *Bṛhat-saṃhitā* description of Viṣṇu images[143] shows that at such an early date the representation of Viṣṇu had already been stereotyped: most of what is held as characteristic for Viṣṇu has been part of Viṣṇu images since then.[144] It is worth mentioning that the text already describes varieties of two-, four-, and eight-armed Viṣṇu images. The *śrīvatsa* mark hints at a fusion of Lakṣmī and Viṣṇu cult; the attributes in his hands express his salvific activities.

The Viṣṇu images preserved are very numerous. There are various ways to classify them: according to the content of their representation they are divided into *para*, *vyūha*, and *vibhava* – the former ones are subdivided according to their positioning of the figure into *sthānaka* (standing), *āsana* (sitting), and *śayana* (lying). Each of the twelve subgroups is again subdivided into *uttama* (highest), *madhyama* (middling), and *adhama* (lowest) according to the number of figures that surround the main deity.[145] A less popular classification divides the Viṣṇu images into *yoga*, *bhoga*, *vīra*, and *abhicārika*.[146]

The *Bṛhat-saṃhitā* description suits the *para-sthānaka* definition. There are two main varieties: Viṣṇu standing alone, and Viṣṇu accompanied by Śrī (sometimes also by Bhūmī). The attributes express salvific activities of Viṣṇu: he kills Madhu and Kaitabha with the *gadā* (club) and Rāhu with the *cakra* (discus); he protects the embryo of Pārikṣit by the arrow and he frightens his enemies by the sound of his bow; he scares away the demons by the sound of the *śaṅkha* (conch) and gives *mukti* through his *abhaya-mudrā*. In later Viṣṇu images, replacing one of the weapons (usually the sword), Viṣṇu holds in one of his hands a lotus – a symbol with a great variety of meanings[147] associated with the highest God since very ancient times. It signifies purity and transcendent bliss: the lotus flower is pure and unstained even growing amidst muddy waters.

The *śayana-mūrti* is the most common Viṣṇu image in South India. Viṣṇu is represented as resting on Śeṣa, the world-snake, attended by Śrī and often also by Bhūmī, who is considered to be his second wife. He represents the highest bliss, the state of absorption of everything in him; through his *darśana* one obtains highest bliss: it is the representation of Viṣṇu in Vaikuṇṭha. The snake itself is a highly symbolic figure in Vaiṣṇavism: though it is the enemy of Garuḍa, it is also the symbol for eternal life and immortality, of secret power and mystery. The association of the serpent with water is also very meaningful: water is the primeval element, the source of everything. From Viṣṇu's navel issues a lotus, on which Brahmā, the demiurge, is seated. Various figures are represented in the company of Viṣṇu; often they are only there to emphasize his importance.

We find the representation of Viṣṇu's *vyūhas* in some four-faced, four-armed North Indian images. One of them shows a human, a lion, a boar, and a demon face. In the *Viṣṇu-dharmottara*[148] we read that the human face is that of Vāsudeva typifying Viṣṇu's *bala*; the lion face is that of Saṁkarṣaṇa typifying *jñāna*; the boar face is that of Pradyumna typifying *aiśvarya*; the demon face is that of Aniruddha, typifying *śakti*.

Very frequent are representations of *vibhavas*, particularly of Rāma and Kṛṣṇa. The stereotyped *daśāvatāras* belong to the standard inventory of many Indian temples. Separate temples exist especially for *Varāha*, *Nṛsiṇha*, and *Vāmana avatāra*. Nonhuman *avatāras* are represented either theriomorphic or hybrid, i.e. a human body with an animal head. *Vāmana* is depicted both as dwarf and as *virāṭa*, the Viṣṇu *trivikrama* of the Vedas. The three Rāmas are always shown in human form with their distinguishing emblems: Paraśurāma with his battle ax, Daśarathi Rāma with bow and arrow, Balarāma with a ploughshare.

Kṛṣṇa is the most popular among the *avatāras* also as regards his images. As early as the second or third century C.E., a representation shows the child Kṛṣṇa, and fourth-century reliefs illustrate Kṛṣṇa lifting up Govardhana mountain, Kṛṣṇa stealing butter, the child Kṛṣṇa subduing Kalīya-nāga. With the growth of the romantic element in Vaiṣṇavism, the representations of Kṛṣṇa in the company of Rādhā and other Gopīs increase. Kṛṣṇa with the flute is one of the most popular motifs; the sweet sound of Kṛṣṇa's music attracts people to him so that they forget everything else and follow him into his enjoyments.

The *Kalki-avatāra* is described in two varieties: one two-armed, the other four-armed. In the *daśāvatāra* slabs we find usually the two-armed variety described in the *Viṣṇudharmottara Purāṇa* as "a powerful man angry in mood, riding on horseback with a sword in his raised hand."

Noteworthy also are representations of the *viśvarūpa* aspect of Viṣṇu or Kṛṣṇa, and representations of Viṣṇu delivering the king of the elephants from the alligator.

The representation of Śrī is earlier than that of Viṣṇu; she is found as consort of Viṣṇu in all the *para* images: *sthānaka*, *āsana*, and *śayana*. In the first two varieties she is usually shown in a regal hieratic attitude – one of her hands often holding a full-blown lotus, another in a *varadā-mūdra*. In the *śayana-mūrtis* she is usually shown at the foot-end, massaging the feet of Viṣṇu.

Sītā in the company of Rāma is usually shown as a dignified lady; Rādhā in Kṛṣṇa's company is depicted either responding to Kṛṣṇa's flute or in a hieratic royal pose.

The images of Viṣṇu are his physical presence for the sake of receiving formal worship; ritual image-worship is one of the main means of winning God's grace. The worship of Viṣṇu in images is as variegated as these images themselves: sometimes Viṣṇu is worshiped in the *para*-form, sometimes in the *vyūha*-form, sometimes in the *vibhava*-form.

The individual acts of formal worship are not exclusively Vaiṣṇava, some may even be Vedic: *mantra-japa* is a very universal practice and the particularity of Vaiṣṇavism lies only in the choice of a *Viṣṇu-mantra*. Vaiṣṇava in a more specific sense may be the congregational singing known as *saṅkīrtaṇa*, or also *nāma-kīrtaṇa* which seems to be of rather recent origin. The worship of the *mūrti* by prostration, by offering incense and light, is also part of non-Vaiṣṇava image worship. But for Viṣṇu worship only specific materials, flowers of certain colors, are allowed.

A universal characteristic of Vaiṣṇavism is its rejection of bloody animal sacrifices. The element of communion with Viṣṇu through a material object either touched by the image or through eating the remnants of the food offered to the *mūrti* (*prasāda*) is quite prominent. Usually Vaiṣṇavas enjoin exclusivity of worship: only Viṣṇu must be worshiped, only through Viṣṇu worship can salvation be attained; a Vaiṣṇava who worships other gods is considered a heretic who has no chance to attain *mukti*.

In the devotional literature Viṣṇu is implored under his different names as helper in various needs. The *avatāras* are invoked severally – the worshiper usually recounts the deed of the *avatāras* as a guarantee for help in similar distress. The *Nārāyaṇa-kavaca* enumerates the *avatāras* with the corresponding evils from which the devotee asks to be delivered.

Hymns to Viṣṇu and his manifestations abound both in Sanskṛt and the vernaculars. They are still used at the gatherings of devotees in *satsaṅgas* – they repeat the feats of Viṣṇu in his different *avatāras*, they glorify his greatness, they contain prayers for deliverance. Some places of pilgrimage are associated with certain *avatāras* of Viṣṇu and they usually celebrate the particular feast of the *avatāra* with great pomp. Very often the worship of Viṣṇu is fused with the worship of one of the great Vaiṣṇava saints, locally considered as *avatāras* themselves. In some sects the worship of Śrī or of Rādhā plays an important role. In later Vaiṣṇavism the worship of the *guru* becomes an integral part of Viṣṇu cult, the *guru* being the living presence of Viṣṇu for the disciple.

The rules laid down for worship in the numerous Vaiṣṇava sects are very complex and it is said that only scrupulous fulfillment will merit the grace of Viṣṇu.[149] Feasts observed in honor of Viṣṇu or of his *avatāras* are too numerous to be mentioned here and they are often only of local importance. The great ones like *Kṛṣṇajanmāṣṭamī*, Kṛṣṇa's birthday, have become national festivals. Observance of *vratas* like fasting on ekādaśī is a very common practice among Vaiṣṇavas, considered essential for the attainment of the goal of religion. So is the observance of a strict vegetarian diet and a certain number of practical rules in daily life.

Viṣṇu *bhakti* has found its systematics in *Bhakti-sūtras* attributed to Śāṇḍilya and Nārada; they imitate even in their literary form the *Brahma-sūtras* of Bādarāyaṇa. The *bhāṣyas* on the *Vedānta-sūtras* by Vallabha, Nimbārka and Baladeva Vidyābhūṣaṇa expound a Kṛṣṇa-Vedānta. There is also a large number of scholastic writing on the subject of *bhakti*, such as the *Bhakti-sandarbha*, a section of the *Ṣaṭsandarbha* by Jīva Goswāmi.

The real source of the vitality of the *bhakti* religion, however, was always the enthusiasm of its poets and mystics, who traveled the length and breadth of India to sing the glories of their God.[150] There is very little difference between Viṣṇu-, Śiva-, and Devī-*bhaktas* when they extol the need to practice *bhakti*. A very striking feature of almost all the *bhakti* poets and mystics is their insistence on the cultivation of high moral virtues such as purity, truthfulness, patience, forbearance, love, renunciation, selflessness, contentment with one's state of life, self-control, pity, freedom from greed and hypocrisy, sincerity, and humility. They usually recommend as means to liberation the traditional Vaiṣṇava *sādhana*: holy company (*satsaṅga*), *kīrtaṇa* and *nāma-japa*, worship of a *mūrti*, submission under the guidance of a *guru*.

All of them emphasize that it is God's grace that saves humans; our own activities only prepare us for it. In many beautiful verses they express the intense longing for God so typical for Vaiṣṇavism. Very often the *bhakti* poet-mystics use Vedāntic expressions when describing their religious experiences. Side by side they also use traditional Vaiṣṇava mythology and imagery. They take the historical humanity of Rāma-Sītā or Kṛṣṇa-Rādhā literally in every detail, but at the same time they see these as the manifestation of an ineffable Absolute.

The Āḷvārs, a group of twelve South Indian poet-mystics flourished between the sixth and the ninth century C.E. in the Tamil country. Devotees of Māl (the Tamil name for Kṛṣṇa and Viṣṇu Nārāyaṇa), they composed thousands of stirring hymns that they sang while moving from place to place. Many of these hymns were later collected in the *Nalayira Divya Prabandham*, "The Book of 4000 Verses," which became recognized as a revealed text by the Śrīvaiṣṇava Ācāryas at Śrīraṅgam, still widely used in temple worship in South India today. The greatest of the āḷvārs was Nammāḷvār, also called Śathakopan (seventh century C.E.). There was one woman among them, Āṇṭāl, also called Goda (725–755 C.E.) who was so overwhelmed by her love for Viṣṇu that she refused to marry anyone else. According to tradition she bodily merged into the

Viṣṇu image at Śrīraṅgam after having formally married him. Her birthplace Śrīvilliputtur, which keeps her memory alive, boasts the tallest Gopura in India.

In later centuries a powerful Vaiṣṇava revival movement began in Karṇāṭaka under the name of "Dāsa Kuṭa", the association of the Servants of God. Its founder Śrīpadirāja, also known as Lakṣmīnārāyaṇa Tīrtha, was the head of the Padmanābha Tīrtha at Mulbagal in the former Mysore State.[151] He wrote poetry under the pen name of Raṅga Viṭhala, indicating thereby his devotion to Viṭhala (a name of Viṣṇu) in Pandharpur, a place of pilgrimage later claimed by the Mahrattas.

The scholar Vyāsarāya, a follower of Madhva, was also a gifted poet of mystical Viṣṇu devotion. Virtually all the great *ācāryas* of the various Vaiṣṇava schools also composed inspired poems that are used in congregational worship today.

The Dāsa movement spread beyond the borders of Karṇāṭaka and influenced the development of a group of Mahārāṣṭrian poet-mystics whose songs are much alive today. Among the most famous of these is Jñānadeva (*c.*1275–1350), the author of the *Jñāneśvarī*, a lengthy commentary on the *Bhagavadgītā*, and composer of many *abhaṅgas* (hymns) in praise of Viṭhoba. His disciple Nāmadeva (1270–1350), who reputedly had lead a life of brigandry before his conversion, spent most of his later life in Pandharpur, singing the praises of God. Another famous bhakta, Ekanātha (1533–1598) wrote a commentary on part of the *Bhāgavata-Purāṇa* and composed many *abhaṅgas*. Tukārām (1608–49), born into a low-caste family in Dehu near Pune, became such an ardent devotee of Viṭhoba that he neglected his family business. He is one of the most popular poet-saints of Mahārāṣṭra and his memory is kept alive by the Vārkarīs, a group of devotees of Viṭhobha, who continue singing Tukārām's *abhaṅgas* at their fortnightly gatherings in Dehu.

When Muslim power was at its height in northern India, and Brahminism perhaps at its lowest ebb, popular singers of God's love arose whose vernacular compositions moved the large masses to fervent expressions of *bhakti* to their traditional deities. The greatest among them is probably Tulsīdās (Tulasīdāsa) (1511–1637), author of the celebrated *Rāmcaritmānas*, a vernacular (Avadhī, Eastern Hindī) recreation of the *Rāmāyaṇa*, which has become the most popular religious classic in northern India. Tulsīdās also composed numerous hymns which are widely used in religious services.[152]

Another famous name in northern India is Sūrdās (1479–1584), the blind poet of Kṛṣṇa's and Rādhā's love, who reportedly deeply moved the Muslim Emperor Akbar through his singing. The collection of his songs is known as *Sūrsāgar*, "Sur's Ocean" of devotion.[153] He exhorts his listeners to utilize their time of life well in the service of Viṣṇu: "Someone who has received a human body and does not worship God is just a morsel for the god of death. Sūrdās says: Without doing *bhajan* you have wasted your life."[154]

The poet-mystics usually place very little importance on the performance of Brahmanic ritual; they even ridicule many customs of the Brahmins. They do not attach much importance to pilgrimages, to rules of conduct fixed for the *varṇas* and *āśramas*, to ritual purity, and the like, but emphasize the importance of moral qualities and spiritual enlightenment.[155] For them the most important means of God realization is not a material sacrament or a ritualistic concept of duty, but the living Word. This tendency has continued to our own time. Contemporary Vaiṣṇava teachers such as Swāmi Rāma Tīrtha emphasize the necessity of cultivating moral virtues and purity of heart, selfless service and spirituality, and they point out the instrumentality of the Word in achieving life's ultimate aim.

VAIṢṆAVISM TODAY

As the largest branch of mainstream Hinduism, Vaiṣṇavism in its great variety of expressions is very much alive today. In hundreds of thousands of Viṣṇu temples the daily ritual attracts millions of worshipers and many of the largest and most popular places of pilgrimage are dedicated to Viṣṇu. The major Vaiṣṇava *saṃpradāyas* are flourishing, guided by theologically and administratively capable leaders, many of whom exercise great influence on the lives and thoughts of a great number of ordinary people. They are usually less well known, especially in the West, than the jet-set gurus, who concoct their own brand of Hinduism.

Part of the Vaiṣṇava ethos is fidelity to tradition and faithful following of rules of life and ritual. Since the major Vaiṣṇava *saṃpradāyas* have been in existence for many centuries and regularly meet at the Kumbhamelās, which take place every three years (as well at the yearly Ardhamelās in Prāyāg), they are stricty regulated and their members have to conform to the norms set down for each. This may be unspectacular but it makes for perseverance and character formation.

Most of present-day Vaiṣṇava worship and thought is medieval, not "modern" – but it has charm and strength and sustains spiritually and socially hundreds of millions of Hindus.

Vaiṣṇavism has also lately been discovered by Westerners. While they were first attracted by Advaita Vedānta, especially in its reinterpretation by Swami Vivekananda around the turn of the century, the most successful Hindu mission to the West in the late twentieth century was the Gauḍīya Vaiṣṇava movement represented by Swāmi Bhaktivedānta, which spread rapidly all over the globe after its establishment in the United States in the late sixties. Mention should also be made of Ronald Nixon, an Englishman, who became known in India as Śrī Krishnaprem Vairāgi; he was not only accepted as a true convert but also as a teacher of Vaiṣṇavism to Hindus.[156]

Western scholarship, too, increasingly turns toward Vaiṣṇavism, after having for a long time focused on Śaṅkara and his school. Part of this scholarship is generated by the members of ISKCON who are systematically exploring the rich scholarly heritage of Gauḍīya Vaiṣṇavism. In numerous references in this chapter recent Western scholarship has been indicated: in the past few decades many translations of Vaiṣṇava texts have appeared, as well as numerous monographs on Vaiṣṇava history and theology, and several conferences were held dealing with *bhakti* movements.[157]

While much of that interest has been generated by the inherent loveliness and charm of Vaiṣṇava poetry and the depth and sophistication of Vaiṣṇava theology, some of it also has to do with the prominent use of Vaiṣṇava symbols such as Rāma and Kṛṣṇa, Rāmarājya and Dharmakṣetra, by Hindu political parties whose activities arouse worldwide attention. While one need not necessarily applaud this usage, it certainly serves as a further indication of the wide and deep fascination that symbols and ideas associated with age-old Vaiṣṇavism still evoke among millions of Hindus.

NOTES

1. S. K. Chatterji, in *HCIP*, vol. I, p. 165. L. Renou, *L'Inde Classique*, vol. I, p. 323 envisages a non-Āryan origin of the name of Viṣṇu. He mentions among the etymologies suggested by different scholars *vi-śaun*, "crossing the heights," and *vis* "active," and notes the epithet *śipiviṣṭa* as indicating a possible phallic origin. Cf. A. Daniélou, *Hindu Polytheism*, p. 149.
2. Sudhakar Chattopadhyaya, *The Evolution of Theistic Sects in Ancient India*, p. 4.

3. *Ṛgveda* I, 154–156; VII, 99 and 100.
4. Cf. *Bṛhaddevatā* II, 64.
5. *Taittirīya Brāhmaṇa* III, 2, 9, 7; *Śatapatha Brāhmaṇa* I, 2, 5; XIV, 1, 1.
6. D. C. Sircar and V. M. Apte in *HCIP*, vol. II, p. 432: "The historical character of Vāsudeva, as the son of Vasudeva of the Vṛṣṇi (known also as Sātvata) set of the famous Yādava or Yadu clan need not be doubted." R. G. Bhandarkar, *Vaiṣṇavism*, pp. 35–38. A. D. Pusalker, *Studies in Epics and Puranas*, pp. 49–81. D. C. Sircar, "Early History," in *CHI*, vol. IV, pp. 108–145.
7. Sircar and Apte, *HCIP*, p. 437. In *Mahābhārata*, Sabhāparvan, chap. 37. Śiśupala, scolding Bhīṣma for worshiping Kṛṣṇa, says of the latter: "This wretch born in the race of Vṛṣṇis, unrighteously slew of old the illustrious King of Jarasandha."
8. Sircar and Apte, "Early History", *HCIP*, vol. II, pp. 450ff.
9. Ibid.
10. Ramdas Lamb, "The Magh Melā: Prāyāg's 'other' Holy Festival," *Journal of Vaiṣṇava Studies* 7/2 (Spring 1999), pp. 195–205
11. The hymns addressed to Viṣṇu are *Ṛgveda* I, 154; 155; 156; VII, 99, 100.
12. Cf. A. A. Macdonell, *Vedic Mythology*, Strasbourg, 1897.
13. In *Ṛgveda* I, 22, 18 Viṣṇu is called the guardian (*gopa*), "he whom none deceives." The great importance of his "three steps" are always emphasized. As friend of Indra he assists in killing Vṛtra.
14. *Ṛgveda* VII, 99; Cf. *Atharvaveda* XIX, 6.
15. *Ṛgveda* I, 154, 5f.; I, 22, 20f.
16. Ibid., I, 155, 4B.
17. *Śatapatha Brāhmaṇa* I, 1, 2, 13; I, 9, 3, 9; III, 6, 3, 3.
18. *Bṛhaddevatā* II, 66.
19. Ibid., 69.
20. *Kaṭha Upaniṣad* III, 9
21. *Ṛgveda* X, 184, 1; VII, 36. 9; *Atharvaveda* III, 23; V, 25; *Bṛhadāraṇyaka Upaniṣad* I, 4; *Chāndogya Upaniṣad* VI, 2; *Taittirīya Upaniṣad* II, 6.
22. *Ṛgveda* X, 121.
23. A comprehensive discussion of "Viṣṇu in the Veda" is offered by R. N. Dandekar in *Vedic Mythological Tracts*, pp. 68–90.
24. *Śatapatha Brāhmaṇa* I, 2, 5, 1–10; *Taittirīya Brāhmaṇa* III, 2, 9, 7.
25. *Śatapatha Brāhmaṇa* 1.c., v. 11.
26. Ibid., III, 1, 3, 1.
27. Ibid., V, 11.
28. Ibid., I, 2, 1ff.
29. Ibid., I, 4, 1ff.
30. *Kaṭha Upaniṣad* III, 9.
31. *Maitri Upaniṣad* IV: VI, 23, 35, 38; VII, 7.
32. *Bṛhadāraṇyaka Upaniṣad* I, 4, 7; *Taittirīya Upaniṣad* II, 6 and parallels.
33. *Bṛhadāraṇyaka Upaniṣad* I, 4, 5.
34. A. D. Pusalkar, "The Rāmāyaṇa, Its History and Character," in *CHI*, vol. II, p. 21. C. Bulcke, *Rāmakathā*. N. Chandrasekhara Ayer, *Indian Inheritance*, vol. I, p. 37 holds that Vālmīki's intention was from the beginning to portray Rāma as a divine being.

35. Swami Nishreyasananda, "The Culture of the Rāmāyaṇa," in *CHI*, vol. II, p. 49.
36. The following are considered *Vaiṣṇava Purāṇas* (dates given according to R. C. Hazra, *CHI*, chaps. 16 and 17).
    1. *Viṣṇu Purāna*: belongs to the Pāñcarātra school and is "purely Vaiṣṇava from beginning to end" (*c.*275–325 C.E.).
    2. *Matsya Purāṇa*: originally Pāñcarātra (*c.*275–325 C.E.).
    3. *Bhāgavata Purāna*: "the most popular among the extant Purāṇas ... expounding exclusively Bhāgavata Vaiṣṇavism" (*c.*530–550 C.E.).
    4. *Kūrma Purāṇa*: "originally a Pāñcarātra work with a considerable Śākta element" (*c.*500–650 C.E.).
    5. *Padma Purāṇa*: "belongs principally to the Vaiṣṇavas" (the nucleus of it composed *c.*600–750, but many later additions).
    6. *Vāmana Purāṇa*: "originally Vaiṣṇava – probably Pāñcarātra" (*c.*900 C.E.).
    7. *Varāha Purāṇa*: "mainly a Vaiṣṇava work ... written mainly by the Pāñcarātras and Bhāgavatas in different ages" (*c.*800–1100 C.E.).
    8. *Agni* and *Garuḍa Purāṇa*: "spurious Vaiṣṇava works" (*c.*900–1000 C.E.).
    10. *Brahma Purāṇa*: partly Vaiṣṇava (*c.*900–1200 C.E.).
    11. *Brahmavaivārta Purāṇa*: (*c.*800 C.E. with additions till 1600 C.E.).

    Among the more important *Vaiṣṇava Upapurāṇas* the following may be mentioned:
    1. *Viṣṇudharma*: "a voluminous work dealing mainly with Vaiṣṇava philosophy and rituals" (*c.*third century C.E.) "definite intention to spread the Vaiṣṇava faith against the heresies, especially Buddhism."
    2. *Viṣṇudharmottara*: "the most important and interesting in the whole range of *Upapurāṇa* literature" (*c.*400–500 C.E.).
    3. *Nṛsiṃha Purāṇa*: "a work of the Pāñcarātras with Bhāgavata inclination," "one of the oldest of the extant Upa-purāṇas."
    4. *Bṛhannāradīya Purāṇa*: "preeminently a work on devotion to Viṣṇu" (750–900 C.E.).
    5. *Kriya-yoga-sāra*: (*c.*900 C.E.).
37. *Sabhāparvan*. Arghābhiharaṇaparvan addition after Chapter 35, 29 (Critical Ed.). Cf. Critical Ed., vol. 2, Appendix I, pp. 386ff. The Vāmana episode: vv. 331ff.
38. *Rāmāyaṇa* I, 28.
39. *Viṣṇu Purāṇa* III, 1, 42
40. *Bhāgavata Purāṇa* VIII, 17: some details of Viṣṇu's incarnation.
41. *Bhāgavata Purāṇa* VIII, 20, 34/4.
42. Cf. *Agni Purāṇa* 3ff.
43. For example, Hiraṇyakaśipu is reborn as Rāvaṇa; Kṛṣṇa liberates Pūtanā by killing her (*Bhāgavata Purāṇa* X, 6, 35).
44. Anuśānaparvan, chap. 126 (Critical Ed. XIII, Appendix I, 14).
45. Sabhāparvan, chap. 35; *Viṣṇu-dharmottara* I, 15; Gajendra-mokṣadāna: *Vāmana Purāṇa* 85.
46. *Śatapatha Brāhmaṇa* XII, 3, 4. Also the *Mahābhārata* knows a *ṛṣi* Nārāyaṇa, who in the company of Nara does *tapasya* in the Himālayas.

47. L. B. Keny, "The Origin of Narayana," *ABORI*, XXIII (1942), pp. 250–256.
48. *Mahābhārata*, Vanaparvan, 187, 3 (Critical Ed.).
49. R. G. Bhandarkar, *Vaiṣṇavism*, p. 30, referring to *Mahābhārata* Śāntiparvan, 341 (Critical Ed., 328).
50. Ibid. Cf. *Manusmṛti* I, 10. According to *Mahābhārata*, Karṇaparvan, chap. 34, Nārāyaṇa is issuing out of the shaft of Śiva's weapon.
51. *Mahābhārata*, Śāntiparvan, chap. 321ff (Critical Ed.).
52. Cf. Bhandarkar, *Vaiṣṇavism*, p. 32. See also: B. N. Seal, *Comparative Studies in Vaishnavism and Christianity with an Examination of the Mahabharata Legend about Narada's Pilgrimage to Svetadvipa and an Introduction on the Historico-Comparative Method*. Private Publication. Calcutta, 1899.
53. Śāntiparvan, chap. 326.
54. From the root *tṛ-+ava-*: to come down, to descend (for the purpose of salvation).
55. *Bhagavadgītā* IV, 7f.; *Bhāgavata Purāṇa* III, 242ff.
56. *Mahābhārata*, Śāntiparvan, chap. 335. H. Glasenapp, *Heilige Stätten* shows (plate 9) a figure of "Dämon Hayagriva – Schutzgott der Pferde".
57. Hopkins, *The Great Epic*, p. 97.
58. *Bhāgavata Purāṇa* III, 24ff.
59. Ibid., V, 3ff.
60. *Bhāgavata Purāṇa* V, 4.
61. Ibid., VI, 8.
62. Kṛṣṇa is the central figure in the most authoritative scriptures of the Vaiṣṇavas: The *Mahābhārata*, *Bhagavadgītā*, *Viṣṇu Purāṇa*, *Bhāgavata Purāṇa*, etc. Also *Liṅga Purāṇa* I, 69; *Devī Bhāgavata* IV, 25. Kṛṣṇa is mentioned several times in the *Ṛgveda*, but it is highly doubtful whether he is in any way associated with the Kṛṣṇa-Vāsudeva of the *Bhāgavata*. *RV* VIII, 74: a Kṛṣṇa invites the gods with songs to drink Soma. *RV* VIII, 85: a Kṛṣṇa-*asura* is mentioned whom Indra defeated. Sāyaṇa apparently identifies him with the Purāṇic Kṛṣṇa. *RV* I, 116: again a Kṛṣṇa-singer is mentioned.
63. The usual definition of an *avatāra* is *kapaṭamānuṣa*, a "sham man," while Kṛṣṇa is *svayam bhagavān*, the apparition of the Lord himself in His proper form.
64. Cf. A. D. Pusalker, *Epics and Purāṇas*, chap. V, "Historicity of Kṛṣṇa," with copious notes and references to literature.
65. Cf. D. C. Sircar, *Early History*, pp. 115ff (*HCIP*, vol. I, 302: Deification of Kṛṣṇa before second century B.C.E.).
66. G. Bhandarkar, *Vaiṣṇavism*, pp. 35ff. M. M. Chandham, "The Indian Cowherd-god," in *Journal of the Bihar and Orissa Research Society*, 28 (December 1942).
67. The chief sources for this are the *Harivaṃśa* and the *Bhāgavata Purāṇa*, the former being not earlier than third century C.E. – the latter sixth to tenth century C.E. M. S. Randhawa, *Kangra Paintings of the Bhāgavata Purāṇa*, (Delhi, 1960), Introduction, p. 22: According to M. R. Iyengar "the Bhāgavata was the ripe fruit of the Āḷvār-Vaiṣṇava renaissance and bears the indelible impress of the living mystical experience of the Āḷvārs . . ." According to South Indian tradition the *Bhāgavata Purāṇa* was

composed in the city of Kāñcī, an ancient seat of Sanskrit learning in the country of the Pāndyas in Tamil Nādu. Thus the *Bhāgavata Purāṇa* is a synthesis of Āryan and Dravidian traditions and ideas and provided a link which forged the unity of Hindu India.

68. Cf. J. Gonda, *Die Religionen Indiens*, vol. II, pp. 150ff.
69. Kṛṣṇa is worshiped as *Madan Mohan*, the charmer of the God of Love, outdoing him. S. K. Chaterji, *HCIP*, vol. I, p. 165: "Kṛṣṇa (in Prākṛt Kaṇha, in Tamil Kannan) is a demon opposed to Indra in the *Ṛgveda*; according to P. T. Śrīnivasa Aiyangar, he represents, partially at least, a Dravidian God of Youth, who has later been identified with Viṣṇu as an incarnation of his."
70. A. D. Pusalker, *Studies in Epics and Purāṇas*, p. 56: "Kṛṣṇa ... was originally a real man as evidenced by the pre-epic literature and the earliest parts of the Mahābhārata itself." Rādhākamal Mukherji, *The Culture and Art of India*, p. 67: Kṛṣṇa the statesman and builder of united India: "Vāsudeva Kṛṣṇa is not a legendary but a historical figure who flourished about 1000 B.C. and was one of India's greatest warriors and sages . . . Vyāsa, alias Kṛṣṇa-Dvaipāyana, as the author of the core of the *Mahābhārata* and *Bhagavadgītā* justly deserves honour." The great Bengali writer Bankim Chandra Chatterjee's *Kṛṣṇacaritra* is a "biography" of Kṛṣṇa as founder of India's principal religion.
71. For example, the apparition of Kṛṣṇa in the *Virāṭ* form (*Bhagavadgītā* XII) which is a cosmic, a-historical element; repeatedly mentioned in *Bhāgavata Purāṇa*.
72. Cf. J. Gonda, *Die Religionen Indiens*, vol. II, pp. 150ff. In some Purāṇas Rādhā appears as a goddess. In poetry she is mentioned from the eighth century onwards. Rādhā is identified with Lakṣmī by Jayadeva in *Gītāgovinda* (twelfth century C.E.). Vidyāpati composed poems in Maithilī about the love of Kṛṣṇa and Rādhā (fifteenth century), Chandī Dās wrote *Śrī Kṛṣṇa Kīrtana* (*c.*1420 C.E.). The Gauḍīya Vaiṣṇavas consider the *Gītāgovinda* as literary sequel to the *Bhāgavata Purāṇa*. Mīrābāī wrote a commentary on *Gītā Govinda*. Vallabha, Sūr Dās, Bihāri Lāl are poets of Kṛṣṇa's love for Rādhā. The last great poet of Kṛṣṇa-Rādhā love was Guru Gobind Singh (1675–1758). He wrote *Kṛṣṇa Āvatāra* (in Brajbhāṣa).
73. Cf. V. Ranghacharya, "Historical Evolution of Śrī-Vaiṣṇavas in South India," in *CHI*, vol. IV, pp. 163ff. See also Sanjukta Gupta "The Pāñcharātra Attitude to Mantra," in H. P. Alper (ed.), *Mantra*, Albany: SUNY Press, 1987, pp. 224–248.
74. *Bhāgavata Purāṇa* III, 24–33.
75. *Viṣṇu Purāṇa* I, 2.
76. Lokācārya, *Tattvatraya*, p. 138.
77. Rāmānuja, *Śrībhāṣya*, I, 1 explains that he is going to give the views of these former teachers who had abridged the lengthy *vṛtti* of Bodhāyana.
78. About the Āḷvārs: cf. V. Ranghacharya, "Historical Evolution of Śrīvaiṣṇavism in South India," in *CHI*, vol. IV, pp. 166ff. A. Hooper, *Hymns from the Āḷvārs*. S. N. Dasgupta, *HIPh*, vol. III, pp. 63ff. K. V. Varadachari, *Āḷvārs of South India*.

79. *Śrīcatuśśloki, Stotraratna, Siddhitraya, Āgama prāmānya.*
80. V. Ranghacharya, *CHI*, vol. IV, pp. 174ff.; S. N. Dasgupta, *HIPh*, vol. II, pp. 100ff. J. Sinha, *Indian Philosophy*, vol. II, pp. 653ff. See J. B. Carman, *The Theology of Rāmānuja*. New Haven & London: Yale University Press, 1974. J. Lipner, *The Face of God*, SUNY Press, 1986.
81. According to a legend Yāmunācārya kept in his death three fingers bent. Rāmānuja inferred that he had died with three unfulfilled wishes which he was going to redeem: to give to the Vaiṣṇavas a *Brahmasūtrabhāṣya*, to perpetuate the memory of Parāśara (the author of the *Viṣṇu Purāṇa*), and to spread the glory of Nammāḷvār.
82. *Gītābhāṣya* VII, 18.
83. These form the central theme of J. B. Carman's masterly study *The Theology of Rāmānuja. An Essay in Interreligious Understanding*. New Haven and London: Yale University Press, 1974.
84. *Gītābhāṣya* VII, 18.
85. *Śrībhāṣya* II, 3, 41.
86. Ibid.
87. *Taittirīya Upaniṣad* II, 7.
88. *Vaikuṇṭhagadya* 4.
89. *Vedārthasaṁgraha*, No. 217 (referring to *Viṣṇu Purāṇa* VII, 70).
90. *Śrībhāṣya* I, 1, 4.
91. Rāmānuja, *Vedāntasāra* I, 1, 1.
92. *Tattvatraya.*
93. *Śrībhāṣya* IV, 4, 5.
94. The development and the substance of the controversy is analyzed in P. Y. Mumme, *The Śrīvaiṣṇava Theological Dispute*. Madras: New Era Publications, 1988.
95. In matrimonials the Vadagalai or Tengalai affiliation of a bride or bridegroom is always mentioned.
96. B. N. K. Sharma, *A History of the Dvaita School of Vedānta and its Literature*, 2 vols. *Philosophy of Śrī Madhvācārya*, Bombay 1962; S. Siauve, *La doctrine de Madhva*, Pondicherry, 1968.
97. Hari is one of the most frequently used names of Viṣṇu; Hara is a name of Śiva.
98. B. N. K. Sharma, *Philosophy of Śrī Madhvācārya*, pp. 218ff.
99. *Aṇuvyākhyāna* 1 (translation: B. N. K. Sarma), p. 89.
100. *Mahābhārata Tātparya Nirṇāya* I, 86.
101. B. N. K. Sharma, *Philosophy of Śrī Madhvācārya*, p. 140. For Madhva the instruction and guidance by a competent *guru* and his *prasāda* are absolutely necessary for *śravaṇa* and *manana* to bear fruit. The grace of the *guru* is more powerful for release than one's own effort. He proves his view by commenting on *Brahma Sūtras* III, 3, 44–46.
102. *Brahmasūtrabhāṣya* IV, 4, 6: "The released have their own separate body consisting of simple intelligence and by that they enjoy their blessings."
103. *Aṇuvyākhyāna* III, 3.
104. *Brahmasūtrabhāṣya* IV, 4, 19; *Aṇuvyākhyāna* III, 3.
105. Ibid., IV, 4, 5.

106. 2 vols., B. N. K. Sharma, *History of Dvaita Vedānta*, Bombay: Booksellers Publishing Co., 1960–61
107. Cf. Roma Bose, *Vedānta Parijāta Saurabha*, 3 vols.; R. G. Bhandarkar, *Vaiṣṇavism*, pp. 62ff.; Roma Chaudhuri, "The Nimbārka School of Vedānta," in *CHI*, vol. III, pp. 333ff.; Umesha Mishra, *Nimbārka School of Vedānta.*
108. Roma Bose (trans) *Vedānta-parijāta-saurabha*, vol. III, p. 116
109. Ibid.
110. *Prabhā* on *Brahmasūtra* IV, 3, 5. Vallabha (an exponent of Śuddhāvaita), knows two kinds of *mokṣa*: (a) for *jñānis*: self-dissolution in Brahman; (b) for *bhaktas*: tasting of Viṣṇu's *līlā*!
111. *Kausthubha* IV, 4, 1.
112. "Life of Vallabha," in S. N. Dasgupta, *HIPh*, IV, 371–372. See also: R. Barz, *The Bhakti Sect of Vallabhācārya*, Faridabad: Thompson Press, 1976 and M. C. Parekh, *Śrī Vallabhāchārya: Life, Teachings and Movement*, Rajkot: Śrī Bhagavata Dharma Mission, 1943.
113. M. I. Marfatia, *The Philosophy of Vallabhācārya*, Delhi: Munshiram Manoharlal, 1967, 70–76: "Puṣṭi or the Doctrine of Grace."
114. An extensive summary is given in the article on Vallabha in *Encyclopedia of Religion and Ethics*, vol. XII, pp. 580–583 by D. Mackichan. The most recent discussion is in D. L. Haberman, "On Trial: The Love of Sixteen Thousand Gopees," *History of Religions*, 33/1 (1993), pp. 44–70.
115. *History of the Sect of the Maharajas or Vallabhacharyas, in Western India*, London, 1865.
116. A good survey of recent English and Hindī literature on Vallabha is provided by J. R. Timm in his article "Vallabha, Vaiṣṇavism and the Western Hegemony of Indian Thought," *Journal of Dharma* XIV/1 (1989) pp. 6–36.
117. Bhatt, "The School of Vallabha," p. 356.
118. Dasgupta, *Obscure Religious Cults*, p. 355.
119. Bhatt, *op.cit.* p. 357: "One may be constantly angry with the Lord and still get *sāyujya*".
120. Bhatt, pp. 354–355.
121. Bhatt, p. 349.
122. *Bhakti* develops in the following seven stages: (1) *bhāva*, (2) *preman*, (3) *prānaya*, (4) *sneha*, (5) *rāga*, (6) *anurāga*, and (7) *vyasana*. Compare these with the stages as developed by Rūpa Gosvāmi, discussed in the next section.
123. Dasgupta, *Obscure Religious Cults*, p. 356.
124. Ibid., p. 332.
125. O. B. L. Kapoor, "The Saṃpradaya of Śrī Caitanya," *Indian Philosophy and Culture*, XVIII/3 (Sept. 1973) points out significant differences between the teachings of Madhva and Caitanya and suggests that Gauḍīya Vaiṣṇavism is a different *sampradāya*.
126. Cf. Rādhā Govinda Nath, "A Survey of the Caitanya Movement," in *CHI*, vol. IV, pp. 186ff.; W. Kennedy, *The Caitanya Movement*; S. K. De, *Early History of the Vaiṣṇava Faith*. A. K. Majundar, *Caitanya: His Life and Doctrine.*

127. Cf. W. Kennedy, *The Caitanya Movement*, pp. 29ff. See also Rādhā Govinda Nath, "The Acintya-Bhedābheda School," in *CHI* III, pp. 366–386 and S. N. Dasgupta, *HIPh*, IV, chap. 32: Caitanya and his followers; and chap. 33: The Philosophy of Jīva Gosvāmi and Baladeva Vidyābhūṣana.
128. *Caitanya Caritāmṛta* III, 20; cf. W. Eidlitz, *Kṛṣṇa-Caitanya, Sein Leben und Seine Lehre*, pp. 490–499.
129. Cf. S. K. De, *Vaiṣṇava Faith and Movement.*
130. Cf. W. Kennedy, *The Caitanya Movement*, p. 92.
131. Ibid., I, 4; II, 8.
132. *Caitanya Caritāmṛta* II, 6.
133. S. K. De, *Vaiṣṇava Faith and Movement*, pp. 388ff.
134. *Caitanya Caritāmṛta* II, 9; III, 20.
135. Cf. S. K. De, *Vaiṣṇava Faith and Movement*, pp. 408ff. See also R. V. Joshi, *La rituel de la devotion kṛṣṇaite.*
136. "Service of God" means for the Vaiṣṇava largely service of a *mūrti* which, therefore, is an indispensable part of his religion. Almost all Vaiṣṇava scriptures contain long sections on rituals, especially the *Āgamas* and *Saṃhitās* of the *Pāñcarātrins.*
137. *Yatīndramatadīpikā* IX, 27ff. Lokācarya Pillai, *Mumukṣupadi*, 139ff.: "The extreme limit of the easy accessibility that is mentioned here is the worshiped image ... This form of the Lord is our refuge. He holds the divine weapons in his hands. He keeps one of his hands in a posture asking us not to fear. He wears a crown. His face is smiling. His feet are firmly pressed on a lotus. His sacred body reveals that He is the protector and an object of enjoyment."
138. It seems that this is one of the most ancient "formless" images under which Viṣṇu receives worship.
139. Ibid., pp. 128ff.
140. D. C. Sircar, *Early History*, pp. 117ff.; cf. Megasthenes' "testimony."
141. Cf. D. C. Sircar, *Early History*, p. 127; Banerjea, *Development*, pp. 408ff.
142. Banerjea, *Development*, pp. 137, 152, 358ff. Ahichchhatra coins with (Viṣṇu symbol) Sudarśaṇacakra and name Acyuta (Viṣṇu), *CHIP*, vol. II, p. 173.
143. *Bṛhatsaṃhitā*, chap. 57, 31ff.
144. It mentions the statues as eight-, four-, or two-armed; the *Śrīvatsa* and the *Kaustubha*, the various objects associated with Viṣṇu (discus, conch, mace, arrow, etc.).
145. That is the system adopted by J. N. Banerjea, *Development*, pp. 396ff.
146. Ibid., p. 398. T. A. G. Rao, *Iconography*, vol. I, pt. 1.
147. L. B. Keny, "The Iconography of Viṣṇu Nārāyaṇa," pp. 171ff. See also H. Zimmer, *Myths and Symbols*, pp. 90–101.
148. *Viṣṇudharmottara Purāṇa* III, 85.
149. Without due initiation into Vaiṣṇavism and application of all prescribed paraphernalia all worship is considered useless.
150. See K. Schomer and W. H. McLeod (eds.), *The Sants: Studies in a Devotional Tradition of India*. Delhi: Motilal Banarsidass, 1987, esp.

A. Vaudeville, "Sant Mat: Santism as the Universal Path to Sanctity," pp. 21–40, with an extensive bibliography.

151. For more information see B. N. K. Sharma, "The Vaiṣṇava Saints of Karṇātaka," in CHI, vol. IV, 349–355.
152. More detail in S. C. K. Handoo, "Tulasīdāsa and His Teachings" *CHI*, vol. IV, pp. 395–407 and in previously mentioned literature on the Sants.
153. English translation by J. S. Hawley and M. Juergensmeyer.
154. Sūrdās, "Ja din mēn-panchi urī jaihai ..." My own translation. A translation of the complete poem will be found in *Hinduism: A Short Reader.*
155. Cf. Kshitimohan Sen, "The Mediaeval Mystics of North India," in *CHI*, vol. IV, pp. 381ff.
156. More about him in the author's *Hinduism: A Short Introduction* and "The Response of Modern Vaiṣṇavism," in H. Coward (ed.), *Modern Indian Responses to Religious Pluralism*, Albany: SUNY Press, 1987, pp. 129–150.
157. It cannot be the purpose of that Short History to provide an exhaustive bibliography – it will suffice to mention a few titles that exemplify that new development: F. Hardy, *Viraha-Bhakti: The early history of Kṛṣṇa devotion in South India*, Delhi: Oxford University Press, 1983; V. Deheja, *Āṇṭāl and Her Path of Love. Poems of Woman Saint from South India*, Albany: SUNY Press: Albany, 1990; N. Cutler, *Songs of Experience. The Poetics of Tamil Devotion*, Bloomington; Indiana University Press, 1987; Jayant Lele (ed.), *Tradition and Modernity in Bhakti Movements*, Leiden: Brill, 1981; D. N. Lorenzen, *Bhakti Religion in North India. Community Identity and Political Action*, Albany: SUNY Press, 1995.

6 A SHORT HISTORY OF ŚAIVISM

Many different traditions, elements, cults, and philosophies have, in the course of some five or six thousand years, coalesced into what we call today Śaivism, part of mainstream Hinduism, the second largest religious community in today's India.

There is evidence for worship of Śiva in the Indus civilization. Sir John Marshall termed one of the figures found on a soapstone seal "Proto-Śiva." He thought he recognized in it the Śiva Trimukha, Paśupati, and Mahāyogi. Another seal is reminiscent of the Hunter, a well-known mythological theme of later Śaivism. A further element of Śiva cult can be seen in the numerous *liṅgas* that have been found all over.

Another important source of Śaivism is the ancient Dravida culture. The most plausible etymology of the name Śiva traces the name to Tamil roots.[1] Several features of Śaivism too can be explained more satisfactorily by comparison with Dravida culture. The basic Śiva mythology and philosophy seems to have grown in the Dravida country. While *liṅga* worship may have come to Tamil Śaivism from outside,[2] the idea of the cooperation of Śiva and Śakti in the image of Śiva-Umā belongs to ancient Tamilian mythology.

Another noteworthy source of Śaivism lies in tribal religions. The very name of the ancient Śibi[3] seems to associate them with Śaivism. Their original home had been in the Punjab and names of places like Śivapura and descriptions in ancient historic records of the Śibis going about clad in skins of wild animals and using a club as their weapon seem to indicate that their tradition did have an influence in the development of Śaivism.

A further trace of tribal elements in Śaivism may be the numerous Rudras, mentioned even later in classical Vedic and Śaiva literature. It is quite possible that these Rudras were particular gods of various tribes which had certain qualities in common: fierceness, howling, dread, and destruction. It is not difficult to think of these Rudras merging into the one Rudra-Śiva that became the chief god of the Śaivites. Tribals of our day are often worshipers of Śiva, whom they invoke under many names, but it seems that their Śaivism is derived from their Hindu neighbours, and not vice versa.[4]

As a fourth source we can mention the Veda. It knows a Rudra as one of the gods to whom hymns are addressed, also a plurality of Rudras. The name Śiva is not used in the Veda as a proper name, but more as a general attribute ascribed to several gods. The fact that Rudra (or Rudras) play a far greater role in the *Atharvaveda* than in the *Ṛgveda* seems to prove that Rudra worship, or the beginning of Śaivism, was more a cult of the lower strata of population and not so much part of Brahmanic ritual. The worship of the *liṅga* must have been frowned upon for a long time by orthodox Brahmanism. We read several disparaging remarks with regard to *śiśna* worshipers, described as hostile to the Āryans.[5] According to B. K. Ghosh, the Vedic Rudra is "an apotropäic god of aversion – to be feared but not adored."[6] Offerings to Rudra and the Rudriyas are not sacrificed in the fire as to the other gods, but laid down at crossroads or deposited in forbidding places.[7] Another tradition seems to combine with this Vedic Rudra when he is worshiped as *Rudra Bhūpati*, "a dread figure who (according to the *Aitareya Brāhmaṇa*) usurped the dominion of *Prajāpati* over all cattle when the latter committed incest with his daughter. He appears at the sacrifice in black raiment and claims the sacrificial victim."[8] Some scholars think that this form of Śiva also goes back to aboriginal religion: non-Āryan tribes worshiping a god of vegetation, closely connected with pastoral life.

It is difficult to say when a sect of Śaivites, worshipers of Śiva (-Rudra) as the highest god, came into existence. References in the *Atharvaveda* may indicate that at such an early date there had been Śaivites.[9] The eight names given to Śiva in the *Śatapatha Brāhmaṇa* seem to prove that he received worship both as the benevolent and as the terrible one at that time.[10]

The earliest reference to the (probable) existence of a sect of Śiva worshipers is found in Pāṇini, mentioning Śiva-bhāgats;[11] Patañjali refers to Śiva images.[12] When Megasthenes writes about Dionysos and Herakles as being very popular in India he probably refers to the cult of Śiva and Kṛṣṇa.[13] According to Haribhadra, Gautama, author of the *Nyāya-sūtras*, and Kaṇāda, author of the *Vaiśeṣika-sūtras*, were Śaivas.[14] According to numismatic evidence some of the early Kuśāna kings have been Śaivas.[15]

The oldest Śiva sect known seem to be the Pāśupatas, with various sub-sects. They believed that Śiva himself descended in the form of Nakulīśa or Lakulīśa in order to teach the tenets of the Pāśupata religion. Modern research tends to accept Lakulīśa as a historical figure. Sir R.G. Bhandarkar thought that the Pāśupata sect began in the second century B.C.E.; the Mathurā inscription of the reign of Candragupta II proves that Lakulin flourished in the first quarter of the second century C.E.

The Epics contain numerous references to Śiva; the older versions of the Śiva myths are usually found in the *Rāmāyaṇa*. In one hymn a number of names and titles of Śiva are enumerated, and it is said that "from that time on Śaṅkara was called Mahādeva."[16]

The *Śiva-Purāṇas* are comparatively late compositions, though they contain ancient myths and tales.[17] They seem to have been written in imitation of the earlier *Vaiṣṇava-Purāṇas*.

Under the Guptas, as pointed out before, Hinduism experienced a renaissance. Though most of the Guptas were devotees of Viṣṇu-Kṛṣṇa-Vāsudeva, some were Śaivas, and others also allowed Śaivism a share in worship beside Vaiṣṇavism. Kumāra Gupta I (415–55 C.E.) had been a Śaiva. So were the famous poets Kālidāsa[18] and Bhāravi. Even the Hūṇa king Mihirakula seems to have been a Śaiva. Also many contemporary kings in Bengal and Deccan were Śaivas. In South India, Śaivism became the dominating religion very early. Mahendra Varman I (600–630 C.E.) had been a Jaina first, persecuting followers of other religions. After his conversion to Śaivism, his capital Kāñcīpura became a stronghold of Śaivism, embellished with temples and statues of Śiva. His successors continued his work. Many of the sixty-three *Nayanmārs* ("lords") flourished at this time and helped to propagate Śiva-*bhakti* among the masses.[19] Between 700 and 1000 C.E. Śaivism seems to have been the dominant religion of India and many ruling families were Śaivites.[20]

The great Śaṅkarācārya was a Śaiva by family background, believed by his followers to be "an incarnation of Śiva, born for the purpose of consolidating Hindu *dharma*, in answer to the implorings of Śaiva-guru and Āryāndā at Kāladī."[21] However, in his time Śaivism was already split into several rival sects. Śaṅkara himself is said to have battled against left-hand Śaiva practices and to have vanquished at Ujjain an *ācārya* of the Pāśupatas, described as a "worshiper of Mahākāla." According to tradition he also visited Kashmir, and it is not improbable that Kashmir-Śaivism was influenced by him. We find, during this time, royal patrons of Śaivism in most parts of India: in Kashmir, Assam, Bengal, Kanauj (Benares), Ujjain, Tripura, Mysore, Tamilnadu (Tanjore, Kāñcī).[22] From the twelfth century C.E. onward tension between Śaivas and Vaiṣṇavas mounted in the South. In the following centuries the North experienced a renaissance of Vaiṣṇavism. The early rulers of Vijayanagara were Śaivas; they considered themselves the vice-gerents (deputies) of Virūpākṣa (Śiva). Later they became Vaiṣṇavas but tolerated Śaivism.

In the twelfth century a powerful new Śaiva movement arose in Karṇāṭaka – the Liṅgāyats. The last great achievement of Śaiva scholarship seems to have been the *Śrīkarabhāṣya* written by Śrīpati (*c.*1400 C.E.), which explains the *Brahmasūtras* in light of the tenets of Vīraśaivism. It cannot be determined definitely when the various other Śaiva sects originated. Rather early on, Śiva seems to have been connected with *saṃnyāsa*, Yoga, and asceticism.

According to a widespread tradition, Śiva became incarnate as Śveta in order to originate the *Śaiva-Āgamas*. Śrīkaṇṭha enumerates twenty-eight teachers of Śaivism–founders of Śaiva sects. The *Bhāmatī* on the *Śaṅkara-bhāṣya* mentions four sects of non-Vedāntic Śaivites: Pāśupatas, Śaivas, Karuṇaka-siddhāntins, and Kāpālikas. Rāmānuja mentions Kālamukhas and Kāpālikas, whereas Mādhava describes at length Nakulīsas (Pāśupatas), Śaivas, Pratyabhijñās, and Raseśvaras. In South India, Śaiva-siddhānta became the dominating Śaiva philosophy. In Kashmir an advaitic type of Śaivism developed from the tenth century onward, whose main exponent was Abhinavagupta.

THE DEVELOPMENT OF ŚIVA MYTHOLOGY

Śiva in the Vedas

The Veda is only one of the sources of Śaivism, perhaps not even the most important. But it is the only source that provides us with literary documents ancient enough to trace at least some components of Śaivism. The main element of Vedic religion that went into the making of Śaivism is the figure of Rudra, who was identified in later times with Śiva. Here already we encounter the predominantly terrifying aspects of Śiva-Rudra: Rudra himself is a terror to those whom he visits. Whereas Viṣṇu is invoked to come and destroy his enemies who molest humans, Rudra is asked to stay away from men. Well-being consists in the absence of the god rather than in his presence. Fever and all kinds of sickness are his work; natural calamities and enmities are his manifestations.

Only three hymns are addressed to Rudra in the *Ṛgveda*.[23] *Śiva* is used as an epithet for several gods in its original meaning "propitious."[24] The name Rudra itself was apotropaic; the very utterance of it was dangerous. Some scholars, who take Śiva to be a solar deity, find references to Śiva in other hymns also, directed, for example, to *sūrya*.[25]

The Rudra hymns themselves are quite revealing: it is plain fear of Rudra that makes the Vedic singer ask Rudra "not to harm either great or small of us, not the growing boy nor the full-grown man, not to slay the sire, nor the mother, not to harm our dear bodies, not to harm us in our seed and progeny, not to slay our heroes."[26] But Rudra is not only the inflicter of evil, he also saves from evil. He can be asked either not to send evil to his devotees or to provide for them a remedy against the evils sent by him. Thus the Vedic singer implores Rudra to give health, strength, grace, bliss, to protect cattle, to heal all sickness, to help the devotee out of his troubles, to repel all assaults of mischief, to give strengthening balm to the heroes. Rudra is the great physician who possesses a thousand medicines, the giver of health and the remover of the woes which the gods have sent, whose gracious hand brings health and comfort.

One of the most interesting texts in the whole of Vedic literature is the famous Śatarudriya in the Yajurveda.[27] A. P. Karmarkar sees in it "a non-Āryan document *par excellence*."[28] J. Eggeling calls it "a dismal litany;" it is of interest, however, insofar as it reflects "popular belief in demoniac agencies to which man is constantly exposed."[29] The hymn is connected with the Śatarudriya offering described in the *Śatapatha Brāhmaṇa*. "Agni has on completion become Rudra and this ceremony is performed to avert his wrath and secure his favour."[30] This Śatarudriya certainly displays many features of classical Śaivism. Śiva is both terrifying and gracious. After homage to Rudra's wrath his auspicious Śiva form is addressed and asked to give health and well-being to all people, as he is the great divine physician. Several verses of the Ṛgvedic Rudra hymns are included. Thus, either the Śatarudriya is a collection of otherwise unconnected Rudra invocations, or the Ṛgvedic Rudra hymns are excerpts from the longer hymn, most of which were not acceptable to the priests who edited the *Ṛgveda*. The most striking feature of the Śatarudriya is its constant change from one Rudra to many Rudras, from praise to imploration not to do harm. The bow, the constant companion of Rudra, is dreaded as harmful and also invoked for protection; homage is paid to it, after it has been unstrung. Also, the act of "grace" of Rudra consists not so much in doing good to his devotees but in refraining from doing harm, not exposing them to his wrath and his arrows. It is beyond doubt that the author of the Śatarudriya believed in a great number of Rudras – "innumerable Rudras are on the face of the earth"[31]–but the epithets given to "Him," i.e. Rudra in the singular, are often names which play a great role in later Śaivism and make Rudra appear the Supreme Being. Apart from names like Nīlakaṇṭha, Sarva, Paśupati, N̄ilagrīva, Śitikaṇṭha, Bhava, and Śobhya, Rudra is the one who stretched out the earth, who is immanent in places and objects, in stones, plants, and animals. There is also the paradoxical ascription of contradictory attributes. After being praised as the great Lord of all beings, he is called "cheat" and "Lord of the thieves"; he is a dwarf and a giant; he is fierce and terrible and the source of happiness and delight. These elements make Rudra appear as the Supreme Being, responsible for the creation, maintenance and destruction of the universe, as the giver and taker of all goods. Certain groups of people are mentioned: thieves, robbers, pilferers, troops and soldiers, deformed people, carpenters, car-makers, potters, blacksmiths, dog-leaders, hunters. Perhaps these were the sections of the population among whom Rudra worship developed first. Several times Rudra is addressed as *kapardin* and as *vyuptakeśa*. He may have had worshipers in two sects: one who used to wear a *kaparda* and one who used to shave the head completely, customs which we notice even today amongst Śaiva ascetics.

As in the Ṛgvedic Rudra hymns, the singer of the Śatarudriya asks Śiva-Rudra to turn away his fearful form and to approach the worshiper with the auspicious, friendly form. Since the Śatarudriya forms part of the *Yajurveda*, it also is part of a Vedic ritual as described in the *Śatapatha Brāhmaṇa.*[32]

Only a few hymns in the *Atharvaveda* are addressed to Rudra. In one of them Rudra and Soma are mentioned as redeemers from disease and sin; in another the two forms of Rudra – Śarva and Bhava – are treated as two distinct persons. They are implored "not to harm our bipeds and quadrupeds." Vultures and flies, as the consumers of dead bodies, are evidently connected with Rudra. But he is also the Lord of Cattle who can prevent death. "Yours are the four directions, yours the heaven, yours the earth, yours this wide atmosphere, you terrible one. Yours is all this that has *ātman*, that is breathing upon the earth." The best thing he can do is to stay away from his worshipers: "Do not harm us, bless us, avoid us, be not angry, let us not come into collision with you."[33] As in the Śatarudriya, here, too, Rudra is asked to spare the worshipers and harm their foes: "Be not greedy for our kine, our men; be not greedy for our goats and sheep; elsewhere, o you formidable, strike out, strike the offspring of our detractors."[34]

Śiva-Rudra in the Brāhmaṇas

The *Śatapatha Brāhmaṇa* offers in connection with the Śatarudriya recitation a very interesting myth explaining the origin of Rudra-Śiva:

> When Prajāpati had become disjointed the deities departed from him. Only one god did not leave him, *manyu* (wrath). Extended he remained within, he cried and the tears of him that fell down settled on *manyu*. He became the hundred-headed, thousand-eyed, hundred-quivered Rudra. And the other drops that fell down spread over this world in countless numbers, by thousands; and inasmuch as they originated from crying (*rud*) they were called Rudras (roarers). That hundred-headed, thousand-eyed, hundred-quivered Rudra with his strong bow strung and his arrow fitted to his string, was inspiring fear, being in quest of food. The gods were afraid of him.[35]

The purpose of the Śatarudriya offering was to appease the wrath of hungry Rudra. Both Rudra in the singular and Rudras in the plural are met with here. It is noteworthy that the sacrificer is to undergo a purificatory ceremony whenever he mentions the name Rudra; the same ceremony as prescribed when uttering *rakṣasas*, *asuras*, *pitṛs*, or enemies, or his own body.[36] Another text states that to Rudra is due whatsoever is injured in sacrifice. Several times Paśupati, Śarva, and Bhava are mentioned as names of Rudra. Only in one place is he Rudra-Śiva;[37] here too the kindliness of Rudra is only the effect of the appeasement made by the sacrificer. His region is the North. In several places he is identified with Agni and even called "Agni's immortal form." One text represents a Śiva magic in order to save cattle from Rudra Paśupati. Rudra is treated in the ritual quite differently from the other gods. At the end of the sacrifice a handful of straw is offered to him to propitiate him; at the end of the meal any food left over is placed in a spot to the North for him to take. The bloody entrails of the victim are made over to his hosts, which attack men and beast with disease and death, in order to avert their anger. Snakes are also connected with him. When the gods reached heaven Rudra was left behind. In a place infested with snakes one should offer to Rudra who is Lord of cattle.[38] The *Aitareya Brāhmaṇa* states that "Rudra is an embodiment of all the dread forms of whom gods are afraid."[39] The bull that is to be sacrificed for Rudra is sacrificed outside the village. The character of Rudra in the *Brāhmaṇas* is still predominantly that of a fierce power, the enemy of civilization rather than its protector.

Śiva in the Upaniṣads

The oldest Upaniṣads do no more than mention Rudra and Rudriyas in the catalogues of gods and their offices. The first and the most important of *Śaiva Upaniṣads*, in which Śiva is identified with Brahman, is the *Śvetāśvatara Upaniṣad*.[40] It refutes at length many other schools and systems – a sign that it cannot be very early, since it presupposes the formation of definite tenets of different groups. The Supreme Being in the *Śvetāśvatara Upaniṣad* is Śiva. The way of salvation which it teaches is Yoga in its practical aspect, and Vedānta in its theoretical aspect. "The immortal and imperishable Hara exercises complete control over the perishable *prakṛti* and the powerless *jīva*: this radiant Hara is one alone."

The way to perfect knowledge is *dhyāna*. The doctrine of *māyā* is intimately connected with Śaivism. Śiva Paramātman is compared to a "fisherman with a net, the arch-juggler that brings to bear the *iśānis* or illusory powers begotten of his *māyā*." His *māyā* is also the means by which he directs the world. To those who realize the truth, that Rudra is the one absolute being, it promises immortality or *videha-kaivalya*. A close parallel to the Viṣṇu-viśva-rūpa is offered by the following passage: "Rudra, the Paramātman, assumes the form of the Virāḍātman, possessed of the eyes of all beings, as his own eyes, the faces of all beings of the universe as his own face ..." Salvation according to the *Śvetāśvatara Upaniṣad* depends on Śiva's grace: in a prayer Śiva is asked to manifest to all seekers his pure form. His forms are only his *māyā* – in reality he is formless.[41] Only the realization of Śiva's formlessness brings bliss and immortality. Śiva manifests himself variously: as *viśva-rūpa*, as *liṅga-śarīra* in the hearts of all beings, as omnipresent on account of his all-pervasiveness, as *antarātman* of the "size of a thumb" (about an inch in height). Śaivites interpret the Puruṣasūkta in a Śaivite sense; Śiva is called the immanent being in all beings. One who perceives through direct intuition the Antarātman-Śiva becomes free from all sorrows. All beings are *īśvara* and the perception of difference between *jīva* and *īśa* is an illusion. "Know then that *prakṛti* is *māyā* and that the great God is the Lord of *māyā*. The whole world is filled with beings who form his parts."

Realization of Śiva brings about peace of soul: "One attains infinite peace on realizing that self-effulgent, adorable Lord, the bestower of blessings who, though one, presides over all the various aspects of *prakṛti* and in whom this universe dissolves, and in whom it appears in manifold forms."

The three elements of later Śaiva systems seem to be quite clearly visible: Śiva, though immanent in all beings, is the Lord of both *puruṣa* and *prakṛti* and not identical with either of them.[42] "He is the controller of Matter and Spirit and the Lord of the *guṇas*. He is the cause of liberation from the cycle of birth and death and of bondage which results in its continuance." The Upaniṣad also quotes from *Ṛgveda* to underline the continuance of the Vedic Rudra-Śiva: the basic belief is still that "normally" Rudra acts as destroyer, deluder, deceiver. He has to be appeased to be favorable, to undo his own work of death and deceit.

Another important text in the same class is the *Atharvaśira Upaniṣad*;[43] it is younger than the *Śvetāśvatara*. It explains the various names and epithets of Śiva. As a means to release, the Upaniṣad recommends the Mahāpaśupata *vrata* "through which alone could be successfully accomplished the *kaivalya* by the *paśus*, bound by the *pāśa* of the deluded belief in the real existence of things apart from *ātman*, through the attainment of the knowledge of the identity of the *paśu* with *pati* and the consequent vanishing of the *pāśa*." The ritual practice of this *vrata* consists of besmearing one's body with ashes.

Other Śaiva Upaniṣads, like *Bṛhajjābāla Upaniṣad*, *Bhāsmajābāla Upaniṣad* etc., deal with sectarian practices: besmearing one's body with ashes, wearing Rudra-*mālā*, applying the *tripuṇḍra* to one's forehead,[44] practicing *japa*, and so forth.

Śiva in the Epics and Purāṇas

Some motifs found in the Vedic literature emerge as fully developed myths in Epics and Purāṇas. Besides these, many new ones appear, whose origin and roots we are unable to trace: some may have been folk-tales, some may have been invented for a particular purpose, some are clearly etiological myths.

The oldest version of epic and puranic Śiva myths is probably found in the *Rāmāyaṇa*, where Śiva is called Śitikaṇṭha, Mahādeva, Rudra, Trayāṃbaka, Paśupati, and Śaṅkara. We find in it the narration of Dakṣa's sacrifice in its simplest form,[45] later it is expanded almost into an epic by itself; the marriage of Śiva with Umā; Śiva drinking the poison; Śiva destroying Andhaka; Śiva conquering Tripura; Śiva cursing Kaṇḍarpa.

The *Mahābhārata* narrates Śiva myths at great length. Though the main figures of both epics are manifestations of Viṣṇu, the epics are rather liberal and allow ample space for Śaivite mythology and doctrine. Thus the *Anuśāña-parvan* narrates how Kṛṣṇa had been initiated by Śiva, remaining for his whole life a Śiva bhakta, the *Śanti-parvan* explains that Hari and Śiva are one and the same, the *Anuśāsana-parvan* enumerates among the thousand names of Viṣṇu also Śiva, Śarva, Sthaṇu, Iśāna, and Rudra. But not in all its forms are Śiva and Viṣṇu mythology integrated in the *Mahābhārata*; there are certainly large sections of pure Śaiva mythology which were incorporated into the epic without trying to harmonize them with existing Viṣṇu myths. It is in the Purāṇas, however, that Śiva mythology reaches its fullest development. In the Purāṇas Śaivism is usually an exclusive religion in which the Supreme Being of other religions is placed lower than Śiva. The oldest among the Śaiva Purāṇas is probably the *Vāyu Purāṇa* (before the second century C.E.); practically identical with it is the (more recent) *Brahmāṇḍa Purāṇa*. The existing revised form of *Matsya Purāṇa* has been ascribed to the age of the Guptas (*c.*325 C.E.). The original *Kūrma Purāṇa* must also be very ancient: the existing revised form, however, is rather late (*c.*710 C.E.). Approximately from the same time are *Skanda Purāṇa* (*c.*700 C.E.) and *Śiva Purāṇa* – called by Śaivites today a *Mahāpurāṇa*, but in most books referred to as one of the Upapurāṇas. The important *Liṅga Purāṇa* (*c.*600 to 1000 C.E.) and the *Vāmana Purāṇa* (revised *c.*900 C.E.) are the last among the Śaiva-Purāṇas. The main myths recur in all the Purāṇas – they differ only in the emphasis given to certain aspects.

Dakṣa's Sacrifice

The myth of Śiva interrupting Dakṣa's sacrifice has always been considered the oldest among the Śiva myths.[46] It is first mentioned in the *Taittirīya Saṃhitā*. The gods had excluded Rudra from a sacrifice: Rudra in anger pierced the sacrifice with an arrow. The *Rāmāyaṇa* briefly refers to it as a well-known episode. It is recounted several times in the *Mahābhārata* and the *Purāṇas* in various versions: in most of them the result is the acknowledgment of Śiva's supremacy by Dakṣa, the anti-Śaivite. In the *Hari-vaṃśa*, however, the myth concludes with an intervention of Viṣṇu, who forces Śiva to submit to him.

The story of Śiva wrecking the sacrifice of Dakṣa and Śiva's pardoning of Dakṣa after he has acknowledged the supremacy of Śiva is recounted at great length in the *Mahābhārata* and in several *Purāṇas*. The *Mahābhārata* narrates the story in two consecutive chapters. The first chapter begins by stating that the story is the explanation of the origin of fever (in connection with the Vṛtra story),[47] and the second chapter begins with the statement that what follows is the story of Dakṣa's sacrifice and how Śiva wrecked it. Both chapters narrate the same story.[48] Since the *Vāyu Purāṇa* version contains the whole story in one continuous chapter and, it seems, in a more logical sequence than the *Mahābhārata*, and since it is the *Vāyu Purāṇa* that had been apparently the model for *Śiva-* and *Brahma Purāṇas*, we take this to be the basic, and probably oldest, version of the Dakṣa myth. The Śiva-sahasranāma, which succeeds both in Vāyu Purāṇa and in the Mahābhārata the narration of the episode, may or may not have been interpolated at a later date. There could have been a common source from which these four texts drew. If this is so, the *Vāyu* seems to have been nearest to it and preserved the most authentic version of the myth, since the *Mahābhārata* was certainly known to the authors of *Śiva-* and *Brahma Purāṇas*.

The story as *Vāyu Purāṇa* tells it runs like this. Dakṣa has prepared an *aśva-medha* and invites all the gods, except Śiva. His daughter Umā, who is Śiva's wife, comes to Dakṣa pleading that he should also invite her husband; she feels wronged and dishonored, being the eldest and foremost of Dakṣa's daughters.[49] Dadhīca also remarks that he fears Dakṣa's sacrifice will have a bad end if Śiva is not invited. Dakṣa retorts that this sacrifice is prepared for Viṣṇu. He does not know of any Rudra other than the eleven Rudras. Viṣṇu is the master of all; to him should sacrifices be offered. Umā is sad and asks her husband why he is not going to his father's sacrifice, while all the other gods are going there. Śiva himself explains that the gods in ancient times decided that Rudra should not have any part in the sacrifice. Umā is silent, reflecting how to obtain for her husband a share – a half or a third – of the sacrifice. Śiva then decides to create a "Terrible Being" that will destroy Dakṣa's sacrifice. There follows a description of this embodiment of Śiva's wrath and of a host of evil and ugly beings that accompany it. They descend upon Dakṣa's sacrifice, scatter everything, drive the gods away, and kill the sacrifice which had assumed the form of a deer. Brahmā, together with the gods and Dakṣa, fold their hands and question the "Terrible Being" about its nature. Vīrabhadra explains his nature and his mission and tells them that they should take refuge with Umā's husband, whose wrath is more propitious even than the boons of other gods. As soon as he hears it, Dakṣa begins praising Śiva. Śiva, pacified, accepts Dakṣa, and grants to him that the sacrifice, though spoilt, be of benefit to him, having spent so much time and pains on it.

The grateful Dakṣa then praises Śiva in a thousand and eight names. At the end he points out that it is always Rudra-Śiva alone who is in all creatures. He did not invite him, because he was creator and all. Or else, he was deluded through the god's subtle *māyā*. But now he takes refuge to Śiva alone. Śiva accepts the praise and devotion and promises Dakṣa his companionship and the fruit of a thousand horse sacrifices and a hundred *vājapeyas*. He then tells him that he had extracted from the Vedas and its six branches the *pāśupatavrata* – the method of liberating the *paśu* ("cattle", designation of an unenlightened human being) from the *pāśa* ("noose", designation of the fetters that bind humans into *saṃsāra*). This Pāsupata religion is open to all, regardless of *varṇa* or *āśrama*. The mere recitation of the text is supposed to bring about freedom from sickness and fear and to let one journey towards Rudraloka whence there is no return.

This myth is one of the oldest and most basic of the Śiva myths. The character of Śiva, the destroyer and the savior, comes out very clearly. Apart from the standard assurances given at the end of the chapter, that its reading or hearing makes one free from sin and free from disease, the story is clearly intended to prove the necessity of Śiva worship in order to be saved from his wrath, and the power of the grace of Śiva, once he is pleased with his devotees. In the older Pāśupata version Satī does not burn herself nor does Dakṣa get killed. In the more recent version both are killed and revived again by Śiva. It is remarkable that even in the oldest version Dakṣa is a Viṣṇu worshiper, recognizing Viṣṇu as the highest God to whom all sacrifices are due. Also remarkable in this oldest version is a trace of Vedānta, according to which Śiva considered himself as immanent in everything, and yet the other element is stronger. The ritualistic, sacrificial aspect according to which the gods individually are keen to get a share of the sacrifice, decides the outcome of the myth. The older versions just refer to "an ancient decree of the gods" according to which no share in the sacrifice is given to Rudra; the ritual texts give full evidence of it. People to whom this version was narrated must still have had the knowledge of it. The more recent version introduces an elaborate story to explain the mutual disaffection of Dakṣa and Śiva. The explanation is again typical of later times: because Śiva fails to pay honor to Dakṣa, Dakṣa curses him and immediately decrees that Śiva should receive no share. It is not only the omission of a gift from the sacrifice, but a harsh and lengthy curse that in this version brings about Śiva's wrath and revenge. The original story certainly intended to persuade people, who for the most part followed the Vedic ritual and religion, to accept Śiva as a Great God and not to neglect him if they wanted to avoid his anger and to receive his blessing. The more recent version emphasizes much more the cruelty of Śiva, and his dreadful companions: it adds many details which have nothing to do with the story of Śiva-savior; it enlarges the role of Umā, and it often ends with an emphasis on Viṣṇu rather than Śiva.

The *Śiva-sahasra-nāma*, though not necessarily part of the Dakṣa story, uses many epithets and attributes of Śiva, which make him appear as the great Savior. All his salvific deeds are mentioned; he is identified with the Sun; he is the artificer of the universe; he is in all things; he is master and lord of all creatures. He gives boons; he destroys and creates again; he smites and heals. But even here, on an occasion when the auspicious character of Śiva has to be proven, his fierce and frightful character still predominates in this litany, which largely repeats the Śatarudriya. He is still worshiped as thousand-eyed, three-eyed, Bhava, Śarva, and Rudra; he is the wielder of the trident; he is red and tawny and has a blue throat; he is white and stainless; he is the embodiment of all kinds of destruction; he is armed with bones and fond of cremation grounds; his bell and his *akṣa-mālā* are mentioned; he is fond of the heart-flesh of all creatures; he is called a tiger and a snake; he is the one who cuts down and pierces and smites; he is time, that is inauspicious. "You are the killing, the instrument to kill and that which is killed."[50] Some of the attributes may refer to the habit of Śiva worshipers and their apparel. Śiva is not a pleasant god; whatever is frightful, dangerous, odd, destructive is identified with him.

The very fact that the *Śiva-sahasra-nāma* refers to all the other deeds of Śiva, while the Dakṣa story, according to the testimony of the text, is the oldest and first of Śiva's exploits, make it appear a later addition.

Śiva Drinks the Poison

For later Śaivism, the myth of Śiva drinking the poison which appeared after the churning of the ocean is perhaps the most important one. In it Śaivas see the clearest image of Śiva the savior – Śiva's blue throat is a permanent reminiscence of the deed by which he saved humankind from perishing through poison.[51]

The oldest version seems to be preserved in the *Rāmāyaṇa*[52] – not only as a passing reference, but as a full-fledged story. Dānavas and Daityas are engaged in churning the ocean to obtain *amṛta*. The snake, which they use as a rope, emits poison, which like a consuming fire, engulfs everything. The frightened gods approach Śaṅkara and ask him to save them. Viṣṇu appears, telling Śiva that the first product of the churning should be Śiva's, whom he calls *sura-śreṣṭha* (the first god) and *surāṇām-agrata* (at the head of all gods). Thus he should accept the "first offering." Śiva then drinks the poison, *halāhala*, and thus saves gods and humans. The next difficulty in the process of churning the ocean is solved by Viṣṇu, and it is again Viṣṇu who distributes *amṛta*, for whose sake *devas* and *daityas* had worked.

The account in the *Mahābhārata* differs in many details.[53] From the very beginning the Tortoise-king (not Viṣṇu) serves as a basis for the mountain Mandara; many products are churned out from the ocean before the poison, here called Kālakūṭa, appears. "Engulfing the earth it suddenly blazed up like a fire attended with fumes. And by the scent of that frightful Kālakūṭa the three worlds were stupefied. And then Śiva, being solicited by Brahman, swallowed that poison for the safety of the creation. The divine Maheśvara held it in his throat, and it is said that from that time he is called Nīlakaṇṭha."

The Vaiṣṇava scriptures also recount the story of the churning of the milk ocean: characteristically the *Viṣṇu Purāṇa*[54] tells us that one of the products that came out from the ocean – neither the first nor the last – was poison. Śiva is not even mentioned; snakes consume it, thus explaining the existence of venomous snakes. The *Bhāgavata Purāṇa* gives the most detailed account of the myth, apparently combining the various traditions that must have been known to the author: Viṣṇu in the form of a tortoise forms the support of Mandara, after the first attempt at churning has failed,[55] and personally takes part in the churning. The first product of the churning is the poison Halāhala, issuing, however, not from the mouth of the snake, but from the sea. It spreads over the whole earth and threatens to consume all beings. The gods flee to Sadāśiva and ask him for protection. Prajāpati addresses Śiva in a long hymn, "O god of gods, supreme deity, the protector and the self of created beings, save us that have sought refuge in you from this poison, which is burning the three worlds. You are the one Lord able to bind and to free the world." A good deal of Śaiva philosophy is woven into this hymn. Śiva, "the friend of all living beings" first consults with Satī, his spouse, before he undertakes anything. In this address to Satī the author of the *Bhāgavata Purāṇa* subtly asserts his Vaiṣṇavism: Śiva remarks that Hari is pleased with a man who sacrifices his life for others – "the universe's soul" – and that he, Śiva, is also happy, when Hari is pleased. It looks as if Śiva was prepared to die for the sake of the mortals. Satī gives her permission and Śiva, "squeezing into his palm the Halāhala, which was spreading all round, swallowed it out of compassion. The poison showed its power even on his person: it made him blue at the throat, but this spot became a special ornament to that benevolent soul." This act pleases Viṣṇu; the act of Śiva constituted the highest worship of Viṣṇu, declares the author of the *Bhāgavatam*. "Scorpions, snakes and poisonous herbs as well as what other biting creatures there were, took in what little poison leaked from the palm of Lord Śiva while he drank it."

Certainly there had been various traditions: in one the poison is the first product of the churning, in others the last. In one, Śiva is coaxed into taking it by Viṣṇu, in others he takes it freely out of compassion. The Śaivite version, however, makes it clear that the importance of this myth lies in establishing Śiva as the Savior of the whole world; the very name Nīlakaṇṭha denotes Śiva as savior. Modern Śaivites even use the expression of Śiva's "vicarious suffering" in this connection.

Śiva Destroys Tripura

Another very popular and important Śiva myth is the legend of Śiva destroying Tripura. It is alluded to as well known in the *Rāmāyaṇa* in several places, but the legend itself is not narrated. The oldest complete version seems to be that in the *Mahābhārata*.[56] The whole scene is reminiscent of a Vedic setting: Śiva plays the role of Indra as the liberator of gods and men from demons. That, in fact, is the scene's main purpose, to show that Śiva saves gods and men from the wicked and powerful *asuras*. The background of the myth is provided by one of the numerous fights between *devas* and *asuras*. Three of the *asuras* practice *tapas* and approach Brahmā for the "boon of immortality from death at the hands of all the creatures of all time." They are told that this is impossible to obtain. Thus they choose to "reside in three cities over this earth. After a thousand years we will come together and our three cities also will be united into one. That foremost one amongst the gods who will with one shaft pierce these three cities united into one will be the cause of our destruction." Māyā, the divine artificer, constructs three cities for the *asuras*: one of gold, one of silver, one of black iron, all of enormous proportions and wonderfully equipped, with everything conceivable obtainable in them. The Dānavas from their aerial fortresses terrorize the whole earth, gods and men alike. The denizens of earth and heaven complain to Brahmā, who tells them that "those three cities are to be pierced with one shaft; by no other means can their destruction be effected. None else save Sthāṇu is competent to pierce them with one shaft. You *adityas*, select Sthāṇu, otherwise called Iśāna and Jiṣṇu, who is never fatigued with work, as your warrior. It is he who will destroy those *asuras*." There follows a very interesting description of a vision of Śiva: "the dispeller of fear in all situations of fear, the universal soul, the supreme soul." In the hymn which the gods address to Śiva they remember his previous mighty deeds – the destruction of Prajāpati Dakṣa's sacrifice, his blue throat, his mighty weapon, his fierceness, his three eyes. They call him Lord of trees, of men, of animals, "Death's self," the destroyer. Brahmā, by asking Śiva to destroy the *asuras*, emphasizes the role of Śiva as saviour of gods and men: "Slay the Dānavas, O wielder of the trident; let the universe, through thy grace, obtain happiness. Lord of all the world, you are the one whose shelter should be sought. We all seek thy shelter." Śiva first offers half of his own energy to the *devas* to defeat the Dānavas – but the *devas* cannot bear it. Thus Śiva takes away half of the energy of the *devas* in order to kill the Dānavas all by himself. "From that time Śaṅkara came to be called Mahādeva."[57] The *devas* have a car constructed, a bow and a shaft fashioned. All the parts of the universe are used for it. Śiva's charioteer is Brahmā: Viṣṇu, Soma, and Agni form his arrow. The roar of Śiva's bull frightens the worlds. "The Sthāṇu armed with trident became deprived of his senses in wrath." The car appears to be sinking into the ground. Nārāyaṇa, in the form of a bull, issues out from the point of the shaft and pulls the car out. Śiva is described as standing on the head of the bull and on the back of the horses.[58] Finally Śarva strings his bow and when Tripura appears before him in the sky he pierces it with a single shot.

"Thus was the triple city burnt and thus were the Dānavas exterminated by Maheśvara in wrath, from desire of doing good to the three worlds. After this the gods, the *ṛṣis* and the three worlds became all restored to their natural disposition."[59]

Śiva Kills Andhaka and Other Demons

Śiva as the destroyer of hostile demons is the topic of the many minor myths that, with many variations, are retold in most of the *Purāṇas* and alluded to as well known in the Epics. One of the titles given to Śiva in invocations is Andhaka-ripu (enemy of Andhaka) and the *Rāmāyaṇa* uses the episode as a term of comparison in another fight between Rāma and Khara.

The *Śiva Purāṇa*, however, narrates the story of the fight between Śiva and Andhaka at great length.[60] Andhaka, an *asura*, son of Hiraṇyākṣa, asks for immortality from Brahmā, after having performed austerities; he obtains the boon of immunity from danger from all classes of beings which he mentions. Andhaka roams about the world and sees Śiva in a cave, clad like an ascetic. He arouses the anger of Śiva's company and a battle ensues. Only Śiva can decide the outcome: he kills Andhaka with his *triśula* (trident).[61]

A similar legend is connected with the name of Śaṅkhacūḍa.[62] Śiva, with Viṣṇu's blessings, had given to Dambhi, at his urging, a son Śaṅkhacūḍa, who became the king of the *asuras*, fought against the *devas*, and was killed by Śiva himself. Parallel stories are connected with the names of Dundubhi, Vidala, Utpala, etc. The *Śiva Purāṇa* abounds in tales recounting the fights of Śiva with numerous demons and Śiva's victory over them. It seems that this "killing of demons" was considered one of the most important functions of a savior-god: the Śaiva Purāṇas never admit that any demon could be killed by anyone other than Śiva, and similarly the Vaiṣṇava Purāṇas do not narrate a single story in which Śiva could slay a demon without Viṣṇu intervening at the decisive moment.

One rather delightful example of such sectarian bias is offered in a story told by the *Bhāgavata Purāṇa*:[63] Vṛka, an evil demon, enquired which of the gods "was quick to propitiate." Nārada tells him: "Go to Śiva. He is soon pleased with a small measure of merit and gets angry equally quickly through a slight offence." He tells him that Śiva granted boons to Rāvaṇa and to Bana, who afterwards caused him serious trouble. Vṛka begins his austerities and promptly wins the appearance of Śiva, who tells him to ask for any boon. Vṛka asks for the gift, that on whomsoever he would place his hand, that person should die. Śiva laughingly grants it. Now Vṛka tries to exercise his boon on Pārvatī, even on Śiva himself. Śiva is helpless: he cannot revoke the boon and is fleeing from the demon and from his own boon conferred on him. Śiva has no other resort left but Vaikuṇṭha. Viṣṇu now saves the situation. He tells the *asura* to try Śiva's boon out on his own head – calling Śiva the "ruler of Pretas and Piśācas" and a liar – and Vṛka promptly dies.

Śaivas in turn also invented or reshaped stories to show the dependence of Viṣṇu on Śiva when a demon had to be killed. Thus Śiva is depicted as giving the Sudarśanacakra to Viṣṇu and it is through Śiva's grace that Kṛṣṇa is able to defeat his enemies.

One of the central themes in Śaiva Purāṇas is Śiva's burning of Kāmadeva, who tries to disturb him in his meditations.[64] In some sources Pārvatī is said to have instigated Kāma to distract Śiva and to marry her. Śiva's first reaction is wrath, and he burns Kāmadeva to ashes. At the wailing of all creatures he restores him to life.

The marriage of Śiva and Pārvatī is usually dealt with at great length in the Śaiva Purāṇas: later philosophy sees in the union of Śiva and Śakti the cause of all activity in the universe, the cause also of all salvation. In fact, Śiva is active as saviour only after his marriage to Pārvatī, and he does his salvific deeds either together with Pārvatī or with her permission.

Finally, among the episodes in which Śiva appears as destroyer of his enemies, there is the death of Yama (the god of death) himself at the hands of Śiva. Śiva is Mṛtyuñjaya; he is the giver of *mokṣa* in this form, when meditated upon. The *mantra* that overcomes death describes Śiva as the overlord of death.

Śiva the Dancer

Śiva Naṭarāja has been immortalized in South Indian art. The images, however, are not found before the sixth century C.E. Śaiva philosophy, especially in the Śaiva-Siddhānta, has developed a sophisticated philosophy around Śiva Naṭarāja, seeing in it Śiva's fivefold activities symbolized.

We find some elements of Śiva Naṭarāja in the Purāṇas: both the *tāṇḍava*, the dance of world destruction, and the Śiva-*līlā*, the dance of the enamoured Śiva. The other forms of Śiva's dance, as described in later Śaiva literature, especially of South India, may have been taken over from the *Nāṭyaśāstra* or may be logical further developments of the idea that Śiva's dance is expressive of his being and acting.

The earliest form of Śiva's dance seems to be that of destruction: already the most ancient references speak of his dancing like a madman. Śiva's dance at the time of universal destruction is used as a standing reference. Only the *Liṅga Purāṇa* offers a detailed description of it.[65] The *tāṇḍava* dance is connected with Vīrabhadra, Śiva's terrific form. It is held on the burning *ghats* and is performed in the company of ghosts and goblins. Śiva's *tāṇḍava* dance is always connected with Devi-Śakti; sometimes Śāktism and Śaivism become indistinguishable. In some places the *tāṇḍava* dance is even described as Śakti's frenzied dance upon Śiva's corpse.

The "beautiful dance," Śiva's *nāṭyalīlā*, is described in various sections of the *Śiva Purāṇa*, characteristically in connection with Śiva's marriage to Umā. The first narration brings Śiva's dance in connection with his wooing of Pārvatī:[66] he appears before Menā and her group and begins a beautiful dance which enchants everybody. He is described as holding in his left hand a horn, in his right a drum; he is dressed in a red garment and wears on his back a carpet. He is also singing a beautiful song. Śiva then appears at the actual wedding with all his strange companions and there again he assumes various forms.

The description of the fully developed Śiva Naṭarāja is given only in the late *Koyil Purāṇa*, a South Indian *sthala-purāṇa*.[67] Here he is described in the pose that became classic: Śiva went out into a forest in which many Mīmāṃsakas were living. Śiva tried to argue with them, but they only got angry with him and created a fierce tiger to devour him. Śiva seized it and stripped off its skin with the nail of his little finger, wrapping it round like a cloth. Next the Mīmāṃsakas let loose a fierce serpent on Śiva. Śiva took it and put it round his neck like a garland. When Śiva began to dance, the Mīmāṃsakas created a fierce dwarf, Muyalaka, to kill Śiva. Śiva put his foot on the back of Muyalaka and broke his neck. Then he resumed his dance. It is this scene which we see in the South Indian bronzes of the Śiva Naṭarāja. The philosophy explaining it has a clear salvific import: the dwarf under Śiva's foot personifies evil, which is subdued by Śiva. The sound produced by his drum is the *anahaṭa* sound, indicative of salvation. The hand which is outstretched shows the *abhaya-mūdra*, the sign of grace. The fire circle in which he dances indicates the consumption of the *māyā*-universe by the appearance of Śiva-reality. The raised foot again is a symbol of freedom. Śiva wears the skull of Brahmā around his neck: all creatures are mortal; Śiva is immortal. The snake around his neck also symbolizes immortality. Many later hymns glorify Śiva's dance. It is again especially the South Indian Śaivite tradition that dwells on this theme and out of it develops an entire philosophy of salvation.

Śiva-avatāras

"Mahādeva is exceedingly difficult to be known ... his forms are many. Many are the places in which he resides. Many are the forms of his grace."[68] Śaivism has never succeeded in developing anything close to the Pāñcarātra systematics of the manifestations of Viṣṇu; its enumerations and classifications are always somehow chaotic and incomplete. The *Mahābhārata* prefers to describe Śiva as assuming all forms: the form of Brahmā and Viṣṇu, of men and women, of *pretas* and *piśācas*, of *kirātas* and *śabaras*, of tortoises and fishes, of *rakṣasas* and *yakṣas*, of snakes and reptiles, of Daityas and Dānavas, of tigers and lions, of jackals and wolves, of crows and peacocks. He sometimes becomes six-faced and sometimes has many faces; he sometimes has three eyes, sometimes three heads; he is sometimes a boy, sometimes an old man.[69] In short, he can assume any form, gentle or fierce, auspicious or inauspicious, gracious or destructive.

Already the *Śatarudriya* described Rudra in paradoxical terms. Some of his forms seem to be hypostatized at an early date, as, for example, Śarva, Bhava, Iśāna, and so forth, but they are always aspects of Śiva. The term *avatāra* is used for certain manifestations of Śiva; the classification seems to be rather late and an imitation of Viṣṇu-*avatāras*. The Śiva-*avatāras* were not universally accepted; in Śaiva scriptures we always find various classifications of diverse Śiva manifestations side by side. They also never gained the importance and popularity of the Viṣṇu-*avatāras*, and among the numerous so-called Śiva-*avatāras* there is none that could be compared with, for example, Rāma or Kṛṣṇa. The individuality of the Śiva-*avatāras* remained rather vague and indistinct. The important salvific events in Śaivism are always ascribed to Śiva himself, never to his *avatāras*. As manifestation of Śiva and as his salvific presence, the *liṅga*, the "presence of Śiva in abstract form," is far more important than the Śiva-*avatāras*.

The *Śiva Purāṇa* deals with the Śiva-*avatāras* under the subtitle of *Śatarudra*, with the *liṅgas* of the more important places of worship under *Koṭirudra*, the myriads of Śiva manifestations.

The first group are the Pañcabrahma *avatāras*: Sadyojata, Vāmadeva, Tatpuruṣa, Aghora, and Iśāna. The names themselves are already found in Vedic texts and in the Epics, but only the *Śaiva Purāṇas* make them appear *avatāras* of Śiva.

The next well-known group is called Śivaṣṭamūrti: Śarva, Bhava, Rudra, Ugra, Bhīma, Iśa, Mahādeva, Paśupati, names that occur already in Vedic texts. The Śaivas of later times usually do not consider them as *avatāras*, but as aspects of Śiva. Śiva *ardhanārī* is also considered as an *avatāra*. In the *Śiva Purāṇa* there follows a list of nineteen *avatāras*, whose names are given with their functions briefly described. They are manifestations of Śiva at different ages and in different places.[70]

The *Śiva Purāṇa* explicitly says that Śiva assumed these different forms in order to give grace to the world and to do good to the Brāhmaṇas. The incarnations begin in the seventh Manvantara of Varāha-kalpa; for each successive Dvāpara-yuga one Śiva-*avatāra* is provided. The narration first mentions the Prajāpati for each of the Dvāparayugas and then the Śiva-*avatāra* and his four foremost disciples together with the function which he fulfilled.

Nandīśvarāvatāra is described next. A *muni* named Śilāda practices austerities to obtain an immortal son. He approaches Indra who confesses to be unable to give such a boon and advises him to go to Śiva. Śiva is pleased by the *muni*'s penance and promises him that he himself would become the son of Śilāda and be his immortal son as Nandin. The *Purāṇa* deals at length with Nandin's birth, penance, *abhiśeka*, and his marriage.

Next we read of a child-incarnation of Śiva from Śuciṣmati. He is called Bhairavāvatāra, whose *līlā* is described in a separate chapter. Then follow Śārdūlāvatāra, and Śalabhāvatāra. A longer section is devoted to Gṛhapatyavatāra and his exploits. Then comes Yakṣeśvarāvatāra. Again a series of ten *avatāras* is introduced with names and salvific functions mentioned, but without further description of the exploits. A group of eleven is mentioned collectively as fighting against demons. Since many names in these groups are identical with previously mentioned ones, we can assume that the *Śiva Purāṇa* merely brought together several existing Śiva-*avatāra* systems without attempting to coordinate them.

In the *Śiva Purāṇa* the Kirātāvatāra is connected with the well-known story of Arjuna's penance and the killing of a demon named Muka, who tried to disturb Arjuna. It also brings the strange story of Arjuna fighting with Śiva in the form of a hunter and the consequent blessing of Arjuna. The last group of Śiva-manifestations described in this section are the twelve *Jyotir-liṅga-avatāras*, which are mentioned together with the effect of their worship.

The following section, called *Koṭi-rudra-saṃhitā*, deals extensively with the *tīrthas*, and sub-*tīrthas* of these twelve *jyotir-liṅgas*, the symbols of Śiva made of light. That the *liṅgas* are understood as a salvific presence of Śiva becomes very clear from their praise. The section that deals with a description of Śiva's manifestations ends with the *Śiva-sahasra-nāma-stotra*, spoken by Viṣṇu. It is noteworthy that many of the Śiva-*avatāras* described above are not mentioned in this litany, while many other forms, not described, are enumerated. The *Śiva-sahasra-nāma* seems to belong to a Śiva tradition different from that from which the description and enumeration of Śiva-*avatāras* were taken. A second list with twenty-eight Śiva-*avatāras*, different from the lists in the *Śatarudriya*, is found in the latter section of *Vāyavīya-saṃhitā*: only the names of the Yoga-*avatāras* and their prominent disciples are enumerated. Since later Pāśupatas accept the standard number of twenty-eight *ācāryas* and *āgamas* we can assume that they incorporated this list into the revised Pāśupata edition of the *Śiva Purāṇa*.

Parallel to Viṣṇu's Śrī-*avatāras*, the *Śiva Purāṇa* knows also female counterparts to the Śiva-*avatāras*. They are found in the second section of the *Vāyavīya-saṃhitā*, in all probability a later addition to the *Śiva Purāṇa* which in its main corpus does not describe any of the Pārvatī-*avatāras*. A later addition from a time in which philosophical Śaiva systems had been established seems to be the section in which Śiva and his various manifestations are identified with the categories of epistemology and ontology, with cosmic processes and elements. Only this section speaks of the duality of Śiva and Śivā, *puruṣa-prakṛti*, as the cosmic principle. The main text of the *Śiva Purāṇa* knows Śiva as an Overlord of the World and not as metaphysical principle together with another principle. This section also knows a form of Śiva called *mukti*, a clear proof that no longer mythology but philosophical speculation determined religion. The *avatāras* must have been considered from a certain time onward an essential part of the image of a savior-god. We find in the Purāṇas of all sects descriptions of *avatāras* of the Supreme God, and none of the rival sects. The Śaiva Purāṇas do not even mention Viṣṇu-*avatāras*, though they most probably borrowed the very idea of *avatāras* from the Vaiṣṇavas. Similarly, the Vaiṣṇava books do not mention any Śaiva-*avatāras*, though at the time of their final redaction they must have known Śaiva Purāṇas which glorified a large number of Śiva-*avatāras*. The *avatāra* was an ultimate and absolute manifestation of the salvific will and power of God that had to be jealously guarded by every religion. In his *avatāras* God becomes, time and again, visibly Savior for all times. Those stories of the rival sects that were too well known, and which involved an act of salvation, were usually reinterpreted and reframed, so as ultimately to give credit to one's own saviour-god, though the apparent salvific deed had been performed by the rival.

A minor role in Śaivism is given to Kārtikeya, who is introduced as the son of Śiva. According to one version it is Kārtikeya who defeats the demon Tāraka and his army.

Far more important than all the Śiva-*avatāras* have always been the visible appearances of Śiva, Śiva *sākṣātkāra*, both in his propitious (Śiva) and in his terrible (Rudra) form. The penances performed by Śiva worshipers have usually no other purpose but to obtain a Śiva vision and to ask a boon from Śiva. In this form he is the easily accessible savior, always ready to come and to help if people only honor him and please him.

Śaivism is characterized by two extremes: Śiva and Rudra, creativity and destruction, grace and curse, asceticism and licentiousness, spirituality and sensuality, highest reason and absurd irrationality. This paradoxical description of Śiva applies also to Śaivite eschatology. Already in the Epics and *Purāṇas*, Śaivism accepts two ultimate states of existence corresponding to the two forms of Śiva: one is personal, individual, bodily immortality enjoyed in Kailāsa; the other is the merging of the individual consciousness in the universal impersonal Śiva-spirit.[71]

Since the Purāṇic period there was no significant development of Śiva mythology. Not a single new Śiva myth of general acceptance or real importance has been framed. We possess, however, a great many Sthala Purāṇas connected with important places of Śiva worship, whose legends and myths belong to later times, commemorating miracles and revelations associated with famous *tīrthas*.

ŚAIVA SCHOOLS OF THOUGHT

"The Śaiva Philosophy," writes S. S. Suryanarayana Sastri,[72] "is, in a sense typical of the entire range of Hindu thought. While in all its forms it subscribes to the belief in three *padārthas* and thirty-six *tattvas*, in the reality ascribed to *tattvas* and in the independence assigned to souls and matter, it varies from idealistic monism at one end of the scale to pluralistic realism at other end. But all through there will be found the typically Hindu insistence on knowledge as essential to salvation."

In Śaivism the *Śvetāśvatara Upaniṣad* occupies about the same position as the *Bhagavadgītā* in Vaiṣṇavism; while its philosophical position is more monistic, dualistic elements are not lacking.[73] Different schools developed early within Śaivism, associating the various *darśanas* with Śaiva tenets. There are some early authors who call the *darśanas* of Yoga, Nyāya and Vaiśeṣika, Śaivite.

Various titles and epithets of Śiva, used already in Vedic literature, would suggest that there had been definite groups of Śiva worshipers bearing these names. In the case of Pāśupatas and Kāpālikas we have early testimonies to this effect.[74] Many of these sects may not have developed any specific system of thought but may have differed from other sects only through certain external signs and practices. Śaiva systems of philosophy are comparatively few.

Śaṅkara in his commentary on *Vedānta-Sūtra* II, 2, 37, as well as Vācaspati Miśra in his *Bhāmatī* upon the *Śaṅkara-bhāṣya*, mention four non-Vedāntic Śaiva systems, which are condemned as erroneous: Śaiva, Pāśupata, Kāruṇika-siddhāntina, and Kāpālika. Rāmānuja mentions at the same place only two systems: Kālamukhas and Kāpālikas. Mādhava, in his *Sarva-darśana-saṁgraha*, deals extensively with four systems: Nakulīṣa (Pāśupata), Śaiva (Śaiva-Siddhānta), Pratyabhijñā (Kāśmīr Śaivism), and Raseśvara.

The Pāśupata System

The earliest among the Śaiva sects were the Pāśupatas; they were divided into various subsects, but possessed a common basic philosophy. The Pāśupatas believe that Śiva himself originated their system.

Paśupati is one of the oldest names of Śiva. The *Mahābhārata* narrates that Paśupati, the consort of Umā, also called Śrīkaṇṭha or Śiva, the son of Brahmā, revealed the *jñāna* known as Pāśupata.

The *Vāyu Purāṇa*, in its enumeration of Śiva-*avatāras*, mentions as the last one Nakulin: Śiva tells Brahmā that in the twenty-eighth Mahāyuga, when Viṣṇu will incarnate as Vāsudeva, he will incarnate as a *brahmacarin*, by name Nakulin, after entering a dead body at a burial ground. He will have four disciples – Kuśika, Garhya, Mitraka, and Ruṣṭa – who, after initiation into Maheśvara-yoga, will reach Rudraloka, from where there is no return. The Śiva Purāṇa and the Liṅga Purāṇa have the same narrative, calling the *avatāra* Lakulin instead of Nakulin.

That Lakulin was regarded by the Pāśupatas as a Śiva-*avatāra* is testified by inscriptions.[75] There is little doubt that Lakulin had been a historical figure and he probably was the founder of the Pāśupata system. Modern research places him in the second century C.E. The basic text of the Pāśupatas are the *Pāśupata-sūtras*, not necessarily the oldest text, since we find elements of Pāśupata doctrine already in the *Mahābhārata* and numerous chapters on Pāśupata-*vrata* in several *Purāṇas*, notably the *Vāyu*, *Śiva*, *Liṅga*, *Brahma*, and *Skanda Purāṇa*.

Mādhava devotes a chapter to the Lakulīṣa-*darśana*, in which he restricts himself to an exposition of a few of the *sūtras* of the *Pāśupata-sūtras*. There is an old (fourth to six century C.E.) *bhāṣya* on the *Pāśupata-sūtras* by a certain Kauṇḍinya which is much more philosophical than the *sūtras* themselves, which deal mainly with rituals. Most of the Purāṇa texts dealing with the Pāśupata-*vrata* are also almost exclusively concerned with certain practices of Śaiva-Yoga. All agree that Śiva taught five topics whose knowledge is essential for the total annihilation of all sorrows: *kārya* (the soul in bondage), *kāraṇa* (the Lord who redeems), *yoga* (ascetical practices), *vidhi* (ritual), and *duḥkhānta* (final release). Pentads play a great role in this system; apart from the five basic categories the whole process of liberation is again represented in eight pentads. Bondage is due to fivefold *mala* ("stain"), in this system called *pāśutva* ("bovine-ness"). The five *malas* are *mithyā-jñāna* (false thinking), *adharma* (unrighteousness), *āsaktihetu* (attachment), *cyuti* ("fall"), and *paśutva mūla* (basic bovine-ness). Liberation consequently consists in the removal of these "stains." The means for this are *vasācaryā* (ethical life), *japa* (repetition of a sacred formula), *dhyāna* (meditation), *rudra-smṛti* (remembering Śiva), and *prapatti* (self-surrender).

Paśu is eternal and the *malas* are superimposed on it: their removal can only be effected when *īśvara* so desires, after the *paśu* has practiced the *pāśupata-yoga* and performed *pāśupata vidhis*. These consist largely of practices like *japa*, *dhyāna*, bathing in ashes, lying upon ashes, laughing and dancing like a madman, singing, muttering *hum hum*, "like the bellowing of a bull," snoring, trembling, limping, acting absurdly, and talking nonsense.

Duḥkhānta, final liberation, in this system is twofold: "impersonal" and "personal." It consists in "being like *īśvara*" with regard to knowledge and active power. The Pāśupatas emphasize that the *summum bonum* is not *kaivalya*, but being with the Supreme Lord who terminates all pain. They also insist that works do bring real fruit, depending on God's will. Therefore the *pāśupata-vrata*, as expressing God's will, is the only way to *mokṣa*.

The Pāśupata system as explained in the *Śiva Purāṇa* differs in several important details. The *Śiva Purāṇa* seems to contain various versions of Pāśupata religion in its different parts. In one chapter the whole process of liberation is reduced to a knowledge of *paśu*, *pāśa*, and *pati*. All sorrows are due to ignorance. *Jīvas* are *akṣara* (indestructible), while *pāśas* are destructible. The *jīvas* are *puruṣa*; *pāśas* are *prakṛti*; and the Supreme Lord, *pati*, moves both to action. *Puruṣa-paśu* is encircled by *prakṛti-māyā-pāśa*. *Pāśa* or *mala* consists in the power of *prakṛti* to conceal the true self-consciousness. When the *paśu* is freed from this *mala*, he attains to his former pure condition. The association of *puruṣa* and *mala* is due to previous evil deeds.

In another section the process of emancipation is described as follows: renouncing the fruits of *karma*, one becomes associated with Śiva faith, either through a *guru*, or without one. Knowing Śiva means to realize the sorrows of *saṃsāra*. The consequences are *vairāgya* and *bhāva* toward the Lord. The devotee becomes inclined to meditate on Śiva. Concentrating on the nature of Śiva, the devotee attains *yoga*, which in its turn further increases devotion and draws down more of Śiva's grace. Finally the *jīva* becomes *śiva-sama*.

The *Śiva Purāṇa* also knows two kinds of final emancipation, corresponding to the "impersonal" and "personal" ones in Mādhava's description. The monistic version says that at the *mahāpralaya*, *māyā* itself will vanish and with it the whole universe and all the individual *jīvas* will merge into Śiva.

The other version distinguishes four kinds of *mukti*: *sārūpya* (assuming the same form as Śiva), *sālokya* (dwelling in the same place with Śiva), *sānnidhya* (sharing Śiva's contemplation), and *sāyujya* (becoming one with Śiva). Śiva alone grants *mukti*. The ultimate aim is to be "similar" or "equal" to Śiva, not to be identical with him. The interaction of God's will and personal effort is one of the most prominent features of the Pāśupata system. Śiva's will is the criterion of the goodness or wickedness of acts. Śiva does not remain indifferent but punishes evil and rewards good. Śiva's will acts in consonance with the intrinsic nature of things, and he delivers a person only after he or she is prepared for liberation. Grace only provides assistance; a person's exertion is as essential for liberation as Śiva's help. *Jīvas* are different on account of the difference in their *malas*, which are the root cause of all suffering. The more free *jīvas* are from *malas*, the clearer they can perceive Śiva. Śiva, the true doctor, leads the soul through true knowledge away from impurities.[76]

The Śaiva System or Śaiva-siddhānta

The *darśana* that Mādhava introduces as Śaiva[77] is better known under the name of Śaiva-siddhānta. It is the predominant form of Śaivism in South India today. It is based upon the twenty-eight *Śaiva Āgamas* and also incorporates the teaching of the eighty-four *Nāyanārs*. Mādhava quotes from the most important Śaiva Āgamas – the *Mṛgendra*, *Kāmika*, *Kāraṇa*, *Kiraṇa*, and *Pauṣkara* – but he does not mention the famous teachers of Śaiva-siddhānta: Meykaṇḍa (thirteenth century), Haradatta Śivācārya (*c.*1050), Śrīkaṇṭha (*c.*1125), Bhojarājā (*c.*1125), Aghoraśivācārya (*c.*1150). In addition to the *Āgamas* and the teachings of the *Nāyanārs*, Meykaṇḍa's *Śivajñānabodham* has acquired a high authority and has been commented upon by many other authors.[78]

Śaiva-siddhānta acknowledges three principles: *pati*, *paśu*, and *pāśa*. It accepts four *pādas* or means of liberation: *vidyā*, *kriyā*, *yoga*, and *caryā*. Śiva is the supreme reality: he is greater than the Trimūrti of Viṣṇu-Brahmā-Rudra and is the only eternal being. Śiva has eight qualities: independence, purity, self-knowledge, omniscience, freedom from *mala*, benevolence, omnipotence, and blissfulness. The most comprehensive terms to circumscribe the essence of Śiva are *sat* and *cit*. Śiva *aṣṭa-mūrti* means the immanence of Śiva in the five elements, in sun, moon, and sentient beings. Śiva is male-female-neuter; he is also *viśva-rūpa*. A very important feature to note is that Śaiva-siddhānta does not accept Śiva *avatāras*: Śiva cannot incarnate, because that would mean birth and death, which are the results of *karma* and *saṃsāra*, whereas Śiva is eternally independent. Śiva appears only in a bodily form as the *guru*; as such he can be worshiped by his devotees. Out of his great love for the souls he comes as a *guru* to save his people from *saṃsāra*. The Siddhāntins constantly emphasize that Śiva is Love, and the whole system of Śaiva-siddhānta has only one great theme, the Grace of God.

One more interesting feature of Śaiva-siddhānta is its insistence that Śiva's activity with regard to the *paśu* depends on the *jīva's karma.*

Śiva's fivefold activities – *anugraha* (giving grace), *tirobhava* (concealment), *ādāni* (binding), *sthiti* (maintenance), and *sṛṣṭi* (creation) – are exercised through his forms as Sadāśiva, his body formed out of pure Śakti. "The Supreme has Īśāna as his head, Tatpuruṣa as his mouth, Aghora as his heart, Vāmadeva as his secret parts, Sadyojāta as his feet."[79] The purpose of his assuming the Śakti body is to be able to give grace to the *bhakta*. The title "Śiva" includes all beings "who have attained to the state of Śiva," Mantreśvara, Maheśvara, the *muktas* who have become Śivas, the *vācakas* and all the means to obtain the state of Śiva.

Despite this universal use of the word Śiva the Śaiva-siddhānta is a pluralistic system, and it insists on the individuality of the souls even after they have reached *śivatva*, the highest aim. That *śivatva* is the highest aim is only known through *śruti*, which alone also provides the means to attain it – hence the great importance of the *Āgamas*. The Śaiva-siddhāntins explicitly reject other understandings of *jīva*. The difference between Śiva and the liberated souls is that Śiva is eternally free; the *jīvas* are liberated by his grace.

The *paśus* or the souls that can be liberated are of three kinds: some are fettered only by *aṇava* or *mala*, that is, without any *karma* or *māyā* fetters. Some are fettered by *mala* and *karma*, others are fettered by *mala*, *karma*, and *māyā*.[80]

Pāśa, the fetter, is the cause of the state of bondage of the *jīva*. We have mentioned three forms of it: *aṇava*, *māyā*, *karma*. "*Karma*, *māyā*, and *aṇava*, like sprout, bran, and husk hide the real nature of the soul and delude it. They cause enjoyment, embodiment, and the state of being the enjoyer."[81]

Māyā comprises the whole process of evolution and involution. *Karma* leads to the fruition of heaven and hell, as ordained by Śiva. The goodness of an action is determined by scripture. "Pleasures and pains are the medicine administered by Śiva, the physician, to cure the diseases and delusions caused by *mala*."[82]

Aṇava, beginningless and eternal, is the primal bondage of the souls; it is something like an "original sin": if *aṇava* is removed the souls will be restored to their essential nature as pure spirits. *Aṇava* is the (positive) limitation of the soul's knowledge.

With this background it becomes possible to understand the process of salvation as envisaged by the Śaiva-siddhantins. *Dīkṣā* (formal initiation) is the direct cause of liberation, but *dīkṣā* is not possible without *vidyā*; *vidyā* is not possible without *yoga*; *yoga* is not possible without *kriyā*; and *kriyā* is not possible without *caryā*. Thus we have steps of liberation, corresponding to four different *mārgas* (paths), leading to four different kinds of *mukti* (liberation).

Dāsa-mārga (the path of the servant) consists of the practice of *caryā* and leads to *sālokya* (living in the same place as Śiva). *Satputra mārga* (the path of the true son) consists of the practice of *kriyā* and leads to *sāmīpya* (nearness to Śiva). *Saha mārga* (the path of the companion) consists of the practice of *yoga* and leads to *sārūpya* (having the same form as Śiva). *San mārga* (the true way) consists of the practice of *jñāna* and leads to *sāyūjya* (complete identity with Śiva). There are three kinds of *jñāna*: *paśu-jñāna* and *pāśa-jñāna* do not lead to *mokṣa* but give only the knowledge of the soul, of words and things. Only *pati-jñāna* leads to *mokṣa*, which is self-luminous and reveals both itself and others. "It is *pati-jñāna* that reveals the three entities: *pati*, *paśu*, *pāśa*. Śiva's *śakti* is the natural eye of Śiva and the artificial eye of the soul. This Śiva *śakti* illumines the natural eye of the soul and reveals the nature of Śiva and also his nature as the life of the soul. Śiva is in a relation of inherence with his *śakti* which is the manifestor of the soul's *cit śakti*."[83] The way to *pati-jñāna* leads through the *guru*'s teaching: the soul's subjection to the three fetters is not open to perception. It is Śiva who appears in the form of a *guru*, who opens the eyes of the devotee, performs the purificatory rites, and removes the *malas*. Śiva appears to the three different groups of *paśus* in different forms and performs various forms of *dīkṣā* on them, which directly causes liberation.

Śaiva-siddhāntins emphasize that it is only in a human birth and only as a Śaiva that the possibility of putting an end to the cycle of births and deaths is given. "Those who, instructed in the great Siddhānta, worship the Lord who wears the crescent, get rid of their *mala* and attain release."[84] A birth in a human form is required to worship Śiva who is bathed in these five manners: he is contemplated by the mind; praises are uttered with words; he is worshiped by exerting the body in a certain manner. Such worship is not possible in any other birth. The celestials like Viṣṇu come to this world because Śiva cannot be worshiped in this manner elsewhere. Those born as human beings seldom realize the uniqueness of their birth and the facilities it offers for release. If release is not sought for in this life, it will be hard to attain it hereafter.

The Siddhāntins claim that all other faiths lead their followers only to one of the thirty-six *tattvas* as the last end. Śaiva-siddhānta alone leads to Śiva, who is above the *tattvas*. "Śiva comes in the form of a preceptor and subjects mature souls to purification by look, etc. He immerses them in the ocean of wisdom and enables them to have *Śivānanda*. Even in this birth he removes their *malas*, makes them *jīvan-muktas*, prevents further births and finally helps them to attain his feet. It is through the Siddhānta that all these can be achieved."[85]

If somebody ignored the Siddhānta it would be a great delusion and a grave sin, and he would go to hell for it. *Mukti* is the appearance of the hidden *śivatva* in the soul through *jñāna*: the state of *mukti* is *jñāna niṣṭha* (steadfastness in knowledge). This state (of jñāna niṣṭha) can be obtained in this body in the case of *jīvan-muktas*, and this goes well together with various kinds of behavior, because of the *prārabdha* of different kinds: "*Śiva-jñānis* may do any good or bad deed – they remain unaffected by the changes and never get away from the feet of the Lord. It is difficult to determine the nature of the *jīvan-muktas*: some of them may be short-tempered, some sweet-tempered, some free from desires, some lustful."[86] One of the best-known examples is Saint Sundaramūrti, "who was free from attachment though outwardly he seemed to live a life of sensual pleasures."[87]

For those who have achieved *jñāna niṣṭha* there is neither good nor evil. Even if they engage in activities, they do so without caring for their results. They need not perform the ceremonies prescribed by their religion. They need not practice *tapas*. They need not observe their duties pertaining to the *varṇa-āśrama dharma*. They need not practice contemplation. They need not put on the external signs of their faith. "Coming to have the qualities of children, mad people, and people possessed of evil spirits, they may even give themselves up to singing and dancing by reason of their ecstasy."[88]

Śiva always resides in the soul, but only the enlightened soul will consciously live a Śiva-life and follow Śiva's grace. Union with Śiva therefore means freedom from egotism: if the free soul does anything, it is Śiva's work: "Śiva takes the good and evil deeds done to the soul as done to himself in order that the soul may be freed from births. Because the soul serves God by being with him, the good as well as the evil it does become service of God. Again, the good and evil done by this soul are auxiliary causes leading to an increase of merit and demerit acquired by others through doing good and evil to this soul."[89]

Because Śiva in the condition of *jīvan-mukti* actuates the soul, all the good and evil that the soul does is Śiva's action. It is Śiva who actuates other people so that all the good and evil that they do, is, again, his action. Those who realize this are aware of nothing but his grace, and completely lose themselves in his grace. Such people will not be affected by ignorance or *karma*. Śiva makes people who seek him as their refuge pure like himself and protects them. Maraijñāna Deśikar says: "Śiva's nature is to help souls without expecting any return. Since he is free from desire and aversion he has the good of all in view."[90] Śaiva-siddhāntins distinguish seven degrees of *jīvan-mukti* that have individual names and are likened in their sweetness to sugarcane, fruit, milk, honey, sugar-candy, sugar, and nectar.

Śaiva-siddhānta knows a complementarity between love of God and love of people: one's love for Śiva's devotees is a sign of one's love for Śiva. Because Śiva exists in all souls, those who love him will really love all souls.

In the state of *mukti* the three entities *pati*, *paśu*, and *pāśa* are present: the Lord grants enjoyment to the soul, the soul experiences this enjoyment, and *mala* makes the enjoyment possible.

In *mukti* the soul remains conscious of its dependence on God and that it owes everything to him: it experiences the bliss of Śiva compared with which all other things are as nothing. No longer does the soul experience through the senses, that is, through *mala*, but through *pati*, the Lord: *patijñāna* is not only knowledge of Śiva, but through Śiva.

In no other system is salvation so much at the center of all reflections as in Śaiva-siddhānta: all the functions of God are ordered toward salvation. God's essence is to be full of grace. Śiva creates the world in order to provide the soul with a body and a stage on which it can act, and only through its efforts in this condition can the soul achieve liberation. *Pralaya* too has its place in the economy of salvation. Repeated births and deaths often weary the soul. To provide some respite and rest to the souls, Śiva withdraws from time to time the world, so as to provide relief and rest to the souls. Śiva acts as a *guru* to the soul; without Śiva's guidance the soul would not be able to reach *mukti*. Through Śiva's love the soul passes from *iruḷ*, darkness, to *maruḷ*, confusion, and from there to *aruḷ*, or grace. At every stage the soul is in need of God, and at every stage God's presence is acting for the salvation of the soul.

Śrīkaṇṭha's Śaiva-Vedānta – classified within Vedānta under *bhedābheda* – may be considered as a special form of Śaiva-siddhānta.[91] It is also called "Viśiṣṭa-Śaiva-Vedānta," indicating by its very name its relation to Rāmānuja's thought. His aim is to reconcile the Upaniṣadic and Āgamic traditions; in fact he quotes extensively from both sources. He accepts the triad of *paśu*, *pāśa*, and *pati*, calling the bondage of man *paśutva* and the state of liberation *śivatva*. He makes use of the Purāṇic images and myths, and interprets Śiva-Nīlakaṇṭha as a symbol "for showing care."[92]

In his system the Brahman of the Upaniṣads is the Śiva of the Āgamas; the grace of Śiva is Brahman's body. "The *muktas*," he writes, "realize the *saviśeṣa* form of Brahman. The *jīvas* do not lose their own nature in Brahman even though he is their material cause; but only become non-distinct from him."[93]

Śrīkaṇṭha maintains that during one's lifetime one can become "knower of Brahman;" he asserts that the mode of departure of knowers and not-knowers are different: "Through the might of the *vidyā* which consists in the worship of the Supreme Lord, as well as through meditation on the Path which is a subsidiary part of this, he the favourer of all, becomes pleased and looks upon the knower with favour, which destroys all his sins that so long concealed his real nature from him. Then he, 'with the door revealed' by His grace, comes out through the 101st vein that passes through the crown of the head. Others do not so but come out through other veins."[94]

Also Śrīkaṇṭha insists that Śiva's abode is higher than Vaikuṇṭha and Satyaloka, and the stage reached by one who has been saved by Śiva is above the *turīya* of the Upaniṣads. *Mukti* means "to realize one's own proper form": "Although the real nature, sinless and consisting in attributes similar to those of Brahman, of one who has attained Brahman is existent in him beforehand, yet it is manifested in him through the removal of sins."[95] The freed soul is similar to Brahman, but not identical with him. The *mukta* obtains "equality in point of enjoyment only."[96]

A slight difference between Śrīkaṇṭha and classical Śaiva-siddhānta may lie in Śrīkaṇṭha's assertion that the *mukta*, after having attained *śivatva*, is "without another ruler," that is, independent. "The Supreme Lord is no longer its ruler, as it is then beyond the scope of all scriptural injunctions and prohibitions which embody his commands and apply to transmigratory mundane existence."[97] When *paśutva* disappears, *śivatva* becomes the nature of the soul: *Śivatva* means being similar to Śiva in nature, i.e., having a supremely auspicious form, free from the slightest vestige of sins. "Omniscience" and the rest constitute the nature of Śiva. Hence the freed soul, who is similar to Śiva, is omniscient, eternally knowing, eternally satisfied, independent, omnipotent, with ever-manifested powers having infinite powers. Transmigratory existence consists in a contraction of one's self-knowledge. When the causes of such a contraction, viz. sins, are removed, then it becomes omniscient. For this very reason, there being a total extinction of ignorance which causes earthly existence, the wrong identification of the unlimited soul with the limited body ceases. Due to this, it becomes free from old age, death, and grief. Thus, not being subject to *karma*, it becomes independent. As it finds pleasure in its own nature, so it is "eternally satisfied." For this very reason it has no hunger, thirst, and the like.[98]

According to Śrīkaṇṭha the *mukta* is independent, has the "eight qualities" of Śiva, and can assume and discard bodies at will. A peculiarity of Śrīkaṇṭha's teaching is his assumption that the *mukta* is all-pervasive: "It is said that the freed souls with their bondage rent asunder by the Great God or the Supreme Brahman – who does good to all like a friend and a father and who has become pleased – become immortal; and attaining the places that are full of illumination and that are placed in His World or the Supreme Ether abide therein. The freed souls pervade the Heaven and the earth by means of the rays of their own powers. Hence the freed souls, who are one in essence with Śiva, are indeed all-pervasive."[99] Like Rāmānuja, Śrīkaṇṭha says that the freed souls do not share the power of God to create, sustain, and destroy the world.

He also maintains that there is only One God! The *muktas*, however, enjoy the same bliss as God enjoys, and they enjoy it eternally: there is no return for them. Śrīkaṇṭha describes the heavens of Śaiva-Vedānta in the following words: "The place of the husband of Umā is like millions of suns, the first, full of all objects of desires, pure, eternal, indestructible. Having attained that celestial place they become free from all miseries, omniscient, capable of going everywhere, pure, full. Further they come to have pure sense-organs and become endowed with supreme Lordship. Then, again they assume bodies or discard these at will. Those men who, being engaged in the pursuit of knowledge and concentration attain this Supreme Place, do not return to the frightful earthly existence."[100] The *muktas* "have Śiva as their souls" and "shine forth with Śiva in all places at all times."[101]

Śiva-Advaita or Kashmir-Śaivism

Kashmir-Śaivism, the main Śaiva school of North India – also called Śaiva-Advaita, Trika, Trikaśāsana, Rahasya Saṃpradāya, Trayaṃbaka Saṃpradāya – is possibly pre-Saṅkarite. The earliest written testimonies go back to the eighth or ninth centuries C.E., but the roots of the system may be several centuries older. It has two main branches, *Spaṇḍa-śāstra* and *Pratyabhijñā-darśana*, which have much in common. It has a long and brilliant history, but today it seems to be practically defunct, quite contrary to Śaiva-siddhānta, which is still very much a living faith for numerous Śaivites.[102] The *Śiva Purāṇa* has several chapters in which Śaiva-Advaita is explained and advocated as a system leading to salvation. The *Liṅga Purāṇa* also has clear statements of Śiva-Advaita. In the *Kailāsa-saṃhitā* the *Śiva Purāṇa* identifies the unity of *sat-cit-ānanda* with the unity of Śiva Śakti. In the connection of Śiva and Śakti there is bliss. It is because of the *malas* in the soul that the *cit-śakti*, which is in the soul, is impeded and man is deprived of perfect bliss. But it is ultimately Śiva himself who contracts himself and manifests himself as the individual *puruṣas* who enjoy the qualities of *prakṛti*. This enjoyment takes place through the function of fivefold *kala*: *kriyā*, *vidyā*, *rāga*, *kāla*, *niyati*.[103] In the *Koṭirudra-saṃhitā* in the same *Purāṇa*[104] it is said that the plurality of appearances is due to nescience. Śiva bestows *mukti* on those who are devoted to him. *Jñāna* comes from *bhakti*; *bhakti* engenders *prema*; and "from *prema* one gets into the habit of listening to episodes about the greatness of Śiva, and from that one comes into contact with saintly people, and from that one can attain one's *guru*. When in this way true knowledge is gained one becomes liberated."[105] The *Koṭirudra-saṃhitā* knows four kinds of *mukti*. Though the basic tenor of those sections of *Śiva Purāṇa* is Advaitic, the theistic elements of *bhakti*, *gurūpasati*, and so forth are mixed with it. Śiva-Advaita proper as a system of thought is connected with the *Śiva-sūtras* of Vasugupta (around 825 C.E.) that became the basic text of both Spaṇḍa-śāstra and Pratyabhijñā-darśana. Many celebrated compendia of both subsects of Śiva-Advaita are commentaries upon the *Śiva-sūtras*.

Pratyabhijñā is the philosophy proper of this system. It is associated mainly with the names of Utpala and Abhinavagupta (950–1020 C.E.) whose disciple Kṣemarāja (975–1050 C.E.) wrote the famous *Pratyabhijñā-hṛdayam*, a concise and authoritative exposition of Kāśmīr Śaivism.

Mādhava in his *Sarva-darśana-saṁgraha* bases his account of the Pratyabhijñā *darśana* on Utpala's and Abhinavagupta's works. The main difference between Śaiva-siddhānta and Pratyabhijñā-darśana, which have many elements in common, lies in that, according to Pratyabhijñā, there is no causality other than Śiva's: no internal or external efforts of the *jīva* have any influence on salvation, but all that is required is "introspection." All reality, Śiva and Śakti and their union, are mirrored in one's own *ātman*. Liberation consists in the recognition of this mirrored image. There is no need of any *dīkṣā*, no need of any external paraphernalia.

Whereas in most other systems qualifications play an important role, here it is said explicitly "that there is no restriction of the doctrine to a previously qualified student."[106] All that matters is the recognition of the Śiva who resides in all beings. One of the qualities of Śiva is *ānanda*, bliss; if a person acquires the nature of Śiva, that person acquires also Śiva's blissfulness. The aim of the follower of this system is to become a "slave of Śiva," that is, "one who is being given everything according to the pleasure of the Lord." In Pratyabhijñā, will and effort play a decisive part: everything owes its existence to the will of Śiva; effort from the side of the *jīva* is necessary to recognize Śiva.

Bondage is limitation or restriction of the Śiva-hood of the *ātman*: through the five limiting factors the All becomes an atom, the universal, omniscient, eternal, blissful Śiva becomes a finite, ignorant, limited, and unhappy *puruṣa*. Kuṇḍalinī, the manifestation of Śakti in the individual, is usually dormant. The innermost core is *caitanya* or Śiva. *Mokṣa* is nothing but the recognition of the true nature of *jīva* as Śiva.[107]

Bondage is a work of *śakti*. *Śakti* helps to overcome it too: *śaktipatā*, the descent of Śakti, is the same as *anugraha*, the advent of grace. Also the *jīva*, being an atom-sized Śiva, partakes of the fivefold activities of Śiva; the full unfolding of the Śakti in the *jīvas* is "the becoming Śiva."

Ontologically and externally nothing happens when liberation is reached: it is only the "recognition" of one's own true nature, remembering of one's identity with Śiva. In Abhinavagupta's words: "It is Śiva himself of unimpeded will and pellucid consciousness who is ever sparkling in my heart. It is his highest Śakti herself that is ever playing on the edge of my senses. The entire world gleams as the wondrous delight of pure I-consciousness. Indeed I know not what the sound 'world' is supposed to refer to."[108] In this stage subject- and object-consciousness become one and the same: the individual experiences itself as the universe and as Śiva. Liberation means removal of all the limitations, the breaking through of the Great Freedom of unlimited being-consciousness. The last *sūtra* sums up the ultimate perfection to be achieved: "Then, as a result of entering into the perfect I-consciousness or Self which is in essence *cit* and *ānanda* and of the nature of the power of the great *mantra*, there accrues the attainment of lordship over one's group of the deities of consciousness that brings about all emanation and reabsorption of the universe. All this is the nature of Śiva."[109]

The stage of consciousness achieved by Pratyabhijñā is considered to be above the *turīya* of the Upaniṣads: *turyātīta*. This again is considered to be of two kinds: *śāttodita* (broken consciousness) and *nityodita* (unbroken consciousness). The means to reach this consciousness is the specific *yoga* of Pratyabhijñā, which has much in common with later Kuṇḍalinī-yoga.

Vīra-Śaivism

The youngest among the major schools of Śaivism is Vīra-Śaivism, connected closely with the name of Basava.[110] The sect itself and its main tenets may, however, go back to a much more remote time. Under Basava's inspiration, Vīra-Śaivism developed into a vigorous missionary movement. The Vīra-Śaivas or "heroic Śiva-worshipers" differ from the Sāmānya and Miśra-Śaivas, who worship both Śiva and Viṣṇu, and also from the Śuddha-Śaivas, who worship Śiva alone but do not wear a *liṅga*. For the Vīra-Śaivas the *liṅga* that they always wear on their bodies – the so-called *iṣṭa-liṅga* – is not only a symbol but the real presence of Śiva. The Vīra-Śaiva wears it in order to make his body a temple of Śiva, fit for him to dwell in.

The Vīra-Śaivas consider as the sources of their religion the twenty-eight *Āgamas*, the teachings of the sixty-three Tamil Nāyanārs and later writers. They have a *Vedānta-sūtra-bhāṣya* of their own in Śrīpati's *Śrīkara-bhāṣya*.[111] His system is called Śakti-viśiṣṭa-advaita, whose essence is: "There is no duality between the soul and the Lord, each qualified by Śakti."[112] The *jīva* is the body of Śiva. Para-Śiva is both the material and the instrumental cause of the universe. Śakti resides eternally in Parama-Śiva: it is the creative principle, also called *māyā*. Out of Śakti all beings come in creation – back into Śakti they return in *pralaya* (final dissolution of the universe) and remain there in a seminal form.[113] *Jīva* is in fact an *aṃśa* (part) of Śiva which on account of *avidyā* imagines itself to be different from him.

The Supreme Brahman, also called *sthala*, by the agitation of its immanent Śakti, divides into Liṅgasthala and Aṅgasthala. Liṅgasthala is Śiva himself, to be adored. Aṅgasthala is the individual soul and the adorer. Śakti also divides herself into two parts, each clinging to one part of the divided *sthala*: *kala* unites with Śiva, *bhakti* unites with *aṅga*. *Bhakti* is the means of final deliverance; through it the *jīva* becomes a Śiva-worshiper. Through *bhakti*, *liṅga* and *aṅga* are reunited. Śakti is again the source of both division and union, bondage and liberation.

The *liṅga* is Śiva himself. It is threefold: Bhavaliṅga is *niṣkala* Śiva – to be perceived by faith alone. It is pure *sat* – not conditioned by space or time. Prāṇaliṅga is *sakala-niṣkala* Śiva – to be perceived by the mind. It is *cit*. Iṣṭaliṅga is *sakala* Śiva and visible by the senses. It confers all desired objects, removes afflictions, and is pure *ānanda*. Each is again subdivided into two forms, and each one is operated by a different form of Śakti. Thus Śiva appears in six forms as Mahāliṅga, Prasādaliṅga, Caraliṅga, Śivaliṅga, Guruliṅga, and Ācāraliṅga. It is the last form under which Śiva appears and acts as the redeemer of the soul.

Bhakti is the characteristic form of *śakti* inherent in *jīva*: it has three stages which correspond to the three divisions of Aṅgasthala. Through Yogāṅga one obtains happiness by union with Śiva. Through Bhogāṅga ("enjoyment stage") one enjoys together with Śiva. Through Tyagāṅga one abandons the world as transient and illusory.

Each of the three forms is again subdivided into two: *Aikya-bhakti* or *sama-rasa-bhakti* is the union of God and soul in blissful experience. *Śaraṇa-bhakti* is the condition in which one sees the *liṅga* in the self and everything else besides. *Prāṇa-liṅgin-bhakti* is disregard for one's own life, renunciation of egotism, and concentration of the mind upon the *liṅga*. *Maheśvara-bhakti* means mainly following the injunction of the sect. The last form is *bhakta-bhakti*, which implies turning away one's mind from all objects and practicing rites and ceremonies, leading a life of indifference to the world.

The soul has to start from the last form and ascend to the first in order to find its bliss in Śiva. Vīra-Śaivas lay great stress upon religious practices without which it is not possible to reach *mokṣa*: these are Pañcācāra and Aṣṭāvaraṇa. Pañcācāra comprises *liṅgācāra* (daily worship of the *liṅga*), *sadācāra* (a moral and decent life and work), *śivācāra* (considering all Liṅgāyats as equal), *bhṛtyacāra* (humility toward Śiva and his devotees), *gaṇācāra* (active fight against those who despise Śiva or mistreat his devotees).

Aṣṭāvarana comprises *guru* (obedience toward the spiritual master), *liṅga* (wearing of a *liṅga*), *jaṅgama* (worshiping an ascetic as an incarnation of Śiva), *pādodaka* (sipping the water in which the feet of a *guru* or of a *jangama* have been bathed), *prasāda* (offering food to a *guru*, a *liṅga* or *jaṅgama*, oneself taking the remains), *bhasma* (smearing ashes obtained from cowdung on one's body), *rudrākṣa* (wearing a *mālā* of *rudrākṣa*-beads), and *mantra* (recitation of the *pañcākṣara*, *Śivāya nāmaḥ*).

Release is more the result of the faithful observance of these rules and ceremonies than of meditation or introspection.

Śrīpati, however, introduces a Vedāntic element into Vīra-Śaivism, in addition to its external rites. According to his teaching the *jīva* originated through Parabrahma Śiva by the agency of Hiraṇyagarbha.[114] Through constant meditation on Hiraṇyagarbha the *jīva* comes within sight of Hiraṇyagarbha through whom he is brought into the presence of Parabrahman and within sight of him. The *mukta* meditates only on Parabrahman and enjoys the bliss of his sight. Meditation on Śiva alone is the means to become free from rebirth. The highest place is Śivaloka, above the highest Viṣṇupada. After fully knowing Śiva through *jñāna*, the *jīva* can attain *śivatadātmya*, *sāyujya mukti*. The Ativahikas, the holy servants of Śiva, will lead the one who meditates on Śiva to holy Kailāsa.

The relationship between *jīva* and Śiva in the state of *mokṣa* is expressed by the simile of the river flowing into the sea: in *mokṣa* the individual is released from the state of *jīva*, that is, from limitations which make Śiva *jīva*; the individual attains the all-pervading, undivided, and supreme *ākāśa*-form and bears the characteristics of *sat*, *cit*, and *ānanda*. It becomes possessed of the supreme quality of omniscience and acquires the *guṇas* of Parabrahman, Paraśiva, Śivaśankara, Rudreśvara, and Mahādeva and claims all the terms by which Parabrahman is called.

Śiva is worshiped under a *mūrta* (embodied) and an *amūrta* (unembodied) form; though his own Parabrahman form is formless, he assumes a *līlā maṅgala vigraha*, a form in which he engages in auspicious playfulness, indicating to the *bhakta* the way to *mukti*. The person who is desirous of liberation and worships the *mūrta* form of Śiva finally reaches the *amūrta* form and attains *kaivalya mukti* (close to the Advaitic dissolution of all personality).

There is the case of the *jīvan-mukta*, who still lives in the world: though free from bondage, he undergoes the experiences of different worlds as long as he possesses a *liṅga-śarīra*. Śrīpati explains that even Mahādeva performed several acts such as the destruction of Vyāghrāsura,

Gajāsura, Tripurāsura, drinking the poison, and protecting his *bhakta* Mārkaṇḍeya. He did this in order to show his *bhaktas* that they should do all that has been ordained.

Śrīpati holds that "a *mukta* in the beginning having obtained a status equal to that of Śiva as the result of his meditation and worship, will proceed from one heavenly place to another with a heavenly body and finally become absorbed in Śiva."[115] Thus there is a growth in Śivahood, an increasing participation in the functions of Śiva after the essence of Śiva has been obtained. The *jīva* gradually acquires a controlling power over *karma* and the existence in a *sūkṣma* form like Parameśvara, which enables him according to his desire to create any number of bodies simultaneously. After this the *mukta* will realize the state of lordship of speech and observation, of hearing and knowledge, which constitutes Śivapada in Mahākailāsa, to continue there for an endless time in the company of *muktas*. The liberated ones eventually become the all-pervasive supreme ether in which the highest brahman manifests itself. They lose all sense of difference between themselves and the Supreme: "Having realized the state of *sarvajñātva* (omniscience), having obtained a large part of the *mukta* world and being released from all *puṇya* (merit) and *pāpa* (sin), they see nothing except Mahādeva."[116]

So much for the doctrine of the Vīra-Śaivas. They are reformist in social matters: they work toward the abolition of caste differences and the development of the community. Today they are a well-organized and politically active community, concentrated mostly in Karṇātaka. They are open to economic and technical progress and are quite affluent.

ŚIVA IMAGES AND WORSHIP

Śiva worship has been associated with the people of the Indus Civilization. Besides the images on soap stone seals interpreted as Paśupati and Śiva the Hunter, many phallic emblems have been found. The *liṅga* has been the most universal form in which Śiva has been worshiped throughout the ages. In Vedic times Śiva-Rudra had been an apotropaic god: his name was not even to be mentioned in order to prevent him from coming, far less would people have wanted his image. The *liṅga*, now closely associated with Śaivism, had been an old symbol of fertility and immortality and was therefore planted on graves and cremation grounds. It is found not only among high cultures but also among tribal ones.[117]

From the third and second centuries B.C.E. we have indigenous coins with both phallic and anthropomorphic representations of Śiva. In later times the form of the *liṅga* becomes more stylized and less realistic, but there are exceptions. One of the earliest sculptures is the *liṅga* of Guḍimallam in South India, still worshiped by Śaivites and considered to date from the second century B.C.E. In the Gupta period so-called *mukhaliṅgas* become frequent: *liṅgas* whose top-portions show one or more heads, very often the famous Sadā-śiva combination of Sadyotjata, Vāmadeva, Aghora, Tatpuruṣa, and Iśāna, the Pañcabrahmaśivāvatāras of the *Śiva Purāṇa*. Though the artistic possibilities in representing the Śiva-*liṅga* are limited, its importance far surpasses that of any other form of Śiva representation. After the consecration (in case it is a human-made *liṅga*), it is considered to be the salvific presence of Śiva. The myth of *Śivaliṅgodbhava*, also represented in sculptures, in which Śiva in a human form comes out from the *liṅga*'s opening sides, is meant to underline the real presence of Śiva in his symbol.[118] The *Śaiva Purāṇas* contain many narrations of the salvific effect of the worship of the *liṅga*, which according to some, are the safest way to attain *mukti*. Śaivas today see in the Śiva-*liṅga* an "abstract image" of Śiva, that is, a symbol of Śiva's formlessness.[119]

The cult-image in the *garbha-gṛha* of Śiva temples is usually a Śiva-*liṅga*, not an anthropomorphic figure. Yet anthropomorphic images are important, as the great number and sublime art of many Śiva representations prove. A well-known system divides them into twenty-five *līlā-mūrtis*, perhaps in line with the twenty-five *tattvas* of Śaiva Siddhānta.[120]

Most of the Śiva images are of the *sthāna* and *āsana* type, either Śiva alone (Candraśekhara), or with Umā (Umāsahitā), or with Umā and Skanda (Somaskanda). *Śayaṇamūrtis* of Śiva are not known except in the Śiva-Sāva images which belong to the Śāktas.

Nandi, Śiva's *vāhana* and symbol, is often represented by himself, and sometimes Śiva and Pārvatī are shown seated on him. Kārttikeya, also a savior connected with Śiva, usually appears seated on a peacock. A local variety of Śiva worshiped in Mahārāṣhṭra is Kaithaba.

Among the anthropomorphic images of Śiva we can distinguish two basic types: *ugra* (*ghora*) and *saumya* (*śānta*) images. Both types are found in many forms. The *ugra-mūrtis* generally refer to one of the Śiva myths in which an enemy had to be destroyed by Śiva or one of his *avatāras*. Thus we find numerous Vīrabhadra images, Bhairava figures, and Aghora representations. Generally these figures are illustrations of the scenes described in the *Purāṇas*.

The *saumya*-representation of Śiva also has a twofold expression: one is Śiva standing with one hand showing the *abhaya-*, the other showing the *varadā-mudrā*. Śiva is thus savior from fear and death, and dispenser of grace and boons. The other kind of *saumya-mūrti* is the *dakṣiṇā-mūrti*: Śiva as teacher of various arts, of Yoga and of *mokṣa*.

Strictly speaking, Śiva Naṭarāja images belong to this group of *dakṣiṇā-mūrtis*. But because of their frequency and their peculiar position within Indian art, they deserve to be dealt with separately. Some of the *saṃhāra-mūrtis* also show movement that could easily be taken as dancing, but the Śiva Naṭarāja images proper have a philosophy of their own: they show Śiva's five main activities of *udbhava*, *sthiti*, *ādāna*, *tirobhāva*, and *anugraha*.

Although the South Indian Śaivites know Seven Dances of Śiva, the most important is usually the *ānānda tāṇḍava*. A Tamil text, the *Unmai ulakham*, thus explains the symbolism underlying the dance of Śiva: "Creation arises from the drum; protection proceeds from the hand of hope; from fire proceeds destruction; from the foot that is planted upon Mūyalahan proceeds the destruction of evil; the foot held aloft gives *mukti* ..."[121] The *tiruvasi* surrounding him symbolizes the act of obscuration (*tirobhāva*). There is another variety of Śiva Naṭarājas, especially in northern and northeastern India: Śiva with ten or twelve arms, dancing in deep ecstasy upon the back of Nandin. In course of time many details have been added to the representation of Śiva Naṭarāja, each of which was given some particular meaning in the context of salvation through Śiva's grace.

Śiva's smile shows his transcendence, his absence of involvement in the process of which he is the master; his dance is his *līlā*. The circle of flames within which he dances is the symbol of *saṃsāra*. His three eyes have been interpreted variously as sun, moon, and fire, or as the three *śaktis* of Śiva, *icchā*, *jñāna*, and *kriyā*. The crescent in his hair indicates his being *cit*. Śiva usually wears a garland of skulls around his neck, symbol of his being *kāla*, the Great Killer. The single skull which he is wearing in some images represents the skull of Brahmā: all the gods, from Brahmā downward, and all living beings are subject to death, Śiva alone is immortal. The snakes on his body are symbols of immortality: that their heads and ends are visible signifies that Śiva is the cause of the beginning and the end of the World. The Gaṅgā, the salvific purifying stream from heaven, passes through Śiva's matted hair; he is the dispenser of all salvation.[122]

Apart from this *ānanda tāṇḍava*, two other forms of Śiva's dance are found on images: *tripura tāṇḍava* representing in a symbolic way the destruction of the three *malas*, identified with the three demon-cities destroyed by Śiva. *Vyūrtha tāṇḍava* is also called *anugraha tāṇḍava*; it expresses the bestowing of grace by Śiva upon the devotee, and makes the soul ready to receive *mukti*. In images it is shown in such a way that Śiva raises one leg up to his head while he dances. "The supreme place, however, where Śiva performs his dance, as agreed by all Siddhāntins, is the heart of the devotee."[123]

In later times, after Śaiva systems had been developed, images have been produced which illustrate certain teachings of Śaiva sects: besides the Sadāśiva-images, with five faces and ten arms, we have Mahāsadāśiva-*mūrtis* with twenty-five faces, representing the twenty-five *tattvas*. In the Śiva *trimūrti* images the central face represents the blissful rest of supreme contemplation.

Worship of Śiva, recitation of certain names or hymns in honor of Śiva, rituals performed before his images are usually the only requirement to win Śiva's grace. Even inadvertently performed acts of worship can win *mokṣa*.[124] No wonder, then, that worship is the central feature of Śaiva religion. Though *mukti* is a gift of Śiva, Śiva will give *mukti* unfailingly as soon as he receives worship from one of his devotees. Lengthy portions of the Śaiva scriptures deal with Śiva worship in its different forms.

In Śiva worship the most prominent place is occupied by the *liṅga*, which is normally the only object found in the *garbha-gṛha*, the *Sanctum Sanctorum* of a Śiva temple. Śiva worship centers on the Śiva-*liṅga*. Śivarātrī, celebrated universally on the seventh day of Phalguṇa even by Vaiṣṇavas, is the most solemn and most universal ritual worship of the Śiva-*liṅga*. The legend that explains its origin is meant to inculcate the necessity and the merit of the worship of the *liṅga*. The hunter who inadvertently dropped some dewdrops upon the Śiva-*liṅga* obtained *mokṣa* from Śiva. Certainly those then, who with devotion consciously worship the *liṅga*, will obtain *mokṣa*.

There are various kinds of *liṅgas*, made from different materials: Śaiva scriptures explain in detail what merit accrues from the worship of each of them. Many chapters in the Śaiva scriptures deal with the worship of the *liṅga*: many more deal with various other forms of Śiva worship. The purpose of all is to obtain Śiva's grace and ultimately *mukti*.

Certain other objects that are considered sacred to Śiva are also conducive to salvation and are worshiped: thus, for example, *rudrākṣas*, *bhasma*, Bilva leaves, and others.

The Śaiva scriptures also speak of a Śiva-*bhakti* as a means to salvation: it consists largely in the performance of Śiva worship and the observance of certain modes of life. Śaivas also believe in the redemptive function of practices like Śiva-*śravaṇa*, Śiva-*kīrtaṇa*, Śiva-*manana*. Śiva-*japa* plays a large role in this context: the "five-syllable *mantra*," *Śivāya namaḥ*, is the most effective *mantra* and invokes *mukti*. The recitation of Śiva hymns, especially the *Śivasahasranāma*, is also an integral part of Śiva worship. To show its importance, the *Śaiva Purāṇas* state that these hymns had been recited by Viṣṇu and Brahmā and other gods who came to Śiva suppliantly. Merit of good deeds is also extolled by Śaivas.

Śaivism from very early times on has been connected with asceticism and with extreme practices.[125] Śaivism has produced many sects and religious orders, which have developed a great variety of practices, supposedly revealed by Śiva himself as necessary and conducive to salvation. Many of the epithets given to Śiva as early as in the *Śatarudriya* reflect practices of Śaiva ascetics: his deerskin dress, his matted hair, his wild dancing and laughing, his behaving like a madman, his besmearing the body with ashes, his living on cremation grounds. It is unclear whether Śiva received these attributes because groups of his worshipers followed such practices or whether his worshipers took up such practices, because they wanted to be "like Śiva."

Śaivism is linked up closely with *saṃnyāsa*. Śaiva scriptures devote many chapters to the description of *dīkṣā* and the life of a *saṃnyāsi*.[126] Śiva is called Mahāyogi and Maheśvara, and many images show Śiva in Yoga position. As to his becoming a *saṃnyāsi* there are several not very flattering stories, probably put into circulation by Vaiṣṇavas.

As Śiva has a *ghora* and a *saumya* aspect, so Śaiva *saṃnyāsis* are divided into *aghoras* and others, who follow the more pleasant features. Many *aghori saṃnyāsis* have revolting practices, imitating Rudra, the god of death and destruction, rather than Śiva.[127] The followers of the highest form of Śiva are the Daśanāmis, whose realization of the "nothingness" of relative existence does not lead them to identify themselves with the death aspect of reality but with pure Spirit.

As in mythology and philosophy, so also in ritual is Śaivism often inextricably connected with Śāktism: many rites practised by Śaivites and many forms of their worship contain tantric elements.

Purāṇic Śaivism opens the door to *mukti* to everyone who is prepared to worship Śiva: man and woman, *brahmin* and *caṇḍāla*, god and animal. But a good many Śaiva *saṃnyāsis* maintain that final liberation, especially in the form of final merging with Śiva, can be achieved only through *saṃnyāsa* in one of the Śaiva orders. Śaivites generally believe in the possibility of *jīvan-mukti*, liberation while still in this body.

Yogis are generally Śaivas. They worship Śiva both as Mahāyogi and the Māyīn. Among the Yogis there are many subsects with numerous rites. One of the most universally practiced rites is *prāṇāyāma*. One of the larger sects, the Kanphati Yogis, have their earlobes perforated and enlarged by heavy iron rings. In many images from rather early dates Śiva displays this type of perforated and enlarged earlobes.

Mādhava describes a Raseśvara-darśana whose followers had the very peculiar habit of taking mercury in order to obtain an immortal body.[128] The use of narcotics and stimulants is quite widespread among Śaivas even now, and many of the states of the *ugra* type of Śaiva-*sādhus* are induced by such drugs.

Between the sixth and the twelfth centuries C.E. South India, especially the land of the Tamils, became the home of a fervent Śiva *bhakti*. The collection of songs and poems called *Tirumurai*, organized into twelve books, contains thousands of fervent invocations of Śiva. K. Zvelebil, one of the foremost experts, calls it "not only an amazing literary and musical achievement and the embodiment of the religious experience of the entire Tamil nation, but also a tremendous moving force in the lives of the people of Tamilnad." These hymns "have played, since the very days they have been composed until the present time, an immense, indispensable and often decisive role in the religious, cultural and social life of the entire Tamil people." Zvelebil holds that "to a great extent the contemporary Tamil culture is still based on the *bhakti* movement."[129] Collectively the Śaiva *bhakti* poets became known as the sixty-three Nāyanārs, beginning with Campantar (also spelled Sambandar) in the sixth century and ending with Cekillar's twelfth-century *Periya Purāṇa*, described as "the crown of Śaivite literature." Only a few names can be mentioned here.

Tirumūlār aimed toward reconciling the *Vedas* and the *Āgamas*. "Becoming Śiva is Vedānta Siddhānta," he says.[130] He considers four forms of Śaivism: *śuddha* (a combination of Śaivism and Vedānta), *aśuddha* (only an application of external means without Vedānta), *mārga* (the so-called *sanmārga* consisting of *cārya*, *kriyā*, *yoga*, and *jñāna*), and *kadumśuddha* (no external rites but only direct meditation on Śiva). When the last stage is reached, the grace of God descends upon the *sādhaka* and by that he achieves *mukti*. Tirumūlār calls this *śakti-nipāta*.

Mānikkavācakar is the author of the famous *Tiru-vācakam*.[131] He suffered persecution from a non-Śaiva king and Śiva in person appeared to him as Māyin. He calls Śiva "brilliance," "nectar," "river of mercy," "inner light," Śiva is everywhere. "He also comes in the form of a *guru* to save the souls that pine to reach his state."[132] He sings: "O highest Truth, you came to the earth and revealed your feet to me and became the embodiment of grace." A good deal of the *Tiru-vācakam* is an ardent appeal to Śiva's grace.

Appar, who had been a Jaina and turned into an ardent foe of Jainism, became a martyr for Śiva's sake. He conceived Śiva as being beyond the twenty-five *tattvas*. He knows three forms of Śiva: Śiva, the destroyer of the universe; Śiva Parāpara (*paranjoti*), the unity of Śiva and Śakti; and Stambha, the pillar of light and consciousness, the ultimate goal of spiritual life.[133]

Campantar too had been fighting vehemently against the Jainas and Bauddhas, who were still quite strong in South India.[134] According to his teaching, Śiva, the highest god, is formless. Attainment of the state of Śiva is *mokṣa*. The soul should release itself from its *mala*. For this Śiva's grace is necessary. The most powerful means to reach it is the *pañcākṣara*. Thus he says: "The five letters are the final *mantra* through which one must reach Śiva. Worship Śiva with all your heart and you will be saved."

In later times, up to our own age, there have also been many Śaiva saints. Most of them were appropriated by one of the schools outlined above. However, it is one of the characteristics of many popular religious leaders ("Saints" in popular parlance) in today's India that they overcome the barriers through which traditional *saṃpradāyas* divided their followers against each other. Thus it is not uncommon to find someone from a Śaivite background also to use Vaiṣṇava, or even non-Hindu, scriptures and figures and to offer a non-sectarian teaching that knows no denominational boundaries. Thus Satya Sāī Bābā, one of the best-known religious personalities in today's India, who originally belonged to a Śaivite tradition, preaches a universal message of love and hope and dispenses his miraculous powers on behalf of anyone, regardless of sectarian affiliation.

CONTEMPORARY DEVELOPMENTS IN ŚAIVISM

The traditional expressions of Hinduism, including Śaivism, continue to be practiced by the vast majority of Indians today. Similarly, the theological training that is imparted to the future leaders of the various *saṃpradāyas* in the traditional schools (usually attached to major temples) is that of the medieval masters. Among the numerous Hindu temples built inside and outside India in the last few decades, there are also a large number of Śaiva sanctuaries, built in the traditional style. What is new is an attempt to express Śaivism in a Western idiom, to relate it to other religions and to modern scientific ways of thinking.

Christian missionaries, intrigued by the rich literary heritage of the Tamils, began translating Śaivite religious texts into Western languages and wrote monographs on it. Two names in particular stand out: George Uglow Pope (1820–1908), who spent many years as an educator in South India and became a well-respected scholar of Tamil. He translated the Tamil classics *Tirukkural* and *Tiruvācakam* into English. The other is Hilko Wiardo Schomerus (1879–1945) who wrote a monograph on the system of Śaiva Siddhānta and translated Śaivite hymns and legends into German. These missionary scholars found a large amount of agreement between Śaiva Siddhānta and Christianity. Following these pioneers, a fair number of Western scholars have focused their research on Śaivism. Some, like Alain Danielou or Stella Kramrisch, even took initiation from Śaivite gurus. Among the noteworthy major recent scholarly publications on Śaivism by Westerners in English are W. Doniger O'Flaherty's *Asceticism and Eroticism in the Mythology of Śiva* and S. Kramrisch's *In the Presence of Śiva*, a veritable encyclopedia of Śaivite mythology and theology.

Among the Hindu scholars with modern training, writing in English, a few names stand out: K. Śivaraman's *Śaivism in Philosophical Perspective* is a most thorough insider presentation of Śaiva Siddhānta. V. A. Devasenapathi's *Śaiva Siddhānta as Expounded in the Śivajñāna-siddhiyar and Its Six Commentaries* is an excellent source for further studies. Devasenapathi also founded and edited for many years the quarterly *Śaiva Siddhānta*, the official organ of the Śaiva Siddhānta Mahāsamajam (later called Śaiva Siddhānta Perumanran). In the 1980s a Department of Śaiva Siddhānta was established at the University of Madras, dedicated to the scholarly study of that school of thought.

A Śaiva Siddhānta mission was started around the turn of the century in the United States by Ponnambalam Ramanathan, a former Attorney

General of Sri Lanka, whose message was that God could be approached through any religion. A more specific Śaiva-siddhānta mission began in Australia in the sixties and has meanwhile spread to other countries. Its most prominent representative was probably Śivaya Subramuniyaswami, who founded and for many years edited the monthly *Hinduism Today*, established the "Himalayan Academy" in Hawaii, and produced numerous popular books on Śaivism.

NOTES

1. S. K. Chatterji ("Race Movements and Prehistoric Culture," in *HCIP*, vol. I, pp. 164ff.) thinks that Śiva is "at least partly of Dravidian origin." Tamil *sivan* (*chivan*) means red – to the early Āryans the divinity was known as *nīla-lohita*: "The Red one with Blue (Throat)" referring to the famous myth of Śiva drinking the poison. Śambhu, another common epithet of Śiva, he derives from Tamil *chempu* or *śembu*, meaning copper, i.e., "the red metal."
2. S. K. Chatterji, *HCIP*, vol. I, p. 165: "The phallic symbol of Śiva appears to be, both in its form and name, of Austric or Proto-Australoid origin. The Mon Khmer and the Kols set up right conical stones for religious purposes. These are reminiscent of the digging stick, which is used as a primitive plough. According to Jean Przyluski the words *liṅga*, *lokuṭa*, *laguḍa*, *laṅgula* are of Austric origin."
3. A. D. Pusalker, *HCIP*, vol. I, pp. 258ff.: The Śibis were intimately associated with the Usinaras. *Aitareya Brāhmaṇa* VIII, 23, 10 refers to Amitratapana, a King of the Śibis. *RV* X, 179 has been ascribed by the *Anukramāṇi* to Śibi Ausinara. The Greek authors refer to the Śibis as "Siboi." Cf. R. C. Majumdar, *The Classical Accounts of India*, p. 136 (Qu. Curtius Rufus), p. 174 (Diodorus Siculus): "(Alexander) ... landed his troops and led them against a people called the Siboi. These, it is said, were descended from the soldiers, who under Herakles, attacked the rock Aornus, and after falling to capture it were settled by him in this part of the country. Alexander encamped near their capital and thereupon the citizens who filled the highest offices came forth to meet him, and reminded him how they were connected by the ties of a common origin."
4. Malavan, Mala Pantaran, Kadar, Chenchu and other South Indian tribes invoke their Highest God as "Parama Śiva." Though they seem to have accepted Śaivism from the neighboring caste-Hindus they attribute certain features to Śiva, not otherwise connected with him: thus, for example, they consider Śiva to be the ancestor of the tribe, make him a forest deity, depict him as riding on horse or elephant, hunting; whosoever sees him, must die.
5. *Ṛgveda* VII, 21, 5; S. Chattopadhyaya, *Evolution of Theistic Sects*, p. 162 suggests that Ahirbudhnya may be a name of Śiva.
6. B. K. Ghosh, *HCIP*, vol. I, pp. 207ff.
7. R. Arbmann, *Rudra*: "In the oldest ritual texts care is taken not to mention directly the name of this terrible god, he is indirectly referred to

as 'this god' or 'the god whose name contains the word *bhūta* or *paśu*. In one case (*RV* II, 3, 1) the name was purposely pronounced different as Rudriya according to *Aitareya Brāhmaṇa* III, 3, 9ff."

8. V. M. Apte, in *HCIP*, vol. I, pp. 448ff.: "This Rudra is (in all probability) not merely a development of the Ṛgvedic Rudra, but an adaptation of him by amalgamation with a popular god."
9. *Atharvaveda* VII, 42 and XI, 2.
10. *Śatapatha Brāhmaṇa* I, 7, 3, 8 and V, 3, 3, 12.
11. Pāṇini *Aṣṭādhyayī* II, 387; R. Agravala, *India as known to Pāṇini*, pp. 358ff.
12. Ibid., p. 365.
13. Megasthenes was a Greek ambassador to the court of the Mauryas around 300 B.C.E. Cf. *HCIP*, vol. II, pp. 453ff.
14. Guṅaratna, a commentator on Haribhadra, specifies this statement saying that the Nāyaikas were Śaivas, the Vaiśeṣikas Pāśupatas. Also the followers of the Sāṁkhya and the Yoga systems were considered Śaivas.
15. There are some coins of Kadphises II with a Śiva image, the inscription calling Kadphises II Maheśvara. A king Gautamīputra Vindhyāvedhana received, according to a coin, his kingdom from Maheśvara and Mahāsena. His banner shows a bull. Cf. *HCIP*, vol. II, p. 177; 140; 150; 152; 455ff. According to D. C. Sircar, "The Sākta Pīṭhas," in *JRASB*, SIV, 1(1948), the *Śvetāśvatara Upaniṣad* is earlier than the *Bhagavadgītā* (third century B.C.E.). In it Śiva is identified with the Bhagavat Maheśvara in whose power are Māyā and Prakṛti. "Knowing Śiva, who is minuter than the minutest, the creator and protector of the universe, the one having many forms and the one alone encompassing the world and concealed in all beings, men become free from all fetters and attain eternal peace." Sircar further maintains: "The exceptionally large number of Indian rulers of all parts of the country in records dating from the first century A.D., the mention of ten generations of Pāśupata *ācāryas* in a Mathurā inscription of 381 A.D. and the evidence of the Epics and Purāṇas show beyond a doubt that Śiva's status at least in the early centuries of the Christian era was practially the same as it is today in the religious life of India" (p. 104).
16. *Mahābhārata*, Karṇaparvan (Critical Ed.) 24, 41ff; 24, 63.
17. *Matsya* and *Śiva Purāṇa* are ascribed to the Gupta period.
18. Kālidāsa's *Śakuntalā* opens with a beautiful hymn to Śiva in which eight forms of Śiva are mentioned: water, fire, sacrificer, sun, moon, ether, sound, earth. Similar *maṅgalas* in Śiva's honor are also found before *Mālavikāgnimitra* and *Vikramorvaśīya*.
19. S. Satchidanandam Pillai, "The Śaiva Saints of South India," in *CHI*, vol. IV, pp. 339ff.
20. *HCIP*, vol. IV, pp. 300ff.
21. Ibid. See also the interesting essay by Paul Hacker, "Śaṅkara der Yogin und Śaṅkara der Advaitin: Einige Beobachtungen," in *WZKS*, XII/XIII (1968), pp. 119–148.
22. *HCIP*, vol. V, pp. 442ff.

23. Ibid., I, 114; II, 33; VII, 46. Partly concerned with Rudra are: I, 43: V, 3; V, 42; VI, 74; VII, 59.
24. *Ṛgveda* X, 92, 9.
25. A. P. Karmarkar, *The Religions of India*, finds evidence for the solar character of Śiva-Rudra in the following texts:
    1. *Ṛgveda* I, 115, 1: Sūrya is the *ātman* of the universe
    2. *Atharva Veda* XI, 2, 4: Rudra is called thousand-eyed = Sun
    3. *Maitri Upaniṣad* VI, 7: "Bharga" is Rudra
    4. *Padma Purāṇa* V, 24, 687: Śiva is Sūrya; V, 20, 13: Sun is *rudravapuṣa*
    5. *Saura Purāṇa* II, 47: "Rudra stands in the skies"
    6. *Garuḍa Purāṇa*, Acāra Khaṇḍa 23, 6 mentions as a Śivamantra: *Śivasūryāyāḥ nāmaḥ*
    7. *Mahābhārata*, Sāntiparvan 290, 86: Śiva is addressed as sun

    The same author also thinks that Śiva had been originally worshiped under the form of a fish.
26. *Ṛgveda* I, 114. Here Rudra is addressed as *kapardin* and asked for health, bliss and well-being.
27. The *Śatarudriya* forms the 16th chapter of the *Yajurveda* according to the Vajasaneyasaṃhitā. English translation by J. Eggeling in *SBE*, vol. XLIII, *Śatapatha Brāhmaṇa*, vol. IV, pp. 150ff., and R. T. H. Griffith, *The Texts of the White Yajurveda*, pp. 168ff.
28. A. P. Karmarkar, *The Religions of India*, vol. I, p. 58.
29. J. Eggeling, *SBE*, vol. XLII, p. 150.
30. R. T. H. Griffith, *Hymns of the Yajurveda*, p. 168.
31. Ibid., v. 54.
32. Another major invocation of Rudra is found in *White Yajurveda* (Vajasaneya Saṃhitā) III, 57ff.; (Griffith, pp. 28ff.).
33. *Atharvaveda* V, 20.
34. Ibid., v. 21.
35. *Śatapatha Brāhmaṇa* IX, 1, 1, 6 (translation by J. Eggeling).
36. *Śatapatha Brāhmaṇa* I, 1, 1, 1. *Kauśītaki Brāhmaṇa* VI, 1–9: the eight names of Rudra (Bhava, Śarva, Paśupati, Ugra, Mahādeva, Rudra, Iśāna, Aṣaniḥ) are explained.
37. Ibid., V, 4, 4, 12.
38. *Aitareya Brāhmaṇa* III, 34, 7.
39. Ibid., I, 3, 9 and 10.
40. S. Radhakrishnan, *Indian Philosophy*, vol. I, p. 142 says that it is certain that the *Śvetāśvatara Upaniṣad* is post-Buddhistic; it is difficult to say whether it is pre-Christian too.
41. *Śvetāśvatara Upaniṣad* III, 1.
42. Ibid., V, 14.
43. A. Mahadeva Sastri (ed.), *The Śaiva Upaniṣads*, No. 3: *Atharvaśira Upaniṣad*, pp. 20–38. English translation by Srinivasa Ayangar, pp. 28–53.
44. The efficacy of the Tripundra is explained in *Kālāgnirudra Upaniṣad* (*Śaiva Upaniṣads*, No. 4): by applying the Tripuṇḍra on one's forehead illumination follows – without it, it is impossible.
45. *Vālmīki Rāmāyaṇa* I, 65, 9–12.

46. D. C. Sircar, *The Śākta Pīṭhas*, pp. 5ff. connects the Dakṣa story of the Epics and Purāṇas with the ancient myths of Prajāpati's incest with his daughter (*RV* X, 61, 57). According to *Śatapatha Brāhmaṇa* I, 7, 4, 1ff., Rudra pierced Prajāpati, identified with the sacrifice, with an arrow. The injured portion blinds Bhaga and knocks out the teeth of Puṣan – it is finally allotted to Rudra. In my paper "The Original Dakṣa Saga" (*Journal of South Asian Literature* XX/1, 1985, 93–107) I attempt to prove that the core of the Dakṣa myth consists of the record of the Śaivite conquest of Kaṇakhala, a *tīrtha* on the Ganges close to today's Hardwār. It was of great importance to Śaivites, Vaiṣṇavas and Śāktas alike, and linked to an important Vedic settlement associated with a famous patriarch Dakṣa.
47. *Mahābhārata*, Śāntiparvan, chap. 274 (Critical Ed.).
48. Critical Ed. XII, 274 takes only the first version into the text and brings the second one (interpolation) in Appendix I, 28 (vol. 16, pp. 2049ff.), Southern Recension. The editor remarks: this passage is substantially the same as *Vāyu Purāṇa* I, 30, 79ff. and *Brahma Purāṇa* 38–40.
49. In a former chapter (I, 30) it explains the mutual hatred of Dakṣa and Śiva.
50. *Vāyu Purāṇa* 30, 249.
51. This forms one of the most important topics in Śaiva-siddhānta. The *Nāyanārs* who dwelt at length on Śiva's love and grace were probably responsible for this emphasis on Śiva Nīlakaṇṭha as the merciful redeemer, whose vicarious suffering they celebrate.
52. *Vālmīki Rāmāyaṇa* I, 45, 20–26 (I, 44, 14ff. Critical Ed.).
53. *Mahābhārata*, Adiparvan, chap. 16.
54. *Viṣṇu Purāṇa* I, 9, 92ff.
55. *Bhāgavata Purāṇa* VIII, 7ff.
56. *Mahābhārata*, Karṇaparvan 24.
57. Ibid., v. 63.
58. Ibid., 34, 104 (Critical Ed., App. I, 4).
59. Ibid., 34, 115ff.
60. *Śiva Purāṇa*, Rudrasaṃhitā, Yuddhakhaṇḍa 44ff. Also Andhakavadha: *Matsya Purāṇa*, chap. 179.
61. *Śiva Purāṇa*, Rudrasaṃhitā, Yuddhakhaṇḍa 46.
62. Ibid., chaps. 26ff.
63. *Bhāgavata Purāṇa* X, 88: a rather wicked question is put at the beginning of the story: Parīkṣit wonders why the worshipers of Śiva are usually wealthy and enjoy life – while the worshipers of Viṣṇu are poor. Śuka's answer is that Śiva is endowed with the three *guṇas* and the "deity presiding over *ahaṁkāra*," whereas Viṣṇu is beyond *prakṛti*. Therefore the worshipers of Śiva acquire wealth – and those of Viṣṇu obtain transcendental Vaikuṇṭha.
64. *Śiva Purāṇa*, Rudrasaṃhitā, III, 18; *Liṅga Purāṇa* I, 101.
65. *Liṅga Purāṇa* I, 106.
66. *Śiva Purāṇa*, Rudrasaṃhitā, Pārvatīkhaṇḍa, 30.
67. A. K. Coomaraswamy, *The Dance of Śiva*, pp. 85ff.
68. *Mahābhārata*, Anuśāsanaparvan 14, 134ff.

69. *Mahābhārata*, Anuśāsanaparvan, 14, 140ff.
70. The text itself says explicitly so: every *avatāra* is located in one of the many *dvāpara-yugas*.
71. *Śiva Purāṇa*, Vāyavīyasaṃhitā defends both the Pāśupata (personalistic) viewpoint and the Vedāntic (a-personalistic) viewpoint.
72. S. Suryanarayana Sastri, "The Philosophy of Śaivism," in *CHI*, vol. III, pp. 387ff.
73. Text and English translation S. Radhakrishnan, *The Principal Upaniṣads*, pp. 707ff.
74. K.A. Nilakantha Sastri, "An Historical Sketch of Śaivism," in *CHI*, vol. IV, pp. 63ff.
75. T. M. P. Mahadevan, "Śaivism," in *HCIP*, vol. II, p. 453 refers to one inscription of C.E. 971 at the temple of Nātha near Ekaliṅga north of Udaipur.
76. *Śiva Purāṇa*, Rudrasaṃhitā, Sātīkhaṇḍa 23.
77. Mādhava, *Sarvadarśaṇasaṁgraha*, chap. VII. The most comprehensive modern treatment of Śaiva Siddhānta is found in K. Śivaraman, *Śaivism in Philosophical Perspective*, Benares: Motilal Banarsidass, 1973.
78. Cf. S. N. Dasgupta, *HIPh*, vol. V, pp. 10ff. fixes the date of Meykaṇḍadeva at *c.*1235 C.E. and that of Śrīkaṇṭha at 1270 C.E.
79. Ibid.
80. Ibid.
81. V. A. Devasenapathi, *Śaiva Siddhānta*, p. 192.
82. Ibid., p. 175: "Not acting according to the precepts of scriptures is sin; acting in accordance with the precepts of the scriptures but without being actuated by love for all beings is virtue. Hence both are to be treated as diseases. The Lord causes those who disobey the scriptures to be hurled into hell and removes their sins after they have been properly punished. By causing them to experience the joys of heaven he removes their virtues."
83. Ibid., p. 266 (quoting Jñānaprakāsar).
84. Ibid., p. 244.
85. Ibid., p. 249.
86. Ibid., p. 258.
87. Ibid., p. 259.
88. Ibid., p. 257.
89. Ibid., p. 274.
90. Ibid., p. 277.
91. Roma Chaudhuri, *The Doctrine of Śrīkaṇṭha*, and English translation of *Śrīkaṇṭha Bhāṣya*, 2 vols.
92. *Śrīkaṇṭha Bhāṣya* III, 3, 39.
93. Ibid., IV, 2, 14ff.
94. *Śrīkaṇṭha Bhāṣya* IV, 2, 16
95. Ibid., IV, 4, 1.
96. Ibid., quoting *Śvetāśvatara Upaniṣad*.
97. Ibid., p. IV, 4, 9.
98. Ibid., quoting *Śvetāśvatara Upaniṣad*
99. Ibid., IV, 4, 15.

100. Ibid., IV, 4, 22.
101. Ibid. End of the *bhāṣya*.
102. Jaideva Singh in his edition of *Pratyabhijñahṛdayam* (Delhi, 1963), mentions his Guru Lakṣamana Joo as "practically the sole surviving exponent of this system in Kāśmīr" (p. i).
103. Ibid., chap. 16. According to S. N. Dasgupta, *HIPh*, vol. V, p. 102 the sixteenth chapter of Kailāsasaṃhitā of this *Purāṇa* was written "somewhere about the ninth or tenth century C.E."
104. *Śiva Purāṇa*, Koṭirudrasaṃhitā, 41ff.
105. Ibid., 43.
106. Ibid.
107. Ibid., pp. 16ff. quoting Abhinavagupta *Tantrāloka* I, 192.
108. Ibid., quoted p. 21.
109. Ibid., *Sūtra* XX.
110. Sri Kumāraswami, "Vīraśaivism," in *CHI*, vol. IV, pp. 99ff. S. C. Nandimath, in *A Handbook of Vīraśaivism*, points out some interesting parallels between Buddhism and Vīraśaiva. The reforms of both are directed against orthodox Brahminism and both reject all Vedic rituals.
111. C. Hayavadana Rao, *The Śrīkara Bhāṣya*, 2 vols,. vol. I: Introduction; Vol. II: Text. Srīpati (*c.*1400 C.E.) is not accepted by all Vīraśaivas as an orthodox interpreter of Vīraśaivism.
112. Cf. *HICP*, vol. V, pp. 445ff. The final goal of the soul is *aikya* or unity with Paraśiva – the soul in union with Śiva enjoys unexcelled bliss: *liṅgāṅga-samrasya*; identity between *liṅga* (Śiva) and *aṅga* (soul).
113. Ibid.
114. Śrīpati, *Śrīkara Bhāṣya*, IV, 3, 9; cf. vol. I (Introduction), p. 575.
115. Ibid., IV, 4, 14; vol. I, p. 460.
116. Therefore those who are called *jīvas* at first finally develop into the *mukta* state by virtue of the *saddharma* of Mahādeva and will be afterwards called after Mahādeva . . ."
117. A. P Karmarkar, *The Religions of India*, vol. I, p. 88.
118. Cf. H. Zimmer, *Myths*, p. 130: "The Phenomenon of Expanding Form."
119. Swami Yatiswarananda, "A Glimpse into Hindu Religious Symbolism," in *CHI*, vol. IV, p. 437: to Śiva worshipers "the *liṅga* is just a non-anthropomorphic, aniconic form or symbol of the Supreme Spirit which, though manifest in forms, transcends them all."
120. Cf. T. A. G. Rao, *Iconography*, vol. II/II, pp. 369ff.
121. *HCIP*, vol. IV, p. 307; J. N. Banerjea, *Development*, p. 473. A. Coomaraswamy, *The Dance of Śiva*, p. 87.
122. V. Paranjoti, *Śaiva Siddhānta*, p. 54.
123. Ibid.
124. Thus, for example, the elephant, snake and spider at Kalahasti. N. Ramesan, *Temples and Legends of Andhra Pradesh*, pp. 70–79.
125. K. A. Nīlakantha Sastri, "An Historical Sketch of Śaivism," in *CHI*, vol. IV, p. 63: "Śaivism has exhibited a close alliance with Yoga and thaumaturgy, and a constant tendency to run into the extremes of ascetic fervour."

126. Almost the entire Kailāsasaṃhitā of *Śiva Purāṇa* deals with *saṃnyāsa* and its various stages; also *Skanda Purāṇa*, Kāśīkhaṇḍa I, 41ff.; *Liṅga Purāna* II, 21 (Śiva-*Dīkṣa*); *Śiva Purāṇa*, Vāyavīyasaṃhitā II, 15, 21. The ascetic element is emphasized also in the *Śaiva Upaniṣads*, beginning from *Śvetāśvatara Upaniṣad* in which *tapas* is said to be the only true means to reach *mokṣa*. The examples of Śaiva saints also show an emphasis on *tapas*.
127. G. S. Ghurye, *Indian Sādhus*, pp. 114–140; H. H. Wilson, *Religious Sects*, 131ff.
128. Ibid. They quote the *Taittirīya Upaniṣad* text "raso vai sa . . ." as being said of mercury!
129. Kamil Zvelebil, "Śaiva Bhakti", chap. 12 in *The Smile of Murugan. On Tamil Literature of South India*, Leiden: Brill, 1973. While Zvelebil deals here only with Śaivite Tamil *bhakti* poetry, he states that as far as the importance and vitality of this genre is concerned, the same can be said of the Vaiṣṇava hymns of the Āḷvārs.
130. T. M. P. Mahadevan, "Śaivism," in *HCIP*, vol. II, pp. 433ff.
131. G. U. Pope: *The Tiruvācagam*.
132. T. M. P. Mahadevan, "Śaivism," p. 434, Manikkavācakar is considered to be the embodiment of the *Cārya-mārga*.
133. Ibid., pp. 434ff. S. S. Pillai, "The Śaiva Saints," p. 341 (Appar is considered to be the embodiment of *Kriyā* or *Satputramārga*).
134. T. M. P. Mahadevan, "Śaivism." S. S. Pillai, "The Śaiva Saints," p. 341 (Sambandhar is seen as the embodiment of *yoga* or *Sahāmārga*).

7 A SHORT HISTORY OF ŚĀKTISM

"The later patriarchal religions and mythologies," wrote Erich Neumann in a richly documented study, *The Great Mother*,[1] "have accustomed us to look upon the male god as a creator . . . But the original, overlaid stratum knows of a female creative being." Neumann assumes for the whole region of the Mediterranean a universally adopted religion of the Great Mother Goddess around 4000 B.C.E., which was revived about 2000 B.C.E. and spread through the whole of the then known world. In this religion the Great Goddess was worshiped as creator, as Lady of men, beasts, and plants, as liberator and as symbol of transcendent spiritual transformation.

The Indus civilization also belonged to that tradition in which the cult of the Great Goddess was prominent. Numerous *terracotta* figurines have been found: images of the Mother Goddess of the same kind that are still worshiped in Indian villages today. Several representations on seals that appear connected with the worship of the Great Goddess also exist. On one of these we see a nude female figure lying upside down with outspread legs, a plant issuing from her womb. On the reverse there is a man with a sickle-shaped knife before a woman who raises her arms in supplication. "Obviously it depicts a human sacrifice to the Earth Goddess."[2]

The connections between Śāktism, Mohenjo-Daro civilization, and Mediterranean fertility cults seem to be preserved even in the name of the Great Mother: "Umā for her peculiar name, her association with a mountain and her mount, a lion, seems to be originally the same as the Babylonian Ummu or Umma, the Arcadian Ummi, the Dravidian

Umma, and the Skythian Ommo, which are all mother goddesses."[3] The name Durgā seems to be traceable to Truqas, a deity mentioned in the Lydian inscriptions of Asia Minor.[4] There is a common mythology of this Great Mother: she was the first being in existence, a Virgin. Spontaneously she conceived a son, who became her consort in divinity. With her son-consort she became the mother of the gods and all life. Therefore we find the Goddess being worshiped both as Virgin and Mother.

Another important current of Devī religion comes from indigenous village cults, "the most ancient form of Indian religion."[5] The worship of the *grāma-devatās* practiced today may not be much different from the village religion of thousands of years ago. The villager's world is inhabited by a host of spirits, good and bad, who are the causes of all unusual events. All catastrophes, diseases, epidemics, and so forth, are brought into connection with these spirits. In order to defend oneself against the evil spirits one has to propitiate and worship the good ones. It is quite revealing that the majority of village deities are female. "It is highly probable that the non-Āryan tribes (who worshiped the Great Mother, viz., Śabaras, Vāvaras, Pulindas, Kirātas and many others) had a matriarchal system of society and that it was due to this system that the custom of worshiping female deities grew among them."[6] The worship of these goddesses has always been connected with bloody sacrifices (of buffaloes, goats, pigs, and cocks), with partaking of meat and wine, with frantic revels and sexual excesses.

Human sacrifice too was generally connected with worship of the goddesses.[7] The Goddess of the aboriginal tribes and of primitive village religion was mainly worshiped to drive away evil spirits, wild beasts, and human enemies. But the Goddess was always the Mother of Life – saving children from diseases, granting cattle wealth, and providing mankind with vegetables. Village religion is earthy. In fact both its strength of feeling and its weakness of uncontrolled emotions must be traced back to this source: the worship of the Great Mother is nourished from the emotional depth of the unconscious, and its aim is always a return to the darkness of all-embracing matter in which nothing is divided or analyzed or distinguished.

Often the worship of deceased women of a village merges with the worship of the Goddess; the process of "making religion" by repeating what had been done for thousands of years still continues.[8] Many names of the Goddess that are found in the *Purāṇas* are probably names of such local village goddesses; many of the functions too are unmistakably taken from village religion.

The *Ṛgveda* sounds hostile toward the cult of the Mother Goddesses, and it took a long time before female deities came to rank as equal to the male gods. Durgā is mentioned as a war-goddess in the *Mahābhārata*. It seems that she superseded Indra in this function at a comparatively early time. The goddess of war played a great role in Tamiḷnādu. She was known as Ayai (Mother), Koṭṭavai (Victorious Mother), and Koṭṭi (Slaughterer) and was predominantly the goddess of the Maravār tribe. Among the hosts of dread figures in the battlefield the Goddess is the principal. She was worshiped by the Maravārs with offerings of toddy, fried rice, and the blood, marrow and entrails of the victims. Thus she became their protector, marching in terrible majesty at the head of their ranks. She is described as moving about the battlefield, with garlands of the entrails of victims on her person, dreadfully laughing at the sight of fallen enemies swimming in their blood. On her flag there is a lion.

That seems to be the same tribal goddess of war which is described in later Tamil works that celebrate the then-accepted cult of Devī:

> Shaking her giant shoulders and dancing to her own song of triumph in the battlefield in the presence of her son Murugan, with dishevelled hair and irregular teeth which adorn an abnormally large mouth, with eyes rolling through rage and with a frightful look, with ears having an owl and a snake as pendants and an awkward large belly, and with an awe-inspiring gait, while she picks out the eyes from a black stinking head, which she is in the act of eating, her mouth dripping with blood.[9]

Another direct allusion to the tribal goddess is offered in the following description:

> The maid of the aborigines, who had her matted hair tied up like a crow on her head, with the shining skin of a young cobra and the curved tusk of a boar fastened in her hair to resemble a crescent. She had a third eye on her forehead and her throat was darkened by drinking poison. A string of tiger's teeth was her necklace. The stripped skin of a tiger was wound round her waist as a garment. She had an elephant's skin as her mantle. A bow bent and ready to shoot was placed in her hand and she was mounted on a stage with branch and antlers. Drums rattled and pipes squeaked in front of her image while the fierce Maravar slaughtered buffaloes at her altar. Oblations with rice mixed with blood and flesh were offered to her, as also perfumed pastes and boiled beans and grain. Offerings of balls, dolls, peacocks and wild fowls were made to her."[10]

In Devī worship as it is practiced today there are, no doubt, elements of Vedic religion, as, for example, the worship of the earth-goddess Pṛthivī, but preeminently she is a deity of non-Vedic origin. Many of the Śākta deities of the *Purāṇas* and *Tantras* are modeled after the village and tribal goddesses, as, for example, the association of the two most important figures, the consorts of Śiva and Viṣṇu with Himālaya and Vindhyās, indicate. The *Mahābhārata* tells us that in early times female deities of different names and forms were worshiped in different parts of India by the followers of the *Vedas* as well as by various non-Āryan tribes. But Vedic religion as such was a patriarchal religion, and its development in the time of the ritual texts and the first systems, with its emphasis on punctilious fulfillment of an elaborate ritual, its insistence on self-control, and its rationality, ran counter to the mainstream of Devī worship, which consists in abandon and ecstasy.

In the Purāṇas an amalgamation of Vedic and non-Vedic religions took place. Significantly, none of the major Purāṇas gives the place of the Supreme Being to Devī. It is only in the Upapurāṇas that Devī is placed above the male gods.

It seems that Umā was the first non-Āryan deity to be regarded as the wife of a Vedic god. Though Umā, the mother goddess, and Durgā, the virgin goddess, were originally different, both became identified as consort of Śiva, since both were associated with the Himālayas. The Vaiṣṇavas then chose Vindhyavāsinī, the most prominent among the female deities of the Vindhya and connected her with Viṣṇu by taking her to be an incarnation of Viṣṇu's *yoga-nidrā* (mystical dream) or *yoga-māyā* (mystical magic power). The dual character of Devī as Virgin and as Mother (Spouse) is clearly discernible. Thus Devī, whether identified with Umā or with Vindhyavāsinī, is found to kill the demons in her virgin state. The earliest form of the Goddess seems to be the virgin who then becomes the Mother of the gods. In the latest phase of Śāktism the Goddess alone was made the Supreme Being, the source of everything.

In Śāktism proper the Great Goddess, *prakṛti* or *māyā*, becomes the active principle of the universe: without her activity the male God, Brahman, Śiva, or Viṣṇu, is unable to do anything. Śakti is all-pervading, the source of creation and of liberation. The aim of the *mantra-śāstras* is the development and discovery of the immanent Śakti, called Kuṇḍalinī. *Mukti* is achieved through a union of the activated Śakti, otherwise dormant in the *mūla-dhāra*, with the Highest Śiva also residing in the body. Without the union of Śakti and Śiva there is no emancipation; it is Śakti who is "the way" to Śiva, who is static and inactive.[11]

Devī in Śāktism is both metaphysical principle and concrete personality. As such she is worshiped under different forms and names, each denoting practically a different hypostasis of the Great Goddess. Sarasvatī, Lakṣmī, and Mahākālī are associated with Brahmā, Viṣṇu, and Śiva, and they appear for all practical purposes as three different deities. Śakti philosophy tried to explain them as manifestations of the three *guṇas* of the one Great Devī.[12] Another important set of titles of Devī is connected with various ages of Devī: thus she is worshiped as one year old under the title Sāndhyā, as two years old under the title of Sarasvatī; as Caṇḍikā she is supposed to be seven years of age, as Durgā or Bālā she is nine, as Gaurī she is a girl of ten, as Mahālakṣmī she is thirteen, and as Lalitā she is a virgin of sixteen years.[13]

There were certain centers of Śakti worship: it seems Kāmarūpa was the most important one.[14] Assam and Bengal are also today strongholds of Devī worship. Another important Śākta center in the Middle Ages was the Bundelkhand region in Central India. Several regions in western India, especially along the coastline, and particularly Kerala, were also important centers of Devī religion. In Tamilnāḍu, in Andhra Pradesh, and in Karṇātaka Devī worship is mostly confined to the worship of the *grāma-devatā*. Worship of the Goddess as the consort of Śiva or Viṣṇu is almost universal among Śaivas and Vaiṣṇavas, though there are remarkable differences. Thus, for example, the worship of Rādhā in some Vaiṣṇava sects comes close to Śāktism; Rādhā is said to be the origin of Kṛṣṇa's grace and that Kṛṣṇa does nothing without Rādhā.

Some of the great religious reformers of modern times came from a Śākta background: Ramakrishna Paramahamsa was a devotee of Kālī and officiated as her priest in Dakṣineśvara. But he took exception to the left-hand (vāmācāra) practices. Śrī Aurobindo Ghose also betrays the influence of Śākta background. Generally Śāktism is an important factor in contemporary Hinduism as a whole.

THE DEVELOPMENT OF DEVĪ MYTHOLOGY

The Goddess in the Veda

The hymns of the *Ṛgveda* are certainly not the mainspring of Śāktism. The prominence of Devī figurines in Mohenjo Daro and Harappa may be a corroboration of the assumption that the Indus civilization represents a late phase of Vedic culture. There are, nevertheless, a few elements in the *Ṛgveda* which are typical for the Devī religion of later times and which helped to make Śāktism acceptable to the followers of the Veda.

The most important of these elements seems to be the worship of *pṛthivī*, the earth as goddess. *Uṣas* (dawn) is called *devānām mātā* (mother of the gods) in one place, but she does not play any significant role in the further development of Śāktism. A more significant element can be seen in Aditi, "the Indian image of the Great Mother."[15] Aditi is the Earth, she is the Infinite, she is the Mother of the gods, she is "filled with splendour."[16]

The *Nirukta* says explicitly: "Aditi, unimpaired, mother of Gods. Aditi is heaven, Aditi is atmosphere, Aditi is mother, father and son. Aditi is all the gods, and the five tribes; Aditi is what is born and what shall be born."[17]

The most important Devī text of the *Ṛgveda* is the so-called Devīsūkta, in which Vāk (Speech) praises herself.[18] The hymn contains an astonishingly large number of allusions to traits of Devī which later become more developed: Vāk, as Goddess, is the mother of the gods, the giver of wealth, the queen. She is immanent in all beings and an all-pervading power, she is connected with Rudra and with battle, with the waters and with infinity. She brings forth the Father and is thus the Great Mother.

Though Rātrī is early understood as one of the names of Devī, the hymn to Rātrī in the *Ṛgveda* hardly contributes anything toward a deeper understanding of Devī: Rātrī is called Goddess, immortal, filling the void. Strangely enough Rātrī is also said to "conquer darkness with her light."[19] She is invoked for protection. The *Śatarudriya* mentions Ambikā as wife and sister of Rudra, perhaps an allusion to customs that prevailed in several ancient countries in which kings married their sisters.[20] *Taittirīya Brāhmaṇa* and *Taittirīya Āraṇyaka* mention Ambikā too in connection with Rudra, invoking her as Durgā, Vairocanī, Kātyāyanī, and Kanyākumārī.[21] She is already called Varadā, the giver of boons. Some early *Upaniṣads* mention Umā Haimavatī, associating the Goddess with the Himālayas.[22] S. Chattopadhyaya considers Devī in the Vedic age as a conglomerate of the wife of Rudra (the god of the mountains), the wife of Agni (showing the terrible, destructive aspect), and Nirṛti (the mother of all evils).[23] But as the *Devī-sūkta* proves, the Goddess seems to have been already in Vedic times a much more complex figure, clearly containing the aspect of universal, all-pervading power and infinity.

We have the testimony of Cosmas Indicopleustes, who visited India around 58 C.E., that in his time Kanyākumārī was worshiped in southern India, and we may infer that the virgin aspect of Devī was already present in Vedic times. From the Maurya age three markedly different types of seals connected with Śāktism are preserved. Seals found in northwestern India show the Mother Goddess united with the Father God. Those from eastern India show *yantras* and symbols of the *yoni*. Those from southern India show the Goddess as virgin. As the title Śakhāmbharī shows, Devī had at an early date been connected with vegetation. We have mentioned already a significant Indus Valley seal. Similar representations occur also in later times and even a custom practiced today in the villages at the time of Durgā-*pūjā* may express the same idea.

It is worth noting that there is no myth relating to Devī in the whole of Vedic literature, nothing, either, about her worship, which, as shown in fertility cults and in village religion, is usually connected with bloody sacrifices. The mainstream Devī religion clearly comes from sources other than Vedic.

The so-called Śākta Upaniṣads are of a very late period and cannot be considered as Vedic. They presuppose purāṇic Devī mythology and the fully developed systems of Sāṁkhya and Vedānta philosophy.

Devī in the Epics

In Vālmīki's *Ramāyāṇa* we can see the transition and gradual fusion of Vedic and *Purāṇic* ideas with regard to the Goddess: the Vedic element is still strong. Aditi plays a comparatively large role as "the mother of the gods," especially as the mother of Viṣṇu, the all-preserving.[24] She is described as one of the eight wives of Kaśyapa. The parallel to the Eight Mothers offers itself, though they are not mentioned by this name. All the eight wives of Kaśyapa become the mothers of a species of living beings. The *Ramāyāṇa* makes a distinction between these four "who obeyed Kaśyapa as true consorts" and the other four "who did not." Tāmrā becomes the mother of five daughters of "immortal fame" who in turn become the mothers of different species of living beings.

Krodhavasā has ten daughters who in their turn also become the mothers of various species. Analā becomes the mother of all fruit trees. Manū becomes the mother of all men: it is from her head that Brahmins spring, from her chest the Kṣatriyas, from her thighs the Vaiṣyas, and from her feet the Śūdras.

It seems evident that the background to this narration is a tradition of Devī as the Great Mother, and the eight mothers represent either various forms of the Great Mother or local goddesses. Almost certainly the five and ten goddesses who become the mothers of living beings other than gods are local goddesses brought into connection with the general system.

The rivers Gaṅgā and Yamunā play a prominent role in Vālmīki's *Rāmāyāṇa*, and they are frankly personified and made into goddesses.[25] To Gaṅgā is ascribed the power to give to dead men the bliss of heaven when she touches their bones, and the long narration of Gaṅgā's descent to earth has the solemnity of a salvation myth.[26]

Vālmīki knows Lakṣmī as consort of Viṣṇu, and Umā as consort of Śiva. Lakṣmī originates from the milk ocean when the gods churn it for amṛta – Umā is one of the daughters of King Himavat and Menā (the other is Gaṅgā). Toward the end of the *Rāmāyāṇa*, Sītā is declared identical with Lakṣmī. Of Umā, Valmīki reports a "long time passed in austere vows and rigid fast" before she got married to Rudra Immortal.[27]

The *Mahābhārata* knows Umā-Pārvatī, the daughter of King Himavat, as the wife of Śiva. In fact, one of the major narratives concerns the wedding of Pārvatī and Śiva. As such her role is not insignificant: she plays a major part in the wrecking of Dakṣa's sacrifice. On this occasion her manifestation Bhadrakālī is mentioned, who is neither Pārvatī herself nor Śiva himself. She is promulgating the "*dharma* for women" which she had extracted from Gaṅgā and other rivers.[28]

Whenever Mount Kailāsa, the residence of Śiva, is mentioned, Pārvatī also is remembered. She grants boons to Kṛṣṇa. And there is something of her *māyā* nature in the myth that she once playfully closed Śiva's eyes with her hands, whereupon darkness befell the world.[29]

There are several accounts of the Goddess in which her connection with Śiva is not mentioned or even presupposed. These reveal an ancient tradition in which the Goddess is connected with battle, death, and night. While describing one of the many cruel battle scenes the narrator includes without further introduction a vision of "Death-Night in her embodied form:"

> A black image, a bloody mouth and bloody eyes, wearing crimson garlands and smeared with crimson unguents, attired in a single piece of red cloth, with a noose in hand, and resembling an elderly lady, employed in chanting a dismal note and standing full before their eyes and about to lead away men and steeds and elephants all tied in a stout cord.

> She seemed to take away diverse kinds of spirits, with dishevelled hair and tied together in a cord as also many mighty car-warriors divested of their weapons.[30]

An interesting detail is added. The Pāṇḍava soldiers had seen in their dreams this dread figure of the Goddess every night since the beginning of their war with the Kurus: "The brave warriors of the Pāṇḍava camp, recollecting the sight they had seen in their dreams, identified it with what they now witnessed."[31] As companions on the battlefield are mentioned the Rākṣasas and Piśācas "gorging upon human flesh and quaffing the blood." Thus we learn: "They were fierce, tawny in hue, terrible, of adamantine teeth and dyed with blood. With matted locks on their heads ... endued with five feet and large stomachs. Their fingers were set backwards. Of harsh temper and ugly features, their voice was loud and terrible. They had rows of tinkling bells, tied to their bodies. Possessed of blue throats, they looked very frightful."[32] The Goddess has now become the deity of war and battleground: Indra, the youthful conqueror-god of the early Āryans is displaced by Durgā, the nightmarish embodiment of senseless murder.

Kṛṣṇa himself exhorts Arjuna to invoke Durgā on the eve of the mighty battle "for defeat of the foe."[33] It is not without significance that immediately preceding the *Bhagavadgītā* we find a Devī-*stotra* in the *Mahābhārata*. Durgā is the Goddess of defeat and of victory; probably this Durgā-hymn had been the original introduction for the narration of the *Mahābhārata* war and not the lengthy philosophical discussion between Kṛṣṇa and Arjuna.[34]

The *Stotra* does not appear as an improvisation for the situation. It looks like an established, well-known hymn for such occasions. Durgā is hymned as "identical with Brahman," "dwelling in the Mandara forest," "free from decrepitude and decay," "black and tawny," 'bringer of benefits to her devotees," Mahākālī, "wife of the universal destroyer," "rescuing from danger," "fierce," "giver of victory," "bearing a banner of peacock plumes," "bearing an awful spear," "holding a sword and shield," "born in the race of the cowherd Nanda," "always fond of buffalo blood," "dressed in yellow robes," "slayer of the *asuras* assuming the face of a wolf," "white in hue," "black in hue," "slayer of the *asura* Kaitabha," "yellow-eyed," "diverse-eyed," "grey-eyed." He implores her: "O great Goddess, let victory always be mine through your grace on the field of battle. In inaccessible regions where there is fear, in places of difficulty, in the abodes of your worshipers and in the nether regions you are at home. You always defeat the Dānavas. You are unconsciousness, sleep, illusion, modesty, beauty. You are twilight, day, Savitrī, mother. You are contentment, growth, light. It is you who supports the Sun and the Moon and who makes them shine." The recitation of the hymn wins an apparition of Durgā, "who is always graciously inclined towards humankind," and she promises victory to Arjuna.

There are promises attached to the *stotra*: "One who recites that hymn rising at dawn need not at any time fear Yakṣas, Rākṣasas, or Piśācas. He can have no enemies; he need not fear animals that have fangs and teeth, snakes as well as kings. He is sure to be victorious in all disputes and if bound he is freed from his bonds. He is sure to get over all difficulties, is freed from thieves, is ever victorious in battle and wins the goddess of prosperity for ever. With health and strength he lives for a hundred years."

A very similar Durgā-*stotra* as preparation for battle is recited by Yudhiṣṭhira.[35] But while the first one seems to imply a connection of Durgā with Śiva, the second one suggests an association of Devī with Viṣṇu, though all the characteristic features are in both cases the same – granting that the second hymn is shorter.

Devī is addressed as "the Divine Durgā, the Supreme Goddess of the Universe, born of the womb of Yaśodā, the giver of prosperity, the terrifier of Kaṃsa, the destroyer of *asuras*, who ascended the skies when dashes on a stony platform, the sister of Vasudeva, armed with sword, and shield, always rescuing the worshipers sunk in sin, the eternal giver of blessings."

The purpose of Yudhiṣṭhira's prayer is to obtain a vision of Devī. It is in this hymn that the Virgin Goddess is particularly invoked: "You who are identical with Kṛṣṇa, O maid, you who has observed the vow of *brahmacarya*." Whereas in the other Devī appearances her frightfulness and ugliness are emphasized, here her beauty and comeliness stand foremost. She is described as having four arms and four faces; or as having ten arms, carrying a vessel, a lotus, a bell, a noose, a bow, a discus, and other weapons. She is "the only female in the universe that possesses the attribute of purity." She has "sanctified the celestial regions by adopting the vow of perpetual virginity." She is the slayer of the Mahiṣa-*asura*, the protectress of the three worlds, the foremost of all deities. She is battle-victory. Her eternal abode is on the Vindhyā – "that foremost of mountains."

She is called Fame, Prosperity, Success, Steadiness, Wife, Offspring, Knowledge, Intellect, Twilight, Night, Sleep, Light, Beauty, Forgiveness, Mercy "and every other thing." She saves her devotees from ignorance, loss of children, loss of wealth, disease, death, and fear. Those are the ever-recurring evils from which Devī saves. Devī appears to Yudhiṣṭhira, promises victory, happiness, long life, beauty, and offspring. The promises of Devī are universal: "For those who invoke me in exile or in the city, in the midst of battle or of dangers from foes, in forests or in inaccessible deserts, in seas of mountain fastnesses, there is nothing that they will not obtain in this world."

Besides this Great Goddess the *Mahābhārata* mentions a great number of "mothers" in the company of Kārttikeya (Kumāra) – another war-god. After describing part of the frightful retinue of Kumāra we hear the names of the "illustrious mothers, the auspicious ones, by whom the mobile and immobile universe is pervaded."[36] It is more than probable that they represent a host of local goddesses, village deities with the same functions. Some of them also occur as names of the Great Goddess, and some seem to indicate a connection with certain localities. Most of them occur only in this place. Their appearance is manifold: "some of them partook of the nature of Yama, some of Rudra, some of Soma, some of Kubera, some of Varuṇa, some of Indra, and some of Agni, some of Vāyu, some of Kumāra, some of Brahman, some of Viṣṇu, some of Sūrya, some of Varāha. Of charming and delightful features, they were beautiful like the *asuras*." They are inconceivably strong and powerful. "They have their abodes on trees and open spots and crossings of four roads. They live also in caves and crematoriums, mountains and springs. Adorned with diverse kinds of ornaments, they wear diverse kinds of attire and speak diverse languages. These and many other tribes of mothers all capable of inspiring foes with dread, followed Kārttikeya at the command of the chief of the celestials."

The *Viṣṇu-parvan* of the *Harivaṃśa*[37] recounts with added details the myth, already alluded to in one of the Durgā-*stotras* of the *Mahābhārata*, in which Viṣṇu asks *nidrā-rūpinī* to become incarnate as the ninth child of Yaśodā at the same time as he would incarnate himself as the eighth child of Devakī. She would join him in heaven after being killed by Kaṃsa. Devī would be responsible for the destruction of the demons Śumbha and Niśumbha, and she would be worshiped with animal sacrifice. The *Harivaṃśa* contains also some brief Durgā-*stotras*[38] but on the whole it does not allot much space to Devī.

The epics do give testimony to a variegated and well-established tradition of Devī worship and the character of Devī as a savior from distress is also present, although her character is predominantly that of a goddess of death and war. It is the *Purāṇas* that depict Devī-religion in all its aspects and develop its philosophy and worship.

Devī in the Purāṇas

All Devī Purāṇas are Upa-Purāṇas of comparatively late date: the major ones are *Devī Purāṇa* (seventh century C.E.), *Kālikā Purāṇa* (*c.*1100 C.E.), *Devī Bhāgavata Purāṇa* (eleventh or twelfth century C.E.), and *Mahābhāgavata Purāṇa* (after twelfth century C.E.).[39] There are references to numerous other *Devī Purāṇas*, which are, however, lost.[40]

Though none of the Mahā Purāṇas are Śākta Purāṇas, several of them contain important sections concerning Devī.[41] Some of these sections may be later interpolations, but they have become integral parts of those Purāṇas, and very often the most popular ones.[42]

The same basic pattern which we have seen in the Epics is repeated in the Purāṇas: Devī is associated with Śiva as Pārvatī-Śakti, and with Viṣṇu as Lakṣmī-Rādhā. But more and more the tendency grows to consider Devī as the Supreme Being, the Mother of the Great Gods, as Prakṛti, and as all-pervading Śakti, who is responsible for bondage and for liberation. The innumerable names and titles given to Devī reveal a multitude of local goddesses who coalesced into the Great Goddess as conceived by the Śākta-theologians of later times. Some of these are personifications of abstract ideas or qualities ascribed to Devī. The *Purāṇas* also preserve the worship of the Mātṛkās, who are treated as different from the Great Goddess.

One of the favorite distinctions of the various forms of the Great Goddess is in "fierce" and "auspicious." However, all the "fierce" goddesses are at times "auspicious" and act as saviors, and all the "auspicious" goddesses can become hostile and "fierce" and destroy those who act as their enemies. It will not be possible, therefore, to construct a consistent and comprehensive Devī mythology; we have to be content with describing some of the individual goddesses and make some tentative generalizations. Even the Śākta Purāṇas, which try to universalize Devī and to make her the One Supreme Goddess, whose various forms and manifestations are locally worshiped, betray their origin and local background: the *Devī Bhāgavata* with its Rādhā mysticism points to a southern form of Devī worship; the *Kālikā Purāṇa*, on the other hand, with its emphasis on *yoni* worship and human sacrifice, reflects the form of Devī worship in Kāmarūpa, where it was written.[43]

It is worth noting that the Devī religion of the Purāṇas consists more of hymns and rituals than of myths, an indication perhaps of the time in which it developed. As regards the myths, they are very often occupied with the origin of the Goddess, a motif completely absent from Vaiṣṇava and Śaiva mythology in which it is always presupposed that Viṣṇu or Śiva have existed from eternity. The entirely different myths concerning the origin of the Goddess again reflect various Devī traditions. Umā-Pārvatī is the daughter of King Himavat and Menā. Sātī is the daughter of Dakṣa. Lakṣmī owes her origin to the gods' churning of the milk ocean. In another version she is the ninth child of Yaśodā.

The *Devīmāhātmya*[44] refers to two different traditions regarding the origin of the Great Goddess: in the first Devī is explained as the Mahānidrā of Viṣṇu embodied as the universe, eternal, incarnated in many forms. She is "drawing herself out from the eyes and the various organs and limbs" of Viṣṇu: when "Great Sleep" leaves Viṣṇu, he awakens. In this form she is the great creator: she creates the entire universe, she is the cause of bondage and transmigration, the cause of final liberation too. She is both fierce and auspicious: she gives to mankind boons for their final liberation.

The second account of Devī's origin has a different ring and seems to be the older one. It not only mentions the Vedic gods but is somewhat reminiscent of the Indra-Vṛtra myth – the fight of the High God against the demon usurper, who has conquered the gods and assumed the place of Indra. Devī here is no longer the *prakṛti* of Viṣṇu but the essence of all the gods, "godhead" in a concrete sense. She surpasses all the individual gods in power and glory because in her all the qualities of the gods are embodied.

Various other Devīs originate from the existing Devī: thus Kauśikī comes out of the body of Pārvatī, Kālī issues from the forehead of Kauśikī, out of Cāmuṇḍā comes Caṇḍikā: all of them act then as individually different Devīs, as the Mātṛkās.

Devī Mahiṣamārdiṇī

The most prominent myth connected with Devī is her killing of the buffalo demon. It is narrated in several *Purāṇas*[45] with significant differences, and even in village religion it seems to feature prominently.[46]

It may in fact constitute an ancient myth connected with an ancient ritual.

The *Mārkaṇḍeya Purāṇa* reports how for a hundred years *devas* and *asuras* fought against one another. The *devas* were defeated and Mahiṣa-asura became the lord of heaven. The gods approached Śiva and Viṣṇu for help. Out of the anger of Śiva, Viṣṇu, and the other gods, Devī was born, "a concentration of light like a mountain blazing excessively, pervading all the quarters with its flames."[47] She received the combination of the essence of all the weapons the gods possess. Several other objects are mentioned that have their importance in Devī worship: bell, noose, string of beads, waterpot, sword, shield, necklace, crest-jewel, ear-rings, axe, lotus, lion, drinking cup filled with wine, and so forth. Specially mentioned is her "loud roar with a defying laugh." This roaring laughter of Devī terrified earth and sky. This roar is also the sign of the beginning of the battle between Devī and Mahiṣāsura. Both Devī and her lion are important for the battle; all the different weapons that she received help her to kill thousands of the demons that follow Mahiṣāsura. Before Mahiṣāsura falls, all the demon-generals, whose names are mentioned, are killed by Devī:

> Mahiṣāsura terrified the troops of the Devī with his own buffalo-form: some he killed by a blow of his muzzle, some by stamping with his hooves, some by the lashes of his tail, and others by the pokes of his horns, some by his speed, some by his bellowing and wheeling movement, some by the blast of his breath. Having laid low her army Mahiṣāsura rushed to slay the lion of Mahādevī. This enraged Ambikā. Mahiṣāsura, great in valour, pounded the surface of the earth with his hooves in rage, tossed up high mountains with his horns, and bellowed terribly. Crushed by the force of his wheeling, the earth disintegrated, and lashed by his tail the sea overflowed all around. Pierced by his swaying horns the clouds went into fragments. Cast up by the blast of his breath, mountains fell down from the sky in hundreds.[48]

This description of the evil incorporated in Mahiṣāsura provides the background for appreciating the great salvific deed of Devī, who saved the universe from this destruction.

First Devī uses the noose to capture Mahiṣāsura. He sheds his buffalo form. Devī uses her sword to cut down the lion form that he assumes. Then the demon assumes the form of a man with sword. Devī assails him with bow and arrows. The demon assumes an elephant form, and Devī cuts him down with the sword. Finally the demon resumes his buffalo form. In this form the final battle takes place: "Enraged, Caṇḍikā, the Mother of the worlds, quaffed a divine drink again and again and laughed, her eyes becoming red."[49] In this form she finally kills Mahiṣāsura in his buffalo form, pressing his neck with her foot and striking him with her spear, finally cutting off his head with her sword.

Thus the salvation of gods and men has been accomplished, and Devī receives praise from all the *devas*. In the course of this prayer all the essential qualities of Devī are mentioned, and the basic Devī philosophy comes to the fore: Devī is "the origin of the universe, the resort of all, the primordial *prakṛti*." She is the "supreme *vidyā* which is the cause of liberation." She is "*durgā*, the boat that carries men across the difficult ocean of worldly existence," she is "Śrī who has taken her abode in the heart of Viṣṇu," and she is "Gaurī, who has established herself with Śiva." Devī offers a boon, and the *devas* choose the following: "Whenever we think of you again, destroy our direst calamities." This feat of Mahiṣamārdinī is repeated in all ages; again and again Devī proves to be savior of gods and men by killing the demons. The *Devī Bhāgavata Purāṇa*[50] devotes a long section to the same theme adding many significant details. Thus before the fight with the *asuras* Indra approaches Viṣṇu and Śiva and Brahmā for help. They decide to fight against Mahiṣāsura and his generals, but, unable to defeat him, they return to their abodes. Only then does Devī come into existence, produced from the combined power and wrath of the gods. Mahiṣāsura first sends his messengers. In the discussions between Mahiṣāsura's ambassadors and Devī she herself explains her nature, her function, and her origin. Mahiṣa repeatedly proposes marriage to Devī, but the enraged Devī only curses him. Devī first kills the messengers of Mahiṣa: Vaskala, Durmukha, Cikṣurakhya, Tamrāksa, Asiloma, Vidalakṣa – and finally kills Mahiṣāsura himself. It is worth noting that there is no mention of the "buffalo-form" of the *asura*, nor of any changes of form. Devī is described as having eighteen arms all equipped with various weapons and instruments. After Mahiṣa has been killed the *devas* praise Devī, the "mother of gods." Devī promises to help the gods in all their troubles in the future.

It is also noteworthy that, after having killed Mahiśāsura, Devī withdraws to Maṇidvīpa, "her own abode," situated in the Ocean-of-Nectar where Devī as *māyā-śakti* is ever sporting in different forms.[51] This may be the explanation of the various forms of the origin of Devī: because she resides in the Ocean-of-Nectar she emerges out from the churned ocean, and in one manifestation she is formed by the energy of the gods.

Devī Kills Various Other Demons

Devī Mahiṣamārdiṇī sets the pattern for the description of many other battles in which Devī kills demons who have terrorized gods and men. A story very similar to that of Mahiśāsura is connected with the names of Śumbha and Niśumbha,[52] two demons who had deprived Indra of his sovereignty and his share in sacrifice. They had also usurped the powers of Sun, Moon, Kubera, Yama, Varuṇa, Vāyu, and Agni. This time the *devas*, remembering the boon granted by Devī on the former occasion, go straight to Devī for help. The praises uttered on this occasion are centered on the "Devī who abides in all beings" as consciousness, as intelligence, as sleep, as hunger, as reflection, as power, as thirst, as forgiveness, as genus, as peace, as faith, as error, as mother.[53] The *Mārkaṇḍeya Purāṇa* combines with this story the episode of the demon's wooing of Devī, to become his wife: solicited by his servants Caṇḍa and Muṇḍa, he sends Sugrīva as a go-between. Devī accepts the offer on one condition: she will marry the man who defeats her in battle.[54] Śumbha dispatches Dhūmralocana, the general of the *asura* army, to defeat Devī and bring her with him. With the sound *hum* Aṃbikā burns Dhūmralocana to ashes. The lion upon which Devī rides destroys the *asura* army. The *asura* king then dispatches Caṇḍa and Muṇḍa to bind and carry off Aṃbikā. As soon as these come near to seize her, "Kālī of terrible countenance, armed with sword and noose, bearing a strange skull-topped staff, decorated with a garland of skulls, clad in a tiger's skin, very appalling owing to her emaciated flesh, with gaping mouth, fearful with her tongue lolling out, having deep-sunk reddish eyes, and filling the regions of the sky with her roars, and impetuously falling upon slaughtering the great *asuras*," issues out of the forehead of Aṃbikā, who herself remains "smiling gently seated upon a lion on a huge golden peak of the great mountain."[55] Kālī now cruelly kills the men and animals of the *asura* army. It is the same goddess of war we had met in the *Mahābhārata*. Kālī severs the heads of Caṇḍa and Muṇḍa and brings them to Caṇḍikā "as two great animal offerings in this sacrifice of battle." The final victory over Śumbha and Niśumbha is reserved to Caṇḍikā herself. Caṇḍikā promotes Kālī to the position of Camuṇḍā. That is the sign for Śumbha to mobilize the entire *asura* army: "Seeing that most terrible army coming, Caṇḍikā filled the space between the earth and the sky with the twang of her bow-string. Her lion made an exceedingly loud roar and Aṃbikā magnified these roars with the clanging of her bell. Kālī, expanding her mouth wide and filling the quarters with the sound *hum*, overwhelmed the noises of the bow-string, lion and bell by her terrific roars."[56]

This triad of Aṃbikā, lion, and Kālī is joined by the Śaktis from the bodies of Brahmā, Śiva, Guha, Viṣṇu, and Indra – each with the attributes and *vāhana* of the god from which she issued. From the body of Devī also a Śakti issues: "Caṇḍikā, most terrific, exceedingly fierce and yelling like a hundred jackals."[57] Śiva is sent by Śakti as ambassador to Śumbha and Niśumbha to offer the netherworld to them provided they return the Trilokas and the oblations to the gods. Each of the Śaktis helps in overpowering the *asuras*: Kālī pierces the enemies with her spear and crushes their skulls with her staff. Brahmāṇī robs them of their valor by sprinkling her water. Maheśvarī slays *asuras* with her trident, Vaiṣṇavī with the discus, Kaumārī with the javelin. Aindrī destroys *asuras* with the thunderbolt, Varāhī tears their breasts open with her tusks, Nārasiṃhī claws and devours them. "Dazed by the violent laughter of Śivadūtī the *asuras* fell down on earth – she then devoured them who had fallen down."

The *asura* army fled. One Raktabīja, however, advanced: whenever a drop of Raktabīja's blood fell to the earth, another *asura* of his stature would rise. These battled the Mātṛs. "And those *asuras* that were born from the blood of Raktabīja pervaded the whole world; the *devas* became intensely alarmed at this."[58] Devī orders Cāmuṇḍā to drink the blood of the *asura* before it falls to earth and to devour the *asuras* that have come already into existence. Finally Devī kills him. Then Śumbha and Niśumbha advance in rage to kill Devī and the lion. Devī intercepts the weapons hurled against her with her own weapons. Śumbha is knocked down by the ax of Devī. Before Niśumbha falls under Devī's trident Devī blows her conch, twangs her bowstring, and fills the four quarters with the sound of her bell. Her lion fills earth and sky with his roar, Kālī produces an enormous noise by striking the earth with both hands, Śivadūtī gives vent to terrible laughter. After Niśumbha is struck by Devī's trident he regains consciousness, resumes fighting, is pierced by Devī's arrow and another demon issues out from him whose head the Devī laughingly severs.

Another interesting feature of Devī philosophy is interwoven with the final killing of Śumbha: the demon challenges Devī by declaring that she is not fighting on her own but resorts to the strength of others. In order to show that she is alone in the world, she reabsorbs all those Śaktis who previously had been fighting separately. A fierce battle follows in which the Devī destroys the weapons of the *asura* by shouting the *mantra hum*. The fight is carried on not only on earth, but also in the sky. Finally Devī pierces Śumbha with a dart through the chest and throws him to the earth, which shakes at the fall. The result of this salvation wrought by Devī becomes apparent in universal relief: "When that evil-natured was slain, the universe became happy and regained perfect peace and the sky grew clear."[59]

The classical symptoms of salvation are enumerated here. The *devas* who are reinstated in their positions praise Devī as saviour. She is addressed as the "cause of final emancipation," as "the bestower of enjoyment and liberation," as "intent on saving the dejected and distressed that take refuge with her," as the one "who removes all sufferings," as the one "who possesses the benevolence of saving the three worlds," as "the one who took away the life of Vṛtra," and as "the one who frees from all fear and from all evils."[60]

Devī promises, to those who worship her, protection and the destruction of future demons: in the twenty-eighth Manvantara under Vaivasvata Manu, Śumbha and Niśumbha will be born again – the Devī promises to destroy them as Vindhyavāsinī, born of Yaśodā. The *dānavas*, descendants of Vipracitti, will be slain by her in an Atirudra form. She will then be called Raktadantā, because her teeth will become red from their blood. At the time of a drought of one hundred years Devī will be born of the *munis* "but not womb-begotten" as the Śatākṣī; maintaining the world with life-sustaining vegetables born of her own body she will be known as Śākambharī. She will slay the *asura* Durgama and will therefore be known as Durgādevī. She will slay the *rākṣasas* in the Himālayas for the protection of the *munis* and will be known as Bhīmadevī. As Bhrāmaradevī she will kill the *asura* Aruṇa "for the good of the three worlds."

Devī makes promises to those devotees who recite the above-mentioned hymns, and who remember her deeds. Those who observe the Devī-*vrata* on the eighth, ninth, and fourteenth *tithi* "shall not experience anything wrong, robbers or kings, of weapons, fire and flood."[61] Devī promises never to forsake a place where her praises are sung. The blessings which are connected with Devī's salvation are: enemies perish, welfare accrues, evil portents subside, the unfavorable influence of planets vanishes, a bad dream is turned into a good dream; it frees children from seizures, promotes friendship, destroys demons, goblins and ogres:

> The chanting and hearing of the story of my manifestations remove sins, and grant perfect health and protect one from evil spirits . . . He who is on a lonely spot in a forest, or is surrounded by forest fire, or who is surrounded by robbers in a desolate spot, or who is captured by enemies, or pursued by a lion, or tiger, or by wild elephants in a forest, or who under the orders of a wrathful king is sentenced to death, or has been imprisoned, or who is tossed about in his boat by a tempest in the vast sea, or who is in the most terrible battle under a shower of weapons, or who is amidst all kinds of dreadful troubles, or afflicted with pain – such a person, on remembering this my story, will be saved from his straits.[62]

Very similar are the myths told in other Upa-Purāṇas concerning Devī killing demons – often the same ones as in the *Mārkaṇḍeya Purāṇa*. The greatest number of such accounts naturally occurs in the *Devī-Bhāgavata Purāṇa*. It describes at length how Devī kills Madhu and Kaiṭabha, Yudhajit and Śatrujit, how a war between Devas and Daityas is decided in favor of the Devas by Devī's intervention; how Kṛṣṇa's salvation from Kaṃsa's sword is ascribed to the intervention of Devī Yogamāyā; how Devī kills Dhumralocana, Raktabīja, Śumbha, and Niśumbha, Taraka-Asura; and how Devī as Bhrāmarī again saves the gods from the Daityas.

In the *Devī Purāṇa* the fight between the demon king Ghora and Devī figures prominently. In connection with this myth the killing of various other demons like Durmukha, Kala, Bhairava, Suṣena, and others by various attendants of Devī is narrated. Finally, Devī kills Ghora, who is no other than Mahiṣa. The gods praise the goddess and offer buffaloes and he-goats to her.

An interesting feature occurs in the *Mahābhāgavata Purāṇa* that connects the Rāma-Sītā story with Devī. Otherwise it contains no myth of Devī killing the *asuras*.

The *Kālikā Purāṇa* is also remarkably devoid of such myths. The *Śiva Purāṇa* narrates in the *Umāsaṃhitā* how Devī killed Dhumralocana, Caṇḍa and Muṇḍa, and Raktabīja. She is also described as savior under the title of Śatakyā. In the *Rudrasaṃhitā* she is described as killing two otherwise invincible demons, Vidala and Utpala. The *Kāśīkhaṇḍha* of the *Skanda Purāṇa* contains an account of Devī battling with *asuras*.

The Various Forms and Manifestations of Devī

It is quite impossible to bring all the different names and forms of Devī occurring in the Purāṇas into one system. The Purāṇas make several attempts to classify the Devīs but succeed finally only in pointing out that all the innumerable forms are but manifestations of the One Supreme Goddess. In fact, the various names are by and large merely local varieties of the goddess: one text in the *Devī Purāṇa* clearly states that Devī is worshiped as Maṅgalā in the region between Vindhyas and Malayās, as Jayantī in the coastal area between Vindhyas and Kurukṣetra, as Nandā between Kurukṣetra and Himālayas, as Kālikā, Tārā and Umā in the mountains, as Bhairavī in Jalandhara, as Mahālakṣmī in the Kola mountain, as Kāla-rātrī in the Sakyā mountains, as Aṃbā in Candhamadana, as Ujjainī in Ujjayani, and as Bhadrakālī in Videha.[63]

Another attempt to systematize the goddesses seeks to connect one goddess with each of the main deities: each of these goddesses having again many subforms. Analogously to Viṣṇu (and Śiva) *avatāras*, Śāktism has also developed a theory of Devī-*avatāras*: manifestations of Devī at different ages for various deeds.[64]

Another division is given by the association of Devī with the main functions of creation, preservation, and destruction of the universe, and with the division into three *guṇas*.

The Mātṛkās are usually a class apart, though there are also instances where they are considered as various forms or emanations of Devī.[65] The different forms of Devī appear on various occasions and they are described in several Purāṇas; though their number is very great they tend to repeat a basic pattern, apart from certain peculiarities expressed in their name.

The *Kālikā Purāṇa* has a peculiar system of differentiating the Goddess according to the different parts of her body.[66]

The *Devī-Bhāgavata Purāṇa* has the most numerous descriptions of forms of Devī: it knows a *virāṭ-rūpa* of Devī;[67] it describes at great length stories connected with Durgā, Śatākṣī, Śākāmbharī, Mahāgaurī, Mahālakṣmī, Siddhapīṭha-Śakti, Kālikā, and Jagadambarī; it has chapters on the Bhāgavatīs, i.e., Bhuvaneśvarī, Mahālakṣmī, Lakṣmī, Svahā and Svadhā, Dakṣinā, Puṣṭī, Maṅgalacaṇḍī, Manasādevī, Śurabhīdevī, Rādhā and Durgā.[68]

Devī-*avatāras* are also found in the Purāṇas. They have the same function which Vaiṣṇavas ascribe to Viṣṇu-*avatāras*, namely to protect the world in successive ages from demons and other evil. This theory also helps to explain the numerous goddesses as manifestations of One Supreme Goddess: "Bhāvanī is worshiped by the gods in all her repeated incarnations. She always kills demons by incarnating herself on earth and she protects all creation in heaven, earth and the nether world.

This Mahādevī was again born from the womb of Yaśodā and killed the demon Kaṃsa by placing her foot on his head. From that time on people on earth have installed this 'giver-of-joy-to-Yaśodā' on the Vindhya mountain and re-introduced her worship."[69]

In connection with *tīrthas* and feasts sacred to Devī, many more goddesses are named in the Purāṇas. In these Devī also functions as teacher of the way of salvation: Devī teaches *jñāna* to various gods, including Indra. She explains her own nature according to Advaita: "I and Brahman are one."[70]

Various forms of Devī are explained as a hypostatical union between several goddesses or of a god and a goddess.

In large sections of the Śākta Purāṇas the influence of Tantricism is very noticeable, so much so that without an understanding of the Tantric idea of the goddess the *Purāṇa* account remains incomplete.

Devī in the Tantras[71]

It is in the Tantras that the Goddess comes to occupy the supreme place: according to the Tantras, Brahman, being neuter and incapable of creation, produced Śiva and Śakti. Śakti is the cause of liberation, Śiva the cause of bondage. There is a large number of texts which bear the title *Tantras*.[72] Besides those, Tantric doctrines are professed also in many other books, including the Purāṇas. Tantricism is not restricted to Hinduism only: there is also a Buddhist Tantric tradition. Possibly the development of Hindu Tantricism during the tenth to the twelfth centuries is due to Buddhist Mahāyāna cults, especially those connected with the goddess Tārā.[73] This association shows already an intense affiliation with the idea of salvation: Tārā, the personification of Buddha's kindness, is the means to salvation. And that exactly is the purpose of Tantric religion, as explained in several Tantras: since all the other means to salvation practiced by people in former times have become inaccessible due to circumstances, only the Tantra way, the worship of the Goddess, can help people to attain salvation in the *kali-yuga*.[74]

Tāntrikas distinguish three *bhāvas* or *mārgas* (paths): *paśu-*, *vīra-*, and *divya-mārga*. The first consists of four *ācāras* (ways of behaviour): *Veda-ācāra*, *Vaiṣṇava-ācāra*, *Śaiva-ācāra*, and *Dakṣiṇa-ācāra*. The second path consists of two *ācāras*: *Vāma-ācāra* and *Siddhānta-ācāra*. The third consists of only one *ācāra*: *Kaulācāra*, which constitutes the highest perfection of a Tāntrika.[75]

The first three of these *ācāras* are practically identical with practices that are found among the non-Tāntrikas: *Veda-ācāra* consists of external worship of the common type; *Vaiṣṇava-ācāra* consists of devotion to Viṣṇu; *Śaiva-ācāra* consists of meditation on Śiva. From *Dakṣina-ācāra* onward the *ācāras* represent the typical Śākta-Tantra forms of worship.

Dakṣiṇa-ācāra consists of worshiping the Devī as the Supreme Goddess with Vaidic rites and rituals. At daytime a Dakṣinācāri will perform his duties as enjoined by the Vedas: at night he will practice *japa* with a name of the Goddess on the *mahāsakha-mālā*.[76]

Vāma-ācāra ("left-hand mode") consists of the "worship with *cakras*" or "secret rites": in these the *pañca tattvas* or *pañca makāras* – *maṃsa*, *matsya*, *mudrā*, *mada*, *maithuna* – play a great role.[77] It "requires proper training at the hands of a *guru* and the acquisition of the necessary courage to disregard social conventions about sexual purity, to defy taboos about food and drink, and to look upon all women as manifestations of Śakti and all males as representatives of Śiva."[78]

The next stage is *Siddhānta-ācāra* in which the Vāma-ācāra practices are no longer kept secret: "the *sādhaka* ... is not afraid of following socially disapproved practices openly. He is relentless in the pursuit of what he thinks to be true ... there is nothing that cannot be purified by the appropriate means."[79] The *pañca makāras* are the means to eliminate all conventional judgments and all distinctions of pure and impure, and to attain complete freedom. The highest stage is reached with *kulācāra*, the *divya-bhāva*: "The aspirant transcends the likes and dislikes of earthly life like God himself to whom all things are equal. Pity and cruelty are equally unmeaning in an ultimate reference, and so are also approbated and unapprobated conduct. Just as one of the Upaniṣads has said that to one who has attained Brahma knowledge no sin attaches for any kind of antinomian act, so also the Tantras place the *kaula* above all moral judgment and put no prohibitions and restraints in his way, as they are unnecessary for one who has pierced the veil of space and time, process and differentiation. A *kaula* roams in all *ācāras* at will – being at heart a Śākta, outwardly a Śaiva, and in social gatherings a Vaiṣṇava. He sees himself in all things and all things in himself."[80]

The *Mahānirvāṇa Tantra* describes the Bhairavī Cakra as a mode of worship of the Kaula.[81] Ānanda Bhairavī is in the center of its meditation – the worshipers are considered as *aṃśas* of the Goddess during the performance itself. As a side effect all the different classes of demons flee away. Its main effect is that the "corrupt sinners of Kali are liberated from the trammels of their sins."[82]

Dīkṣā becomes of utmost importance in Tāntricism: a special initiation is necessary for anyone who wishes to enter the Tantra-*ācāra*. It is open to all without distinction of caste or sex, and even a Brahmin has to apply for it, otherwise he is not entitled to take part in the *cakra*. Terrible punishment is in store for those who take part in the rites without initiation and also for those who invite uninitiated persons.

A very important part is also played by the different rites of purification – especially purification of the *pañca makāras*. The Tāntrikas are aware that the enjoyment of these five *ma* involves the violation of all moral laws which are binding for ordinary men. They are the great temptations of ordinary people. Tantricism is interpreted as a spiritual homoeopathy: by the very poison of the snake the snakebite is cured. But the administration of this antidote has to take place in a controlled way under an expert physician: the *pañca makāras* have to be purified and are to be taken only under the guidance of a *guru*. The purification takes place with a number of *mantras*, whose meaning is clear only to the initiated.[83] Before taking any of the *ma* the *sādhaka* has to recite the *mantra* – then only is the *makāra* a sacrament and not a sin.

One of the most important items in Tantricism is the *yantra*. It is indispensable for Tantra worship.[84] *Yantra* and *mantra* are closely combined. The *yantra* is a symbol of the Goddess and upon it the letters of the alphabet, or short monosyllabic *mantras*, are inscribed which constitute the *mantra*- or *śabda*-body of the Goddess. By the letters of the alphabet the body of the Goddess is constituted. The worshiper will identify certain parts of his own body with certain letters and thus will identify himself with the Goddess.[85] The process of placing the letters in different parts of the body is called *nyāsa*. The *sādhaka* should think of his own body as consisting of *mantras*. *Nyāsa* presupposes a purification by which the body is made fit to receive the *mātrika-mantras*. The *yantra* inscribed with the specific *mantras* represents the body of the Goddess whom the *sādhaka* wants to worship.[86] "Every deity has his or her own *yantra* but the most famous of these *yantras* is the *śrī-yantra* on which lavish praise has been bestowed. In its various parts it is supposed to represent the origin, maintenance and dissolution of the world of things, the dot in the middle representing the unitary world-ground. The *bīja-mantra* of the Śakti goddess is mentally placed in the various projections of its constituent titles and lotuses and in its circles and squares."[87]

In most forms of Tantric worship the awakening of the Kuṇḍalinī Śakti in the body plays a great role: Śakti lies dormant, coiled up at the base of the human body. Through Tantric practices, especially the employment of *mantras*, she is awakened and sent through the main nerves of the body through the other *cakras*, absorbing the *mantras* and elements in them, thereby identifying the *sādhaka* with Kuṇḍalinī Śakti until Kuṇḍalinī and Śiva unite blissfully in the highest of the *cakras*.[88] The aim of the Tāntrika is always the union of Śakti and Śiva, the merging into Śakti. The details of Tantraśāstra are very complex and obscure. It does not have any specific mythology of its own and only develops the idea of the Goddess as the ground of everything.

> The Goddess is the great *Śakti*. She is *Māyā*, for of her the *māyā* which produces the *saṃsāra* is. As Lord of *Māyā* she is *Mahāmāyā*. Devī is *avidyā* because she binds, and *vidyā* because she liberates and destroys the *saṃśara*. She is *prakṛti* and as existing before creation is the *Adyā Śakti*. Devī is the *Vācaka Śakti*, the manifestation of *Cit* in *Prakṛti*, and the *Vācya Śakti* or *Cit* itself. The *Ātma* should be contemplated as Devī. Śakti or Devī is thus the Brahman revealed in its mother aspect (*Śrīmātā*) as creatrix and nourisher of the worlds. Kālī says of herself in Yoginī Tantra: "I am the bodily form of *Saccidānanda* and I am the *brahman* that has emanated from *brahman*."[89]

Possibly in imitation of the Vaiṣṇava *daśa-avatāras*, the Tāntrikas know *dasā-vidyās*: Kālī, Tārā, Ṣodaśī, Bhuvaneśvarī, Bhairavī, Chinnamaṣṭā, Dhūmāvatī, Bagalā, Maṭaṅgī, Kāmalātmikā.[90]

DEVĪ WORSHIP AND ICONOGRAPHY

Since it is the aim of the Tāntrika to become one with the Goddess, conceived as present in flesh and blood, it becomes understandable that bodily worship and physical acts of devotion play a central role in Tāntricism. The earliest Tantric texts are hymns to the Goddess and the bulk of later Devī religious literature consists of hymns, *mantras*, description of rituals, feasts, and ceremonies. Whereas Devī mythology is comparatively uniform, Devī worship takes innumerable forms. It is usually connected with some material object that represents Devī; she is *prakṛti*, never "pure spirit".[91]

The material object may be a *yantra* – either drawn on the ground, or on a piece of paper, or engraved in metal or stone[92] – or a *ghaṭa* (an earthen pot) covered with red cloth, or a sculpted or painted image of the

Devī. These again are much more diversified than the images of any other deity. Devī is represented either as the consort of Śiva or Viṣṇu, as the Great Mother, as Śakti of Śiva or Viṣṇu, as Virgin, or in any other of the many forms under which she is invoked by Śāktas.

As the consort of Śiva she is represented with two, four, six, or ten arms – holding lotus, *pāśa* (noose), *aṅkuśa* (goad), *śaṅkha* (conch), *cakra* (discus), and showing *varadā* (boon-giving) and *abhaya mudrā* (reassuring gesture) while one hand may be hanging free.[93] Sometimes she is represented as having three eyes. She is standing at the side of Śiva, sitting at his side, or sitting on his left thigh.

There is another representation of Devī in which she is still associated with Śiva but not subordinated. As Durgā she has nine forms: in all of them she has four, eight, or more arms, three eyes, a dark complexion and she is standing either on a *padmāsana* or on the head of a buffalo or seated on the back of a lion. Her breast is bound with a snake. She is the "dear younger sister of Viṣṇu who came out of the Ādiśakti." Her nine forms are worshiped for various ends: as Nīlakaṇṭhī she is the bestower of wealth and happiness, and as Kṣemaṅkarī she gives health. Harasiddhī is worshiped for the "attainment of desired ends," as Rudrāṃśa Durgā, Vana Durgā, Agni Durgā, Vindhyavāsinī Durgā, and as Ripumārī Durgā she has a predominantly terrific aspect. One of the most popular images is that of Devī Mahiṣamārdinī or Kātyāyanī. She has usually three eyes, wearing on the head the *jaṭa-makuṭa* (crown of matted hair) and the *candra-kalā* (crescent moon); her body is of the color of the *atasī* (Jasmine) flower. She has ten hands: in the right ones she carries *triśula* (trident), *khadga* (sword), *śaktyāyudha* (missile), *cakra* (discus), and *dhanus* (bow); in the left ones *pāśa* (noose), *aṅkuśa* (goad), *kheṭaka* (club), *paraśu* (battle-axe), and *ghaṇṭa* (bell). At her feet should be a buffalo, decapitated, with blood gushing from its neck. The *asura* emerging from it in human form should be half visible, pinned down by the *nāga-pāśa* of the Goddess. The right foot of the Devī is on the back of the lion, the left one on the head of *mahiṣa*.

There is also an image of Navadurgā, depicting Devī with eighteen hands, that is "capable of granting all powers."

Many of the forms of Devī mentioned in the myths are represented in figures too: Bhadrakālī, Mahākalī, Aṃbā, Aṃbikā, Maṅgalā, Sarvamaṅgalā, Kālarātrī, Lalitā, Gaurī, Umā, Pārvatī, Rambhā, and so forth. Totalā is said to be able to destroy all sins. As Tripurā she is the object of worship of the Tāntrikas, often represented as residing in *maṇi-dvīpa*, the jewel-island, often combined with the Śiva-Śava.

As Bhūtamāta Devī she is worshiped by *bhūtas* (ghosts), *pretas* (restless souls of dead people), and *piśācas* (evil spirits), by Indra, Yakṣas, and Gandharvas.

There is a group of eight Devīs with a predominantly terrific function who are worshiped for the destruction of enemies and the removal of fear from devotees: they are Jyeṣṭhā, Raudrī, Kālī, Kalavikarṇikā, Balavikarṇikā, Sarvabhūtadamanī, Balapramathanī, Manonmanī.

The various *avatāras* of Devī mentioned in the *Devī Purāṇas* are also represented figuratively: thus we find statues of Varuṇī-Cāmuṇḍā, Rakta-Cāmuṇḍā, Śiva-dūtī, Yogeśvarī, Bhairavī, of Śivā, Kīrti, Siddhi, Riddhi, Kṣamā, Dīpti, Rati, Śvetā, Bhadrā, Ghaṇṭākarṇī, Diti, Arundhati, Aparājitā, Surabhi, of Kṛṣṇā, Indrākṣī, Annapūrnā, Tulasīdevī, Aśvārūḍhadevī, Bhuvaneśvarī, Bālā, and Rājamātaṅgī. Of special importance is the image of Kālī. Associated with Viṣṇu, Devī is represented as Lakṣmī, Bhūmī, Sītā, Rukmiṇī, Satyabhāma, and Rādhā. With Brahmā she is associated as Sarasvatī.

The Sapta-mātṛkās (Seven Mothers) are usually represented as a group in the temples of South India.

The hymns by which Devī is addressed consist, as usual, of an enumeration of her titles, qualities, and achievements. Again we have differences stemming from the various conceptions of Devī: as consort of Śiva or Viṣṇu she is praised as faithful wife; as "Great Mother" she is identified with *brahman*, with *prakṛti*, and with *ātman*. The five functions of creation, preservation, attraction, liberation, and destruction are ascribed to her.[94] In Tantric worship she is identified with certain *mantras*, and letters and the worship of the *yantra* play a great role. In other forms of worship she is seen incorporated in a woman who receives worship as Devī. Some of the most popular and profound hymns to Devī are ascribed to Śaṅkarācārya.[95] She is praised as Mother, as Eternal, as granting both enjoyment and liberation, as the body of Śambhu, identified with the material universe and with the subtle elements: "O mother, may all my speech, howsoever idle, be recitation of *mantra*; may all my actions with my hand be the making of *mudrā*; may all my walking be *pradakṣina*; may all my eating and other functions be *homa* rites; may my act of lying down be prostration before thee; may all my pleasures be an offering to the *ātman*. Whatsoever I do may it be counted for the worship of thee."[96]

Much of *Tantra* hymnology is written in the so-called *sāṃdhya* ("twilight") style, that is, with a double meaning: one gross and sensual, the other sublime and spiritual. Only the initiated will discover the true sense.

Promises are usually attached to the recitation of Devī hymns: the devotee is assured of the forgiveness of sins, of *mukti*, of all sorts of blessings, of an appearance of Devī. The same blessing is usually attached to the listening to, and recitation of, texts related to Devī worship as, for example, the *Devī-Bhāgavata Purāṇa*.

Devī worship consists largely of the same acts as that employed in the worship of Viṣṇu or Śiva. But a few peculiar features are worth mentioning. One of them is bloody sacrifice. The proper worship of Devī is done through the killing of a victim. In former times human sacrifice was connected with several important centers of Devī worship, and assuredly a large number of people met their death as offerings to Devī.[97] Now, usually the sacrifice of fowls and goats takes the place of human sacrifice. Sexual promiscuity also often formed part of Devī worship at certain places. Black magic and sorcery are also closely connected with several centers of Devī worship.

Tāntrikas in former times did not attribute any importance to pilgrimage since the union of Devī and Śiva could be found in one's own body. But later on fifty-one Śakti-pīṭhas came to be recognized as centers of Śakti pilgrimage, according to legend they were the places where the parts of Satī fell to the earth.[98] Every one of these places has its own legends and promises of merits and gain in this world and in the next.

Assam has been the center of Śāktism as far back as our knowledge of Śāktism goes. The most famous of the Assamese temples, Kāmākhyā near Guwahatī, is the most important of the Śakti-*pīṭhas*, the place where the *yoni* fell down, appearing as a cleft rock.[99] She is worshiped there under the title Kāmeśvarī. According to the *Kālikā Purāṇa* the mountain upon which it fell is Śiva's body.

Thus Kāmākhyā is both a cemetery and the place of the activity of Śiva-Śakti. Both these aspects, death and life, seem to be essential for Śāktism. Reportedly, even now both right-hand and left-hand practices are performed in this temple and animals are slaughtered at its altars.[100]

The main feast in honor of Devī is Devī-nava-rātra, popularly known as Durgā-Pūjā in Bengal where it is the greatest festival of the year.[101] It is celebrated to commemorate the visit of Pārvatī at her parents' home after her marriage to Śiva, and even now married daughters continue the custom by returning for this occasion to their parents' homes. Numerous images of Devī-Mahiṣamārdiṇī are put up in houses and public places; at the end of the festival these images are immersed in the Gaṅgā or the sea. Often worship is performed before earthen vessels draped in red cloth, symbols of Devī.

Major centers of Devī worship have their own peculiar feasts. One of these is Aṃbuvācī, when Mother Earth is supposed to have her menses and the temple remains closed for three days.[102] Only red flowers are used in worship at this time, and devotees receive red cloth.

Devī worship is particularly intense in times of epidemics. These are interpreted as signs of the wrath of the Goddess, because her worship had been neglected. Then she has to be appeased by the sacrifice of buffaloes, pigeons, and goats.[103] Similarly, Devī is invoked when somebody has been bitten by a snake or shows signs of poisoning.[104] Usually it is Devī herself who in the Purāṇas and Tantras exhorts people to worship her and also gives instructions as to how people should do it.

ŚĀKTA PHILOSOPHY

Much of Śākta ideology forms an integral part of certain schools of Śaivism.[105] Śiva and Pārvatī are considered to be the "world-parents," their mutual dependence is so great that one cannot be without the other, and thus we find, in the figure of Śiva *ardha-nārī*, Śiva and Pārvatī combined into one being which manifests a dual aspect. It is not improbable that the original Sāṁkhya system had the same basic philosophy. It is, then, only a matter of emphasis whether a certain system is called Śāktism or Śaivism, depending largely on the relative importance attributed to either the male or the female principle.

The peculiarity of Śāktism is the acceptance of material creation as basic reality, and its emphasis on the existence of *māyā* as an entity: Śakti is called Ādya- or Mūla-Prakṛti and Mahāmāyā. The *Tripurā Rahasya*, a Śākta Tantra, explicity says: "Do not conclude that there is no such thing as the world. Such thinking is imperfect and defective. Such a belief is impossible. One who tries to negate the whole world by the mere act of thought brings it to existence by that very act of negation. Just as a city reflected in a mirror is not a reality but exists as a reflection, so also this world is not a reality in itself but is consciousness all the same. This is self-evident. This is perfect knowledge."[106]

At the same time it is not possible to classify Śāktism proper as either Dvaita or Advaita: the *Mahānirvāṇa Tantra* calls it *Dvaitādvaita vivarjita*. For Śāktism the fetters that bind are neither illusionary as

Advaita claims nor are they pure evil to be removed from the *ātman* as Dvaita intends to do, but they are the means to liberation. The imperfections or fetters "have their place and function in the descent of the universe from its ultimate perfect source and have therefore got to be resolved and not simply 'by-passed' when ascent is thought from cosmic limitations to the purity, freedom and perfections of the ultimate source. The *Jīva* has to work out his salvation not by simply negating his limitations and his evil, but by so working them up that they become his allies, his helpers, and ultimately his liberation."[107]

The oneness of *bhukti* and *mukti*, of means to fetter and to free, of *māyā* and *vidyā*, is one of the characteristic signs of Śākta soteriology. Thus the *Tripurā Rahasya* says: "There is no such thing as bondage or liberation. There is no such thing as the seeker and the means for seeking. Partless, Non-Dual, Conscious Energy, Tripurā alone pervades everything. She is both knowledge and ignorance, bondage and liberation too. She is also the means for liberation. This is all one has to know."[108]

The metaphysical principle behind this teaching is the realization that the body is not evil, but the incarnation and manifestation of Śiva-Śakti, taking part in his divine play (*ullāsa*). In poison there are healing qualities if rightly applied by a wise physician. In the body, seemingly the prison of the spirit, lies the coiled-up energy that enables one to reach limitless freedom. This Kuṇḍalinī Śakti has to be awakened, and that awakening constitutes one of the main practices of Śāktism which is only partly accessible through theory.[109]

The philosophy of Śāktism does not intend to isolate the spiritual self from *prakṛti* but to immerse the spiritual self in *prakṛti*, to reunify the two basic principles of reality which are seen as polarity in the phenomenal world, but have in reality but one ground and source. The details of the way to ultimate bliss vary according to different schools. Many accept a plurality of Śaktis which are instrumental in the process of liberation.

Śāktism accepts the possibility of *jīvan-mukti*. According to the *Devī-Bhāgavata Purāṇa*[110] one thought of Devī in her revealed form can transform one instantly into a *mukta*. The *Mahānirvāṇa Tantra* writes: "He who sees everything in Brahman and who sees Brahman everywhere is undoubtedly known as a true Kaula, who has attained liberation while yet living."[111] Śakti is considered instrumental in bondage and liberation also in Vaiṣṇavism and Śaivism, though her functions are defined differently. Thus Śaṅkara recognizes *śakti* as the root of all phenomenal existence, as the root of bondage and creation: "This world, when being dissolved, is dissolved to that extent only that the *śakti* of the world remains and is produced from the root of that *śakti*."[112] And: "Belonging to the Self, as it were, of the omniscient Lord, there are name and form, the figments of Nescience not to be defined either as being or as different from it, the germs of the entire expanse of the phenomenal world, called in *śruti* and *smṛti*, *māyā*, *śakti* or *prakṛti* of the omniscient Lord. Different from them is the omniscient Lord himself."

In Śrīvaiṣṇavism *śakti* has a much more positive function and the tendency to ascribe to the Ultimate a plurality of Śaktis as his hypostases becomes clearly marked out. Thus Rāmānuja writes, quoting first from the *Viṣṇu Purāṇa* (VI, 7, 61–63): "'The *śakti* of Viṣṇu is the highest, that which is called the embodied soul is inferior; and there is another third energy called *karma* or Nescience, actuated by which the omnipresent *śakti* of the embodied soul perpetually undergoes the afflictions of wordly existence.' These and other texts teach that the highest Brahman is essentially free from all imperfection whatsoever, comprises within itself all auspicious qualities, and finds its pastime in originating, preserving, reabsorbing, pervading, and ruling the universe; that the entire complex of intelligent and non-intelligent beings in all their different estates is real and constitues the *rūpa* or *śakti* of the highest Brahman." The lessons which he draws from the *Purāṇa* text is the following: "It declares that the highest Brahman, that is, Viṣṇu possesses two *rūpas*, called *śaktis*, a *mūrta* and an *amūrta* one, and then teaches that the portion of the *mūrta*, namely the *kṣetrajñā* (embodied soul) which is distinguished by its connection with matter and involved in nesciences – that is termed *karma*, and constitutes a third *śakti* – is not perfect."[113] He also declares Bhāgavat to be the abode of the three *śaktis*.

Still more explicit and nearer to Śāktism is Caitanya's form of Vaiṣṇavism in which a number of Śaktis are ascribed to Viṣṇu-Kṛṣṇa, the highest of which, *hlādinī śakti*, gives bliss (by sharing) to all his *bhaktas*.[114]

In the Śaiva system of Pratyabhijñā a number of Śaktis of Śiva play a great role.[115] In the Śaiva system as described by Mādhava the grace of Śiva is personified as *rodhaśakti*.[116]

The most characteristic teaching of Śāktism, however, comes close to Advaita Vedānta: Śakti is considered to be identical with Brahman. Śakti is the creative force which creates the world and the creation is one with the force which pervades it.[117] The earliest evidence for Śakti-Advaita can be found in some *Purāṇas*, in which Devī is explaining her own identity with

Brahman.[118] The *Śākta Upaniṣads*, which belong to the period from the twelfth century onward, teach Śakti-Advaita and liberation through Śrīmahāvidyā. Quite significant also are the narrations in the *Purāṇas* where Devī is described as imparting *jñāna* as a means to liberation. The *Tantras* are built on a basis of Śakti-Advaita, considering the world – which is seen as real – as an expression of Śakti. Śakti as Cit-Śakti has two basic powers: *prakāśa* and *vimarṣa-śakti*. The latter makes self-experience possible through the manifestations of the world.

Since Śakti is both *avidyā* and *vidyā*, matter and spirit, the *sādhana* taught by Śāktas often emphasizes the oneness of *bhukti* and *mukti*, the merging of matter and spirit instead of their discrimination (*viveka*) as advocated by other systems. The perfection of the *jīvas* is achieved through an assumption of all the different forms of Śakti into their own subtle bodies, thus becoming one with the force that sustains the universe.

ŚĀKTISM TODAY

Śāktism has deeply influenced many recent movements of religious and philosophical renewal. As outstanding examples we may mention Ramakrishna Paramahamsa, the ecstatic priest of the Goddess at Dakṣineśvara, and Aurobindo Ghose, the recluse of Pondicherry with a worldwide audience. Many people find in Śāktism a basis for a religion for our age, a religion which takes material reality as seriously as spirit.[119] As V. S. Agrawala writes: "Mother Earth is the deity of the new age ... the *kalpa* of Indra-Agni and the *yuga* of Śiva-Viṣṇu are no more. The modern age offers its salutations to Mother Earth whom it adores as the super-goddess ... Mother Earth is the presiding deity of the age, let us worship her."[120]

Goddess worship is an integral part of contemporary Hinduism both in India and abroad. Recently in India, two large new Śākta temples have been added to the countless traditional ones of the past: the Aṣṭalakṣmī Temple in Cennai (Madras), and the Kailās Ashram in Bangalore. One of the largest Hindu temples outside India, the Mahālakṣmī temple in Boston, is dedicated to the Goddess, and so is the more recent Mīnākṣī temple in Houston. During the last few years a large Durgā temple was completed in Toronto. Of the 17,000 Hindu temples registered in Malaysia, 10,000 are Śākta temples. Wherever there are larger numbers of emigrant Hindus, in countries such as South Africa, Trinidad, Fiji and Surinam, new Goddess shrines are built.[121]

Not surprisingly, the Goddess, especially in her fierce form, as Durgā, has also become the patron deity of the Indian women's liberation movement. Many feminist groups add her name to their self-description, indicating a new confidence in the power of the female aspect of the creator, preserver, and destroyer.

NOTES

1. E. Neumann, *The Great Mother*, translated by R. Manheim.
2. A. D. Pusalker, "The Indus Civilization."
3. R. C. Hazra, *Upapurāṇas*, pp. 23ff.
4. Cf. S. K. Chatterji, "Race Movements and Prehistoric Culture," in *CHIP*, vol. I, pp. 165f.
5. H. Whitehead, *Village Gods*, p. 11.
6. R. C. Hazra, *Upapurāṇas*, pp. 18f.
7. The Thugs who murdered thousands of people were Śāktas and considered every murder as an offering to Devī. Cf. R. C. Hazra, *Upapurāṇas*, pp. 18f.
8. See, for example, Ruth S. Freed and Stanley A. Freed, *Ghosts: Life and Death in North India*. Seattle: University of Washington Press, 1993.
9. *Paṭtupāṭṭu*, I, 370f.
10. *Śilappadikāram* XII, 21, 10f.; quoted by A. P. Karmarkar, *The Religions of India*.
11. Cf. P. C. Bagchi, "Evolution of the Tantras," in *CHI*, vol. IV, chap. 12, pp. 211–226.
12. Cf. *Mārkaṇḍeya Purāṇa*: out from the Supreme Mahālakṣmī issue Sarasvatī, Lakṣmī and Mahākālī as manifestations of her *sattva*, *rajas*, and *tamas guṇas*. Each of these divide again into a male and female form that are wedded among themselves: out from Sarasvatī issue Gaurī and Viṣṇu; from Lakṣmī come Lakṣmī and Hiraṇyagarbha; from Mahākālī come Sarasvatī and Rudra. Gaurī is wedded to Rudra, Viṣṇu to Lakṣmī, and Hiraṇyagarbha to Sarasvatī.
13. Another important set of titles of Devī is connected with her activities: as Mahākālī she is connected with *sṛṣṭi*, as Mahāmārī she is causing *pralaya*; as Lakṣmī she bestows wealth, as Alakṣmī or Jyeṣṭhādevī she destroys wealth.
14. *Kālikā Purāṇa*, one of the most important scriptures of Śāktism, was probably written in Kāmarūpa. It describes the various sanctuaries of the Mother Goddess Kāmākhyā, the main deity of Assam. Cf. Bani Kanta Kakati, *The Mother Goddess Kāmākhyā*.
15. L. Rénou, *Vedic India*, p. 120. The interpretation of Aditi as Great Mother is Przyluski's.
16. *Ṛgveda* I, 136, 3.
17. *Nirukta* IV, 22ff.
18. *Ṛgveda* X, 125, Translation T. R. H. Griffith, vol. I, pp. 572f. K. F. Geldner, *Der Ṛgveda*, vol. III, p. 355, calls the hymn "eine der Vorstufen der Prāṇa-Brahman-Ātman Lehre."

19. Ṛgveda X, 127, 2 b.
20. S. Chattopadhyaya, *The Evolution of Theistic Sects in Ancient India*, pp. 49ff. *Yajurveda* III, 5ff: *Aṃbikā* as *svasrā* of Śiva-Rudra.
21. Cf. S. Chattopadhyaya, *The Evolution of Theistic Sects in Ancient India*, pp. 51f.
22. E.g., *Kena Upaniṣad* III, 25. *Muṇḍaka Upaniṣad* I, 2, 4. Pāṇini mentions the same goddess Indrānī, Varunāṇī, (IV, I 49) Agnāyī, Vṛṣikapāyī (37). Prithvī-Dyānī; Uṣas (IV, 2, 31). Four names of Pārvatī, namely, Bhāvānī, Śarvānī, Rudrānī, Mṛdāṇī (IV, 1, 49). "The names of Śarvānī and Bhavānī were local designations of the one and the same Mother Goddess." According to *Śatapatha Brāhmaṇa* II, 1, 3, 18, Śarva was popular in Prācya, Bhava in Vātūka. Cf. A. Agravala, *India as Known to Pāṇini*, p. 359.
23. *The Evolution of Theistic Sects in Ancient India*, pp. 52ff.
24. *Rāmāyāṇa* II, 86.
25. Ibid., I, 35; I, 43.
26. Ibid., I, 43f. See also: H. v. Stietencron, *Gaṅgā und Yamunā*. Wiesbaden: Harrassowitz, 1973.
27. Ibid., I, 35.
28. *Mahābhārata* Anuśāsanaparvan, 134.
29. Ibid., 127.
30. *Mahābhārata* Sauptikaparvan, 8, 64ff.
31. Ibid., 8, 82.
32. Ibid.
33. *Mahābhārata* Bhīṣmaparvan, 23, 4–16 (Critical Ed., App. I, 1, pp. 710ff.).
34. The date of the Durgā hymn in *Mahābhārata* according to E. Payne's *Śāktas* (p. 39), is third or fourth century C.E. According to Sircar's *Śāktapiṭhas* the Devīstotra is earlier than the *Bhagavadgītā*. S. K. Belvalkar, the editor of the *Bhīṣmaparvan*, relegates the Durgāstotra to the Appendix (I, 1, p. 710), considering it an interpolation later than the *Bhagavadgītā* (pp. 768/22).
35. Raghu Vira, the editor of the *Virāṭaparvan*, relegates the entire Durgāstotra of the Vulgate (6) to the Appendix I, 4, D.
36. *Mahābhārata* Śalyaparvan, 45.
37. *Harivaṃśa* III, 3.
38. *Harivaṃśa* I, 3; II, 120.
39. According to R. C. Hazra, "The Upapurāṇas," in *CHI*, vol. II, pp. 280ff.
40. Cf. R. C. Hazra, *Upapurāṇas*, vol. II, pp. 466ff.
41. The main texts concerning Devī in the *Mahāpurānas* are: *Mārkaṇḍeya Purāṇa* 81–93; *Vāmana Purāṇa* 17–21; 51–56; *Varāha Purāṇa* 21–28; 90–96; *Kūrma Purāṇa* I, 11–12. *Śiva Purāṇa* and *Bhāgavata Purāṇa* contain many materials too.
42. Thus the Devī-māhātmya of the *Mārkaṇḍeya Purāna*, is almost certainly interpolated into a text that originally had nothing to do with Śāktism and which is the main source for Devī-pūjā.
43. R. C. Hazra, "The Upapurāṇas," in *CHI*, vol. II, pp. 280f.
44. The *Devīmāhātmya* consists of chaps. 81 to 93 of the *Mārkaṇḍeya Purāṇa* (sixth century C.E.). It has been edited separately many times;

English translation (with Sanskrit text and notes) by Swami Jagadisvarananda.

45. Cf. R. C. Hazra, *Upapurāṇas*, pp. 19f; *Devī Bhāgavata* V, 1–19; *Vāmana Purāṇa* 17–20. For translation of major passages, see W. D. O'Flaherty, *Hindu Myths*, pp. 238–249.
46. The buffalo sacrifice features prominently in village rituals (cf. H. Whitehead, *Village Gods*).
47. *Devīmāhātmya* I, 12ff.
48. Ibid., II, 21–27.
49. Ibid., III, 34.
50. *Devī Bhāgavata* V, 1–19.
51. Ibid., V, 20; III, 1f. describes a vision of Devī in her Dvīpa. Ibid., X, 2: Devī in the Vindhyās.
52. *Devīmāhātmya* V, 1ff.; *Devī Bhāgavata* V, 30f.
53. *Devīmāhātmya* V, 14–80.
54. Ibid., vv. 101ff.
55. Ibid., VII, 2ff.
56. Ibid., VIII, 8–11.
57. Ibid., v. 23.
58. Ibid., VIII, 52.
59. Ibid., X, 28–32.
60. Ibid., v. 27: the bell is invoked as a means to protect from all evil.
61. Ibid., vv. 4–6.
62. Ibid., vv. 20–30.
63. *Devī Purāṇa*, chap. 38. A highly interesting study of one of these goddesses is provided by Pratyapaditya Pal in his article "The Pilgrimage of Nanda," *Purāṇa* XXXII/2 (1989) pp. 112–141.
64. *Śiva Purāṇa*, Umāsaṃhita 28–45 (Umā's *avatāras*); Rudrasaṃhitā 14ff. *Devī Bhāgavata*, passim.
65. *Devīmāhātmya* X, 4–8. "The name 'Mothers' had apparently to do with the placing of children on the laps or by the side of these mother-goddesses, who were virtually looked upon as the guardian angels of small children. The Mahāyāna deity Hārītī ... had a similar figure and function. She had ectypes in Manasā, the serpent goddess and also Śītalā, the goddess of smallpox who begins to figure towards the end of this period in temples in Kathiawad and Gujarat (Sejakpur and Sunak). Later on the goddess Saṣṭī took over this protective function from the Mothers ... Probably the name 'Mothers' was euphemistic when extended to the Yoginīs and was designed to cover up their destructive or terrible aspect ... number fluid ... sixty-four and more in *Purāṇas* ... names vary." H. D. Bhattacharyya, *HCIP*, vol. IV, pp. 342f.
66. *Kālikā Purāṇa*, chaps. 15ff., describes how Satī attends uninvited Dakṣa's sacrifice, is insulted and gives up her life. Śiva takes Satī's body on his shoulders. Brahmā, Viṣṇu, and Śanaiścara enter it and cut it into pieces and let them fall to earth. Chap. 18 describes where the different parts of Satī's body fell and how she was called in those places: Satī's feet fell at Devīkta, where she was called Mahābhāgā; her thighs at Uḍḍiyāna, where she was called Kātyāyanī; her *yoni* at Kāmagiri in

Kāmārupa, where she was called Kāmākhyā; her navel east of Kāmārūpa, where she was called Pūrṇeśvarī; her breasts at Jālandhara, where she was called Caṇḍī; her neck at the eastern borders of Kāmarupa, where she was called Dikkaravāsinī and Lalitākāntā.

67. *Devī-Bhāgavata* VII, 33f.
68. Ibid., IX, 50.
69. *Bhaviṣya Purāṇa* IV, 138; R. C. Hazra, *Upapurāṇas*, vol. II, p. 29.
70. Ibid., III, 6.
71. Tantrism has been defined as "systematic quest for salvation or spiritual excellence by realizing and fostering the bipolar, bisexual divinity within one's own body." Teun Goudriaan and Sanjukta Gupta, *Hindu Tantric and Śākta Literature*, p. 1.
72. H. D. Bhattacharya, "Tantrik Religion," in *HCIP*, vol. IV, p. 135. The most exhaustive account is found in T. Goudriaan and Sanjukta Gupta, *Hindu Tantric and Śākta Literature*, A History of Indian Literature (ed. Jan Gonda) vol. II, fasc. 2; Wiesbaden: Otto Harrassowitz, 1981.
73. There is a large number of goddesses in the Mahāyāna Buddhist Pantheon, gentle ones and fierce ones: Vasudhārā, Nairātmā, Parnaśavarī, Prajñā-Pāramitā, Mārīcī, Vajravārāhī, etc. Cf. Nalinaksha Dutt, "Buddhism: Iconography," in *HCIP*, vol. IV, pp. 275ff. *The Way of the Buddha*, pl. 209, 210, 226.
74. In *Mahānirvāṇa Tantra* I, 37ff., Devī speaks to Śiva: "By Thee also have been spoken for the Liberation of good men Tantras, a mass of Āgamas and Nigamas, which bestow both Enjoyment and Liberation, containing Mantras and Yantras and rules as to the *sādhana* of both Devīs and Devas . . ." In the Tantras Devī is mainly worshiped as "Tripurā-sundarī, bright as millions of rising suns, armed with the noose, the elephant hook, the bow of sugar-cane and the arrows of flowers." Cf. *Lalitā Sahasranāma* with Bhāskara's commentary. Translated by R. Ananta Krishna Sastry.
75. H. D. Bhattacarya, *HCIP*, vol. IV.
76. A. T. B. Ghosh, "The Spirit and Culture of the Tantras," in *CHI*, vol. IV, pp. 241ff.
77. Cf. *Mahānirvāṇa Tantra*, chaps. 5 and 6. The description of Vāmacāris in H. Wilson, *Religious Sects*, p. 142; also text of the *Śakti Sudhanā*.
78. H. D. Bhattacarya, *HCIP*, vol. IV, p. 320.
79. Ibid., p. 320.
80. Ibid., p. 321.
81. *Mahānirvāṇa Tantra* X; VIII, 154–175.
82. Ibid., in No. 202 it is also said: "Those who with devotion worship the Kaulas with Pañcatattva cause the salvation of their ancestors and themselves attain the highest end." D. N. Bose, *Tantras*, p. 155.
83. *Mahānirvāṇa Tantra*, chap. V.
84. D. N. Bose, *Tantras*, chap. X, "Tantric Symbols and Practices," explains a number of Yantras.
85. J. Woodroffe, *Introduction to Tantra Śāstra*, pp. 106ff.
86. Ibid., pp. 91ff. "The ritual which aims less at beseeching than compelling the goddess, consists chiefly in the correct use of spells, magical or

sacramental syllables and letters, diagrams and gestures. The worshipper seeks union with the divine, seeks indeed to become divine. It is believed that man is a microcosm corresponding to the macrocosm of the universe." "The Tantras not merely sanction the lowest rites of primitive savagery and superstition, they are guilty of the crime of seeking philosophical justification for such things." Payne, *The Śāktas*, pp. 59f.

87. H. D. Bhattacharya, *HCIP*, vol. IV, p. 325. "No wonder that before the recognition of the fifty-one Śakti-pīṭhas distributed all over India, pilgrimages to sacred places should have been considered unnecessary by Śāktas who located these symbolically within their body."
88. J. Woodroffe, *Introduction to Tantra Śāstra*, pp. 135ff.
89. Ibid., p. 12; quoting *Yoginī Tantra* I, 10.
90. D. N. Bose, *Tantras*, chap. XVI, "The Ten Mahāvidyās."
91. Cf. J. Woodroffe, *Introduction to Tantra Śāstra*, pp. 74ff.
92. The most famous *yantra* is the Śrīcakra consisting of forty-three triangles. Regular *pūjā* is offered to it twice daily in South Indian Śakti *pīṭhālayas*. Other *yantras* are engraved upon thin gold, silver or copper plates, which are rolled into a cylinder and then put into a golden or metallic case so that they may be worn on the body of a person with a view to avoid diseases, possession of devils and other such evils, which, it is supposed they have the power to ward off. Occasional worship is also offered in this case containing the magical *yantra* and the wearer's faith in its efficacy may well affect cures in many cases. (T. A. G. Rao, *Iconography*, vols. I–II, p. 332). Cf. Moti Chandra, "Our Lady of Beauty and Abundance: Padmaśrī," in *Nehru Abhinandan Granth*, pp. 497–513 (with illustrations).
93. Cf. T. A. G. Rao, *Iconography*, vols. I–II, pp. 320ff.
94. *Devī Bhāgavata* III, 4; Hymn to Gaṅgā and other rivers *Bṛhadstotra-ratnākara*, pp. 255ff.
95. Thus, for example, the famous *Ānandalaharī*, *Saundaryalaharī. Tripur-asundarī*, etc. (*Bṛhadstotraratnākara* No. 5). About their authenticity, cf. S. K. Belvalkar, *Lectures on Vedānta*, Lecture VI.
96. Ibid., v. 28. The recitation of a litany of names and titles of Devī is a very common practice. The following purāṇic texts contain the one hundred and eight names of Devī: *Matsya Purāṇa* 13, 26–53; *Devī Bhāgavata* VII, 30, 55–83; *Padma Purāṇa* Sṛṣṭikhanda 17, 185–211; *Skanda Purāṇa*, Āraṇyakhaṇḍa 98, 6–92; *Varāha Purāṇa* 90–95; *Kūrma Purāṇa* I, 11–12 (1000 names of Devī).
97. A description of a human sacrifice to Devī is found in *Bhāgavata Purāṇa* V, 9, 12f. A. P. Karmarkar, *The Religions of India*, p. 213, cites many historic instances of human sacrifice. Up to the nineteenth century every Friday one human sacrifice was offered in the Kālī temple at Tanjore. Marathas were keen observers of this cult. The head was placed on a golden plate before Kālī; the lungs were cooked and eaten by Kandra Yogis; the royal family ate rice cooked in the blood of the victim. Many tribes, for example, Khonds, Nāgas, Bhumji, Bhuviyayas, knew the practice of human sacrifice. Guru Gobind Singh offered a disciple to Durgā. About the practice of human sacrifice at the notorious

Tamreśvarī temple in Sasya (Assam), cf. Barua-Murthy in *Temples and Legends of Assam*, p. 86. The human sacrifice was an annual feature there. In 1565 Nara Narayan, a ruler of Kutch, rebuilt the temple of Kāmākṣī. For its consecration, one hundred and forty men are said to have been sacrificed. Also in Bhāvabhuti's *Mālatī-mādhava* we find the description of a human sacrifice before the image of the Devī. D. C. Sircar, *Śakti-Pīṭhas*, p. 16, brings ample historical evidence of regular human sacrifice to Devī. Even today newspapers report from time to time cases of human sacrifice and self-immolation to Devī.

98. According to D. C. Sircar, *The Śakti-Pīṭhas*, the origin of the Śakti Pīṭhas is due to a further evolution of the Dakṣa-*yajña* story at the beginning of the Middle Ages. Early Tantras (eighth century?) mention four *pīṭhas*: Ātmapīṭha, Parapītha, Yogapīṭha, and Guhyapīṭha. Later texts mention eight, ten, eighteen, forty-two, fifty-one and even one hundred and eight *pīṭhas*.
99. Barua-Murthy, *Temples and Legends of Assam*, pp. 19ff. F. Pratt, *Hindu Culture and Personality*, pp. 234ff., calls Devī worship "worship of the Terrible for its own sake." He thinks that Devī worship is connected with the urge to self-castration, suicide, murder. There are many instances in literature of people cutting their own throat in honor of Kālī in Durgā temples.
100. Cf. Bani Kanta Kakati, *The Mother Goddess Kāmākhyā*.
101. In *Devī Bhāgavata Purāṇa* III, 26ff. the Devī-Navarātravrata is explained. Cf. P.V. Kane, *HDhS*, V/I, describes some other common Devī feasts: *Manasāpūja* (p. 125, worship against snakebite); *Haritālikā* (pp. 144f.); *Śrīpañcamī* (pp. 432f.); *Sartī-devī* (p. 434); *Śambhayugā* (p. 455); *Śabavotsara* (p. 105). For the history of present-day worship of Devī during Durgā-Pūjā in a mud-image, cf. D. C. Sircar, *The Śakti-Pīṭhas*, pp. 74f., N. 1.
102. Barua-Murthy, *Temples and Legends of Assam*, p. 37.
103. The Purāṇas contain a large number of chapters on the mode of worship of Devī. The bulk of Tantras also consists of rituals and ceremonies. Cf. *Devī Bhāgavata Purāṇa* VIII, 24f.; V, 32f.; IX, 4ff.; IX, 15, 25; XII, 13ff. Cf. *Kalyāṇa Upāsanāṅgka* (1968), pp. 350ff.
104. H. Whitehead, *Village Gods*, pp. 112ff.
105. Śāktism is intimately connected with Kāśmīr Śaivism; Śrīpati's system of Śaivism is called Śakti-viśiṣṭādvaita. *Śiva Purāṇa* and *Liṅga Purāṇa* contain many chapters in which Śaivism and Śāktism are combined.
106. *Tripurā Rahasya* (Jñānakhaṇḍa), English translation, A. U. Vasavada, p. 156.
107. Swami Pratyagatmananda, "Tantra-Philosophy," in *CHI*, vol. III, pp. 437ff.
108. *Tripurā Rahasya* (English translation), p. 156.
109. D. N. Bose, *Tantras*, pp. 188ff. J. Woodroff, *The Serpent Power* (Kuṇḍalinī Śakti), pp. 18ff. Swami Satyananda, *Taming the Kuṇḍalinī*, pp. 111ff.
110. *Devī Bhāgavata Purāṇa* XI, 1, 44.
111. *Mahānirvāṇa Tantra* X, 209f.

112. Śaṅkara, *Brahmasūtrabhāṣya*, I, 3, 30.
113. Rāmānuja, *Śrībhāṣya*, I, 1, 1.
114. *Prameyaratnāvalī* XX.
115. Jaideva Singh (ed.), *Pratyabhijñāhṛdayam*, pp. 67ff.
116. Madhava, *Sarvadarśanasaṁgraha*, chap. V.
117. *Tripurā Rahasya* (English transl.), p. 154: "The omnipotent Goddess who is consciousness, who is truly the 'I-consciousness,' creates appearances of the world upon its own essence like reflections in a mirror by her willpower or the power of *māyā* known as freedom."
118. Thus in *Kūrma Purāṇa* I, 1, 58. According to R. C. Hazra the *Kūrma Purāṇa* was originally a Pāñcarātra work with a considerable Śākta element and was composed between 500 and 600 C.E. Toward the beginning of the eighth century, it was recast by Pāśupatas; Śāktas made further additions (*CHI*, vol. II, p. 259f.). A similar statement is found in the *Devī Bhāgavata Purāṇa*. According to R. C. Hazra (*Upapurāṇas*, pp. 281 f.), the *Devī Bhāgavata Purāṇa* belongs to the eleventh or twelfth century.
119. Also, such popular contemporary figures as Ānandamayī Mā or Sathya Sāī Bābā teach "new religions" with a strong Śākta component.
120. V. S. Agrawala, "Mother Earth," in *Nehru Abhinandan Granth*, pp. 490–496.
121. Much of this information is taken from an article by June McDaniel, "Four Schools of Śāktism," in *Hinduism Today*, Feb. 1993.

8 *SMĀRTAS* – TRADITIONAL HINDU UNIVERSALISTS

Besides the adherents of the many Vaiṣṇava, Śaiva, and Śākta *saṃpradāyas* who maintain strict separation between their communities and who not infrequently engage in sectarian denunciation of each other, there is a large group of traditional Hindus called *Smārtas*. They characteristically pay devotion to Viṣṇu, Śiva, and Devī (and in addition to Śūrya and Gaṇeśa, and often also to Kārttikeya or Brahmā), and follow a non-sectarian path, according to the regulations of the traditional law-books.[1]

The name *Smārta* is derived from *smṛti*, literally "remembrance," "memory," alluding to the class of writings called *Smṛtis*, such as the *Manusmṛti*, which codify the right behavior of traditional ("orthodox") caste Hindus, and also to a general attitude of respectful acknowledgment of the traditional "Vedic" way of life. They de-emphasize the exclusivity of sectarian worship of specific deities and advocate a return to Vedic religiosity.

The *Ṛgveda* already declares that Indra is known by many names and that the learned understood these many names as referring to One.[2] It leaves it open who this One really is. The Upaniṣads go further and relativize the individual deities and the sacrifice offered to them; an attitude that leads in the *Bhagavadgītā* to Kṛṣṇa's assurance that all prayers and offerings, to whichever deity made by sincere worshipers, were made to him, and that he would reward the devotees of all the gods.[3]

With the rise of narrowly circumscribed communities of Vaiṣṇavas, Śaivas and Śāktas, based on scriptures and rituals of their own, a sense of separateness increased among Hindus and very often they no longer felt belonging to one and the same Great Tradition. They competed against each other and mutually ridiculed each others' beliefs and practices. When Buddhism and Jainism arose, this disunity of Hindus proved to be their undoing. It was easy for the Buddhists and Jains to point to the self-contradictory nature of Hinduism and to highlight the mutual hostility between Hindu sects. The more liberal among the Vaiṣṇavas, Śaivas, and Śāktas tried to bridge the differences between the sects. According to R. C. Hazra, "the *smārta* adherents of the different sects changed the character of their respective deities to a great extent and brought them nearer to the Vedic gods. Their intention was to preach their own reformed Brahmaism, Vaiṣṇavism and Śaivism, as against the heretical religions, and to popularize thereby the Vedic ideas as far as possible among all."[4]

Śaṅkara, the great reformer of Hinduism, following the lead provided by the *smārtas*, introduced *pañcāyātana pūjā*, the simultaneous worship of five deities, viz. Gaṇeśa, Viṣṇu, Śiva, Devī and Sūrya, accommodating the major Hindu sects under one umbrella. Instead of playing one of these great gods out against the other, as the sectarians did, he insisted on the undivided (*advaita*) nature of the Ultimate, that could not be named and could not be separated from anything. Śaṅkara himself is credited with having composed hymns to all these deities as well as hymns that address the Ultimate as impersonal and nameless.[5] The members of the religious orders which he reorganized, the Daśanāmis, are *smārtas*. The successors to Śaṅkara, the heads of the *maṭhas* founded by him, who are universally respected religious leaders, continue to propagate the *smārta* viewpoint.

Sri Chandrasekharendra Sarasvati, the Śaṅkarācārya of Kāñcī Kāmakoti Pīṭha for most of the twentieth century, introduced the custom to sing at every *pūjā* in temples and homes during the month of Margaśirṣa both Āṇṭāl's *Tiruppavai*, a hymn in praise of Viṣṇu, and Manikkavācagar's *Tiruvembavai*, a hymn glorifying Śiva. He organized *Tiruppavai-Tiruvembavai* conferences to foster a feeling of unity between Vaiṣṇavas and Śaivas. As he said: "Among us there is the concept of the *iṣṭa-devatā*, of the particular form of God which one chooses for his worship and meditation. To get at the One Supreme, you must start from some manifestations of It and you choose it as your *iṣṭa-devatā*. Another man may choose another manifestation. As each progresses in his devotion and concentration, he will be led on to the

One where the differences disappear. That has been the experience of great sages and saints. A true Śiva-bhakta has no quarrel with a true Viṣṇu-bhakta."[6]

The Śaṅkarācārya himself performed *pūjā* to both deities and insisted that Advaita, the underlying philosophy, not only bridged sectarian boundaries but also transcended Hinduism – indeed it was the one insight that was the foundation of all religion and science.[7]

It is hard to say how many Hindus are Smārtas – they often would not identify themselves as such. They assume that it is the typical non-sectarian Hindu approach that need not be named. While believing in the Oneness and Namelessness of the Ultimate, they usually choose an *iṣṭadevatā*, one particular form and name of God which most appeals to them (or as they would often say, has chosen them!) to worship. Thus some Smārtas may worship Viṣṇu or Kṛṣṇa, others Śiva or Devī, as their favourite object of devotion. What distinguishes them from the members of particular Vaiṣṇava, Śaiva, or Śākta *saṃpradāyas* is their non-sectarian approach and their conviction that other forms of worship are as valid as their own. Often *smārtas*, true to the root-meaning of their designation, are also staunch upholders of traditional austere living practices: they observe the ancient rules of purity often under great hardship and uncompromisingly follow the regulations of their *dharma*.[8] Where members of other *saṃpradāyas* may often make concessions to circumstances and human weakness, the *smārtas* would show iron will and discipline as part of their tradition.

A contemporary essay entitled *Smārta-yoga*[9] offers extracts from the Smṛtis that have relevance for the conduct of life with a view to finding ultimate liberation. Its author, a Smārta himself, attempts to show that the rituals prescribed in the Vedic texts "are not concerned only with the outer physical actions but aim at an all-round development of human personality." He continues: "This Smārta Yoga does not require that the aspirant should give up the household life and run away from society. While advising to do the personal, social and other duties when traversing on the path of emancipation, this Yoga also pays attention to building up the character and developing integrity."[10] He cites the definition of Yoga given in the Vedic Āpastamba Sūtras: "Freedom from anger, from contempt and from envy, generosity, sincerity, not hankering after sense-enjoyment, peace of mind, sense control, harmony with all living beings – this is Yoga."[11]

NOTES

1. R. C. Majumdar, "Evolution of Religio-Philosophic Culture in India," in *CHI*, vol. IV, pp. 31–62.
2. *Ṛg-Veda* I, 164, 46.
3. *Bhagavadgītā* IX, 23.
4. R. C. Hazra, "The Purāṇas," *CHI*, vol. II, pp. 240–270. The reference is on p. 250.
5. A selection, with English translations and commentaries, is provided in T. M. P. Mahadevan, *The Hymns of Śaṅkara*. Madras: Ganesh, 1970.
6. T. M. P. Mahadevan, *The Sage of Kanchi*, Secundarabad: Sri Kanchi Kamakoti Sankara Mandir, 1967 p. 45.
7. Ibid., p. 44.
8. R. C. Hazra, an acknowleged Purāṇa scholar, makes the Smārtas responsible for inserting Smṛti topics into the Purāṇas. Cf. his essay "The Purāṇas," in *CHI* vol. II, pp. 240–270.
9. R. Kokaje, *Smārta-yoga*, translated from the original Sanskrit by C. T. Kenghe, Lonavla: Yoga-Mimamsa Prakasana, 1970.
10. Ibid., p. 30.
11. *Āpastamba Dharma Sūtra* I, 23, 6 (my translation).

9 A SHORT HISTORY OF HINDU PHILOSOPHY

Reflection and speculation, the characteristics of what we call "philosophy," have been the hallmark of Hinduism from its earliest times to the present. The *Ṛgveda* contains hymns that could be called philosophical: the famous "Hymn of Creation"[1] begins by stating that in the beginning "there was neither being nor non-being, neither air nor sky, and goes on to ask: "Whence came this world? The gods were born after this world's creation: who can know from whence it has arisen?"

The Upaniṣads, the basis for later Vedānta philosophy, are a string of profound sayings and insights into the nature of reality. They suggest that our ultimate destiny depends on finding out the truth about the world and ourselves.

Not satisfied with the aphoristic wisdom of these sources, and keen to construct an all-embracing world-view, Hindu thinkers developed a number of philosophical systems, called *darśanas*, "theories," in the original Greek sense of this word.[2] Already in the Upaniṣads we find a great number of different worldviews side by side. In later times regular schools developed that became known under specific names. The older sources refer to a very large number of such schools, many of them no longer existent. In the early (Indian) middle-ages Hindus began to differentiate between *āstika*, "orthodox," and *nāstika*, "heterodox," schools:[3] among the latter were listed Buddhism, Jainism, and Cārvāka (an early Indian form of materialistic philosophy). The orthodox systems were classified in a stereotypical six,[4] paired into three groups: Nyāya-Vaiśeṣika, Sāṁkhya-Yoga, Pūrva and Uttara Mīmāṃsā.

Hindus took their philosophy very seriously indeed: they believed that to gain a true understanding of reality was the most important task of a human being. As Śaṅkara has it: "There are many different opinions, partly based on sound arguments and scripture, partly based on fallacious arguments and scriptural texts misunderstood. If one would embrace any of these opinions without previous examination, one would bar oneself from the highest beatitude and incur grievous loss."[5]

Hinduism has always shown great respect for scholarship. A brahmin, according to traditional Hindu law, had to devote the first part of his life to study, and *svādhyāya*, study on his own, was one of the permanent duties imposed upon him for his whole life. Study, according to Manu, was enjoined by the creator himself "in order to protect the universe" and it was also the most effective means to subdue sensual desires and obtain self-control. The true centers of Hinduism were always centers of study: be it the *āśramas* of classical India or the *pāthaśālas* of later times, the private libraries of individual scholars or the large university-like centers of major denominations.[6]

A common characteristic of all *darśanas* is that at some time their basic teachings were condensed into *sūtras*, "leading threads" which helped to express precisely the content of the systems in a technical terminology and also served as texts for students to memorize. Instruction would largely consist of commenting upon the pithy *sūtras* and expanding on the meaning of the terms used in them, pointing out differences between one's own system and others and providing proof for the truth of the *sūtra*. Since many of the *sūtras* are (almost) unintelligible without a commentary and explanation, often the commentary (*bhāṣya*) has become the most important exposition of a system. These *bhāṣyas* in turn have become the object of sub-commentaries (*vṛttis* and *ṭīkas*) and further glosses (*tippaṇis*) which constitute the material which an expert in that particular branch of learning has to study. Hindu scholars have invented most peculiar names for their subcommentaries and glosses.[7] The *sūtras* which we possess today are not always the oldest texts of the schools and they are not always the work of the authors to whom they are ascribed. But they can be relied upon as containing the gist of the teaching of the systems, and they provide the technical terminology for each.

NYĀYA-VAIŚEṢIKA

The *Vaiśeṣika Sūtras*, ascribed to Kaṇāda, are, in the words of Dasgupta, "probably the oldest that we have and in all probability are pre-Buddhistic".[8] That does not entitle us, however, to make any statement about the age of the system itself, which is known particularly for its interesting early atomistic theory and its classification of categories. Vaiśeṣika may initially have been a school of Vedic thought, as its emphasis on *dharma* and its traditional opinion on *adṛṣṭa* as its fruit would suggest.[9] The book which besides the *sūtras* contains the most complete representation of the system, the *Daśa-padārtha Śāstra*, is no older than the sixth century C.E.[10]

The beginnings of the *Nyāya* systems may go back to the disputations of Vedic scholars; already in the times of the Upaniṣads, debate was cultivated as an art, following certain rules in which the basic elements of logical proofs were contained.[11] The *Nyāya Sūtras*, ascribed to Gautama, the main text of the school, have received very important commentaries. The *sūtras* cannot be assigned to a definite date. All scholars agree that a considerable part of the *sūtras* consists of additions to an original work, additions that suggest early Buddhist interpolations and later Hindu insertions to invalidate the Buddhist arguments. From the probable identification of *nyāya* with the *anvīkṣikī* in Kautilīya's *Artha-śāstra*[12] we may assume that the *Nyāya* system already existed in some form in the fourth century B.C.E. Followers of the *Nyāya* system have produced a large amount of important works and of all the Hindu systems *Nyāya* enjoys the greatest respect on the part of Western philosophers, who are coming to discover the enormous subtleties and intricacies of Indian logic.

A Brief Summary of Vaiśeṣika

"Now an explanation of *dharma* . . ." so begins the Kaṇāda Sūtra. "The means to prosperity and salvation is *dharma*." The attainment of salvation is the result of the cognition of the six categories of substance, quality, action, class concept, particularity and inherence.[13] The substances are: earth, water, fire, air, ether, time, space, *ātman* and mind. The qualities are: taste, color, odor, touch, number, measure, separation, contact, disjoining, prior and posterior, understanding, pleasure and pain, desire and aversion, and volitions.

Action (*karma*) is explained as upward movement, downward movement, contraction, expansion, horizontal movement. The feature common to substance, quality, and action is that they are existent, non-eternal, and substantive; they effect, cause, and possess generality and particularity. A major part of the *sūtra* consists in a further elucidation of the various terms just mentioned, much in the same way in which the early Greek philosophers of nature analyzed and described the elements, their qualities and the interrelations. In the third book the *sūtra* deals with the inference of the existence of the *ātman*, which is impervious to sense-perception, from the fact that there must be some substance in which knowledge, produced by the contact of the senses and their objects, inheres. Thus the *ātman*'s existence may be inferred from inhalation and exhalation, from the twinkling of the eyes, from life, from movements of the mind, from sense affections, from pleasure and pain, will, antipathy and effort. It can be proved that it is a substance and eternal. Eternal (*nitya*) is that which exists but has no cause for its existence. The non-eternal is *avidyā*, ignorance.

In the seventh book we are told that *dṛṣṭa*, insight based on observation and rationality, is able to explain even natural phenomena only up to a certain point. All the special phenomena of nature are caused by *adṛṣṭa*, an unknown invisible cause. *Adṛṣṭa* is also said to be the cause of the union of body and soul, of rebirth and of liberation. This "invisible fruit," which is the cause of ultimate happiness, is produced by ablutions, fasting, continence, life in the *guru*'s family, life in the forest, sacrifice, gifts and alms, observation of the cosmic cycle, and the following of the rules of *dharma*. Thus *Vaiśeṣika* places itself quite explicitly in the tradition of Vedic orthodoxy. The *sūtra* also discusses at some length the means and instruments of valid knowledge, topics that are dealt with more thoroughly in the sister-system of *Nyāya*. The *Vaiśeṣika Sūtras* do not contain any polemics against the Buddhists, although they are opposed to some of their quite fundamental tenets: Buddhism denies the "thing in itself" and explains all phenomena merely as a chain of conditions that ultimately can be reduced to non-existence; the Vaiśeṣikas, on the contrary, hold fast to the real existence of things.

Later works of the school, the commentaries on the *Sutra* by Śaṅkara Miśra and Candrakānta, the *Padārtha-dharma-saṅgraha* by Praśasta-pāda and the *Daśa-padārthī* by Maticandra (preserved only in a Chinese version), also give a more detailed explanation of Indian atomism. What we hear, feel, see, etc. are not *continua* but *discreta* (*quanta* we would say today), and these again are not units but compounds of infinitely small indivisible parts (*aṇu*) which clearly differ from one another. Things are products, therefore, and not eternal.

The primordial elements, earth, water, fire and air, are partly eternal, partly temporal. Only ether is completely eternal. The first four elements have mass, number, weight, fluidity, viscosity, velocity, characteristic potential color, taste, smell, or touch. *Ākāśa*, space or ether, is absolutely inert and structureless, being only the substratum of *śabda* or sound, which is thought to travel like a wave in the medium of air. Atomic combinations are possible only with the four basic elements. Both in dissolution and before creation, the atoms exist singly; in creation they are always present in combination. Two atoms combine to form a *dvyaṇuka*, a molecule. Also *tryaṇukas*, *caturaṇukas*, etc., i.e., aggregates consisting of three or more molecules, are possible. Atoms are possessed of an inherent incessant vibratory motion; but they are also under the influence of the *adṛṣṭa*, the will of *īśvara*, who arranges them into a harmonic universe. Changes in substances, which are limited within the frame of possible atom combinations, are brought about by heat. Under the impact of heat-corpuscles a molecule may disintegrate and the characters of the atoms composing it may change. The heat particles which continue to impinge on the individually changed atoms also cause them to reunite in different forms so that definite changes are effected through heat. In many details the Vaiśeṣikas reveal a keen observation of nature and describe in their books a great number of phenomena, which they try to explain with the help of their atom-theory. Similar to modern physicists, the ancient Vaiśeṣikas explained heat and light rays as consisting of indefinitely small particles which dart forth or radiate in all directions rectilineally with inconceivable velocity. Heat also penetrates the inter-atomic space or impinges on the atoms and rebounds, thus explaining the conducting and reflecting of heat. All the *paramāṇus* are thought to be spherical. Attempts have been made to link the atomism of the Vaiśeṣika *darśana* with the teachings of Democritus – so far without any positive evidence.

Leaving out most of the technicalities of the system, a brief explanation of *viśeṣa* – the term that gave the name to the whole system – may give an idea of the specific approach taken by this school of classical Indian philosophy.[14]

Praśāstapāda writes:

> *Viśeṣas* are the ultimate specificatives or differentiatives of their substrates. They reside in such beginningless and indestructible eternal substances as the atoms, *ākāśa*, time, space, *ātman* and *manas* – inhering in their entirety in each of these, and serving as the basis of absolute differentiation of specification. Just as we have with regard to the bull as distinguished from the horse, certain distinct cognitions – such, for instance as (a) that it is a "bull", which is a cognition based upon its having the shape of other bulls, (b) that it is "white", which is based upon a quality, (c) that it is "running swiftly", which is based upon action, (d) that it has a "fat hump", which is based upon "constituent parts" and (e) that it carries a "large bell", which is based upon conjunction; so have the Yogis, who are possessed of powers that we do not possess, distinct cognitions based upon similar shapes, similar qualities and similar actions – with regard to the eternal atoms, the liberated selves and minds; and as in this case no other cause is possible, those causes by reason whereof they have such distinct cognitions – as that "this is a peculiar substance", "that a peculiar self" and so forth – and which also lead to the recognition of one atom as being the same that was perceived at a different time and place – are what we call the *viśeṣas*.[15]

According to the teaching of the Vaiśeṣikas, there are many different *ātmans*, distinguished by their relative and specific *viśeṣas*. The common man, however, is able to recognize their diversity only on account of externally perceptible actions, qualities and so on. Only the Yogi has the "insight into the essence of the soul itself and thus into the real cause of their diversity." The *ātman* is eternal and not bound to space and time. But the actions of *ātman* – thought, will, emotions – are limited to the physical organism with which it is united at a given time. *Jñāna*, knowledge, is according to the Vaiśeṣikas only an accident of *ātman*, not his nature as such, since in dreamless sleep there is no cognition. Emotions and will are, likewise, mere accidents. The "spiritual" is not substantial but accidental. *Manas*, the mind given to every *ātman*, is merely its instrument and does not produce anything of itself. On the other hand, the cooperation of *manas* is necessary.

The state of *mokṣa* or freedom "is neither a state of pure knowledge nor of bliss, but a state of perfect qualitylessness, in which the self remains in itself in its own purity. It is the negative state of absolute painlessness."[16] Concerning the way to reach it we read in the *Daśa-padārtha Śāstra*:

> One who seeks eternal emancipation ought to devote himself to *śīla* or morality, *dānā* or liberality, *tapas* or austerities, and *yoga*. From these comes supreme merit which leads to the attainment of emancipation and

> *tattva-jñāna* or knowledge of ultimate truth. "Prosperity" is enjoyment of pleasure in *svarga* or heaven. Knowledge of ultimate truth brings *mokṣa* or permanent liberation, when merit and demerit have been completely destroyed and *ātman* and *manas* no longer come in contact with each other, that is when the nine things are no longer produced.[17]

Dharma and *adharma* together form *adṛṣṭa* which supports the cycle of *saṃsāra*, of attraction and aversion, and continuously drives the *ātman* back into bodily existence. The activity which is guided by the feeling of the particular existence depends on *avidyā*; when a person realizes that things as such are only varying combinations of atoms of the particular elements, all affection and aversion ceases. If the right knowledge of the self is achieved, egotism and all selfish activity ceases. When *adṛṣṭa* is no longer produced, the transmigratory cycle comes to an end. On the other hand, *ātman* is never completely without *adṛṣṭa*, because the series of births is beginningless. When the soul has rid itself of its gross body it still is and remains attached to the subtle body, even in *pralaya*, the dissolution of the universe. Time, place and circumstances of birth, family and duration of life are all determined by *adṛṣṭa* and it is not possible ever to destroy it completely.

Kaṇāda's *sūtra* do not require an *īśvara*. The substances are eternal; movement is due to the impersonal, eternal principle of *adṛṣṭa*. Later authors introduce an eternal, omniscient, and omnipresent *Īśvara* who is responsible for the universal order of atoms and their movements. This Vaiśeṣika-God, however, resembles very much the *deus otiosus* of deism. *Ātman* and the *aṇu* do not owe their existence to a creator, they are eternal and independent. *Īśvara* differs from the *ātman* only insofar as he is never entangled in *saṃsāra*. He gives laws to the world but never interferes with it subsequently. He winds up the clockwork and lets it run its course.

Nyāya and Navya-Nyāya

Nyāya was, even in ancient times, composed of two parts: *adhyātma-vidyā*, or metaphysics, and *tarka-śāstra*, or rules of debate, often simply called logic. Thus the *Nyāya Sūtra*, famous for its acute analysis of discursive thought as such, also has substantial sections on suffering, soul, and salvation. It begins with the following aphorism: "It is the knowledge of the true character of the following sixteen categories that leads to the attainment of the highest good: (1) The Means of Right

Cognition; (2) The Objects of Right Cognition; (3) Doubt; (4) Motive; (5) Example; (6) Theory; (7) Factors of Inference; (8) Cogitation; (9) Demonstrated Truth; (10) Discussion; (11) Disputation; (12) Wrangling; (13) Fallacious Reason; (14) Casuistry; (15) Futile Rejoinder and (16) Clinchers."

Logic is here practiced for the sake of salvation. That gives greater weight to the *Nyāya Sūtra* within Hinduism than a book on logic would normally have within a religious tradition. Logic as a way to truth is a means of liberation: "Suffering, birth, activity, mistaken notions, folly – if these factors are cancelled out in reverse order, there will be *mokṣa*."[18]

S. K. Sarma makes an important point when he states: "*Nyāya* is not logic in the strict sense of the word. It is a system of philosophy. It is true that it lays stress on inference or reasoning as a means to correct knowledge, but it is not formal. It is not a mere device for correct thinking, but a well-thought-out and complete metaphysical thesis."[19]

A definite break in the development of *Nyāya* took place in the twelfth century, which marks the rise of *Navya-Nyāya* or the New Logic. Whereas the earlier works had been concentrating on the elucidation of the categories, as enumerated in the *Nyāya Sūtra*, the *Tattva-cintāmaṇi* by Gaṅgeśa, the major work of the new school, emphasized the *pramāṇas*, the means of valid cognition, devoting one chapter each to perception (*pratyakṣa*), inference (*anumāna*) analogy (*upamāna*), and verbal testimony (*śabda*).

In spite of the intention to keep the description non-technical it should be said that *Navya-Nyāya* not only developed a highly complex epistemology but also created a technical language with the help of newly coined terms and thus initiated a quite peculiar style of philosophical writing in India which stands out for its brevity and precision. The development of *Navya-Nyāya* and the focusing upon *pramāṇas* instead on the categories of the *Nyāya Sūtra* did not prevent the continued production of works of the "old school" alongside the flourishing "new logic." Works in both branches keep appearing even in our day.

The special field of *Navya-Nyāya* is epistemology. It acknowledges four legitimate means of finding truth: *pratyakṣa* or sense perception, *anumāna* or inference, *upamāna* or analogy, and *śabda* or scriptural authority. *Pratyakṣa* is the perception that results from the contact of one of the senses with its proper object: it is definite, uncontradicted and unassociated with names. *Anumāna* is of three kinds: *pūrvavat* or from cause to effect, *śeṣavat* or from effect to cause, and *samanyato dṛṣṭa* or from common characteristics. *Upamāna* is the knowing of anything by similarity with any well-known thing. *Śabda* is defined as the testimony of reliable authority, which may also transcend one's own experience.

The objects of knowledge are: *ātman*, the body, senses, sense-objects, *buddhi* or understanding, *manas* or mind, *pravṛtti* or endeavor, rebirths, enjoyment of pleasure and suffering of pain, sorrow and liberation. Desire, aversion, effort, pleasure and pain, as well as knowledge, indicate the existence of the *ātman*. The classical Aristotelian syllogism has three members – major, minor, and conclusion – the Nyāya-syllogism has five:

1. *pratijñā* or the stating of the point to be proved;
2. *hetu* or the reason which establishes the proof;
3. *udahāraṇa* or illustrative example;
4. *upanaya* or corroboration by the instance;
5. *nigamana* or inference, identical with the initial assertion.

The standard example of Indian logic for many centuries has been the following:

- The mountain there in the distance is ablaze (1);
- Because it is wreathed in smoke (2);
- Whatever is wreathed in smoke is on fire, as e.g. a stove (3);
- The mountain there is wreathed in smoke in such a manner (4);
- Therefore: the mountain there in the distance is ablaze (5).

The discussion of fallacies and doubt demonstrates the lucidity and sharpness of the Naiyāyikas' intellects. All kinds of fallacies are analyzed and the causes of doubt are explained, but the general skepticism of the Buddhists, who maintained that nothing can be known with certainty, is refuted. The polemics against Buddhism, especially the *Śūnya-vādins*, plays a large part in *Nyāya* literature. Naiyāyikas dissolve the extreme skepticism of the Buddhists with their critical realism and take the wind out of the Buddhists' sails by disproving their teaching of emptiness and the impossibility of true cognition with the very arguments which the Buddhists have used. The Naiyāyikas seek to demonstrate that real liberation is possible through true cognition of reality. They agree with Vaiśeṣika metaphysics when they define *mokṣa* only in negative terms as "absolute freedom from pain."[20] It is a "condition of immortality, free from fear, imperishable," to be attained only after bodily death – there can be no *jīvan-mukta*.[21]

Quite unique in Indian philosophy are the arguments for the existence of *Īśvara*, which we find in Nyāya works.[22] The *Nyāya Kusumañjalī* states that the experience of contingency, eternity, diversity, activity, and individual existence requires an *adṛṣṭa*, an unseen cause, responsible ultimately for the joys and sorrows of human life. Above the *adṛṣṭa* of the Vaiśeṣikas, the Naiyāyikas postulate a Lord as the cause of right knowledge, of creation and destruction. "From effects, combination, support, etc. and traditional arts, authority, *śruti* and so on, an everlasting omniscient being must be assumed." The commentary on this text explains:

> The earth etc. must have had a maker, because they have the nature of effects like a jar; by a thing's having a maker we mean that it is produced by some agent who possesses the wish to make, and has also a perceptive knowledge of the material cause out of which it is to be made. "Combination" is an action, and therefore the action which produced the conjunction of two atoms, initiating the *dvyaṇuka* at the beginning of a creation, must have been accompanied by the volition of an intelligent being, because it has the nature of an action like the actions of bodies such as ours. "Support" etc.: the world depends upon some being who possesses a volition which hinders it from falling, because it has the nature of being supported ... By traditional arts etc.: The traditional arts now current, such as that of making cloth, must have been originated by an independent being, from the very fact that they are traditional usages like the tradition of modern modes of writing. "From authority": The knowledge produced by the *Vedas* is produced by a virtue residing in its cause, because it is right knowledge, just as in the case of the right knowledge produced by perception. "From *śruti*": The *Veda* must have been produced by a person, from its having the nature of a *Veda* like the *Āyur Veda* ... At the beginning of creation there must be the number of duality abiding in the atoms, which is the cause of the measure of the *dvyaṇuka* but this number cannot be produced at that time by the distinguishing perception of beings like ourselves. Therefore we can only assume this distinguishing faculty as then existing in *Īśvara*.[23]

The Lord is qualified by absence of *adharma*, of *mithyā-jñāna*, or false knowledge, and of *pramāda*, or error, and the positive presence of *dharma*, right knowledge and equanimity. He is omnipotent, though influenced in his actions by the acts of his creatures. He acts only for the good of his creatures and acts toward them like a father toward his children.[24] The Naiyāyikas also develop a theory of grace: "*Īśvara* indeed supports the efforts of people, i.e. if a person tries to attain something special, it is *Īśvara* who attains it; if *Īśvara* does not act, the activity of people is fruitless."

A good deal of *Nyāya* is so technical that it taxes the understanding even of a specialist in Western logic, not to speak of the general reader. Much of it is of interest mainly against the background of inner-Indian disputes, especially with the Buddhist logicians. It is, however, important to note that India, too, has its schools of critical logicians, and that, despite the popular opinion of Indian philosophy being merely opaque mysticism, there is also the disciplined reasoning of logic.

Tarka-śāstra, the study of formal logic, is a difficult business and no more popular in India than anywhere else. Keśava Miśra of the fourteenth century, the author of a concise textbook which is still widely used, starts off his course in the following gruff manner: "I am writing this 'Exposition of Reasoning' consisting, as it does, of short and easy explanations of arguments, for the sake of the dull youth who wishes to have to learn as little as possible for the purpose of entering the portals of the Nyāya *darśana*."[25]

Nyāya-vaiśeṣika has remained a living philosophical tradition even in our age. The more it is studied, the more respect it commands for its incisiveness and brilliance of definition. It could also possibly make a substantial contribution to the contemporary philosophy of science, anticipating, often by many centuries, problems which we are only now discovering.

SĀṀKHYA-YOGA

Yoga is one of the most popular and most ambiguous words in Indian literature, a word with which every Westerner seems to be familiar, as the advertisements of numerous Yoga schools suggest. Etymologically the word is derived from the root *yuj-*, to join, to unite. Pāniṇi, the grammarian, explains the meaning of *yoga* as virtually identical with that of our word "religion," union with the Supreme. Patañjali, in his *Yoga Sūtra*, defines *yoga* as "cessation of all changes in consciousness." According to the Vedāntins *yoga* means the return of the *jīvātman*, the individual being, to its union with the *paramātman*, the Supreme Self. In a more general sense Hindu scriptures use the word *yoga* as a synonym to *mārga*, denoting any system of religion or philosophy, speaking of *karma-yoga*, *bhakti-yoga*, *jñāna-yoga*.

Here we deal with *yoga* only in its technical and classical sense: the Yoga system as explained by Patañjali. It is called *Rāja Yoga*, the "royal way" in contrast to *Haṭha Yoga*, the "tour de force"[26] of most Western

Yoga schools, or the *Kuṇḍalinī Yoga* of the Śāktas. It is also called Sāṁkhya-Yoga, because of its intimate connection with the *darśana* known as Sāṁkhya[27]

Sāṁkhya-Yoga has become, in one form or another, part and parcel of most major religions of India: thus we find Sāṁkhya-Yoga combined with Vaiṣṇavism, Śaivism and Śāktism, and most of the Purāṇas contain numerous chapters on Sāṁkhya-Yoga as a path to salvation.[28] It fell into disfavor at a later time when Vedānta in one of its denominational schools became the predominant theology of Hinduism. The reasons for this development are twofold. Sāṁkhya does not base its statements on scripture; it even explicitly rates *śruti* no higher than reasoning. And Sāṁkhya did not recognize a Lord above *puruṣa* and *prakṛti*, an idea which was crucial to the theistic systems of medieval Hinduism.

The interpretation of some Mohenjo-Daro seals showing figures in what has been interpreted as yoga-posture would suggest a pre-historic root of practices later brought together in the Yoga system. The basis of the Sāṁkhya, the male–female polarity as the source of all development, does not need a specific inventor, it can easily be considered as a "natural system." In some of the earlier Upaniṣads we find allusions to doctrines that could be termed Sāṁkhya, leaving open the question whether the Upaniṣads refer to an already developed philosophical system or whether the system developed out of the elements provided in the Upaniṣads. In order to explain the name Sāṁkhya – in modern Indian languages the word for "number" – some scholars have resorted to the hypothesis of an original Sāṁkhya which, like the school of Pythagoras, was concerned with numbers and conceived of the world as being constructed from harmonious proportions.[29]

The original meaning of Sāṁkhya must have been very general: understanding, reflection, discussion. The name simply came to connote philosophy or system. Kapila, its mythical founder, figures in the Indian tradition quite often as the father of philosophy as such. Later Vedānta, which assumes a different position on many basic issues, polemizes quite frequently against the Sāṁkhya-system, but there is hardly a book that does not deal with it or that would not betray its influence.

Sāṁkhya ideas may be found already in the cosmogonic hymns of the *Ṛgveda*, in sections of the *Atharvaveda*, in the idea of the evolution of all things from one principle, dividing itself, in the Upaniṣads, and also in the Upaniṣadic attempts to arrange all phenomena under a limited number of categories. The *Mahābhārata* has sections explaining the full

Sāṁkhya system, though with significant differences as compared to the classical Sāṁkhya. The Great Epic makes Kapila the son of Brahmā; according to the *Bhāgavata Purāṇa* he is an *avatāra* of Viṣṇu who teaches Sāṁkhya as a system of liberation through which his mother reaches instant release.[30] There is not much historical evidence for the opinion, found in some works on Indian philosophy, that as a historical person Kapila belongs to the sixth century B.C.E. The oldest traditional textbook of the school is the *Sāṁkhya-kārikā* of Īśvara Kṛṣṇa, dating probably from the third century C.E. This work, which has received numerous important commentaries in later centuries, claims to be the complete summary of the entire *Śaṣṭi-tantra*, perhaps an older work. The *Sāṁkhya-kārikā* are a short treatise, containing only seventy aphorisms.[31] The *Sāṁkhya-sūtra*, ascribed to Kapila himself, is a later work, much longer than the *Kārikā* and going into more detail.[32]

Yoga as a system is already dealt with quite extensively in some of the later Upaniṣads, which in fact are sometimes brief compendia of Yoga.[33] The *Tejobindu Upaniṣad* gives a fairly detailed description of *rāja-yoga*. Many of the teachings found in it can be found word for word in Patañjali's *Yoga Sūtra*, which has become the classical textbook, commented upon by great scholars like Vyāsa and Bhoja.[34] This Upaniṣad suggests to the Yogi who is intent on realization to repeat constantly: "I am Brahman." He is advised sometimes to affirm and sometimes to negate the identity of all things with *brahman*. "Renouncing all the various activities think thus: 'I am Brahman – I am of the nature of *sac-cid-ānanda*.' And then renounce even this!"[35]

Most Indian schools, be they followers of the Sāṁkhya or of the Vedānta philosophy, accept Patañjali-yoga as a practical and indispensable means for purification and concentration. Recently a commentary to the Patañjali *Yoga Sūtra*, ascribed to Śaṅkara, has been published from a manuscript in Madras. Many scholars assume it to be genuine, in spite of the polemic against Sāṁkhya-Yoga in the *Brahmasūtrabhāyṣa*.[36]

The Basic Philosophy of Sāṁkhya

The *Sāṁkhya Kārikās* begin with the aphorism: "From torment by threefold misery the inquiry into the means of terminating it."[37] Our frustrations and pains, caused by *devas* and *asuras*, fellow-men, beasts, inanimate and ourselves,[38] are the stimulus for the quest for freedom from misery: Sāṁkhya offers the solution. Sāṁkhya neither denies the reality of experience nor the reality of pain accompanying every experience, but it offers a possibility of terminating this pain of experience. Rejecting all other means, the *Kārikās* establish the thesis that "the discriminative knowledge of the evolved, the unevolved and the knower is the means of surpassing all sorrow."[39]

Basically Sāṁkhya defends, or rather presupposes, a dualistic realism. There are two beginningless realities: *prakṛti* and *puruṣa*, the female and the male principle, matter and spirit. Ideally, before the development of concrete existences, they exist separately in polarity. In actual existence they are combined and interacting. *Puruṣa*, pure consciousness, experiences the changes which *prakṛti*, on account of her three *guṇas*, is undergoing, as if these were his own. *Puruṣas* are originally many – *prakṛti* is originally one. The association with a *puruṣa* makes *prakṛti*, as the evolved being, manifold and makes *puruṣa* interact with it. Under the influence of *puruṣa*, out of the unevolved primordial *prakṛti*, develop macrocosm and microcosm according to a fixed pattern. Each part of it is characterized in a different measure by the presence of the three *guṇas*. Originally the three *guṇas* – *sattva* (lightness), *rajas* (passion) and *tamas* (darkness) – had been in equilibrium in *prakṛti*. Under *puruṣa*'s influence the equilibrium is disturbed and evolution begins. The first product of this evolutionary process, which simply takes its course without needing a creator or a world-soul, is *mahat*, the Great One, also called *buddhi*, the intellect. From *mahat* issues *ahaṁkāra*, the principle of individuation. Having the *tri-guṇa* structure, it communicates it to the further "evolutes" (i.e., the products of the evolution taking place through the interaction between *puruṣa* and *praktṛi*): the senses and the elements which form their object. The enumeration of the twenty-four basic elements is intended to provide a description of the universe and to prepare the ground for the way back to the source. Against those who assume that there is only one spirit in the universe, the *Kārikās* establish the following argument: "The plurality of *puruṣas* follows from the fact of individual death and individual birth, and from the fact that the organs of cognition and action are individual; moreover not all people are active at the same time and the relationship of the three *guṇas* varies from person to person."[40]

In *devas* and saintly people *sattva* dominates; in ordinary people *rajas*, and in animals *tamas*. To dispel the objection that *prakṛti* is mere fiction because she cannot be seen, heard, touched, etc., the *Kārikās* state: "The non-perception is due to its subtlety, not to its non-existence, since it is cognized from its effects."[41]

Knowing *prakṛti* as *prakṛti* is becoming free from her; for *prakṛti* is not only the means to bind *puruṣa* but also the means to free him. If a person is able to analyze experience in such a way as to differentiate *puruṣa* from *prakṛti* in consciousness, seeing in *prakṛti* the reason for the contingence of all things and the basis for all change and multiplicity, he or she is free. Though *puruṣa* is free by nature, he is incapable of acting and thus unable to free himself when associated with *prakṛti*: "Certainly no *puruṣa* is in bondage and none is liberated nor has he to undergo any changes; it is *prakṛti*, dwelling in many forms, which is bound, freed and subject to change. *Prakṛti* binds herself sevenfold and through one form she causes liberation for the benefit of *puruṣa*."[42]

The *Kārikās* compare *puruṣa* and *prakṛti* with a lame man being carried by a blind man: it is the seeing lame one that directs the blind walking one and realizes his own purpose. In another simile the *puruṣa* is compared to a spectator observing a dancer. After the dancer has shown all her skills, she cannot but repeat her performance over and over again. When the onlooker becomes aware of the repeat performance he loses his interest. And the dancer, seeing that the spectator pays no more attention to her, ceases to dance. Although the union still persists, nothing more is produced from it. "*Puruṣa*, because of former impressions, remains associated with the body, just like the potter's wheel continues to rotate for a while without being impelled again, due to the impulse received before."[43]

When the separation from the body finally takes place and the aim has been fulfilled, *prakṛti* ceases to be active and *puruṣa* reaches *kaivalya*, aloneness, perfect freedom. By doing away with objective sense perception, by tracing back egoism and discursive reasoning to *prakṛti*, by coming to know the true nature of *prakṛti*, *puruṣa* becomes emancipated. Spirit, having been restless in connection with matter, realizes matter to be the cause of his restlessness. By realizing the nature of *prakṛti* as contrary to his own nature and recognizing all objective reality as but "evolutes" of *prakṛti* the spirit becomes self-satisfied and self-reliant. The very dissociation of *puruṣa* from *prakṛti* is his liberation.

The Theory and Practice of Yoga

The practical process of discriminative knowledge leading to the actual achievement of the "isolation" of the *puruṣa* is proposed in Patañjali's *Yoga Sūtras*. Yoga is not mere theoretical knowledge but it also implies physical training, exertion of will-power and acts of decision, because it deals with the complete human situation and provides real freedom, not just a theory of liberation.

The *sūtra* itself – a short work of but 194 aphorisms – is clearly structured into four *pādas*, with the subject-titles *samādhi* ("trance"), *sādhana* ("means of realization"), *vibhūti* ("preternatural accomplishments"), and *kaivalya* ("ultimate aim"). The first *sūtra*, defining the aim and meaning of Yoga as *citta-vṛtti-nirodha* ("cessation of all changes of the mind"), goes to the very core of Sāṁkhya metaphysics. *Citta* is identical with the *mahat* of the Sāṁkhya, the first evolved, whose changes ultimately cause all suffering. For *citta* the cessation of all changes means merging into *prakṛti*. *Prakṛti* then becomes again undifferentiated and dissociated from *puruṣa*: the *puruṣa* achieves *ekāgratā*, one-pointedness, *kaivalya*, aloneness, being-with-himself-only, being nothing but consciousness. The changes that may affect *citta* are enumerated as five-fold: perception, delusion, imagination, deep sleep and memory.[44] The means to do away with them is *abhyāsa* and *vairāgya*, the dialectic interaction of positive effort and renunciation. The *Yoga Sūtras* introduce *īśvara*, the Lord, as one of the supports of concentration. *Īśvara* is defined as a *pūruṣa*, untouched by suffering, activity and *karma*. He is the teacher of the ancients and is denoted by the sign Om, whose constant repetition is recommended to the Yogi to attain *kaivalya*.[45] The Lord is also a help in removing the obstacles that hinder self-realization: sickness, suffering, indecision, carelessness, sloth, sensuality, false views, and inconstancy which cause distraction. In the company of these distractions come pain, despair, tremor, hard and irregular breathing. For the purification of the mind the *Yoga Sūtra* recommends truthfulness, friendliness, compassion, contentment together with indifference toward happiness and unhappiness, virtue and vice. Breath-control, too, is advised.

The second part of the *Yoga Sūtra* dealing with *sādhana*, the means to liberation, begins with the aphorism: "The *yoga* of action is constituted by *tapas* or austerities, *svādhyāya* or scriptural study, and *isvara pranidhana* or meditation with the Lord as object." Its goal is to attain *samādhi*, "trance," complete inner peace, and to terminate the *kleśas*, the frustrations and afflictions. The root-cause and source of all suffering is identified as *avidyā*, lack of insight and wisdom. It manifests itself in four principal forms, as *asmitā*, egoism, *rāga*, attachment, *dveṣa,* aversion, and *abhiniveśā*, love of physical life. *Avidyā* is further explained as mistaking the non-eternal for the eternal, the impure for the pure, the painful for the pleasurable, and the not-self for the Self.[46] To combat these afflictions the *Yoga Sūtras* commend *dhyāna* (meditation). The actual vehicle of liberation is *viveka*, discrimination, implying understanding of the Self as the only true and worthwhile being and the rest as illusory. This knowledge arises only after the impurities of the mind have been destroyed by the practice of the eight *yogāṅgas*, limbs of Yoga. These are *yama* and *niyama*, ethical commands and prohibitions, *āsana* (bodily postures), *prāṇāyāma* (breath control), *pratyāhāra* (withdrawal of the senses), *dhāraṇā* (concentration), *dhyāna* (meditation), and *samādhi* (trance).

The *Yoga Sūtras* find that the cause of all sin lies in *lobha*, *moha*, and *krodha* – greed, delusion, and anger – whereas with the practice of the virtues many side effects are produced that are helpful either for the Yogi's own realization or for his fellow-men. Thus when *ahiṃsā*, non-violence, is firmly established, others too will give up their enmity and violence in the presence of the Yogi; not only people but also animals will live peacefully with each other. When *satya*, the love of truth, is perfected it enables a person to perform great deeds. When *asteya*, abstention from misappropriation is practiced, the treasures from which the Yogi runs away will run after him. When *brahmacarya*, perfect continence, is practiced, great strength will come to the Yogi. The practice of *aparigraha*, of generosity in the widest sense, brings with it a knowledge of the round of births and rebirths. *Śauca*, disgust with one's own body, is accompanied by the end of the desire to have bodily contact with others. Purity also helps to attain physical well-being, control over one's senses and concentration. *Santoṣa*, contentment, brings inner peace and happiness to the Yogi. *Tapasya*, practice of austerities, purifies from sins and makes the Yogi acquire *siddhis* or supernatural faculties. Through *svādhyāya*, scriptural study, one can reach the *Īṣṭadevatā*. *Īśvara praṇidhāna*, surrender to the Lord, brings about *samādhi*, "trance," peace and illumination.

Āsana, posture, is defined as a way of sitting that is agreeable and enables the practicant to sit motionless for a long time without falling asleep or straining himself. It is intended to overcome the distraction caused by the *dvandvas*, the pairs of opposites like heat and cold, hunger and thirst, comfort and discomfort. While *Haṭha Yoga* manuals develop a veritable science of the *āsanas*, enumerating altogether eighty-four extremely difficult bodily postures for curing or preventing diseases or attaining certain other results, Patañjali is of the opinion that any position will serve, provided that it allows a person to practice continued concentration and meditation: his aim is neither self-mortification for its own sake, nor the cure of bodily ailments, but spiritual realization.[47]

In the third *pāda* Patañjali speaks about the extraordinary or miraculous faculties of the Yogi, *siddhis* or *vibhūtis* which appear as side effects of Yoga. Despite Patañjali's warning that they should not be cultivated, because they detract from the principal aim of Yoga as spiritual realization, a number of Yogis at all times have practiced Yoga for the sake of those *siddhis* – becoming invisible, reducing one's size to that of a grain of sand or increasing it to the volume of a mountain, adopting a radiant body or leaving the body and reentering it at will.

Patañjali stresses the moral aspects of the preparation for *kaivalya*. If evil desires and intentions are not completely purged, there is the danger that the increased power which a Yogi wins through concentration may be used for evil purposes, rather than for realization of the highest aim.

Dietetic rules are prominent in many books on Yoga; whatever is sour, salty, or pungent should be avoided. Non-stimulating food will allow the body to come to rest; milk alone is the ideal food for Yogis.

The Core of Yoga

In the *Yoga Sūtras* one of the most important topics is *prāṇāyāma*. *Prāṇa*, or life-breath, has always played a significant role in Indian philosophical speculation. *Prāṇāyāma* is one of the most widely practiced disciplines and one of the most ancient methods of purification. Perfect breath-control can be carried so far that to all appearances a person does not breathe any more and the heart-beat becomes imperceptible. Thus we hear quite frequently about Yogis who get themselves buried for days or weeks and let themselves be admired on coming out from their graves. According to all indications there is neither fraud nor miracle involved. The secret lies in the consciously controlled reduction of metabolism to the minimum required for keeping the life-processes going and in the overcoming of fear through concentration; for fear would increase the need for oxygen. The *Yoga Sūtras* end the explanations on *prāṇāyāma* with the statement: "The mind's ability for concentration." Breath control is the basis of body control and of mental realization.

Pratyāhāra, withdrawal of the senses, is dealt with immediately afterwards: "When the senses do not have any contact with their objects and follow, as it were, the nature of the mind."[48] The senses, in this condition, not only no longer hinder the intellect, but the power invested in them actively helps it.

The next section is probably the most crucial one: it deals with three stages of realization. They are briefly explained as follows: "*Dhāraṇā* is the fixation of the intellect on one topic. *Dhyāna* is the one-pointedness in this effort. *Samādhi* is the same (concentration) when the object itself alone appears devoid of form, as it were."[49] The commentaries explain the first stage as a concentration of the mind on certain areas in the body: the navel, the heart, the forehead, the tip of the nose, or the tip of the tongue. In the second stage all objects are consciously eliminated and the union with the absolute is contemplated. In its perfection it glides over into the third and last stage. Here the identification has gone so far that there is no longer a process of contemplation of an object by a subject, but an absolute identity between the knower, that which is known and the process of knowing. Subject–object polarity disappears in a pure "is-ness," a cessation of the particular in an absolute self-awareness.

The three stages together are called *saṃyama*. They are understood not as something that incidentally happens to someone but as a practice that can be learned and acquired and then exercised at will. It is the specific schooling of the Yogi to acquire those tools with which one masters the world. Though we must omit the details here, suffice it to say that as with the mastery of any science, so Yoga requires a certain talent, hard work and progress through many small steps, avoiding numerous pitfalls on the way, before one can competently use the appropriate instruments. If the training is applied to the various objects and the various levels of reality, the Yogi can win knowledge of the future and the past, obtain a knowledge of all languages and the sounds of all living beings, understand the language of the animals, know about former births, read other people's thought, become invisible, foresee the exact time of death, become full of goodwill toward all creatures, gain the strength of an elephant, have knowledge of what is subtle, distant and hidden, know the regions of the firmament, the stars and their orbits, and the whole anatomy of the human body, suppress completely hunger and thirst, see the *devas*, have foreknowledge of all that is going to happen, receive extrasensory sight, hearing and taste, acquire the ability to enter other bodies mentally at will, walk freely on water without even touching it, walk across thorny and muddy ground without getting hurt or dirty; acquire a body which is bright and weightless; leave the body and act without it, become master of all material elements; obtain a body which is beautiful, strong and as hard as a diamond; have direct knowledge of the *pradhāna*, the ground from which all beings come, and mastery over all conditions of being as well as omniscience.[50]

More than anything else those *vibhūtis* have been described and dreamed about in literature about Indian Yogis. Biographies and autobiographies of Yogis are full of reports about such feats. In actual life one hardly ever encounters any miracles of this sort. Living for years in a place where thousands of holy men and women dwelled and where countless rumours about *siddhis* circulated, I never witnessed a single incident corresponding to this idea of the miraculous. Not too many years ago a Yogi called a press conference in Bombay and announced that he would demonstrate walking on water without wetting even his feet, against a purse of one million rupees. The bargain was agreed upon and a tank was built and filled with water. The Yogi could choose the auspicious time for his performance. When the hour had come, scores of journalists and hundreds of curious onlookers were present to watch the Yogi win his million. He lost it, being unable even to swim like an ordinary mortal. Later "unfavorable circumstances" were blamed for the Yogi's failure and another attempt was announced for an undisclosed future date.

According to Patañjali the purpose of many of these *vibhūtis* is fulfilled if the Yogi experiences in trance those miraculous happenings as if they were real. In the overall context of *rāja-yoga* the *siddhis* are an obstacle on the way to *samādhi*.

The fourth and last *pāda* of the *Yoga Sūtras* deals with *kaivalya*, the goal of Yoga. The introductory aphorism states that the above-mentioned *siddhis* are brought about either by imprints left in the psyche from previous births, by drugs, by *mantras*, or by *samādhi*. The proper thrust of *samādhi*, however, is not backward into the world of objects, from which it is freeing the spirit, but forward into the discrimination of *puruṣa* from the *guṇas* that belong to *prakṛti*. *Viveka*, discriminatory knowledge, means freedom from the influence of the *guṇas*: they return to their source as soon as their task is fulfilled. *Prakṛti* withdraws as soon as *puruṣa* has seen her as *prakrti*. When the *guṇas* cease to be effective, activity and passivity, action and suffering also cease. "*Kaivalya* is realized when the *guṇas*, annihilated in the objectives of a person, cease to exert influence, or when *citta-śakti*, the power of consciousness, is established in her own proper nature."[51]

Yoga is the reversal of the evolutionary process demonstrated in the Sāṁkhya system, it is the entering into the origins. It is not, however, simply an annihilation of creation. Sāṁkhya does not think in terms of the model of the genetic method of modern science, but phenomenologically. *Prakṛti*, "matter," is not an object of physics but of metaphysics. Her eternity is not the non-destructibility of a concrete object but of potentiality.[52] When *puruṣa* combines with her, there is no need for any additional cause from outside to set evolution going. It is an unfolding of primeval matter which until then had existed as mere potency, but which is always there. Yoga comes close to what we today would call psycho-science, that is, a detailed observation of human nature, but with a deep conviction of an ultimate that is missing in modern psychology.

Yoga has become part of our spiritual world culture and many Westerners, who have received training from Hindu masters, opened up Yoga schools of their own, often modifying the original teaching and adapting it to Western minds and bodies. One of the best known representatives of Yoga in the West today is Georg Feuerstein, founder and director of the Yoga Research and Education Center in Lower Lake, California. He has written numerous books about Yoga. His latest, *The Yoga Tradition. Its History, Literature, Philosophy and Practice*,[53] is a most comprehensive and exhaustive survey of Yoga not only in the Hindu but also in other traditions. He also publishes *Yoga-World*, an international newsletter for Yoga teachers and students, with many useful and insightful articles and news items. The Indian Government runs a scientific Yoga Research Centre in Lonavla (Mahārāṣṭra) where Yoga treatment is clinically supervised by modern-trained physicians.

PŪRVĀ AND UTTARA MĪMĀṂSĀ

Mīmāṃsā, "enquiry," is the name of two very different systems of Hindu theology which have one thing in common: out of the statements of *śruti* they develop a complete theology.

Pūrva Mīmāṃsā (often simply called *Mīmāṃsā*), the "earlier enquiry" has *dharma* as its proper subject and the *karma-kāṇḍa* of the Vedas as its scriptural source. *Uttara Mīmāṃsā*, the "latter enquiry," better known as Vedānta, has *brahman* knowledge as its subject and the *jñāna-kāṇḍa* of the Veda as its scriptural basis. Though historically there was a considerable amount of friction between the two systems, they are also in many ways complementary and are considered to be the two most orthodox of the six systems. Certainly they are the two *darśanas* that come closest to the idea of theology as developed in the West.

Essentials of Pūrva Mīmāṃsā

At the end of the "Short History of Vedic Religion" (p. 68), Pūrva Mīmāṃsā was mentioned as the most orthodox form of Vedic exegesis, and some of its texts and its history were described, that need not be repeated here.

Athato dharma-jijñāsa, "Now, then, an enquiry into *dharma*," is the first sentence of the *Jaimini Sūtras*. It goes on to explain: "*Dharma* is that which is indicated by Vedic injunctions for the attainment of the good".[54] The Mīmāṃsakas took it for granted that the performance of sacrifices was the means to attain everything and that the Veda was meant to serve this end alone. Despite their insistence that the Veda was *a-pauruṣeya*, not man-made, and infallible revelation, they were prepared to drop all those parts of the Veda as non-essential which had nothing directly to do with sacrificial ritual. "The purpose of the Veda lying in the enjoining of actions, those parts of the Veda which do not serve that purpose are useless; in these therefore the Veda is declared to be non-eternal."[55]

Classical Mīmāṃsā does not admit the existence of any *īśvara* as the creator and destroyer of the universe. Mīmāṃsakas even formulate arguments which positively disprove the existence of God.[56] The world, in their view, has always been in existence and the only real agent of a permanent nature was the sacrifice, or rather its unseen essence, the *a-pūrva*. Sacrifice, therefore, is the only topic that really interests the Mīmāṃsakas. The texts treat of the eternity of the *Veda*, of the means to its correct understanding and of the validity of human knowledge as preliminaries to this question.[57]

Many times we read in the *Brāhmaṇas*: "Desiring heaven one should perform sacrifice." Consequently the Mīmāṃsakas emphasize that "desire for heaven" is the basic presupposition for performing a sacrifice. Besides animals, *devas* and the Vedic *ṛṣis*, women and *śūdras* are categorically excluded from the performance of sacrifices. So are those who lack sufficient wealth or suffer from a physical disability.[58] The theory of *a-pūrva* is intended to explain the infallible effect of a sacrifice. The Mīmāṃsakas say that the *a-pūrva* is related to the verb of the Vedic injunction because this expresses something as yet to be accomplished. More subtly Mīmāṃsa distinguishes between principal and secondary *a-pūrva*.[59]

The *Mīmāṃsā Sūtra* is very brief in its description of the state to be achieved through sacrifice, namely *svarga* (heaven). Mīmāṃsākas are probably convinced that one cannot know much about it. By its very own principles it must come to the conclusion that passages in the Vedas which describe heaven, not enjoining certain acts, cannot be taken as authoritative. One *sūtra* says: "That one result would be heaven, as that is equally desirable for all."[60] To which the commentator adds: "Why so? Because heaven is happiness and everyone seeks for happiness." The *Mīmāṃsā Sūtra* does not mention the term *mokṣa* at all. Śabara declared that the statements concerning heaven found in the *Mahābhārata* and the Purāṇas can be neglected because these books were composed by men; and also that Vedic descriptions of heaven were mere *arthavāda*, without authority.[61] Later Mīmāṃsākas, perhaps influenced by Vedānta, introduce the term *mokṣa* into their vocabulary and describe it as not having to assume a body after death.[62] They also offer a description of the way to liberation: becoming disgusted with the troubles that one has to undergo during life on earth, finding the pleasures of the world to be invariably accompanied by some sort of pain, one comes to lose all interest in, and longing for, pleasures. Turning one's attention toward liberation, one ceases to perform acts that are prohibited and which lead to misfortune, as well as acts that are prescribed but only to lead to some sort of happiness here or hereafter. One attenuates all previously acquired karma by undergoing the experiences resulting from it, and destroys the sole receptacle or abode of these experiences by the knowledge of the *ātman*. Virtues such as contentment, self-control and so forth prevent the further return of the soul into this world. Finally the soul becomes free, a *mukta*.[63]

With their interest in language and analysis the Mīmāṃsakas are often close to the Grammarians, who developed a philosophical school of their own. Important epistemological observations can be found already in the *Śābara-bhāṣya*.[64] The first major commentary on Pāṇini's *sūtras*, the *Mahā-bhāṣya* by Patañjali (which is ascribed to the second century B.C.E.) contains questions concerning the nature and function of words. The most famous name in Indian linguistic philosophy, however, is Bhartṛhari (*c.*500 C.E.) whose *Vākya-padīya* has been studied with great interest by Western scholars in recent years. His system is also called *sphoṭa-vāda* after its most characteristic teaching which compares the sudden appearance of meaning at the enunciation of a word with the process of the sudden ejection of liquid from a boil.[65]

Uttara Mīmāṃsā or Vedānta

Athāto brahma-jijñasa, "Now, then, an enquiry into *brahman*," begins the *Vedānta Sūtra*, also called *Brahma Sūtra*, which is ascribed to Bādarāyaṇa, and forms the basic text of Vedānta *darśana*. The 550 *sūtras*, purporting to summarize the teaching of the Upaniṣads, are usually so short – often consisting of not more than one or two words – that without a commentary they remain incomprehensible. In all probability there had been a living tradition of Vedāntins in which the meaning of the *Vedānta Sūtra* was passed on from one generation to the next. As the Upaniṣads themselves took great care to maintain the *guru paraṃparā*, the succession of authorized teachers of the *vidyā* contained in them, so also the systematized aphoristic *sūtra*-text and its meaning was preserved in a carefully guarded tradition, the beginning of which we are unable to identify.

According to Indian tradition there had been other *Brahma Sūtras* before the one composed by Bādarāyaṇa. The most famous of these predecessors must have been an Ācarya Bādarī who is credited with having written both a *Mīmāṃsā Sūtra* and a *Vedānta Sūtra*.[66] Other *ācāryas*, whose names are found in ancient texts as forerunner to Bādarāyaṇa include Kārṣṇājini, Ātreya, Auḍulomi, Āsmarāthya, Kāśakṛtsna, Kāśyapa, Vedavyāsa – all mentioned in the extant *Brahma Sūtra* – whose works have not been preserved. In all probability Bādarāyaṇa's *sūtra* impressed his contemporaries as being superior, so that in the course of time it completely replaced the others.[67] The *bhāṣyas*, or commentaries to the *Brahma Sūtra*, have gained authoritative position in the recognized ten branches of Vedānta, combining a textual exegesis with other living traditions, as we saw earlier when dealing with Vaiṣṇavism and Śaivism.[68] The oldest of the extant complete commentaries is that by Śaṅkarācārya. We know that there had been earlier commentaries associated with names like Bhartṛprapanca, Bhartṛmitra, Bhartṛhari, Upavarṣa, Bodhāyaṇa (whose authority is several times invoked by Rāmānuja against Śaṅkara), Brahmānaṇḍi, Ṭaṅka, Brahmadatta, Bhāruci, Sundarapāṇḍya, Gauḍapāda and Govinda Bhagavatpāda, the *guru* of Śaṅkaracārya.[69]

As the commentators, expounding the most diverse theological views, demonstrate, the original *Brahma Sūtra* is merely a kind of general frame for a further development of ideas, which are left fairly vague and undetermined. Looking at the bare *sūtras* without a commentary one can only give a general idea of their structure without discussing their import.

The *Vedānta Sūtra* is divided into four *adhyāyas*, chapters, each subdivided into four *pādas*, literally "feet" or parts, which again are made up of a varying number of *sūtras* or aphorisms.

The entire first *adhyāya* is devoted to a discussion on *brahman*: *brahman* is the sole and supreme cause of all things. Systems which teach otherwise are rejected as heretical. The detailed polemics against the Sāṁkhya system is continued into the second *adhyāya* which also refutes Vaiśeṣika theories. Toward the end of the second *pāda* the *Bhāgavata* system is mentioned. The comments on this part of the text (II,2,42–48) are a classic example of the wide diversity that exists in the commentaries. Śaṅkara understands the *sūtra* to say that the *Bhāgavata* system is untenable; Rāmānuja sees in it a recognition and justification for the *Bhāgavata* system. The next two *pādas* show the origin of the various phenomena that go into the making of the universe. The third *adhyāya* discusses the *jīvātman*, the individual living being. The condition and circumstances of the soul after death and the various states of dream, dreamless sleep, etc. are inquired into. A long series of *sūtras* deals with meditation and the types of *brahman* knowledge. The fourth *adhyāya* takes up again the topic of meditation and ends with a description of the *brahman*-knower's fate after death.

Schools of Vedānta

In connection with the history of Vaiṣṇavism, Vaiṣṇava (theistic) schools of Vedānta were mentioned, reacting against the (non-theistic) Advaita interpretation given by Śaṅkara. Similarly, in the context of Śaivism, Śaiva-Vedānta schools were briefly described. In the following, therefore, the focus will be on Advaita Vedānta and its history. Advaita Vedānta is only one of the ten recognized schools of Vedānta philosophy. However, it not only has acquired a certain prominence in India due to Śaṅkara's genius, but is also the best (and often the only) known system of Hindu philosophy in the West.

Śaṅkarācārya, according to many the greatest Vedāntin and perhaps the greatest of India's philosophers, born, according to tradition, in 788,[70] near Kālaḍi in today's Kerala, became a *saṃnyāsi* at the age of eighteen. He vanquished all his opponents in debate, established four headquarters in the South, East, North and West of India for the missionaries of his doctrine, the *Daśanāmi Saṃnyāsis*, wrote numerous books and died at the age of thirty-two.[71] He constructed his Advaita-

Vedānta upon principles set forth by Gauḍapāda in his *Kārikā* to the *Māṇḍukya Upaniṣad*.[72] Gauḍapāda is thought to be Śaṅkara's *prācārya*, that is, his *guru*'s *guru*. Śaṅkara's commentary on these *Kārikās* may be the earliest and most concise statement of his philosophy, later expanded in the *Śarīraka-bhāṣya*, his famous commentary on the *Brahma Sūtras*.

As all Indian philosophical theologians do, Śaṅkara clarifies his epistemological position in the introduction to his main work. He offers his own critique of the process of acquiring knowledge and states that all subject–object knowledge is distorted by *adhyāsa*, superimposition, which falsifies knowledge in such a way that the subject is unable to find objective truth. Quoting the familiar example of the traveler mistaking a piece of rope on the road for a snake (or vice versa) he proceeds to call all sense-perception into question as possibly misleading due to preconceived, superimposed, ideas. But though all object-cognition can be doubted, the existence of the doubter remains a fact. Every perception, be it true, doubtful or mistaken, presupposes a subject, a perceiver. Even if there were no objective perception at all, there would still be a subject. It cannot be proved, nor does it have to be, because it precedes every proof as its inherent condition. It is distinct from all objects and independent. *Ātman* is pure consciousness which remains even after *manas*, rational thought, has passed away. *Ātman* is ultimately *sat-cit-ānanda* (truth/reality–consciousness–bliss). Śaṅkara does not regard the world of things as "pure illusion" (as his opponents accuse him of doing): the world is neither *abhāva*, non-existence, nor, as Buddhist idealism has it, *śūnyatā*, emptiness. For Śaṅkara the Buddhists are the arch-antagonists of *brahman*-knowledge; using Buddhist patterns of thought (which later earned him the title "Crypto-Buddhist" by zealous Vaiṣṇavas) he sets out to reestablish Brahmanism. Sense objects, in his view, are different from fiction, but they also differ from reality in the ultimate sense. In order to understand Śaṅkara's statements one must always see them in the frame of reference in which they are made: all his assertions are explicit or implicit comparisons with absolute reality, which alone is of interest to him. The "natural" person does not know how to distinguish between relative and absolute being, between "things" and "being," between *ātman* and non-*ātman*. This is the congenital *avidyā*, a nescience that we are not even aware of. It is this ignorance which keeps a person in *saṃsāra*. *Ātman* is *brahman* – that is good Upaniṣadic doctrine; the self of a person is identical with the ground of all being. *Brahman*, however, is invisible, impervious to any sense or mind-perception: *brahman* is not identical with any one particular thing. Some Upaniṣadic passages speak of a "lower" and a "higher" brahman,[73] they speak of the immutable supreme *brahman* and also of the *īśvara* who is creator, Lord and ruler of the world. Śaṅkara takes those passages as the occasion to introduce his most controversial distinction between *brahman saguṇa* and *brahman nirguṇa*, the Supreme with attributes and the Supreme without attributes, the *īśvara* of religious tradition, and the absolute and unqualified reality, a no-thing. According to Śaṅkara *īśvara* is only a temporal manifestation of *brahman*, creator for as long as creation lasts. Śaṅkara is credited with numerous beautiful hymns to the traditional Lords of religion, to Viṣṇu, Śiva, and Devī.[74] Devotion is one of the stages which one has to go through, but not a stage to remain at: the ultimate goal is deliverance also from God, a complete identification with the Reality, which neither develops nor acts, neither loves nor hates but just *is*. The process of achieving this complete liberation is a cleansing process that separates the *ātman* from all untruth, unreality, and temporality. The doing away with *avidyā*, obscuring ignorance, is in itself already *vidyā*, knowledge that is identical with being. In this *vidyā* the self experiences its identity with *brahman nirguṇa*, the pure and immutable reality.

Commenting on the first *sūtra* of the *Vedānta Sūtra*, Śaṅkara writes:

> The special question with regard to the enquiry into Brahman is whether it presupposes the understanding of *dharma*. To this question we reply: No! Because for a person who has read the Vedānta it is possible to begin the inquiry into the nature of *brahman* before having studied the *dharma*. The study of *dharma* results in transitory heaven and this depends on the performance of rituals. The inquiry into the nature of *brahman*, however, results in *mokṣa*, lasting liberation. It does not depend upon the performance of ceremonies. A few presuppositions preceding the inquiry into the nature of *brahman* will have to be mentioned. These are:
>
> 1. discrimination between the eternal and the non-eternal;
> 2. renunciation of the desire to enjoy the fruit of one's actions either here or hereafter;
> 3. practice of the basic virtues like peacefulness, self-restraint and so on;
> 4. strong desire for liberation.
>
> If these conditions are fulfilled, then a person may inquire into *brahman* whether before or after the *dharma*-inquiry; but not if these conditions are not fulfilled. The object of desire is the knowledge of *brahman* and complete understanding of it. Knowledge is therefore the means to perfect *brahman*-cognition. The complete knowledge of *brahman* is the supreme human goal, because it destroys the root of all evil, namely *avidyā*, which

> is the seed of *saṃsāra*. One may now ask: is *brahman* known or unknown? If *brahman* is known then there is no need for further inquiry; if *brahman* is unknown we cannot begin an inquiry. We answer: *brahman* is known. *Brahman*, omniscient and omnipotent, whose essential nature is eternal purity, consciousness and freedom, exists. For if we contemplate the derivation of the word *brahman* from the root *bṛh-*, to be great, we understand at once that it is eternal purity, etc. More than that: the existence of *brahman* is known because it is the *ātman*, the self of everyone. For everyone is conscious of the "self" and no one thinks: I am not. *Ātman* is *brahman*. If the existence of the self was not known each one would think: I am not. But if *ātman* is generally known as *brahman*, one does not have to start an inquiry. Our answer is: No. Because there is a diversity of opinions regarding its nature. Uneducated people and the Lokāyatas are of the opinion that the body itself, having *caitanya*, consciousness as an attribute, is the *ātman*. Others believe that the sense-organs, endowed with the potency to experience, are the *ātman*. Others again believe that *cetana*, reasoning or *manas*, mind is the *ātman*. Others again believe the self to be simply a momentary idea, or that it is *śūnya*, emptiness. Some others explain that there is besides the body some supernatural being, responsible for the transmigrations, acting and enjoying; others teach that this being enjoys only but does not act. Some believe that besides these there exists an omniscient, omnipotent *īśvara* and others finally declare that the *ātman* is that enjoyer ... The *sūtra*, therefore presents a discussion of the Vedānta texts with the motto: "Inquiry into *brahma*", which proceeds with appropriate arguments and aims at supreme bliss.[75]

Already his direct disciples and successors considered Śaṅkara a superhuman teacher, the embodiment of divine wisdom. His words were treated on a par with the words of revelation.[76] Extreme care was taken not only to preserve his written works but also to ensure the succession in the *maṭhas* founded by him.[77]

As far as the further elaboration of the system of Advaita philosophy was concerned, a split developed among the immediate disciples of Śaṅkara. The two factions later became known as the "Vivaraṇa" and the "Bhāmatī" schools, named after two celebrated subcommentaries on Śaṅkara's *bhāṣya*, written by Prakāśātman (*c.*1000 C.E.) and Vācaspati Miśra (*c.*850 C.E.). They differed on the role which ritual played in the process of emancipation and also on the question of whether the locus of *avidyā* (ignorance) was in the individual *jīvātman* or in the universal *brahman*.

A recent bibliographical survey of Advaita Vedānta Literature[78] enumerates almost five hundred Advaita philosphers from the seventh century to the present. This chapter cannot do justice to the breadth and depth of the history of Advaita Vedānta and can only highlight a few names.

The two most important immediate disciples of Śaṅkara were Maṇḍana Miśra, the author of *Brahmasiddhi*, a compendium of Advaita Vedānta; and Sureśvara, author of *Naiṣkārmyasiddhi*,[79] another compendium, as well as of longish subcommentaries on Śaṅkara's commentary on the *Bṛhadāraṇyaka Upaniṣad*. The former laid the foundations for the Bhāmatī school; the latter for the Vivaraṇa school, whose "official" founder was Padmapāda (ninth century C.E.), author of the *Pañcapādikā*, a subcommentary on Śaṅkara's *Brahmasūtrabhāṣya* on the first five sūtras. The author of the work *Vivaraṇa*, after which the school is called, was Prakāśātman (*c.*1000 C.E.). One of the most famous and still widely read representatives of this school was Vidyāraṇya, also known under the name Bhārati-tīrtha. According to Advaita tradition he was Prime Minister of the Hindu state of Vijayanagara before becoming head of the Śaṅkara-maṭha at Śriṅgerī. He is the author of *Pañcadaśī*, a widely used handbook for Advaitic meditation, as well as of *Jīvan-mukti-viveka*, a summary of teachings on "liberation while alive in a body." Recently his authorship of the celebrated *Sarva-darśana-saṁgraha*, a critical survey of all (sixteen) Indian schools of thought, has been disputed.[80] The work itself is remarkable for its method of argumentation.Instead of critiquing each school from his own standpoint, Vidyāraṇya lets them eliminate each other in turn before stating the final truth of Advaita in the last chapter.

Vācaspati Miśra (ninth century C.E.), the author of the *Bhāmatī*, a subcommentary on Śaṅkara's commentary on the first four sūtras of the *Vedāntasūtra*, held that the individual self was the locus of ignorance, and not *brahman*. Another representative of this school was Amalānanda (thirteenth century), author of *Kalpatāru*. A major figure in this school, still widely read, was Appaya Dīkṣita (sixteenth century), author of the *Siddhānta-leṣa-saṅgraha*.

Noteworthy representatives of Advaita Vedānta are also Sarvajñātman (tenth century), author of *Samkṣepa-śarīraka*; Vimuktātman (twelfth century), author of the *Iṣṭa-siddhi*; Madhusūdana Sarasvatī (sixteenth century), a great polemicist and author of *Advaita-siddhi*; Sādānanda (fifteenth century), author of a widely used easy compendium of Advaita, *Vedānta-sāra*; and Dharmarāja (seventeenth century) whose *Vedānta-paribhāṣa* is an invaluable introduction to Advaita epistemology.[81]

A widely read nineteenth-century treatise in Advaita Vedānta is *Vicāra Sāgara*, written in Hindī by Niścaldās (and later translated into Sanskrit by one of the twentieth-century Śaṅkarācārayas, Brahmendra Saraswatī Swāmigal).

Not only was Advaita Vedānta eagerly studied by nineteenth-century Western Indologists, who saw parallels to Hegel's philosophy in it, it is also the most widely held philosophy today in Indian professional academic circles. The Advanced Centre for Philosophy at the University of Madras under the leadership of its founder T. M. P. Mahadevan became a stronghold of Advaita Vedānta scholarship. T. M. P. Mahadevan and his colleagues translated numerous major Advaita texts into English and published widely recognized monographs on several aspects of Advaita Vedānta. Advaita Vedānta is certainly the best represented of the Hindu *darśanas* in the West today and a wealth of translations of original texts and scholarly studies is waiting to be explored.

Vedānta does not belong to the past only, but is also perhaps the most important contemporary expression of Indian philosophy and theology. An unbroken tradition of scholars and saints leads from the great *ācāryas* into the present time; all their major institutions are still centers of living Vedānta. Vedānta is not only speculative, abstract thought, but also mysticism, realization and the way to ultimate freedom.

HINDU PHILOSOPHY TODAY

It is worth noting that Hinduism has never known the division between a purely rational philosophy and a purely scripture-based theology, which has been so typical for the intellectual development of the West and so detrimental to both philosophy and theology. For Hindus philosophical reflection on the revelations given to *ṛṣis* and poets is an integral component of religion. Similarly, Indian philosophy has always dealt with questions of ultimate, "religious" significance and has endeavored to be meaningful to real people in their real lives.

While much of Hindu philosophy along traditional lines is pursued by the religious leaders of particular schools of thought in the context of preserving and propagating these schools, there is also a large number of academics teaching philosophy at the public universities all over India. Surprisingly many of these do philosophy in the old Hindu tradition, i.e., dealing with "religious" isssues and applying "theological" methodologies.

The articles published in the prestigious *Indian Philosophical Annual*[82] are as good a proof of this statement as are the presentations given at the biennial *International Vedānta Conferences.*[83] In a collection of essays under the title *Contemporary Indian Philosophy*[84] a number of prominent Indian philosophers expressed the gist of their personal convictions. The majority of them were Hindus and most of these advocated a religiously inspired philosophy, much in tune with Hindu traditions.

Religion is not taboo in Indian intellectual circles, as it is in the West, and the development of Hindu philosophical ideas continues. In 1983 M. P. Rege from the University of Pune organized a highly original and successful dialogue between traditional Hindu pandits and modern Western-trained philosophers. Far from being overwhelmed or put off by such a dialogue, the assembled pandits, all discursing in Sanskrit, expressed very sound opinions on modern philosophical isssues and delighted in the give and take of discussions.[85]

NOTES

1. *Ṛgveda* X, 129.
2. The word *theorīa* comes from a verbal root *theoreīn*, to see, and originally meant a comprehensive in-depth view of the principles of life and being.
3. Literally *āstika* means "it is" and *nāstika* means "it is not." The criterion is acceptance or non-acceptance of the Veda as revealed truth.
4. But even the fourteenth-century Mādhava enumerates in his *Sarvadarśanasaṁgraha*, the "Synopsis of All Philosophical Systems," sixteen such philosophies.
5. *Brahmasūtrabhāṣya* I, 1, 1.
6. Some interesting details are presented in a light-hearted manner by Kuppuswami Sastri in a contribution to "The Library Movement" under the title "Kośavān ācāryaḥ" (i.e., one who has a library is a teacher, or: a teacher is one who has a library). Reprinted in S. S. Janaki, ed., *Kuppuswamy Sastri Birth Centenary Commemoration Volume*, Part I, (Madras, 1981). This claim is also supported by the information on the scholastic engagement of the Śaṅkarācāryas past and present, in W. Cenkner, *A Tradition of Teachers*, esp. chap. 4: "The Teaching Heritage after Śaṅkara," 84–106.
7. Thus the commentaries on Gaṅgeśa's *Tattvacintāmaṇi* were called *Didhiti*, *Gaṅgādhārī*, *Karṣikā*, *Candrakālā*, *Nakṣatramālikā*, etc. See R. Thangasami Sarma, *Dàrśanamañjarī*, Part 1 (Madras: University of Madras, 1985), 64f.
8. S. N. Dasgupta, *History of Indian Philosophy*, Cambridge: Cambridge University Press, 1961, vol. 1, 282.
9. See the evidence offered by S. N. Dasgupta, ibid.

10. It has only been preserved in a Chinese translation; this has been edited and translated and commented upon by H. Ui (1917; reprint Varanasi: Chowkhambha Sanskrit Series, 1962).
11. Early writers use the word *Nyāya* as a synonym with *Mīmāṃsā*.
12. *Arthaśāstra* 2, 30, a text often referred to in this connection. So far I have not seen reference made to *Viṣṇu Purāṇa* I, 9, 121 which has the same enumeration of sciences. In this text the Goddess (after the churning of the Milk Ocean) is addressed as the embodiment of all knowledge (*vidyā*) specifically of *anvīkṣikī*, *trayī*, *vārtā*, and *daṇḍanīti*.
13. *Vaiśeṣikardarśana*, Anantalal Thakur, ed. Darbhanga: Mithila Institute, 1957. N. Sinha, trans., Allahabad: Panini Office, 1911.
14. W. Halbfass in an excursus "The Concept of Viśeṣa and the name of the Vaiśeṣika System," in *On Being* . . ., 269–75, offers alternative suggestions.
15. *Padārthadharmasaṅgraha* No. 156, Ganganatha Jha, trans. (Allahabad: Lazarus 1916).
16. Dasgupta, *HIPh*, vol. 1, 363.
17. These "nine things" are: *buddhi* (understanding), *sukha* (happiness), *duḥkha* (suffering), *icchā* (desire), *dveṣa* (hatred), *prayatna* (effort), *dharma* (righteousness), *adharma* (unrighteousness), *saṃskāra* (innate propensity).
18. *Nyāyasūtra* with *Vātsyāyana Bhāṣya*, Ganganatha Jha, ed., trans. and commentator, 2 vols. (Pune: Oriental Book Agency, 1939).
19. *Maṇikana*, A Navya-Nyāya Manual, E. R. Sreekrishna Sarma, ed. and trans., Adyar: The Adyar Library and Research Center, 1960, Introduction, xvii.
20. *Nyāya Sūtra* I, 1, 22.
21. Ibid., IV, 1, 66.
22. For details see G. Chemparathy, *An Indian Rational Theology. Introduction to Udayana's Nyāyakusumañjalī*, Vienna: Indological Institute of the University of Vienna, 1972.
23. Udayanācārya's *Nyāyakusumañjalī* with the commentary of Haridasa Bhattacarya, E. B. Cowell, trans., Calcutta, 1864.
24. *Nyāya-bhāṣya* IV, 1, 21f.
25. *Tarkabhāṣa of Keśava Miśra*, Ganganatha Jha, ed. and trans., Pune: Oriental Book Agency, 1949.
26. The best-known text of Haṭhayoga is the *Haṭhayogapradīpikā* by Svātmārāma Yogīndra, Adyar: Theosophical Publishing House, 1933.
27. See Chapter 23.
28. E.g., *Bhāgavata Purāṇa* II, 25, 13ff.; III, 28.
29. A. B. Keith, *The Sāṁkhya System*, The Heritage of India Series, Calcutta: YMCA Publishing House, 1949, 18. The most comprehensive recent study of Sāṁkhya is G. J. Larsen, *Classical Sāṁkhya*, Delhi: Motilal Banarsidass, 1969. See also H. Bakker, "On the Origin of the Sāṁkhya Psychology," in: *WZKSA* 26 (1982), 117–148, with an extensive bibliography. G. J. Larsen makes an important point in his essay "The Format of Technical Philosophical Writing in Ancient India: Inadequacies of Conventional Translations," *Philosophy of East and*

West, 30, no. 3 (1980): 375–80. Comprehensive information on the development of Sāṁkhya is contained in E. Frauwallner, *Geschichte der Indischen Philosophie*, Salzburg: Otto Müller Verlag, 1953, vol. 1, 228ff and 472ff.

30. *Bhāgavata Purāṇa* III, 28.
31. The best edition and translation with ample comments is that by S. S. Suryanarayana Sastri (Madras: University of Madras, 1948). Also *Sāṁkhya Kārikā* of Mahāmuni Śri Īśvarakṛṣṇa with the commentary *Sārabodhinī* of Pandit Śivanārayāṇa Śāstrī with *Sāṅkhya Tattvakaumudī* of Vācaspati Miśra, Bombay: Nirnaya Sagar Press, 1940.
32. *Sāṁkhyadarśana*, Pyarelal Prabhu Dayal, ed., Bombay: Nirnaya Sagar Press, 1943; J. R. Ballantyne, trans., London: Truebner 1885 (3rd edn).
33. Edited and translated under the title *The Yoga Upaniṣads* (Adyar: Adyar Library, 1920 and 1952).
34. A good edition is that by Swāmī Vijñāna Āśrama (Ajmer, 1961). A complete English translation of the Pātañjala *Yogasūtra* with Vyāsa's *Bhāsya* and Vācaspati Miśra's *Tattva Vaiśāradī* has been published by J. H. Woods in the *Harvard Oriental Series* Vol. 17 (Cambridge, Mass.: Harvard University Press, 1914). Students may find useful I. K. Taimni *The Science of Yoga*, Wheaton, Ill.: Theosophical Publishing House, 1972 (3rd edn); it offers the text and the translation of the *Yogasūtra* and a good running commentary that avoids the technicalities of the classical commentaries. Valuable recent treatments of Yoga are: S. N. Dasgupta, *Yoga as Philosophy and Religion*, 1924; reprint Delhi: Motilal Banarsidass, 1973; J. W. Hauer, *Der Yoga als Heilsweg*, Stuttgart, Kohlhammer, 1932; G. Feuerstein, *The Philosophy of Classical Yoga*, Manchester: University of Manchester Press, 1982; G. M. Koelman, *Pātañjala Yoga. From Related Ego to Absolute Self*, Pune: Papal Athenaeum, 1970. M. Eliade, *Yoga: Immortality and Freedom*, Princeton: Princeton University Press, 1958; 1969 (2nd edn) has become a classic in its own right: it not only describes Pātañjala Yoga but compares it to other phenomena, and it has an exhaustive bibliography of works up to 1964. Controversial new ideas on classical Yoga are advanced in G. Oberhammer, *Strukturen Yogischer Meditation*, Vienna: Österreichische Akademie der Wissenschaften, 1977.
35. *Tejobindu Upaniṣad*, VI, 107.
36. P. Hacker, "Śaṅkara der Yogin und Śaṅkara der Advaitin: Einige Beobachtungen," *WZKSA* 12–13 (1968): 119–48. A full translation of the work was published by James Legget in 1990.
37. *Sāṁkhya Kārikā* 1.
38. This is the traditional interpretation given to *duḥkhatraya*.
39. *Sāṁkhya Kārikā* 2.
40. Ibid., 18.
41. Ibid., 8.
42. Ibid., 63.
43. Ibid., 67.
44. *Yogasūtra* I, 5ff.
45. Ibid., I, 23ff.

46. Ibid., II, 5f.
47. According to Haṭhayoga the *utthita padmāsana* confers superhuman vision and cures troubles of the respiratory tract; *sūpta padmāsana* cures illnesses of the digestive organs, *bhadrāsana* activates the mind, *dhastricāsana* regulates body-temperature, cures fever and purifies the blood, *guptāṅgāsana* cures venereal diseases, etc. There are centers in India, like the Yoga Research Institute at Lonavla, in which medical research is done on the effects of *yoga* on body and mind.
48. *Yogasūtra* II, 54.
49. Ibid., III, 1–3.
50. Ibid., III, 16ff.
51. Ibid., IV, 34: 51.
52. These notions find a surprising parallel in contemporary scientific thought. See I. Prigogine, *Order Out of Chaos*, New York: Bantam Books, 1948.
53. Hohm Press: Prescott, Arizona, 1998. It has 686 large pages with text and illustrations.
54. *Jaimini Sūtras* I, 1, 2: *codanalakṣano'artho dharmaḥ*.
55. Ibid., I, 2, 1.
56. *Śābara Bhāṣya* I, 1, 22: "There can be no creator of this relation because no soul is cognized as such by any of the means of cognition. If there had been such a creator, he could not have been forgotten." Cf. also: Kumārila Bhaṭṭa, *Ślokavārttika*, XVI, 41ff.
57. Ganganatha Jha, *Pūrvamīmāṃsā in Its Sources*, 178ff.
58. *Jaimini Sūtras* Vi, 1, 6ff.
59. Ganganatha Jha, *Pūrvamīmāṃsa in Its Sources*, 264f.
60. *Jaimini Sūtras* IV, 3, 15.
61. *Śābara Bhāṣya* on VI, 1, 1.
62. *Nyāyaratnākara*: "Liberation must consist in the destruction of the present body and the non-production of the future body." Quoted by G. Jha, *Pūrva Mīmāṃsā*, 38.
63. *Prakāraṇapañcikā, Tattvāloka*, p. 156.
64. O. Gächter, *Hermeneutics and Language in Pūrvamīmāṃsā, A Study in Śābara Bhāṣya* (Delhi: Motilal Banarsidass, 1983) with bibliographic references to both Eastern and Western authors.
65. H. G. Coward, *The Sphoṭa Theory of Language. A Philosophical Analysis* (Delhi: Motilal Banarsidass, 1980), with extensive bibliography. The complete text has been edited by Prof. K. V. Abhyankar and Acharya V. P. Limaye in the University of Poona Sanskrit and Prakrit Series, Pune: University of Puna, 1965.
66. Ramdas Gaur, *Hindutva*, 589.
67. According to S. K. Belvalkar (*Shree Gopal Basu Mallik Lectures on Vedānta Philosophy*, (Pune: Bilvakunja, 1929, Part 1, Chapter 4: "Vedānta in the Brahmasūtras" (142), Jaimini, the author of the *Mīmāṃsāsūtra* wrote a *Śarīrakasūtra*, which sought to harmonize the teaching of the *Sāmaveda Upaniṣads*, particularly the *Chāndogya Upaniṣad*, and this *sūtra* was incorporated within, and forms the main part of the present text of the *Brahmasūtra*.

68. The ten recognized *Vedāntācāryas* are: Śaṅkara, Rāmānuja, Madhva, Vallabha, Bhāskara, Yādavaprakāśa, Keśava, Nīlakaṇṭha, Vijñānabhikṣu, and Bāladeva. They are the founders of separate branches of Vedānta philosophy. There are several comparative studies of the different schools of Vedānta such as V. S. Ghate, *The Vedānta*, Pune: Oriental Bookstore, 1926; reprint 1960; O. Lacombe, *L'absolu selon le Vedānta*, Paris: Geuthner, 1957; reprint 1973. See also B. N. K. Sharma, *A Comparative Study of Ten Commentaries on the Brahmasūtras*, Delhi: Motilal Banarsidass, 1984.
69. Cf. Rāmdās Gaur, *Hindutva* (in Hindī), Kasi: Madhav Visnu Paradkar, 1995, 591ff.
70. Some researchers place Śaṅkara's birth around 600 C.E.
71. A complete list with a critical analysis is given in S. K. Belvarkar, *Shree Gopal Basu Malik Lectures on Vedānta Philosophy*, Poona: Bilkunja, 1929, 218ff. See also R. T. Vyas, "Roots of Śaṅkara's Thought," in: *JBOI* 32, nos. 1–2 (September–December 1982): 35–49.
72. Swami Nikhilananda has brought out an English paraphrase of the *Māṇḍukyopaniṣad with Gauḍapāda's Kārikā and Śaṅkara's Commentary* (Mysore: Ramakrishna Ashram, 1955, 4th edn). See also T. Vetter, "Die Gauḍapādīya-Kārikās: Zur Entstehung und zur Bedeutung von (A)dvaita, *WZKSA* 22 (1978): 95–131.
73. For example, *Maitrī Upaniṣad* VI, 15; *Muṇḍaka* II, 2, 8.
74. Contained in H. R. Bhagavat, ed., *Minor Works of Śrī Śaṅkara-ācārya* (Poona Oriental Series No. 8), Pune: Oriental Book Agency, 1952 (2nd edn), 374–402.
75. Several complete English translations of the *Śaṅkarabhāṣya* are available: G. Thibaut (*SBE*, vols. 34 and 38); Swami Gambhirananda, Calcutta: Advaita Ashrama, 1965, makes use of some major classical commentaries. See also: E. Deutsch, *Advaita Vedānta: A Philosophical Reconstruction*, Honolulu: University of Hawaii, 1969; and E. Deutsch and J. A. B. van Buitenen, eds., *A Source Book of Advaita Vedānta*, Honolulu: University of Hawaii, 1971.
76. Sureśvara in his *Naiṣkārmyasiddhi* refers to Śaṅkara as "the source of pure knowledge . . . and of illumination," he calls him "omniscient," "the guru of gurus," and compares him to Śiva himself. Śaṅkara, as is well known, is one of the names of Śiva. The *Naiskārmyasiddhi* has been edited and translated by K. K. Venkatachari, Adyar: Adyar Library Series, 1982. For Sureśvara's teaching and his relationship to Śaṅkara see the Introduction to R. Balasubramanian, ed. and trans., *The Taittirīyopaniṣad Bhāṣya-Vārtika of Sureśvara*, Madras: The Radhakrishnan Institute for the Advanced Study of Philosophy, University of Madras, 1984 (2nd edn).
77. A. Nataraja Aiyer and S. Lakshminarasimha Sastri, the authors of *The Traditional Age of Śrī Śaṅkarāchārya and the Maths* (Madras: private publication, 1962), not only provide the lists of all the successors to Śaṅkarācārya relying on eminent scholars who "have already proved that the date of Śaṅkara is 509–477 B.C." (Preface) but also bring excerpts from court cases which were initiated in the twentieth century

in order to settle the claims of candidates and counter-candidates to some *gaddīs* (headships of *maṭhas*).

78. By R. Thangaswami (in Sanskrit), Madras University Sanskrit Series No. 36, Madras, 1980.
79. Translated by A. J. Alston, London: Shanti Sadan, 1959.
80. See K. Kunjunni Raja, Preface to English translation of Chapter 16 of *Sarvadarśanasaṁgraha* in *Brahmavidyā: The Adyar Library Bulletin*, vol. 61 (1997), pp. 149f.
81. Extracts (in English translation) from the works of the above-mentioned authors are found in Elliot Deutsch and J. A. B. van Buitenen's *A Source Book of Advaita Vedānta* (Honolulu: The University Press of Hawaii, 1971).
82. Published by the Radhakrishnan Institute for Advanced Studies in Philosophy, University of Madras.
83. Organized by R. R. Pappu from Miami University, Oxford, Ohio.
84. Edited by S. Radhakrishnan and published by Allen & Unwin, London, 1952
85. *Saṃvāda*, ed., by Daya Krishna, M. P. Rege, R. C. Dwivedi, Mukund Lath; Indian Council of Philosophical Research; Delhi: Motilal Banarsidass, 1991.

10 A SHORT HISTORY OF MODERN HINDUISM

Although it should have become clear from the foregoing it has to be restated emphatically in connection with the history of "modern Hinduism" that neither the origin of Hinduism nor its varied histories warrant a periodization "pre-modern" and "modern." What is presented here as "modern Hinduism" consists of sporadic and episodic new movements within mainstream Hinduism that arose in reaction to the presence of European colonial powers on Indian soil from the early nineteenth century onwards. Mainstream Hinduism as described above – Vaiṣṇavism, Śaivism, Śāktism, and a host of minor *saṃpradāyas* – continues to claim the allegiance of the majority of Hindus. As remarked in an earlier chapter when dealing with these branches of "mainstream Hinduism," these too have in many ways changed and adapted to new circumstances and cannot be globally labelled "pre-modern".

The reform movements of the nineteenth and twentieth centuries were effective in transforming Hinduism not so much by attracting large followings – in fact, with few exceptions their followings remained very small and some died out completely – but by stimulating traditional Hindu religion to change and adapt. They were also instrumental for Hindu missions to the West, a reversal of the Christian missions that had established branches of dozens of denominations of Western Christianity in India.

So far the Western world has taken it more or less for granted that its own religious traditions, woven over more than a thousand years into its social and cultural fabric, would take care of its spiritual needs. No longer can we assume this to be the case. The present upsurge of new and mostly Indian religious movements has alarmed many people who consider it out of tune with traditional Western religion as well as with the scientific and rational temper of the contemporary West.

Almost sixty years ago Heinrich Zimmer, a respected scholar of Indian philosophy, art and religion, wrote:

> We of the Occident are about to arrive at a crossroads that was reached by the thinkers of India some seven hundred years before Christ. This is the real reason why we become both vexed and stimulated, uneasy, yet interested when confronted with the concepts and images of Oriental wisdom. This crossing is one to which the people of all civilizations come in the typical course of the development of their capacity and requirement for religious experience, and India's teachings force us to realize what its problems are. But we cannot take over the Indian solutions. We must enter the new period our own way and solve its questions for ourselves, because though truth, the radiance of reality, is universally one and the same, it is mirrored variously according to the mediums in which it is reflected. Truth appears differently in different lands and ages according to the living materials out of which its symbols are hewn.[1]

BEGINNINGS OF MODERNITY IN INDIA

The modern West's contact with India began with Vasco da Gama's historic voyage around the Cape of Good Hope in 1498. Several European powers – besides the Portuguese there were the Dutch, the Danes, the English and the French – expressed their interest in India by establishing first "factories" (trading posts) and then colonies. Together with the merchants and the soldiers came the Christian missionaries. To their great surprise they discovered a large group of indigenous Christians, whom they promptly wanted to convert to their own variety of Christianity, since these had no knowledge of the Pope's authority. While the attitude of many of the early missionaries was hostile and negative towards Hinduism, some seventeenth- and eighteenth-century works provided much useful information also about India's religions.[2]

Scholars who developed an interest in Indian religions were initially severely handicapped by the Brahmins' reluctance to teach Sanskrit and to divulge the contents of their holy books. Far from being interested in contacts with the West, Hinduism by that time had become inward-looking, defensive and secretive. The German philosopher Arthur Schopenhauer (1788–1860), whose enthusiastic praises of the Upaniṣads are frequently cited even now, had to rely on a Latin translation made from the Moghul Prince Dara Shukoh's Persian version of the original Sanskrit text. The situation improved dramatically with the encouragement given by the British East India Company to scholars to provide information about Hindu laws and customs. The first work so commissioned, a Sanskrit digest of Hindu law compiled by Hindu pandits under the title *Vivāda-varṇava-setu* had first to be translated into Persian (the "official language" of the court) before an Englishman could translate it into English. It was published in 1776 under the title *A Code of Gentoo Law.* Already by 1785 Charles Wilkins had acquired sufficient knowledge of Sanskrit to produce the first English translation of the *Bhagavadgītā*, which was eagerly received by the educated Europeans. Less than ten years later, Sir William Jones, the founder of the Asiatic Society of Bengal, published a translation of the *Manusmṛti*. His successor Thomas Colebrook provided the first reliable modern account of the Veda in his paper "On the Vedas or Sacred Writings of the Hindoos."

Soon chairs of Sanskrit and Indian studies were established at the major universities of Europe. Although the Boden Professorship in Oxford was founded in order "to promote the translation of the Scriptures into Sanskrit, so as to enable [our] countrymen to proceed in the conversion of the natives of India to the Christian religion,"[3] the real effects of such studies were a dissemination of genuine knowledge about India, especially its literature, philosophies and religions, on the basis of a study of original materials.

Friedrich Max Müller (1823–1903), to single out one of these early scholars, earned fame among Hindus through his monumental edition of the *Ṛgveda with Sāyaṇas Commentary.*[4] Hindus called him *mokṣa mūla* ("root of salvation"). A number of Max Müller Bhavans, German cultural centers, keep his memory alive today in India. Since his time a great number of Westerners have taken up the study of Indian religions seriously, contributing to textual and thematic researches and making it accessible to large numbers of people.

HINDU REACTIONS TO CHRISTIAN MISSIONS

While the Moghul Empire was crumbling and was unable to withstand the inroads made by diverse European colonial powers, individual Indians were quite capable of resisting the efforts to Westernize and Christianize their homeland. Contact with Western ideas and institutions initiated the "Hindu Renaissance": a restoration and reinterpretation of

Indian tradition against the background of the predominant Western culture. Some traditional Hindus wrote defensive and apologetic tracts (in Sanskrit) against the foreign culture and religion.[5] But there also arose men and women who realized that India had to change if it was to survive in the new age and that it had to recapture its own identity if it was not to lose its own soul.

The early reformers risked a great deal: they had to break the Hindu rules which forbade contact with the *mlecchas*, the impure foreigners, they had to critically analyze their own tradition instead of simply submitting to the decision of their pandits, they had to give up much of what was thought a sacred and inviolable order of life.

One of the first and one of the best known of these early Hindu reformers may serve as an example. Ram Mohan Roy (1772–1833), called the Father of Modern India, born into an orthodox Hindu family, but also conversant with Arabic and Persian, was one of the first brahmins to enter the service of the East India Company and to study English. After 1814 he devoted himself fully to religious propaganda and reform. He wished to purify Hinduism by leading it back to its Upaniṣadic sources. He sought connection with the English Baptist missionaries, who had opened a college at Serampore (Śrīrāmpur) – then a Danish possession – not far from Calcutta. He studied Greek and Hebrew in order to translate the Bible into Bengali. The publication of a little book *The Precepts of Jesus: The Guide to Peace and Happiness* estranged him both from his Hindu friends and the foreign missionaries. The former accused him of canvassing for Christianity, the latter objected to his "Hinduising of Christianity." In the course of quite bitter polemics Ram Mohan Roy accused the missionaries of having misunderstood and misinterpreted the words of Jesus, a charge that has been leveled by Hindus against Western Christianity ever since.

Ram Mohan Roy won a triumph in his battle against the practice of *satī*, the more or less voluntary burning of widows together with their deceased husbands. As a boy he had witnessed the forced *satī* of a much-liked sister-in-law which had stirred him so profoundly that he vowed to devote his life to the abolition of this cruel custom, tolerated by the British administration as part of their policy of non-interference with local religious customs. Ram Mohan Roy succeeded in convincing the government that *satī* did not form part of the original and pure Hindu dharma. In pursuit of this cause he broke the rule which forbade Hindus to "cross the black waters" and went to England to defend his stance.

After several unsuccessful attempts to organize a group of people to begin a new religious movement he founded the Brahmo Samāj, combining Hindu metaphysics with Christian ethics. Ram Mohan Roy kept his sacred thread and intended to remain a Hindu; Hindu orthodoxy however excommunicated him. He also became instrumental in establishing English schools in Calcutta, emphasizing the value of modern, scientific education. Many Europeans in his day thought that the Brahmo Samāj would become the future religion of India.

Ram Mohan Roy's successor Debendranath Tagore (father of the more famous Nobel Prize Winner for Literature [1913] Rabindranath Tagore) founded a school for Brahmo missionaries with the explicit purpose of checking the spread of Christian missions. He openly broke with orthodox Hinduism by declaring the Vedas as neither free from error nor inspired.

While the Brahmo Samāj did not become a Hindu religious movement in the West, it prepared the way for such movements: it gave rise to a new Hindu self-confidence, it modernized Hinduism and it established the opinion that Hindu philosophical religion was superior to that of the West – that Hindus could indeed interpret the true meaning of the Bible for the West.

A more radical parallel Hindu reform movement, the *Ārya Samāj*,[6] founded by Swami Dayananda Saraswati (1824–83) went one step further: it not only resented and resisted Christian missionary activities in Hindu-India, it introduced a *śuddhi*-(purification) ceremony whereby Christians and Muslims who had Hindu ancestry could become Hindus again, and it sent missionaries abroad. The appeal of this Vedic fundamentalism was not large in India; less so in the West. But the dam had been breached. Hinduism, for centuries a non-proselytizing religion, began to proselytize again. Dayananda Saraswati, who was convinced that the Veda was the source of the original and only true *sanātana dharma* for the whole of mankind, believed he had a worldwide mission.

After his death the movement split into a more conservative and a more progressive wing. The former established a Sanskrit-based traditional *gurukula* system, whose flagship, in Kangri near Rishikesh, has recently been given University status by the Indian Government. The progressives wanted a blend of traditional Vedic, modern English, and scientific education. They established the first "Dayanand Anglo-Vedic College" at Lahore in 1886. The model proved so successful that today there are about 500 D.A.V. colleges and schools in India and some other countries. They have dedicated teachers who consider it their mission to instill in their students not only secular knowledge but also love and respect for the Vedic tradition. The Ārya Samāj also runs the Vishveshvaranda Vedic Research Institute in Hoshiarpur (Panjab), which claims to be the largest of its kind. The Ārya Samāj, according to its own sources, today has over 10 million members worldwide.[7]

The best known of all the Hindu reform movements is the Ramakrishna Mission, founded by Swami Vivekananda (1863–1902), favorite disciple of Paramahamsa Ramakrishna (1836–1886). Sent as Hindu delegate to the World Parliament of Religions in Chicago in 1893, Swami Vivekananda became a sensation in the West. He was invited to tour America and Europe to lecture on Hinduism. His Vedanta Ashrams are still centers of Hindu culture and religion, arranging lecture series and distributing Hindu literature. Swami Vivekananda inspired Hindu-India with immense pride and a sense of mission. He articulated the rationale for the new Hindu Religious Movements in the West in the following manner: "We Hindus have now been placed, under God's providence, in a very critical and responsible position. The nations of the West are coming to us for spiritual help. A great moral obligation rests on the sons of India to fully equip themselves for the work of enlightening the world on the problems of human existence."[8] And: "Once more the world must be conquered by India. This is the dream of my life. I am anxiously waiting for the day when mighty minds will arise, gigantic spiritual minds who will be ready to go forth from India to the ends of the world to teach spirituality and renunciation, those ideas which come from the forests of India and belong to Indian soil only. Up India, and conquer the world with your spirituality . . . Ours is a religion of which Buddhism, with all its greatness, is a rebel child and of which Christianity is a very patchy imitation."[9]

The Ramakrishna Mission, as is well known, not only promotes a non-sectarian (Neo-) Hinduism but also a kind of religious universalism. Ramakrishna is the source of the widely accepted "all-religions-are-the-same" theory. Accordingly, the Ramakrishna Mission does not only spread Hinduism in the West but also invites representatives of other religions to its temples and centers in India to speak about their own traditions.

HINDUISM AFTER INDEPENDENCE

As the movement for India's independence from British colonial rule accelerated after the Second World War, it became clear that the tensions between Hindus and Muslims were so strong that the country had to face a division along the lines of religious affiliation. Eventually both British and Indian politicians agreed to create two successor nations to the British Indian Empire.[10] While Pakistan chose to become an Islamic theocracy, the Republic of India (Bhārat) decided to give itself a constitution as a secular democracy. Not all Hindus were happy about that and many continued agitating for a Hindu Rāṣṭra, a state based on traditional Hindu principles, as well as a reunification of the two Indian nations.

Jawaharlal Nehru, the first Prime Minister, came from a nominally Hindu background but repudiated all religious affiliations. His ideal was Democratic Socialism after the European fashion. Nevertheless, the majority of the population of the Republic of India were Hindus and Hinduism began to reassert itself in many ways. Hindu nationalist parties like the Jana Sangh, the Hindu Mahāsabhā and the Rām Rājya Pariṣad, as well as Hindu activist associations like the Rāṣṭrīya Svayamsevak Sangh and later the Viśva Hindū Pariṣad, became more and more articulate and visible in public life.

Even the "secularists" in government had always insisted that "secularism" in India did not mean hostility or even indifference toward religion, but equal respect for, and recognition of, all religions. In spite of this, the history of the past fifty years of independent India has been marred by numerous violent conflicts between Hindus and Muslims, Hindus and Sikhs, Hindus and Christians. And today a militant Hindu minority is pushing towards the creation of a Hindu state to confront the neighboring Muslim state.

The moderate majority of Hindus follows traditional Hindu principles of tolerance, non-violence, and cultivation of genuine religiosity. The great model for this kind of Hinduism had been Mahatma Gandhi, the Father of Independent India, himself a victim of Hindu fanatism. One can justly count Mahatma Gandhi among the great Hindu reformers whose work had considerable impact on the West. Gandhi never left any doubt about his Hindu identity. Thus he declared early on in his Indian career:[11]

I call myself a *sanātani* Hindu because

1. I believe in the Vedas, the Upaniṣads, the Purāṇas, and all that goes by the name of Hindu scriptures, and therefore in *avatārs* and rebirth.
2. I believe in the *varṇāśrama dharma* in a sense, in my opinion, strictly Vedic, but not in its present popular and crude sense.
3. I believe in the protection of the cow in its much larger sense than the popular.
4. I do not disbelieve in idol worship.

He qualified and explained all these points in a lengthy article which began as follows:[12] "I have purposely refrained from using the word 'divine origin' in reference to the Vedas or any other scriptures. For I do not believe in the exclusive divinity in the Vedas. I believe the Bible, the Koran and the Zend Avesta to be as much divinely inspired as the Vedas. My belief in the Hindu scriptures does not require me to accept every word and every verse as divinely inspired ... I do most emphatically repudiate the claim (if they advance any such) of the present Shankaracaryas and Shastris to give a correct interpretation of the Hindu scriptures."

Gandhi's *satyāgraha* has inspired many people outside India. *Sarvodaya* movements have formed after his death in a number of countries. One can hardly call them Hindu religious movements any more, although they do take their inspiration from Gandhi and his understanding of Hinduism.

The great Hindu writers and philosophers of our time – Rabindranath Tagore, Aurobindo Ghose, Sarvepalli Radhakrishnan – have spread an appreciation of the Hindu view of life among thousands of educated Westerners. While of these three only Aurobindo can be associated with a specific movement in the West which bears his name, the writings of the others have not failed to make a major impact especially on the religious scene in the West. It was Sarvepalli Radhakrishnan who pleaded first for a "dialogue of religions" to replace the unedifying competition and mutual denigration between the major religions. While some of his views may be closer to liberal Christianity than to orthodox Hinduism, he projected an image of Hinduism which not only Westerners but also modern Hindus found attractive and appealing.

A brief extract from his autobiographical sketch gives us an insight into the making of this eloquent modern missionary of a universalized Hinduism:[13]

> At an impressionable period of my life I became familiar not only with the teachings of the New Testament, but with the criticisms levelled by Christian missionaries on Hindu beliefs and practices. My pride as a Hindu, roused by the enterprise and eloquence of Swami Vivekananda, was deeply hurt by the treatment accorded to Hinduism in missionary institutions. The challenge of Christian critics impelled me to make a study of Hinduism and find out what is living and what is dead in it. I prepared a thesis on the ethics of Vedānta. That little essay indicates the general trend of my thought. Religion must establish itself as a rational way of living. If ever the spirit is to be at home in this world and not merely a prisoner or a fugitive, secular foundations must be laid deeply and preserved worthily. Religion must express itself in reasonable thought, fruitful actions and right social institutions.

HINDU TEACHERS GOING WEST

In the last few decades the number of Hindu religious movements either imported from India to the West or initiated in the West has proliferated to such a degree that it is impossible to give a complete account or an adequate assessment of them. An Indian writer quipped that nowadays the *abhiṣeka* (ordination) of a Hindu Swami consists of a jet-trip to America. The movements are so diverse and of such varying significance that a global assessment is impossible. Some are extensions of Indian *saṃpradāyas*, not primarily aimed at Western audiences, others have been specifically designed for the West.

Coupled with a declared policy of non-proselytizing, mainstream Hindu movements have always maintained claims of universality. The hagiographies of several great Hindu leaders carry the title *Dig-vijaya*, conquest of the four quarters of the earth, and the heads of the five recognized Śaṅkara *maṭhas* bear the official title of *Jagad-guru*, world-teacher. The word "universal" comes naturally to many Hindus who assume that their religion, the *sanātana dharma*, is by definition the universal religion of humankind. Thus also relatively obscure new movements like the *Bhārata Sevāshram Sangha* (founded by Swami Pranavanandaji) aim toward "Universal Awakening – Universal Re-Adjustment – Universal Unification – Universal Emancipation."

Even pointedly nationalist militant Hindu organizations like the Rāṣṭrīa Svayamsevak Sangh (R.S.S.) uphold universalist claims for Hinduism. As M. S. Golwalkar, a former leader of the R.S.S. wrote:[14] "The mission of reorganizing the Hindu people on the lines of their unique national genius which the Sangh has taken up is not only a process of true national regeneration of Bhārat but also the inevitable precondition to realize the dream of world-unity and human welfare ... It is the grand world-unifying thought of Hindus alone that can supply the abiding basis for human brotherhood. This knowledge is in the safe custody of the Hindus alone. It is a divine trust, we may say, given to the charge of the Hindus by destiny ..."

A great many well-known, respected and popular representatives of Hinduism of the more charismatic type, who have their major audience in India, have also attracted Western followers, who often establish centers in their own countries, propagating the words and works of their masters.

Ramana Maharsi (1879–1950) has been among the most lasting and deepest spiritual influences coming from India in recent years. He was not educated in the traditional sense but he intuited Advaita Vedānta and became something like a Socrates among the Indian yogis. Even after his death the place where he lived is said to be somehow charged with spiritual power, emanating from him.[15]

Swami Sivananda (1887–1963), the founder of the Divine Life Society with headquarters at Sivanandasram in Rishikesh, began as a physician before he turned *saṃnyāsi*. His interest, however, continued to be devoted to body and soul. In Rishikesh his followers collect herbs to produce Āyurvedic medicines. Disciples from many countries live a religious life in Sivanandashram, which intends to synthesize the teachings of the great world religions.[16]

Guruji Maharaj – a still living hereditary *ācārya* of the Vallabhas in India – became an overnight teenage celebrity through his Divine Light Movement in the seventies.

J. Krishnamurti (1895–1990), groomed by Annie Besant of the Theosophical Society to be the *avatāra* of the twentieth century, developed into quite an independent man, denouncing his God-mother. He became known in his own right as a lecturer and writer on spiritual topics.[17] He may have refused to be labeled a Hindu but his roots were clearly Hindu and he found his most attentive audience among Hindus.

Among the better-known women-saints of our time was Anandamayi Ma (1896–1983), with establishments in Benares, Vrindaban and Bombay, and abroad. Her quite considerable following considered her during her lifetime the incarnation of a deity.[18]

Paramahamsa Yogananda (1893–1952), author of *Autobiography of a Yogi* and founder of the Yoga-fellowship of California,[19] is far better known in the United States than in India.

Swami Taposwami Maharaj, quite well known in India in his own right,[20] became famous in the West through his world-touring disciple Swami Cinmayananda (1915–97), who gave well-advertised Gītā-lectures in big cities. He also founded Sandeepany Sadhanalaya, a training institution for Hindu missionaries in a Bombay suburb.[21]

One of the most colorful of the contemporary saints is Śrī Sathya Sāī Bābā (born 1926), who sports a bright-red silk robe and an Afro hairdo. As a boy of fourteen he declared that he had no more time for such things as going to school, declaring that he was Sāī Bābā and that his devotees were calling for him. The present Sathya Sāī Bābā claims to be a reincarnation of the older Sāī Bābā of Śīrdī, who had died in 1918. He is even now supposed to appear to people and initiate them, in their dreams. The first miracle of the now living Sāī Bābā was to create sweets for his playmates and flowers for the villagers of Putharpartha in Andhra Pradesh. The "sacred ashes" which he now creates (following the lead of the "old" Sāī Bābā, on whose images a curious ash-like substance is forming) are said to have miraculous properties to effect cures in sickness and to accord mental relief. Modern as he is, he also creates photographs of his own holy person out of nowhere and distributes them, still damp, to his followers. His healing powers are said to be phenomenal and people come from far and wide so that he may help their bodies and their souls. He is said to be able to read thoughts and to have the gift of prophecy and multilocation. Thus he speaks: "Trust always in me and lay your burden upon me; I shall do the rest; It is my task to prepare you for the grace of Bhagvan, when you receive it, everything else will be simple." He does not demand any special exercises, only trust: "Sāī is mother and father. Come to him without fear, doubt or hesitation. I am in your heart."[22]

A fascinating story is connected with a movement called *Ānandmārg*, Path of Bliss. Founded in 1955 by a former railway employee in Jamalpur (Bihar) the movement grew quickly. P. R. Sarkar or Anand Mūrti, considered the "great Preceptor, the harbinger of a New Civilization and the loving guru" by his devotees, was born in 1921 and believed himself to be the third incarnation of God after Śiva and Kṛṣṇa. Besides expressing opinions on almost everything of importance, be it democracy, morals or communism, the *guru* taught Tantric *yoga*. A political wing of the movement, which in a few years established 2000 centers in India and abroad, claimed five million followers; the Proutist Block of India aimed at "establishing the dictatorship of Baba." It has a large number of special organizations for students, workers, welfare activities, etc., and entered elections in India under the symbol of the swastika. The movement is suspected by many people because of its secrecy and its activities, and its founder was arrested some years ago on a murder-charge. His wife had informed police about thirty-five murders committed at the instigation of Ānand Mūrti and quite horrendous crimes in other areas as well.[23]

Mahesh Prasad Varma (born 1911?), the later Mahesh Yogi Maharishi, founded in 1957 in Rishikesh the "Spiritual Regeneration Movement." Its Transcendental Meditation (T.M.) technique soon became popular in the West as a shortcut to enlightenment. When the Beatles began taking an interest in him in 1967 the movement mushroomed. Millions have since undergone T.M. training and the movement has established major centers in Europe and the United States. Transcendental Meditation members established a Maharishi International University, a Maharishi European Research University, and other academic institutions which have attracted a surprisingly large number of reputable scientists as well. Since 1976 the movement has been governed by "The World Government of the Age of Enlightenment" with ten ministries, each headed by a chief minister. The aims of the movement are lofty and comprehensive:

1. To develop the full potential of the individual.
2. To enhance governmental activities.
3. To realize the highest ideal of education.
4. To solve the problems of crime and all behavior that brings unhappiness to the family of man.
5. To maximize the intelligent use of the environment.
6. To bring fulfillment to the individual, family and society.
7. To fulfil the spiritual goals of mankind in this generation.

The members of the movement believe that their mere presence helps to promote peace and harmony, and eventually this will bring about the "Age of Enlightenment." *TIME Magazine* not long ago carried a two-page advertisement of the Institute of World Leadership, Maharishi International University, Fairfield, Iowa, under the caption "Maharishi Technology of the Unified Field."[24]

The founder of the International Society for Krishna Consciousness (ISKCON), popularly called the "Hare Krishna Movement," Swami Bhaktivedanta Sarasvati (born Abhay Charan De) (1896–1973), became rather late (after marriage and life as a businessman) a disciple of Bhaktisiddhanta Saraswati (1957). Swami Bhaktisiddhanta Saraswati, the son of Bhaktivinoda Thakura (1838–1914), who had reawakened interest in Caitanyism in Bengal, commissioned his own disciples to preach Caitanya's religion of Krishna bhakti not only in different parts of India but also in Western countries. Subsequently Caitanya *maṭhas* were built in Madras and London and one of its members, Swami Bon Maharaj, toured America and Europe before the Second World War. Its impact was modest – some Europeans joined the movement, but the movement did not attract much attention.

Virtually singlehandedly and without material support from his Indian colleagues Swami Bhaktivedanta began in the mid-sixties at an already advanced age to form his movement which blossomed into a world-wide organization with several thousand members and an incredible amount of activity.[25]

While it is the most genuinely Hindu of all the many Indian movements in the West – a transplant of an Indian religion with all its cultural trappings down to the last detail – it is the one which curiously does not wish to be called Hindu at all. In his published conversation with Dr. A. L. Basham, Subhanandadasa, an American Hare Krishna member, raised the following point.[26] Hinduism, he contended, is a highly stereotyped term. "It tends to bring to mind such notions as non-devotional monism and pantheism, as well as polytheism and caste, notions which we are not eager to be identified with." He continued, saying:

> The reason why we tend to avoid applying the designation Hindu to ourselves is that the founder of the Hare Krishna movement, Srila Prabhupada, felt that it has a distinctly sectarian implication. One is Hindu in contradistinction to being Christian, Jewish, Muslim, etc. Krishna consciousness, viewed from within as a universal, transcultural spiritual principle, just doesn't fit neatly into the contrived historical cultural term "Hindu". A more appropriate term for Krishna consciousness, from our point of view, would be *sanātana dharma*, eternal religion. If truth is indeed true it must be true everywhere and for everybody. It must transcend relative cultural orientations. But for the sake of placing Krishna consciousness on the map of the history of religions, the term "Vaiṣṇavism", signifying the cultural and theological tradition based upon the worship of Viṣṇu or Krishna, is an accurate and descriptive term for the historical tradition of Krishna consciousness. We refer to ourselves as Vaiṣṇavas.[27]

What became the biggest practical problem of the Western followers of the Hare Krishna movement in India, was a move by Swami Bhaktivedanta – himself a Vaiśya, not a Brahmin by caste – which was wholly out of tune with Indian orthodoxy: the conferring of brahmin caste status on each member. Throughout, Hindu orthodoxy has maintained that nobody who had not been born a brahmin, can become a brahmin. Moreover, one of the more attractive features of the Indian *bhakti* movements was their disregard for caste and their egalitarianism. Also – and that applies to all denominations of Hinduism – acceptance of *saṃnyāsa* was connected with the giving up of one's caste-affiliation: the sacred thread was burned as part of the initiation ceremony, symbolizing the neophyte's new existence outside caste-structured secular society.

After the founder's death in 1977 the ISKCON administration was placed in the hands of eleven governors appointed by Swami Bhaktivedanta some time before. Its aim is "to spread Krishna Consciousness and through it bring the world back to God and to a state of harmony and peace."

The coming of the Hindu religious movements to the West is in many ways an exact parallel to the Western Christian missionary movement in the East. The presence of Indian religions in the West is incomparably smaller than the presence of Western religions in India. The number of Westerners at present engaged in religious propaganda on behalf of Western religious institutions is much greater than the number of "Orientals" spreading their message in the West. Let us not overlook the fact that some of the more aggressive of the Indian movements in the West have been born out of the desire to counteract and neutralize aggressive Western missionary attacks on the religions of their country in the nineteenth and twentieth centuries. No wonder that Eastern missions carry some of the features of their Western counterparts. The failure of Western religions to prevent the horrors of two world wars and of the atrocities of totalitarian governments, the moral collapse of Western civilization and the ensuing lack of guidance and orientation, has convinced many sincere representatives of Eastern religions that they could and should offer rescue by introducing their religions, their meditation-techniques, and their rituals. Many Indian Swamis, who often under considerable personal hardship began missions in the West, are as highly motivated as Christian missionaries.

If some people find the ways of a group like the Hare Krishna slightly eccentric or even comic, they should consider that these are doing nothing else but what Christian missionaries have done in Asia for several centuries: they expected their Asian converts to wear trousers and jackets instead of the traditional dress, they clothed their indigenous priests and nuns in the same outfit that was prescribed in medieval Europe, built Neo-Gothic churches and introduced a Hebrew and Greek scripture, a Latin theology, English, German and Italian hymns, etc.

Last but not least – when speaking about the Hindu religious movements in the West in present times – we should not overlook the impact which Hindu thought and religion exert on representatives of Western cultural and intellectual life, who may never consider joining a Hindu religious movement but who are eager to integrate Hindu elements into their own work.

Among the major writers, Hermann Hesse may be mentioned, whose *Siddharta* turned many of the young people of the sixties on to Hinduism. Somerset Maugham too made a quite serious effort to come to terms with Indian thought.[28] The work of some specialists in Hindu studies like Heinrich Zimmer, Ananda Coomaraswamy, and Alan Daniélou appeal to a wide circle of educated people in the West. The great violinist Yehudi Menuhin showed an interest not only in Yoga but also in Indian music, and he undertook interesting experiments with Ravi Shankar to combine Indian and Western music. The composer Karl Heinz Stockhausen composed music with Hindu themes and with an intention to lead to a meditative religious experience in the Hindu tradition. George Harrison of Beatles fame had been very close to the Hare Krishna movement for years and his recordings as well as his good relations with the movement have certainly helped it become more acceptable to the broader public.

While the majority of the professional philosophers and theologians of our time, who might be expected to show an eager interest in Hindu thought, have not cared to take up the challenge, there are some prominent Western thinkers like K. Jaspers, Ch. Moore, C. G. Jung and others who exhibited keen professional interest in certain aspects of Hindu thought. So did some leading scientists, especially physicists. Erwin Schrödinger was personally convinced of the true insights of Advaita Vedānta. C. F. von Weizsäcker has paid tribute to, and has tried to suggest parallels between, nuclear physics and Advaita Vedānta.[29] On a more popular level, F. Capra, another physicist, in his best-seller *The Tao of Physics*, has drawn wide-ranging connections between central concepts of contemporary physics and Eastern thought. Although he may not possess enough specialized Orientalist knowledge to avoid misinterpretations and misrepresentations of Hindu thinking at some points, his enthusiastic acceptance of some of its major expressions has again brought many scientifically interested people into contact with Hindu thought. More carefully, David Bohm, another leading physicist of our age, followed clues provided by his spiritual mentor Jiddu Krishnamurti, to arrive at interesting physical theories in which consciousness figures as an essential part of physical reality. It is, frankly, quite surprising, how many quotes from Hindu religious writings one encounters in the works of contemporary scientists like K. Malville (*A Feather for Daedalus*), R. Oppenheimer (*Science and the Common Understanding*), V. Nalimov (*Realms of the Unconscious*) and others.

This is not the place to detail exhaustively the influence of Hindu thought and religion on the contemporary West. The examples referred to will be sufficient to give support to the opinion that the influence is broadening as well as deepening.

Even in the more specifically religious sphere a change is noticeable. A hundred years ago, when Max Müller, himself a deeply religious scholar, fascinated by the religions of India, suggested adding the Bible to his collection of *Sacred Books of the East*, the Churchmen did not give their permission. They did not wish to suggest that the Bible was on an equal footing with other sacred books. Meanwhile more or less successful attempts have been made not only to compare Hindu teachings with those of the Bible, but Christians – Western as well as Indian – have gone some way to existentially appropriate Hindu religiosity and Hindu religious thought as part and parcel of their own. Theologians like Abbé Monchanin, Swami Abhishiktananda, Bede Griffiths, Raimon Panikkar and others have made an impact, and they have cleared a path that leads from Hindu religious thought to the Christian Church.

A quiet but remarkable change has taken place in some texts of Christian theology. Here one can now find many references to parallels with – amongst others – Hinduism, where formerly there was no mention at all or very negative polemics. It has become fairly common for students of theology to take courses in Indian religions as part of their professional education. The great theologian Paul Tillich is reported to have remarked toward the end of his life, that, were he to begin his theological career now, he would do so by studying Eastern religions.

HINDUISM PRESENT AND FUTURE

When R.S.S. activists after months of agitation for a recovery of the birthplace of Rāma in Ayodhyā finally destroyed the Babri mosque in December 1992 – in full view of the T.V. cameras of the whole world – some of the worst Hindu–Muslim rioting broke out all over India. In their aftermath the government banned some of the militant Hindu associations and jailed their leaders. They were soon free again and began rebuilding their political power basis. They did it so successfully that by January 1998 they were able to form the central government. In spite of the horror which many had felt in the aftermath of Ayodhyā it became clear that the Hindu parties enjoyed the sympathies of large sections of the population and that "Hindutva," "Hindu-ness" was a winning political card.

The term had been used as a political tool first in 1923 by Vir Savarkar, a firebrand ideologue of the Hindu Mahāsabhā, who distinguished "Hindutva" as Indianness from "Hinduism" as a religion. He demanded, nevertheless, that every true Indian should consider the country of India as "Holy Land" and that a refusal to do so should exclude people from citizenship in India.

Obviously "Hindutva" is a very vague concept and its meaning depends very much on who is using it. In the minds of some it has ominous implications of Hindu autocracy and fascist ideology. It need not have these implications, however. It could become the legitimate expression of a newly found Indian identity, a recovery of cultural roots and a reconnecting with the historic achievements of "the wonder that was India," to use the title of a well-known scholarly work. India was one of the great ancient civilizations – it suffered during the past thousand years invasions and occupations by foreign powers, who attempted to destroy its native culture and its indigenous religions. To take pride in Indian civilization and to attempt to build on its strengths is no crime. Every reasonable person will welcome such a development. India's ancient civilization had been deeply imbued with spirituality; its revival will also mean a *Hindu jāgaran*, an awakening of Hinduism as a religion. If Hindus reawaken to the cosmic religion of the Vedas, the profound spirituality of the Upaniṣads, the fervent *bhakti* of their singer-saints, the scholarly spirit of their *ācāryas*, the social concern of a Ram Mohan Roy and the inspired world vision of a Mahatma Gandhi, Hinduism will become again a guide for humankind and a light for the whole world.

NOTES

1. H. Zimmer, *Philosophies of India*, ed. J. Campbell, Cleveland and New York: The World Publishing Company; 1956, 1.
2. One of the best known and most informative is Abbé Dubois' *Hindu Manners, Customs and Ceremonies*.
3. Preface to New Edition of M. Monier-Williams' Sanskrit–English Dictionary, Oxford: Clarendon Press, 1899 (Reprint 1964), ix.
4. First published in six volumes, Oxford: Clarendon Press, 1849–74; second edition in four volumes 1892; Indian reprint 1966.
5. A good selection of these is offered by R. F. Young, *Resistant Hinduism: Sanskrit Sources of Anti-Christian Apologetics in Early Nineteenth Century India*, Vienna, 1981.
6. The most scholarly work is J. T. F. Jordens, *Dayananda Saraswati: His Life and Ideas*, Delhi: Oxford University Press, 1978.
7. Information is taken from an article in *Hinduism Today*, vol.14, no. 9 (September 1992). As source it mentions Sarvadeshik Arya Samaj Pratinidhi Sabha, Dayananand Bhavan New Delhi.
8. *The Complete Works of Swami Vivekananda*, Mayavati Memorial Edition, 7th edition, 1946 (Mayavati, Almora), vol. III, 139.
9. Ibid., 274ff.
10. The Buddhist countries of Burma (Myanmar) and Ceylon (Sri Lanka) which had also been part of the British East Indian Empire, became independent nations. As is well known, the former East Pakistan (East Bengal) became independent Bangladesh after Pakistan lost its war with India in 1972.
11. *Young India*, Oct. 6, 1921.
12. Ibid.
13. *My Search for Truth*, Agra, 1946, p. 6.
14. *Bunch of Thoughts*, Vikrama Prakashan: Bangalore, 1966; p. 7f.
15. Arthur Osborne, *Ramana Maharshi and the Path of Self-Knowledge*, Jaico: Bombay, 1962.
16. An appreciation of his life can be found in Swami Chidananda's, his successor, *Light Fountain*, Divine Life Society: Sivanandanagar, second edition, 1967.
17. A very sympathetic insider's account is Pupul Jayakar, *J. Krishnamurti: A Biography*, Delhi: Penguin India, 1987.
18. See C. Das Gupta, *Mother as Revealed to Me*, Benares: Shree Anandamayi Sangha, 1954.
19. *Autobiography of a Yogi*, Bombay: Jaico, 1960. The Yoga Fellowship also publishes a magazine with information about its activities.
20. He is the author of *Wanderings in the Himalayas*, Madras: Ganesh, 1960.
21. He published a monthly *Tapovan Prasād* and a commentary on the *Bhagavadgītā* in twelve volumes.
22. By now there is an immense literature on Sathya Sāī Bābā, much of it recording the numerous miracles worked by him. See e.g. *Satya Sai Baba Speaks*, ten volumes, published by Sri Sathya Sai Education and Publications Foundation, Kadugodi, 1974–75.

23. *The Illustrated Weekly of India* devoted a cover story and several articles to the Ānandmārg in vol. XCVIII/42 (Oct. 30–Nov. 5, 1977).
24. The publications of and about T.M. fill many shelves. T.M. activities are usually well advertised. A sympathetic outsiders' view is *TM. Discovering inner energy and overcoming stress* by H. Bloomfield, M. P. Cain, D. T. Jaffe and R. B. Kory, New York: Dell Publishing Company, 1975.
25. Publications by and about Swami Bhaktivedanta are too numerous to mention here. The most detailed description is provided by Satsvarupa dasa Goswami in his six-volume biography of A. C. Bhaktivedanta, *Śrīlā Prabhupāda-līlāmṛta*, Los Angeles; Bhaktivedanta Book Trust, 1983.
26. *Hare Krishna, Hare Krishna. Five Distinguished Scholars on the Krishna Movement in the West*, New York: Grove Press, 1983, 162–195.
27. Ibid. p. 172.
28. His novel *The Razor's Edge* not only carries a quote from the Bṛhadāraṇyaka Upaniṣad as a motto, the theme of the book itself is concerned with ideas central to Hinduism.
29. T. M. P. Mahadevan (ed.), *Spiritual Perspectives*, Delhi: Heinemann, 1975.

CHRONOLOGY

The chronology of Ancient India up to the time of Gotama the Buddha (including the dates of Gotama the Buddha's life) is at present the focus of vigorous scholarly debates. The majority of Indian scholars assume an indigenous origin and a date of *c.*4000 B.C.E. for the earliest parts of the *Ṛgveda*,[1] based on constellations mentioned in them. The majority of Western scholars maintain the "Aryan Invasion Theory," dating the composition of the *Ṛgveda* to 1500–1200 B.C.E. There is today increasing evidence for cultural continuity between the Indus civilization and the Vedic tradition.[2] The chronology offered here for the earliest period of the history of Hinduism represents mostly the traditional Indian position.[3]

Indians who do not use the Western (Gregorian) calendar have several other systems of dating. The most common eras used in today's India are *samvat* (beginning 57 B.C.E.) and *śaka* (beginning 78 C.E.).

On the basis of the more recent research, based on archeology and astronomy, the following chronology can be tentatively established:

c. 4000 B.C.E.	Earliest Vedic hymns.
c. 3500	Early Harappan civilization.
c. 3100	Traditional dates for the "Great Flood" and Manu Vaivasvata.
c. 3000–2750	Traditional date for Yayāti Period.
c. 2750–2550	Traditional date for Māndhātri Period.
c. 2700–1500	Mature Indus civilization.
c. 2350–1950	Traditional date for Rāmacandra period.
c. 1900	Age of *Rāmāyaṇa*.
c. 1500–500	Major *Upaniṣads*, development of early *Sāṁkhya*, early *Pūrva Mīmāṃsā*.
c. 1400	Great Bhārata War – Age of Kṛṣṇa. Early version of *Mahābhārata*.
c. 1200	Early *Sūtra* literature. Consolidation of Vedic Civilization: *Manusmṛti*.

624–544	Life of Gautama Buddha according to traditional reckoning.
527	End of Jīna Mahāvīra's earthly life according to Jain tradition.
518	Persian invasion under Skylax and conquest of the Indian satrapy for Darius I.
c. 500 B.C.E.–500 C.E.	*Śrauta Sūtras*, *Gṛhya Sūtras*, *Dharma Sūtras*, *Vedāṅgas*; the basis of the orthodox systems; epics and the original *Purāṇas*.
c. 500–200 B.C.E.	*Bhagavadgītā*.
c. 500–200	Bādarāyaṇa's *Vedānta Sūtra*.
c. 490–458	Reign of Ajataśatru, king of Magadha.
c. 400	Pāniṇis *Aṣṭādhyayī* (Grammar).
c. 400–200	Jaimini's *Pūrvamīmāṃsā Sūtra*.
327–325	Alexander of Macedonia's invasion of India.
c. 322–298	Reign of Candragupta of Magadha.
c. 300	Megasthenes, Greek Ambassador to Magadha.
c. 300	Kautilīya's *Arthaśāstra* (according to some scholars: 100 C.E.) Gautama's *Nyāya Sūtra* and Kaṇāda's *Vaiśeṣika Sūtra*.
c. 273–237	Reign of Aśoka.
c. 200 B.C.E.–100 C.E.	Invasions of Śūngas, Iranians, Śakas and Kuśānas, who founded kingdoms in India.
c. 200 B.C.E.–200 C.E.	Peak period of Buddhist and Jain influence.
c. 150 B.C.E.–100 C.E.	Patañjali's *Mahābhāṣya*.
c. 115 B.C.E.	Besnagar inscription of Heliodorus with a mention of Kṛṣṇa worship.
c. 100 B.C.E.–500 C.E.	Patañjali's *Yoga Sūtra*.
c. 100 B.C.E.–100 C.E.	Upavarṣa's Commentary to *Pūrvamīmāṃsā Sūtra* and *Vedānta Sūtra*.
c. 100 B.C.E.–400 C.E.	*Śabara-bhāṣya* on Jaimini Sūtras.
c. 100 B.C.E.–800 C.E.	Composition of *Tirukkural*.
c. 100 B.C.E.	Early Mathurā sculpture; images of gods in temples.
c. 25 B.C.E.	Indian Embassy to Emperor Augustus of Rome.
c. 50 C.E.	First documentation of images of gods with several pairs of arms.
c. 10	Indian Embassy to Emperor Trajan of Rome.
c. 100–500	Expansion of Hinduism in South-East Asia.
c. 100–200	*Yājñavalkyasmṛti*.
c. 100–300	*Viṣṇudharma Sūtra*.
c. 100–400	*Nāradasmṛti*.
c. 200–500	Composition of *Viṣṇu Purāṇa*.
c. 250–325	*Sāṁkhya Kārikā* of Īśvarakṛṣṇa.
c. 300–600	Composition of some of the older *Purāṇas* in their present form.
c. 300–888	Pallava rulers in South India (Kāñcīpuram).
c. 319–415	Gupta Empire of Mathurā.
c. 400–500	Vatsyayana's *Kāma Sūtra*.
c. 400	*Harivaṃśa Purāṇa*, *Ahirbudhnya Saṃhitā*. Age of Kālidāsa, the greatest Indian dramatist. Spread of Vaiṣṇavism, especially Kṛṣṇa cult. Beginning of Tantricism.

c. 400–500	Vyāsa's *Yoga-bhāṣya.*
c. 450–500	Huna invasions.
c. 500	*Devī-māhātmaya* (in *Mārkaṇḍeya Pūraṇa*). Spread of Śāktism into larger areas.
c. 500–800	Āḷvārs; composition of *Kūrma Purāṇa.*
547	Kosmas Indikopleustes travels to India
c. 600–650	Poet Bana, author of *Kādambarī* and *Harṣacarita.*
c. 600–800	Peak of Pāñcarātra Vaiṣṇavism.
c. 600–900	Late (metrical) *smṛtis*; composition of *Agni* and *Garuḍa Purāṇa.*
after 600	Strong development of Vedānta.
c. 600–800	Brahmanical renaissance; successful fight against strongly tantric Buddhism.
c. 640	King Harṣa of Kanauj sends embassy to China.
c. 650–1200	Several independent kingdoms in Western, Central, East and South India.
c. 650–700	Life of Kumārila Bhaṭṭa and Manikavācaka.
since *c.*700	Prevalence of *bhakti* religions.
c. 700–750	Gauḍapāda, author of a *kārikā* on the *Māṇḍukya Upaniṣad* and *prācārya* of Śaṅkarācārya.
since *c.*700	Flourishing of Kāśmīr Śaivism.
c. 788–820	Life of Śaṅkarācārya.
c. 800–900	Composition of the *Bhāgavata Purāṇa* in its present form; *Śukra-ñiti-sāra.*
c. 800–1250	Cola dynasty in Tamilnadu.
c. 825–900	Medathiti, writer of a commentary on *Manusmṛti.*
c. 900	Udāyana's *Nyāyakusumañjalī.*
c. 900–1100	*Śiva Purāṇa*; Śaivite tantricism in Indonesia.
c. 900–1100	Composition of *Yogavasiṣṭharāmāyaṇa* and *Bhaktisūtra.*
999–1026	Mahmud of Ghazni repeatedly raids northwestern India.
1026	Muslims loot temple of Somnāth.
1017–1137	Life of Rāmānuja.
c. 1100	Buddhism virtually extinct in India; life of Abhinavagupta; composition of Hindu Tantra.
c. 1100–1400	Composition of *Śākta Upaniṣads*; rise of Vīrasáivism in South India.
c. 1150–1160	Kalhana's *Rājatarāṅginī.*
c. 1150	*Śrīkaṇṭha-bhāṣya*; building of Jagannath Temple at Puri.
c. 1197–1276	Life of Madhvācārya.
c. 1200–1250	Life of Viṣṇusvami.
1205–1300	Life of Lokācārya Pillai.
c. 1250	Beginning of *Śaiva-siddhānta*; building of Sun Temple in Koṇāraka.
1211–1236	Reign of Iltutmish, first Sultan of Delhi; beginning of Muslim rule over large parts of India.
c. 1216–1327	Rule of Pāndyas at Madurai; foundation of Mināksī and Śiva Temple of Madurai.

1269–1370	Life of Vedānta Deśika.
c. 1275–1675	Jñāneśvara of Mahārāṣṭra and other *bhakti* mystics.
1288	Marco Polo at Kalyan
c. 1300–1386	Life of Sāyaṇa, famous commentator of the Vedic *Saṃhitās* and *Brāhmaṇas.*
1327	Muslims loot temple at Śrīraṅgam.
c. 1333	Ibn Battuta's travels in India.
c. 1340	Life of Mādhava, author of *Sarvadarśanasaṅgraha* and *Pañcadaśī.*
1336–1565	Kingdom of Vijayanagara, last Hindu empire in India as far as Malaysia, Indonesia, and the Philippines.
c. 1350–1610	Vīraśaivism state religion of Mysore.
c. 1350–1650	Composition of many works of the Pūrvamīmāṃsakas.
1365–98	Life of Jāyatīrtha.
c. 1400–1470	Life of Rāmānanda.
c. 1420	Life of Mīrābāī.
1440–1518	Life of Kabīr.
c. 1449–1568	Life of Śaṅkaradeva, great Vaiṣṇava preacher in Assam.
c. 1475–1531	Life of Vallabha.
c. 1469	Birth of Gurū Nanak, founder of Sikhism.
1478–1539	Life of Vyāsarāya.
c. 1485–1533	Life of Caitanya.
1479–1584	Life of Sūrdās.
1498	Vasco da Gama, after having rounded the Cape of Good Hope, lands on the Malabar coast.
c. 1500	Composition of *Adhyātma Rāmāyaṇa* and of Sādānanda's *Vedānta-sāra.*
c. 1500–1800	Peak of Durgā worship in Bengal.
c. 1550	Life of Brahmānanda Giri, author of a famous commentary on Śaṅkara's *Śarīraka-bhāṣya.*
1510	Portuguese occupy Goa.
c. 1526–1757	Moghul rule in India, destruction of most Hindu temples in North and Central India.
1511–1637	Life of Tulasīdāsa.
c. 1542	The Jesuit missionary Francis Xavier lands in Goa.
c. 1548–1598	Life of Ekanātha.
1580	Akbar the Great invites some Jesuit missionaries from Goa to his court for religious discussions.
c. 1585	Life of Hit Harivaṃśa, founder of the Rādhā-Vallabhis.
1608–1649	Life of Tukārāma.
1608–1681	Life of Rāmdās.
1610–1640	Composition of Mitramiśra's *Viramitrodaya*, famous digests of the *dharma-śāstras.*
c. 1630	Composition of Śrīnivāsadāsa's *Yatīndramatadīpikā.*
1631	Death of Mumtaz, in whose honor Shah Jahan built the famous Taj Mahal at Agra.

1651	The East India Company opens first factory on the Hugli (Bengal).
1657	Dara Shikoh translates the Upaniṣads into Persian.
1661	Bombay becomes a British possession.
1664	Śivāji declares himself king of Mahārāṣṭra.
1675	Foundation of the French colony of Pondichéry.
c. 1670–1750	Life of Nagojibhaṭṭa, author of numerous works on grammar, *dharma-śāstra*, yoga, etc.
1690	Foundation of Calcutta through East India Company (Fort St. George).
c. 1700–1800	Life of Baladeva, author of *Govinda-bhāṣya.*
c. 1750	Composition of the (reformist) *Mahānirvāṇa-tantra.*
1757	Battle of Plassey; Clive is master of India.
1784	Asiatic Society founded in Calcutta by Sir William Jones.
1791	Foundation of Banaras Sanskrit College.
1818	Defeat of the last Maratha Peshwa.
1828	Rām Mohan Roy founds Brahmo Samāj.
1829	Law against *satī.*
1829–1837	Suppression of the *thags.*
1834–1886	Life of Ramakrishna Paramahamsa.
1835	Introduction of English school system in India.
1842–1901	Life of M.D. Ranade, great social reformer.
1857	The so-called Mutiny ("First Indian War of Independence" in more recent history books).
1858	The British Crown takes over the administration of India from the East India Company.
1875	Foundation of *Ārya Samāj* by Swami Dāyānanda Sārasvatī.
1885	Foundation of *Indian National Congress* in Bombay.
1909	Foundation of Hindū Mahāsabhā by Pandit Mohan Malaviya.
1913	Nobel prize in literature for Rabindranath Tagore.
1920	Mahatma Gandhi begins first All-India Civil Disobedience Movement.
1925	Foundation of *Rāstrīa Svayamsevak Sangh.*
1947	Partition of India and creation of the Indian Union and Pakistan as independent nations.
1948	Assassination of Mahātma Gandhi. Foundation of *Rām Rājya Pariṣad.* Pandit Nehru Prime Minister of the Indian Union. Sri Cakravarti Rajagopalacari appointed Governor General.
1950	India declared a Republic within the Commonwealth. Acceptance of the Constitution. Death of Śrī Aurobindo Ghose and Ramana Maharṣi.
1951	Inauguration of the *Bhūdān* movement by Vinoba Bhave, Gandhi's successor. Foundation of the *Bhāratīya Jana Sangh.*
1955	The Hindu Marriage Act passed in parliament.
1956	Reorganization of states (provinces) according to linguistic principles.

1961	Goa, Damao and Diu, Portuguese colonies in India, liberated in a military action.
1962	Dr. Rajendra Prasad, the first President of the Republic of India (since 1950), dies. Dr. Sarvepalli Radhakrishnan, Vice-President, succeeds him.
1964	Death of Jawaharlal Nehru. Lal Bahadur Sastri succeeds as Prime Minister. Foundation of Viśva Hindū Pariṣad (VHP).
1965	Conflict with Pakistan (West). Indira Gandhi succeeds as Prime Minister.
1984	Sikh agitation for an independent Khalistan. Central Government forcefully evicts Sikh extremists from Golden Temple in Amritsar/Punjab. Indira Gandhi assassinated by two of her Sikh guards.
1985	Rajiv Gandhi, Indira's oldest son, elected Prime Minister.
1991	Rajiv Gandhi assassinated by Tamil extremist.
1992	Hindu agitation on behalf of temple on Rāma's presumed birthplace in Ayodhyā culminating in destruction of Babri-Masjid and major riots in many Indian cities.
1998	Electoral victory of Hindu parties: establishment of a Bhāratīya Janatā Party minority government. India detonates nuclear devices. Celebration of Kumbhamelā at Hardwar with several million pilgrims attending.
1999	Bḥāratīya Janatā Party wins majority in new elections.

NOTES

1. The present text of the *Ṛgveda* is a later redaction of an earlier collection of hymns that probably were not focused on Indra as much as the more recent version. See A. Esteller, "The Quest for the Original Ṛgveda" in ABORI 48/1 (1969) pp. 1–40 and "The Ṛgveda Saṃhitā as a 'Palimpsest'" in *Indian Antiquary* (3rd Series) 4/1 (January 1967) pp. 1–23 and also R. N. Dandekar "*Vṛtrahā Indra*" in ABORI 30/1 (1951) pp. 1–55.
2. See W. S. Fairservis, "The Harappan Civilization and the Ṛgveda" in M. Witzel (ed.) *Inside the Texts*, pp. 61–8. The last page consists of a comparative table of traits attested in the Ṛgveda paralleled by archeological finds in the Indus civilization.
3. The dates given below are those provided by A. D. Pusalker in the chapter "Historical Traditions" of *The Vedic Age* [Vol. I of *The History and Culture of the Indian People*, General editor R. C. Majumdar, Bombay: Bharatiya Vidya Bhavan, 1965; 4th impression] pp. 271–336.

GLOSSARY

abhaṅga	(Mahratti) devotional poem.
abhāva	nonperception (in the Nyāya-system); nonbeing (in the Vaiśeṣika-system).
abhaya	fearlessness; in iconology: *abhaya mudrā* is the hand pose of a deity, inspiring confidence and trust.
abhideya	conversion.
abhiniveśa	desire; in the *yoga*-system: instinctive craving for life.
abhiṣeka	anointment, part of installation ceremony of a king and an image of the deity.
abhyāsa	exercise, practice, exertion.
ācamana	rinsing of mouth with water before worship and before meals.
acāra	immobile (used as an attribute of the Supreme Being).
ācāra	way of life; mode of behavior.
ācārya	master (also used as equivalent to Master of Arts).
acetana	without consciousness (used as attribute of matter).
acintya	beyond intellectual understanding.
ādāna	taking away.
adbhūta	marvellous, miraculous.
adharma	unrighteousness, evil.
adhikāra	qualification (especially of students of religion).
adhyāsa	superimposition; misidentification.
adhyātma	supreme; spiritual; relating to the Supreme Being.
adhyāya	chapter (of a treatise).
Aditi	Vedic Goddess, "Mother Earth," mother of *ādityas*.
adṛṣṭa	invisible; important technical term in the Nyāya and Vaiśeṣika systems.
advaita	nonduality; name of a school of Vedānta.
ādya prakṛti	primeval matter.

ādya śakti	primeval power, title of the Goddess.
āgama	source, beginning, scriptures; name of a class of writings which are considered revealed.
aghora	horrible; name of a sect of Śaivites.
agni	fire; one of the foremost Vedic gods.
agnicayana	a particular kind of Vedic fire sacrifice.
agnihotra	Vedic fire sacrifice.
agniṣṭoma	fire sacrifice.
ahaṁkāra	principle of individuation; egotism.
ahiṃsā	not killing; nonviolence.
ahi	snake.
ahita	improper, unwholesome, not propitious.
aikya	unity, oneness.
aiśvarya	Lordliness.
aja	unborn (masc.); attribute of the Supreme Being; billygoat.
ajā	unborn (fem.), attribute of Primordial Matter; nannygoat.
ajñāna	ignorance; absence of (redeeming) knowledge.
akala	without parts; attribute of Supreme Being.
ākāśa	ether (one of the five elements of Indian cosmology); space.
akhila	undivided, complete.
akhila rasamṛta mūrti	description of Kṛṣṇa as "perfect embodiment of the nectar of all feelings."
akṛti	uncreated; eternal principle underlying words, etc.
akṣa-mālā	rosary made of beads from a shrub sacred to Śiva.
akṣara	imperishable; syllable (letter); name of Supreme Being.
amarṣa	impatience; anger; passion.
aṃbikā	mother; Mother Goddess.
amṛta	nectar; draught of immortality.
aṃśa	part, fragment.
anādhāra	without support.
anādi	without beginning; eternal.
anahaṭa	"unstruck," mystical sound arising from within the body, signifiying divine grace.
ānanda	bliss; used as last part of the proper name of many *samnyāsis*.
ananta	without end; proper name of the world-snake upon which Viṣṇu rests.
aṇava	veil; congenital ignorance concerning the ultimate; stain.
aṅga	member, constituent part, e.g., of a major work.
aṇimā	smallness; in *yoga* the faculty to diminish one's size.
aniruddha	free, without hindrance; proper name of one of the *vyūhas* of Viṣṇu.
anitya	not permanent; transient.
aṅkuśa	goad; one of the divine attributes.
anṛta	against the (moral) law.
anta	end, death.
antarātman	conscience.

antaryāmī	the "inner ruler," the Supreme Being as present in the human heart (literally understood).
aṇu	atom.
anubhava	experience.
anugraha	attraction; grace of God.
anumāna	inference.
apara	unsurpassed; attribute of the Supreme Being.
aparigraha	without having (and wanting) possessions.
aparokṣa	immediate, present.
apas	water.
apāśraya	supportless.
apauruṣeya	not man-made; technical term for the supernatural origin of the Veda in Mīmāṃsā.
apsarā	nymph.
apūrva	technical term in the Mīmāṃsā system to denote the not-yet realized effect of a sacrifice.
araṇya	forest.
arcā	rites of worship of an image.
arcāvatāra	image of God, who took on this form in order to become an object of worship for the devotees.
ardha	half.
ardhanārīśvara	figurative representation of Śiva, in which one half shows a male figure, the other half a female one.
arjuna	bright; proper name of the hero of the *Bhagavadgītā*.
arka	sun.
artha	object; meaning; wealth.
arthavāda	"eulogy", mere description (without authority).
ārya	noble (man); self-designation of the "Āryans."
āsana	seat, sitting posture.
asat	not true; "not real."
āśirvādam	(ritual) blessing.
asmitā	egoism; from *asmi*, "I am."
āśrama	hermitage; stage in life; proper name of a group of *samnyāsis*.
aṣṭamūrti	"eightfold embodiment," eight proper names of Śiva.
asteya	not stealing.
āstika	someone who accepts the authority of the Veda; orthodox.
aśubha	inauspicious.
aśuddha	impure.
asuras	demons; class of superhuman beings.
aśvamedha	horse sacrifice.
aśvatha	tree (*ficus sacra*).
aśvins	Vedic gods, a pair of brothers; astronomy, Castor and Pollux.
ātmakūṭa	self-deceit.
ātman	self.
ātmanivedana	self-surrender (as part of religious initiation).
avatāra	descent (of god in a bodily form).

avidyā	ignorance (of reality).
avyakta	unmanifest.
āyurveda	traditional Indian medicine; literally, "life-knowledge."
baddha	bound (into *saṃsāra*)
bala	strength, power.
bana	arrow; attribute of images of deities.
bandha	bondage.
bhadra	well, happy; blessing.
bhāga	luck, fortune.
bhagavān	lord; most general title of god.
Bhagavadgītā	"Song of the Lord," celebrated religio-philosophical epic poem, conceived as dialogue between Kṛṣṇa and Arjuna, part of the *Māhābharata.*
bhajana	devotional recitation.
bhakta	devotee.
bhakti	love, devotion.
bhasma	(sacred) ashes.
bhāṣya	commentary.
bhāva	condition; emotion; nature.
bhaviṣya	future.
bhaya	fear, terror.
bheda	difference.
bhoga	enjoyment.
bhū, bhūmī	earth; proper name of Viṣṇu's second consort.
bhukti	enjoyment.
bhūta	being, a spirit.
bibhatsa	trembling.
bīja	seed.
bīja-mantra	"seed-spell," mystical syllables identified with the Goddess, used by Śāktas.
bindu	"drop," crescent.
brahmā	(personal) creator-god.
brahmacarin	student; celibate.
brahmacarya	first period in life, celibate studenthood.
brahmaloka	world of Brahmā; highest abode.
brahman	(impersonal) absolute.
brāhmaṇa	member of the highest caste; class of ritual texts.
brahmārandra	the place from where the soul departs at death (the backside of the cranium).
buddhi	intelligence; in the Sāṁkhya system name of the first product of the union of *puruṣa* and *prakṛti.*
caitanya	spirit, consciousness, also proper name for the Supreme; proper name of a Bengali saint of the sixteenth century.
caitta	consciousness.
cakra	circle, disc; centers in body; one of Viṣṇu's weapons; discus.

cakravartin	universal ruler.
caṇḍa	moon; silver.
candāla	wild; bad; proper name of lowest caste; outcaste.
caṇḍana	sandalwood.
caṇḍī	fierce woman; proper name of Devī.
carita	biography.
caryā	activity; mode of behavior.
caturmukha	four-faced; proper name of Brahmā.
caturvarṇāśrama	the four *varṇas* ("castes") and stages of life.
chāyā	shadow.
cit	consciousness; spirit.
citta	thought.
daitya	a goblin, a slave, a demon.
dakṣina	sacrificial fees.
dakṣinācāra	right-handed path.
dāna	gift; charity.
Dānava	member of a group hostile to Vedic Āryans.
darśana	view; audience; theory; philosophical system.
dāsa	servant; often part of proper name.
dāsa-mārga	"way of the servant", lowest rank in Śaiva-siddhānta.
daśanāmī	ten-named; proper name of a religious order.
dasyu	slave; name for non-Āryan in *Ṛgveda*.
dayā	compassion.
deva, devatā	divine (superior) being.
devayāna	path of the gods.
devī	goddess.
dhairya	firmness.
dhama	area; body.
dhāraṇa	support.
dharma	"law," religion, support, etc.
dharmaśāstras	law books.
dharmakṣetra	"the field of righteousness."
dhatṛ	giver; proper name for God.
dhyāna	meditation; concentration in Yoga.
dig-vijaya	conquest of the four quarters; appellation of the successful competition of a religious teacher.
dīkṣā	initiation.
dīpā	lamp.
divya-mārga	"way of the deities," highest rank in Śaiva-siddhānta.
duḥkha	sorrow, suffering.
dvaita	duality; name of a school of Vedānta.
dvaitādvaita vivarjita	beyond duality and non-duality.
dvandva	pair of opposites (hot-cold, etc.).
dvāpara yuga	second era of each *kalpa*.
dveṣa	hatred.

dvijati twice-born; appellation of the three upper castes whose initiation is considered a second birth.
dvīpa island; continent.
dyaus resplendent; sky; Vedic high god.
ekādaśī eleventh day (of each half-month); sacred to Vaiṣṇavas.
ekāgratā one-pointedness, single-mindedness.
ekaśṛṅga one-horn (unicorn); the fish-descent (of Viṣṇu) with one horn, on which Manu fastened his raft and thus was saved in the great flood.
gaddī throne, seat, headship (as of a *maṭha*).
gandharva celestial musician.
Gaṇeśa lord of the celestial armies; elephant-headed son of Śiva and Pārvatī.
garbha womb; *garbha-gṛha*; innermost sanctuary of the temples.
Garuḍa Viṣṇu's vehicle; gryphius.
ghāṭ(a) steps; especially flight of steps leading to a river or tank.
gopa cowherd
gopī milk maid.
gosvāmī lord of cows; title for high-ranking Vaiṣṇavas of certain communities.
grāma-devatās village deities.
guṇa quality.
guru elder; spiritual master; teacher in general.
gurūpāsati surrender to the master (as part of initiation)
guru-paraṃparā lineage of gurus, succession of guru and disciple.
hala plough, attribute of Bālarāma.
halāhala poison churned up from the Milk Ocean, consumed by Śiva in order to save the world.
hara literally, the one who takes away; name of Śiva.
hari literally, the yellowish green one; name of Viṣṇu.
harṣa joy.
hasyā laughter.
Hayaśirṣa "horse-head," an *avatāra* of Viṣṇu.
hetu cause.
hiṃsā violence, killing.
hindūtva "hindu-dom", Hinduism as a cultural and political over against "hindu-*dharma*" as a religious concept.
hiraṇyagarbha literally, golden womb; in cosmology the first being.
hita beneficial, good.
hitavācana well-intentioned speaking.
hlādinī enjoyment.
hlādinī-śakti "power of enjoyment," one of the three *śaktis* of Kṛṣṇa.
homa fire oblation.
hotṛ class of Vedic priests.
hṛdaya heart; core of something.
icchā wish, desire.

indriya	sense organs.
īrṣyā	envy, jealousy.
iṣṭa	preferred, wished for.
iṣṭa-deva(tā)	the god of one's choice.
īśvara	Lord; God.
itihāsa	history; technical term for the epics.
japa	repetition of the name of God or a *mantra*.
jātī	birth; race, family, "sub-caste."
jaya	victory; also as greeting – "hail."
jīva(-ātman)	life; individual living being.
jñāna	knowledge.
jñānaniṣṭha	state of being firmly and irrevocably established in ultimate knowledge.
jñāni	a knower (of the absolute).
jyotis	light
jyotir-liṅga	"liṅga formed of light," twelve famous Śiva-*liṅgas* which are not made by human hands.
jyotiṣa	one of the auxiliary sciences of the Veda: astronomy and astrology.
jyotiṣṭoma	a seasonal sacrifice for the departed.
kaiṁkārya	"service", used in connection with service of God in heaven as ultimate aim (*kaiṁkārya-prāpti*).
kaivalya	"aloneness;" ultimate aim of *yoga*.
kāla	time; black colour; fate; death.
kālamukha	black-mouth; name of Śiva; name of a Śaivite sect.
kālī	the "black one"; name of the terrible form of the goddess.
kālī-yuga	age of strife; last period in each world-era (*kalpa*).
kalkin	the future (last) *āvātara* of Viṣṇu in the form of a white horse.
kalpa	world-era, day of Brahmā (432 million years); ritual; one of the auxiliary sciences of Veda.
kalpa-sūtras	texts describing sacrificial rituals.
kāma	desire, lust, love; name of god of love.
kāmadhenu	"wish-fulfilling cow."
kāmya-karma	ritual performed to fulfill a particular wish.
kāṇḍa	part (of a text).
kāpalī	literally one with a skull; name of followers of certain Śaivite groups.
kāraṇa	cause; title of the Supreme Being; God.
karma	work; action; result of an action.
kārya	worship of an image through various acts.
kavaca	"armour", "protection"; designation of certain prayers invoking the protection of a deity.
kavi	poet, wise man, omniscient.
keyura	earring, attribute of images of deities.
khadga	sword, attribute of images of deities.
kīrtaṇa	congregational religious singing.

kleśa	suffering; pain.
kośa	sheath; cover; treasury; lexicon.
kriyā	activity; skill; exercises.
krodha	anger.
kṛpā	favor; grace.
Kṛṣṇa	black; proper name of the most famous *avatāra* of Viṣṇu.
kṛta-yuga	the first age in each world era; the golden age.
Kubera	god of wealth, king of the *yakṣas*, friend of Śiva.
kukṣi	chest.
kuṃbha	waterpot; astronomically, sign of Aquarius.
kuṃbha-melā	a great gathering at specific holy places every twelfth year.
kuṇḍalinī	serpent; in Tantricism, life-energy.
Kūrma	tortoise; one of the *avatāras* of Viṣṇu.
lakṣana	characteristic; attribute; sign.
līlā	play.
liṅga	characteristic sign; subtle nature; phallic symbol of Śiva.
lobha	greed.
loka	world; sphere.
loka-nātha	Lord of the world.
loka-pāla	guardian of the world.
mada	intoxication; dementia.
mādhava	sweet like honey (*madhu*); proper name of Kṛṣṇa; proper name of several famous philosophers.
madhurasa	literally, honey sentiment; highest love and affection.
mādhurya bhāva	"feeling of sweetness", highest degree of *bhakti*.
madhya deśa	"middle country", Central (North-) India, the best place for brahmins to live in.
mahā	great.
Mahābhārata	"The Great Bhārata (Narrative)"; a huge epic and a veritable encyclopedia of Hinduism.
mahā-pāpa	"great sin," unforgivable action.
mahant(a)	head of a monastic establishment.
maharṣi	great sage; honorific title.
mahat	great; in the Sāṁkhya system, first evolute (intellect).
mahātmā	great soul; honorific title.
māhātmya	eulogy, text praising a particular place.
maheśvara	great lord; proper name of Śiva.
mahiṣa	buffalo; proper name of a demon killed by Devī.
maithuṇa	copulation; pair; astronomically, Gemini.
makara	crocodile; alligator.
mala	stain.
mālā	garland; chain; "rosary" of beads.
maṃsa	meat.
mānasa	mind borne.
māna	pride; idea, concept; honor.
manas	mind.

māṇava	relating to Manu; human.
mānava-dharma	laws given by Manu (for humankind).
maṇḍala	circle; section of *Ṛgveda*.
maṇḍapa	covered hall; tent.
maṇḍira	palace; temple.
maṅgala	auspicious, lucky.
maṅgala-śloka	an opening verse or prayer of a text to ensure that the undertaking is auspicious.
maṇi	jewel.
mantra	word, formula (especially from scriptures).
Manu	ancestor and lawgiver of humankind.
manvantara	an age of one (of fourteen) Manu (432 million years); according to Hindu tradition we live now in the seventh *manvantara* (seven more are to follow before the end).
mārga	way; street; especially in metaphor, path of salvation.
marjāra	cat, *marjāra-mārga*, "the cat's way."
markaṭa	monkey, *markaṭa-mārga*, "the monkey's way."
Marut	wind; wind god.
maṭha	monastic establishment.
matsya	fish.
māyā	fiction.
melā	fair, assembly.
mīmāṃsā	inquisition; system; proper name of one *darśana*.
mithyā	futility; false; e.g., *mithyā-jñāna* is false knowledge.
mleccha	"barbarian," somebody who does not belong to Hindu culture.
moha	delusion.
mokṣa	liberation.
mṛtyu	death.
mudrā	(hand) pose.
mukta	one who is liberated; e.g., *jīvan-mukta* is one liberated while still living in the body.
mukti	liberation.
mukti-dātā	giver of liberation, title of Viṣṇu.
mūla	root.
mūla-prakṛti	primary matter.
mulayahan	name of demon, personification of evil, subdued by Śiva.
mumukṣu	one who desires liberation.
muni	literally, one who keeps silence; ascetic; "monk."
mūrti	literally, embodiment; figure; image.
muśala	hammer, attribute of images of deities.
nādī	river, (body) vessel, nerve.
nāga	superior being; snake; naked, heretic.
naimittika karma	non-obligatory ritual for the purpose of obtaining a particular object.
nāma-japa	repetition of name(s) of God.

nāmakīrtaṇa	congregational singing of the name(s) of God.
nāma-rūpa	name and form; individuality.
nāmaskāra	greeting in a spirit of worship.
Nandi	Śiva's vehicle; a bull.
nāraka	hell.
nāsadīya	title of a famous Ṛgvedic hymn beginning with *nāsad* ("there was not").
nāstika	heretic; someone who denies the authority of the Veda.
nāstikya	irreligiosity.
nāṭarāja	"King of Dance," title of Śiva.
nātha	lord. *Viśvanātha*, "Lord of the Universe."
nigama	*Veda*; authoritative scripture.
nigamana	quotation (from *Veda*); in logic: deduction, conclusion.
nīla	dark blue. *Śiva nīlakaṇṭha*: Śiva with a dark-blue throat.
nirguṇa	without qualities or attributes.
Nirukta	classical work of etymology.
niṣkala	without part; undivided, complete.
nitya	eternal.
nivṛtti	withdrawal.
Nṛsiṇha	man-lion; one of the *avatāras* of Viṣṇu.
nyāya	rule, method; motto; logic; syllogism.
pāda	foot; verse, part of a text.
padārtha	category (in Vaiśeṣika system).
padma	lotus.
pañca	five; e.g., *pañcāgni* is five fires.
pañcāṅga	the traditional Indian calendar.
Pāñcarātra	branch of Vaiṣṇavism.
pañcāyātana-pūjā	worship of five gods.
paṇḍit(a)	learned man; honorific title.
pantha	path, way; e.g., *Kabīr-pantha* is the religious sect founded by Kabir.
pāpa	sin.
para	beyond; supreme; liberation.
paramārthika	that which concerns ultimate reality.
paraṃparā	tradition.
Paraśurāma	Rama with the battle-ax; one of the *avatāras* of Viṣṇu.
Pārvatī	daughter of the mountains; name of Śiva's consort.
pāśa	fetter.
paśu	animal; cattle; in Śaivasiddhanta: unliberated person.
paśupati	"lord of the cattle," name of Śiva.
piṇḍa	small ball of rice which is offered to ancestors as oblation.
piśāca	imp; ogre.
pīṭha	place sacred to Śāktas
pitṛ	ancestor, forefather; *pitṛyāna* is the path of the ancestor.
prabhā	splendor.
pradakṣiṇā	respect shown through certain actions.

pradhāna	head; source; in Sāṁkhya system, ground from which everything develops.
prajāpati	Lord of creatures; creator.
prakāśa	splendor.
prakṛti	matter; nature.
pralaya	dissolution of the world.
pramāda	error.
pramāṇa	logical proof; means of cognition.
prāṇa	life breath.
prāṇava	the mantra OM.
prāṇayama	breath-control.
prapanna	one who has surrendered to God.
prapatti	(formal) act of surrender to God.
prārabdha	remainder of karma from former births.
prārthana	prayer.
prasāda	grace, share of food offered to deity.
prasthāna trayī	triad of authorities (*Upaniṣads, Bhagavadgītā, Brahmasūtras*).
pratibiṃba	reflection; mirror-image.
pratijñā	recognition; proposition.
pratisarga	dissolution of the universe.
pratisiddha karma	forbidden action or ritual.
pratyabhijñā	recognition.
pratyahāra	withdrawal of the senses
pratyakṣa	immediate (sense) perception.
pravṛtti	inclination; active liberation.
prāyaścitta	atonement (through certain prescribed acts).
prayatna	effort.
premā	love; used as technical term for spiritual love.
preta	soul of a deceased who has not (yet) received offerings.
prīti	amity; love.
pṛthivi	earth.
pūjā	(image) worship.
punarjanma	rebirth.
punarmṛtyu	redeath.
puṇya	merit.
purāṇa	old; proper name of class of authoritative scriptures.
purohita	class of Vedic priests.
puruṣa	man; person; supreme being; spirit.
puruṣārtha	aim of human life.
puruṣottama	supreme person.
puṣpa	flower.
puṣṭimārga	special form of *bhakti*.
putra	son.
putra-mārga	way of the son; third rank in Śaiva-siddhānta.
rāga	passion; in music, basic tune.

rāgānuga bhakti	"passionate love"; special form of *bhakti*.
rajas	excitement; one of the basic three *guṇas*.
rājayoga	"royal way"; name of Patañjali's *yoga* system.
rajñī	splendor.
rakṣasa	goblin.
Rāma	main hero of the *Rāmāyaṇa*; general name for God.
Rāmārajya	Rāma's rule; "kingdom of God."
Rāmāyaṇa	"Rama's Adventures", a large epic poem, ascribed to Vālmīki. There are many vernacular re-creations of this original work like Tulsīdās' *Rāmcaritmānas*.
rasa	juice; sentiment.
rasa-līlā	theatrical reenactment of scenes from the life of Kṛṣṇa.
rati	pleasure; proper name of consort of god of Love.
ratna	jewel; pearl; often used as honorific title.
ratrī	night.
ṛk	hymn.
ṛṣi	seer; wise man.
ṛta	(Vedic) law of the world (moral and cosmic).
rudra	reddish; name of Vedic god; name of Śiva especially in his frightful aspect.
rudrākṣa	"Rudra's eye"; rough, round seed of an Indian shrub, used in garlands by Śaivites.
Rukminī	Kṛṣṇa's spouse.
śabda	sound; word; scriptural authority.
saccidānanda	the Supreme Being (being, consciousness, bliss).
sadācāra	morality; good behaviour.
ṣaḍdarśana	the six orthodox systems.
sādhana	means (to gain liberation).
sādhaka	one who practices a *sādhana*.
sadhāraṇa dharma	common law; religion common to humankind.
sādhu	"holy man"; mendicant.
sādhvī	a female ascetic.
sāgara	sea; great mass of things.
saguṇa	with qualities.
saguṇa brahman	*brahman* with attributes.
sahajā	natural; in-born.
sahāmārga	the way of the companion; the second rank in Śaiva-siddhānta.
sahasra-nāma	"thousand names," litany with 1000 names and titles of a deity.
śākhā	branch; a school of thought or practice.
sākṣātkāra	bodily vision of the supreme.
sākṣī	witness; the Supreme as present in humans.
śākta	follower of Śakti cult.
śakti	power; name of Śiva's consort.
śālagrāma	ammonite; symbol under which Viṣṇu is present.

sālokya	sharing the same world; one of the stages of liberation.
samādhi	deep concentration; death; memorial.
sāman	Vedic tune.
sāmānya	equality; category in *Vaiśeṣika*.
samāvāya	similarity.
samāveśa	togetherness.
sambhoga	enjoyment.
saṃdhya	twilight; dusk and dawn; prayers recited at dawn.
saṃdhya-bhāṣa	words with double meaning.
saṃhitā	collection; name of class of authoritative scriptures.
sāmīpa	nearness; stage of liberation.
samjñā	understanding.
sāṁkhya	figure, number; proper name of philosophical system.
saṁkīrtaṇa	congregational singing.
saṃnyāsa	renunciation.
saṃnyāsī	ascetic, homeless mendicant.
saṃpradāya	a religious order or sect.
saṃsāra	world; connoting constant cyclic change.
saṃskāra	rites; "sacraments."
samskṛta	artfully composed, refined, name of old Indian high language.
samyama	concentration.
sanātana dharma	eternal law; "Hinduism."
śaṅkha	conch shell.
sanmārga	"the true way"; highest stage in Śaiva-siddhānta.
śānti	peace.
santoṣa	contentment.
śaraṇā-gati	seeking refuge.
sarga	creation; emanation.
sāraṅga	bowstring.
śarīra	body.
sārūpa	of equal form.
śāśtra	doctrine; treatise, authoritative teaching.
śāstrī	one who knows the traditional doctrine; Bachelor of Arts.
sat	being, truth.
satī	"faithful," wife who (voluntarily) dies with deceased husband.
satsàng(a)	"gathering of the righteous," religious meeting.
sattva	being; nature; virtue; one of the three *guṇas*.
satya	truth; reality.
śauca	purity.
saulabhya	benevolence.
sauśilya	kindness.
savitṛ	sun God.
sāyujya	togetherness.
śeṣa	"endless," world-serpent upon which Viṣṇu rests.
seva	service.

siddha	accomplished; saint.
siddhi	accomplishment; in *yoga*, extraordinary faculties.
śikhā	tuft on the crown of the head.
śikhara	spire-like elevation over central sanctuary.
śīkṣā	instruction.
śīlā	good behavior; morality.
Sītā	furrow; proper name of Rāma's consort.
Śiva	"propitious," proper name of major Hindu deity.
śloka	double verse.
smasāna	cremation ground.
smṛti	what has been committed to memory; proper name for a certain class of scriptures.
soma	intoxicating drink used in vedic sacrifices.
spaṇḍa-śāstra	treatise of vibrations, branch of Kāśmīr Śaivism.
sphoṭa	boil; idea; connection between letter and meaning.
śraddhā	faith.
śrāddha	last rites.
śrautasūtras	ritual texts dealing with public Vedic sacrifices.
śravaṇa	listening to the recitation of religious texts.
Śrī	fortune; proper name of Viṣṇu's consort; Sir.
śrīvatsa	mark on Viṣṇu's body signifying Lakṣmī's presence.
śṛṅgāra	feeling of erotic love.
sṛṣṭi	creation; emanation.
śruti	what has been revealed and heard, "scripture."
Sthala Purāṇa	collection of legends about a holy place
sthūla	gross, material.
stithi	maintenance (of the world).
stotra	hymn in praise of God.
śubha	auspicious.
śuddha	pure.
śuddhi	ritual of purification (for readmission into caste).
sūkṣma	subtle.
sūkta	Vedic hymn.
śūnya	zero; nothing; emptiness.
sura	divine being.
surā	intoxicating drink.
sūrya	sun.
sūta	bard; charioteer.
sūtra	aphoristic textbook; thread.
svadharma	one's own duties.
svādhyāya	study of Vedic texts.
svahā	invocation at offering to *devas*.
svāmī	Lord; today usually "Reverend."
svarga	heaven.
svayambhu	being of itself; name for Supreme Being.
Śyāma	black; name of Kṛṣṇa.

tamas	darkness; dullness; one of the three *guṇas*.
tantra	loom; system of practices; main branch of Hinduism.
tapas	heat; energy.
tapasvī	ascetic; one who has accumulated much merit through self-mortification.
tarka	logics; debate.
tattva	principle; nature; reality; element.
tejas	splendor; light; heat.
ṭīkā	subcommentary.
tilaka	mark on forehead.
tirobhāva	disappearance.
ṭippaṇī	gloss.
tīrtha	fording place; place of pilgrimage (on holy river).
tīrthayātra	pilgrimage.
tiru (Tamil)	holy; e.g., *tiru-kural* is the Tamilveda.
tithi	moon day.
traividyā	knowledge of the three *Vedas*.
tretāyuga	third world age.
trilocana	three-eyed; name of Śiva.
triloka	the three worlds.
trimārga	literally, "three ways"; the collective name for the paths of works, devotion, knowledge.
tripuṇḍra	Śiva's trident; sign of the forehead.
tristhalī	the three most important places of pilgrimage, viz. Prāyāga (Allahabad), Kāśī (Benares), and Gāyā.
trivarga	the triad of *dharma*, *artha*, *kāma*.
tulasī	a small tree (holy basil), sacred to Viṣṇu.
turīya	the fourth; designation of highest stage of consciousness.
turyātīta	beyond the fourth; highest stage in some Hindu schools who claim to transcend the Vedāntic *turīya*.
tyāgi	renouncer; ascetic.
udāhāraṇa	example, illustration; part of Nyāya syllogism.
udbhava	appearance.
udaṃbara	Indian fig-tree, sacred to Śiva.
udyama	exertion; rising or lifting up.
upadeśa	advice; religious instruction.
upādhi	attribute; title; deceit.
Upa-Gītā	"lesser Gītā."
upamāna	analogy.
upamśū	prayer uttered in a whisper.
upanayana	initiation; investiture with sacred thread.
upāṅga	auxiliary sciences or texts to Vedāṅgas.
upaniṣad	class of authoritative scriptures; secret doctrine.
Upa-purāṇa	lesser *Purāṇa*.
upāsana	worship.
upavāsa	(religious) fasting.

vācya śakti	power of speech.
vāhana	conveyance.
vaicitriya	manifoldness; distraction.
vaidhi-bhakti	devotion expressing itself through ritual worship.
vaidika dharma	"Vedic religion," self-designation of Hinduism.
Vaikuṇṭha	Viṣṇu's heaven.
vairāgi(nī)	ascetic (fem.).
vairāgya	renunciation.
vaiśeṣika	name of a philosophical system.
vaiśya	member of third caste; businessman, artisan.
vajra	diamond; thunderbolt.
vāk	voice; word.
vālmīka	an ant's hill.
vāmācāra	left-handed way (in Tantra).
vāmana	dwarf; one of the *avatāras* of Viṣṇu.
vaṃśa	genealogy.
vānaprastha	forest dweller; third stage in a Brahmin's life.
varāha	boar; one of the *avatāras* of Viṣṇu.
varṇāśramadharma	social system of Hinduism based on a partition into four classes and four stages of life.
vātsalya	love toward a child, one of the stages of *bhakti*.
vāyu	wind; wind god.
veda	knowledge; sacred knowledge: revelation; scripture.
vedāṅga	limb of *Veda*; auxiliary sciences.
vedānta	end of *Veda*; *Upaniṣads*; name of a system.
vedī	altar for vedic sacrifices.
vibhava	emanation.
vibhūti	supernatural power.
videha	without a body.
vidhi	ritual.
vidyā	knowledge.
vijñānamaya	made of knowledge.
vinaya	discipline.
vipra	Brahmin.
vīra	hero.
virajā	purity; name of river separating the world of mortals from Viṣṇu's heaven.
virāṭ	first product of Brahman; universe.
vīrya	heroism.
viṣāda	despair.
víseṣa	propriety.
viśiṣṭa	qualification.
viśva-rūpa	all form; Kṛṣṇa appearing as cosmic person.
vitarka	debate; logical argument.
viveka	descrimination.
vrata	vow; celebration.

vratya	mendicant; class of people; Supreme Being.
vṛddhi	growth.
vṛtti	being; condition; fluctuation; activity, means of subsistence.
vyākaraṇa	grammar.
vyakta	manifest; revealed.
vyāpāra	function.
Vyāsa	arranger; proper name of Vedic sage credited with the compilation of the *Vedas*, the *Mahābhārata* and the *Purāṇas*.
vyavahāra	livelihood; the world of senses.
vyūha	part; special manifestation of Viṣṇu.
yajña	Vedic sacrifice.
yajñopavita	sacred thread.
yajus	rites.
yakṣa	goblin; tree-spirit.
yama	god of the netherworld; restraint (yoga).
yantra	machine; meditational device.
yati	wandering ascetic.
yatidharma	rules for ascetics.
yātrā	pilgrimage.
yoga	yoke; name of a system.
yojana	"mile" (either four, five, or nine miles).
yoni	source; womb.
yuga	world era.

ABBREVIATIONS USED IN NOTES AND BIBLIOGRAPHY

ABORI	*Annals of the Bhandarkar Oriental Institute* (Poona)
CHI	*The Cultural Heritage of India* (H. Bhattacharyya, general ed.)
HASA	*Historical Atlas of South Asia* (J. Schwarzberg, ed., 2nd ed.)
HCIP	*The History and Culture of the Indian People* (R. C. Majumdar, general ed.)
HDhS	*History of Dharmaśāstra* (P. V. Kane)
HIL	*A History of Indian Literature* (Jan Gonda, ed.)
HIPh	*History of Indian Philosophy* (S. N. Dasgupta)
HOS	Harvard Oriental Series
HR	*History of Religion* (Chicago)
IFR	*Indian and Foreign Review*
JAAR	*Journal of the American Academy of Religion*
JAOS	*Journal of the American Oriental Society* (New Haven)
JAS	*Journal of the Asian Society* (Ann Arbor)
JBRS	*Journal of the Bihar Research Society* (Patna)
JIPH	*Journal of Indian Philosophy*
JOIB	*Journal of the Oriental Institute* (Baroda)
JRAS	*Journal of the Royal Asiatic Society*
JVS	*Journal of Vaiṣṇava Studies*
KSBCCV	*Kuppuswami Sastri Birth Centenary Commemoration Volume* (Madras: Kuppuswami Research Institute)
RS	*Religion and Society* (Bangalore/Delhi)
SBE	*Sacred Books of the East* (Clarendon Press, Oxford)
SBH	*Sacred Books of the Hindus* (Allahabad: Panini Office)
WZKSA	*Wiener Zeitschrift für die Kunde Südasiens*
ZMDG	*Zeitschrift der Deutschen Morgenländischen Gesellschaft*
ZRGG	*Zeitschrift für Religions- und Geistesgeschichte*

SELECT BIBLIOGRAPHY

Abbot, J. E. ed. and trans. *The Poet Saints of Mahārāṣṭra*, 12 vols. Poona: Scottish Mission Industries, 1926–41.

Agni Purāṇa, M. N. Dutt (trans.) 2 vols. Reprint Varanasi: Chowkhambha, 1967.

Agrawal, D. P. "The Technology of the Indus Civilization." In *Indian Archeology, New Perspectives*, R. K. Sharma, ed. Delhi: Agam Kala Prakashan, 1982, 83–91.

Agrawala, V. S. *India as known to Pāṇini*, Varanasi: Prithvi Prakasan, 1963 (2nd edn).

—— *Matsya-Purāṇa: A Study*. Varanasi: All-India Kashiraj Trust, 1963.

—— "Mother Earth." In *Nehru Abhinandan Granth*. Calcutta: Nehru Abhinandan Granth Committee, 1949, 490ff.

Aiyer, V. G. Ramakrishna. *The Economy of a South Indian Temple*. Annamalai: Annamalai University, 1946.

Ali, S. M. *The Geography of the Purāṇas*. New Delhi: People's Publishing House, 1966.

Allchin, B. and R. Allchin. *The Rise of Civilization in India and Pakistan*. Cambridge: Cambridge University Press, 1982.

Altekar, A. D. "Hinduism, A Static Structure or a Dynamic Force?" In *Nehru Abhinandan Granth*. Calcutta, 1949, 421–425.

—— *The Position of Women in Hindu Civilization from Prehistoric Times to the Present Day*. Benares: Motilal Banarsidass, 1956.

—— *State and Government in Ancient India*, Delhi: Motilal Banarsidass, 1962 (4th edn).

Sri Anandamurti. *Ānandamārga*. Anandanagar: private publication, 1967 (2nd edn).

Anderson, L. M. *Vasantotsava: The Spring Festivals of India*. D. K. New Delhi; Printworld, 1993.

Anderson, W. K. and S. D. Dhamle. *The Brotherhood in Saffron: The Rāstrīya Swayamesevak Sangh and Hindu Revivalism*. Boulder, CO: Westview Press, 1987.

Aṇuvakhyāna of Madhva. S. S. Rao, Trans. Bombay: Nirnaya Sagara Press. Ṭirupati, 1936 (2nd edn).

Athalye, D. *Life of Lokmanya Tilak*. Poona: A. Chiploonkar, 1921.

Atharvaveda, W. D. Whitney, trans., 2 vols. *HOS*, 1902; reprint Varanasi: Chowkhamba, 1962.

Ātmabodha of Śaṅkarācārya, Swami Nikhilananda, trans. Mylapore: Ramakrishna Math, 1962 (2nd edn).

Auboyer, J. *Daily Life in Ancient India from Approximately 200 B.C. to A.D. 700*. New York: Macmillan, 1965.

Ayyar, C. V. Narayana. *Origin and Early History of Śaivism in South India*. Madras: University of Madras, 1936.

Baird, Robert D., ed. *Religion in Modern India*. Delhi: Manohar, 1981.

The Vedānta-sūtras of Bādarāyaṇa with the Commentary of Baladeva. B. D. Basu, trans. *Sacred Books of the Hindus*, vol. 5. Allahabad: Panini Office, 1934.

Balasubramanian, R. *Advaita Vedānta*. Madras: University of Madras, 1976.

—— *The Mysticism of Poygai Āḷvār*. Madras: Vedanta Publications, 1976.

Balasundaram, T. S. *The Golden Anthology of Ancient Tamil Literature*, 3 vols. Madras: South India Saiva Siddhanta Book Publishing Society, 1959–60.

Banerjea, A. K. *Philosophy of Gorakhnāth*. Gorakhpur: Mahant Dig Vijai Nath Trust, Gorakhnath Temple, 1962.

Banerjea, J. N. *The Development of Hindu Iconography*. Calcutta: University of Calcutta, 1956 (2nd edn).

Banerjea, S. C. *Dharma Sūtras: A Study of Their Origin and Development*. Calcutta: Punthi Pustak, 1962.

Banerjee, G. N. *Hellenism in Ancient India*. Delhi: Munshi Ram Manoharlal, 1961.

Barua, B. M. *History of Pre-Buddhistic Indian Philosophy*. Calcutta: Calcutta University, 1921.

Barz, R. *The Bhakti Sect of Vallabhācārya*. Faridabad: Thompson Press, 1976.

Basham, A. L. *The Wonder that Was India*. New York: Grove Press, 1959.

Beal, S. *Si-Yu-Ki: Buddhist Records of the Western World*. London: 1884; reprint Delhi: Oriental Books Reprint Corporation, 1969.

Beane, W. C. *Myth, Cult and Symbols in Śākta Hinduism: A Study of the Indian Mother Goddess*. Leiden: Brill, 1977.

Belvalkar, S. K. and R. D. Ranade. *History of Indian Philosophy. Volume II. The Creative Period. Volume III: Mysticism in Maharastra*. Poona: Bilvakunja, 1927 and 1932.

Bengali Religious Lyrics: Śākta, E. J. Thompson and A. M. Spencer, trans. Calcutta: Association Press, 1923.

Bhagavadgītā, F. Edgerton, trans. Cambridge, MA: Harvard University Press, 1944.

Bhāgavata Purāṇa, 2 vols. text and transl. Gorakhpur: Gita-Press, 1952–60.

Bhaktirasāmṛtasindhu of Rūpa Goswāmi, Swami Bon Maharaj, trans., 3 vols. Vrindaban: Institute of Oriental Philosophy, 1964–78.

The Bhāmatī of Vācaspati on Śaṅkara's Brahmasūtrabhāṣya, S. S. Suryanarayana Sastri and C. Kunhan Raja, eds. and trans. Adyar: Theosophical Publishing House, 1933.

Bhandarkar, R. G. *Vaiṣṇavism, Śaivism and Minor Religious Systems*. Reprint Varanasi: Indological Book House, 1965.

Bharadwaj, Krishna Datta. *The Philosophy of Rāmānuja*. New Delhi: Sir Sankar Lall Charitable Trust Society, 1958.

Bharati, Agehananda (L. Fischer). *The Ochre Robe*. Seattle: University of Washington Press, 1962.

—— *The Tantric Tradition*. London: Rider and Company, 1965.

Bhardwaj, Surinder Mohan. *Hindu Places of Pilgrimage in India: A Study in Cultural Geography*. Berkeley: University of California Press, 1973.

Bhatt, G. H. "The School of Vallabha." In *CHI*, vol. 3, p. 348.

Bhattacharya, H., general ed. *The Cultural Heritage of India*, 4 vols. Calcutta: Ramakrishna Mission Institute of Culture, 1957–62 (2nd edn).

Bhattacharya, H. D. "Tantrik Religion." *HCIP*, vol. 4.

Bhattacharya, T. *The Cult of Brahma*. Patna: C. Bhatacarya, 1957.

Bhattacharyya, N. N. *History of the Tantric Religion*. Delhi: Manohar, 1982.

Bihari, Bankey. *Minstrels of God*, 2 vols. Bombay: Bharatiya Vidya Bhavan, 1956.

—— *Bhaktā Mīrā*. Bombay: Bharatiya Vidya Bhavan, 1961.

—— *Sufis, Mystics and Yogis of India*. Bombay: Bharatiya Vidya Bhavan, 1962.

Bishop, Donald H., ed. *Thinkers of the Indian Renaissance*. New York: Wiley Eastern, 1982.

Bloomfield, M. *The Religion of the Veda*. New York: G.B. Putnam's, 1908.

Bose, D. N. *Tantras: Their Philosophy and Occult Secrets*. Calcutta: Oriental Publishing Co., 1956 (3rd edn).

Bose, N. K. and D. Sen. "The Stone Age in India." In *CHI*, vol. 1, (1958, 2nd edn), 93–109.

Boyd, R. *An Introduction to Indian Christian Theology*. Madras: Christian Literature Society, 1977 (2nd edn).

Bṛhaddevatā, A. A. Macdonell, ed. and trans. Reprint Delhi: Motilal Banarsidass, 1965.

Briggs, G. W. *The Chamars*. Calcutta: Association Press, 1920.

—— *Gorakhanātha and Kanphata Yogis*. Calcutta: Association Press, 1938.

Brown, C. M. *God as Mother: A Feminine Theology in India: An Historical and Theological Study of the Brahmavaivarta Purāṇa*. Hartford, VT: Claude Stark, 1974.

Brown, L. W. *The Indian Christians of St. Thomas*. London: Cambridge University Press, 1956.

Brunton, P. *Maharsi and His Message*. London: Rider & Co., 1952.

Bühler, G. *The Sacred Laws of the Āryas*. In *SBE*, vols. 2 and 14. Reprint Delhi: Motilal Banarsidass, 1964.

van Buitenen, J. A. B. *Rāmānuja on the Bhagavadgītā*. Delhi: Motilal Banarsidass, 1965.

Śrī Caitanyacaritāmṛtam, S. K. Chaudhuri, trans., 3 vols. Calcutta: Gauḍīya-Math, 1959 (2nd edn).

Candidasa, Baru. *Singing the Glory of Lord Krishna*. M. H. Klaiman, trans. Chico: Scholars Press, 1984.

Carman, J. B., *The Theology of Rāmānuja. An Essay in Inter-religious Understanding*. New Haven and London: Yale University Press, 1974.
Carpenter, J. E. *Theism in Mediaeval India*. London: Constable & Co., 1921.
Cenkner, W. *A Tradition of Teachers: Śaṅkara and the Jagadgurus Today*. Delhi: Motilal Banarsidass, 1983.
Chakladar, H. C. *Social Life in Ancient India*. Calcutta: Greater India Society, 1954 (2nd edn).
Chakravarti, C. *Tantras: Studies on Their Religion and Literature*. Calcutta: Punthi Pustak, 1963.
Chakravarti, S. C. *The Philosophy of the Upaniṣads*. Calcutta: University of Calcutta, 1935.
Chand, T. *Influence of Islam on Indian Culture*. Allahabad: The Indian Press, 1963.
Chatterji, S. K. "Race Movements and Prehistoric Culture." In *HCIP*, vol. 1, 164ff.
Chattopadhyaya, S. *Reflections on the Tantras*. Delhi: Motilal Banarsidass, 1978.
—— *Some Early Dynasties of South India*. Delhi: Motilal Banarsidass, 1974.
Chattopadyaya, S. *The evolution of Theistic Sects in Ancient India*. Calcutta: Progressive Publishers, 1963.
Chaudhuri, N. C. *Autobiography of an Unknown Indian*. London: Macmillan, 1951.
—— *The Continent of Circe*. Bombay: Jaico, 1966.
Chaudhuri, Roma. "The Nimbārka School of Vedānta." In *CHI*, vol. 3, 333ff.
—— *Doctrine of Śrīkaṇṭha*, 2 vols. Calcutta: Pracyavani, 1959–60.
Choudhuri, D. C. Roy. *Temples and Legends of Bihar*. Bombay: Bharatiya Vidya Bhavan, 1965.
Cidananda, Swami. *Light Fountain*. Rishikesh: Divine Light Society, 1967.
Clothey, F. W. *The Many Faces of Murukan: The History and Meaning of a South Indian God*. Religion and Society, No. 6. The Hague: Mouton, 1978.
—— "Tamil Religion." In *Encyclopedia of Religions*, M. Eliade ed. Vol. 12, 260ff.
—— "Pilgrimage Centers in the Tamil Cultus of Murukan." *JAAR*, 40 (1972): 79–95.
Clothey, F. M. and J. B. Lond (eds.). *Experiencing Śiva*. Columbia, MO: South Asian Books, 1983.
Coburn, T. B. *Devī Māhātmya: The Crystallization of the Goddess Tradition*. Delhi: Motilal Banarsidass, 1984.
Coomaraswamy, Ananda. *The Dance of Śiva*. Bombay: Asia Publishing House, 1956 (3rd edn).
Courtright, Paul B. *Gaṇeśa: Lord of Obstacles, Lord of Beginnings*. New York: Oxford University Press, 1985.
Coward, Harold G. *Bhartṛhari*. Boston: Twayne Publishers, 1976.
—— *Jung and Eastern Thought*. Albany: State University of New York Press, 1985.
—— (ed.) *Studies in Indian Thought: Collected Papers of Prof. T. R. V. Murti*. Delhi: Motilal Banarsidass, 1983.

Crawford, S. Cromwell. *Ram Mohan Roy: Social, Political and Religious Reform in 19th century India*. New York: Paragon House, 1987.
Cutler, N. *Songs of Experience: The Poetics of Tamil Devotion*, Bloomington: Indiana University Press, 1987.
Dandekar, R. N. *Some Aspects of the History of Hinduism*. Poona: University of Bangalore, 1967.
Das, Bhagwan. *Kṛṣṇa: A Study in the Theory of Avatāras*. Bombay: Bharatiya Vidya Bhavan, 1962.
Dasgupta, G. *Mother As Revealed to Me*. Benares, 1954.
Dasgupta, S. H. *Obscure Religious Cults*. Calcutta: Firma K. L. Mukhopadhyay, 1962 (2nd edn).
—— *History of Indian Philosophy*, 5 vols. Cambridge: Cambridge University Press, 1961–62 (3rd edn).
Dave, J. H. *Immortal India*, 4 parts. Bombay: Bharatiya Vidya Bhavan, 1959–62 (2nd edn).
De, S. K. *Early History of the Vaiṣṇava Faith and Movement in Bengal*. Calcutta: Firma K.L. Mukhopadhyay, 1961 (2nd edn).
Deheja, V. *Āṇṭāl and Her Path of Love*. Albany: State University of New York Press, 1990.
Deming, W. S. *Rāmdās and Rāmdāsis*, The Religious Life of India Series. Oxford: Oxford University Press, 1928.
Derret, J. D. M. *History of Indian Law* (*Dharmaśāstra*). Leiden: Brill, 1973.
Devasenapathy, V. A. *Śaiva Siddhānta as Expounded in the Śivajñāna Siddhiyar and Its Six Commentaries*. Madras: University of Madras, 1960.
Devī-Bhāgavata Purāṇa (Varanasi: Swami Vijnananda 1962), Pandit Pustakalaya, trans., 2 vols. In *SBH*. Allahabad: Panini Office, 1923.
Diehl, C. G. *Instrument and Purpose: Studies on Rites and Rituals in South India*. Lund, 1956.
Diksitar, V. R. *Studies in Tamil Literature and History*. London: Luzac, 1930.
Dimmit, C., and J. A. B. van Buitenen, eds. and trans. *Classical Hindu Mythology: A Reader in the Sanskrit Puranas*. Philadelphia: Temple University Press, 1978.
Drekmeier, C. *Kingship and Community in Early India*. Stanford: Stanford University Press, 1962.
Eban, Martin, ed. *Maharishi the Guru. The Story of Maharishi Mahesh Yogi*. Bombay: Pear Publications, 1968.
Eck, Diana L. *Banaras: City of Light*. Princeton: Princeton University Press, 1983.
Edwardes, S. M., and H. O. O. Garrett. *Mughal Rule in India*. Reprint Delhi: S. Chand, 1962.
Elliot, H. M., and J. Dowson. *The History of India as Told by Its Own Historians: The Mohammedan Period*, 8 vols. Reprint Delhi, 1964.
Elkman, S. M. *Jīva Goswāmi's Tattvasandarbha*. Delhi: Motilal Banarsidass, 1986.
Entwistle, A. W. *Braj. Centre of Krishna Pilgrimage*. Groningen: E. Forsten, 1987.

Farqhar, J. N. *Modern Religious Movements in India*. Oxford: Oxford University Press, 1914; reprint Varanasi, 1967.

—— *An Outline of the Religious Literature of India*. Reprint Varanasi: Motilal Banarsidass, 1967.

Feuerstein, G. *The Philosophy of Classical Yoga*. Manchester: University of Manchester Press, 1982.

—— *The Yoga Tradition. Its History, Literature, Philosophy and Practice*, Prescott, Arizona; Hohm Press, 1998.

——, with S. Kak and D. Frawley. *In Search of the Cradle of Civilization*. Quest Books: Wheaton Il., 1995.

Fischer, L. *The Life of Mahatma Gandhi*. Reprint Bombay: Bharatiya Vidya Bhavan, 1959.

Frauwallner, E. *History of Indian Philosophy*, V. M. Bedekar, trans., 2 vols. Delhi: Motilal Banarsidass, 1983–84.

Frawley, David. *Gods, Sages and Kings: Vedic Secrets of Ancient Civilization*. Salt Lake City: Passage Press, 1991.

—— *The Myth of the Āryan Invasion of India*, New Delhi: Voice of India, 1994.

French, H. W., and A. Sharma. *Religious Ferment in Modern India*. New York: St. Martin's Press, 1981.

Fuller, C. J. *Servants of the Goddess: The Priests of a South Indian Temple*. Cambridge: Cambridge University Press, 1984.

—— *The Camphor Flame: Popular Hinduism and Society in India*. Princeton: Princeton University Press, 1992.

Gaur, R. C. *Excavations in Atranjikhera. Early Civilization of the Upper Ganga Basin*. Delhi: Archeological Survey of India, 1983.

Gayal, S. R. *A History of the Imperial Guptas*. Allahabad: Kitab Mahal, 1967.

Gazetteer of India. Reprint, 4 vols. Delhi: Ministry for Information and Broadcasting, 1965.

Gelberg, S. J., ed. *Hare Krishna, Hare Krishna: Five Distinguished Scholars on the Krishna Movement in the West*. New York: Grove Press, 1983.

Geldner, H. F. *Der Ṛgveda*, 3 vols. Cambridge, MA.: Harvard University Press, 1955–57 (English translation in progress).

Getty, A. *Gaṇeśa*. Oxford: Oxford University Press, 1936.

Gheraṇḍasaṃhitā, S. C. Vasu, trans. Allahabad: Panini Office, 1914.

Ghose, Aurobindo. *Sri Aurobindo*. Birth Centenary Library, 30 vols. Pondicherry: Sri Aurobindo Ashram, 1972–75.

Ghosh, B. K. "The Āryan Problem." In *HCIP*, vol. 1, 205–21.

—— "The Origin of the Indo-Āryans." In *CHI*, vol. 1, 129–43.

Ghoshal, U. N. *A History of Indian Political Ideas: The Ancient Period and the Period of Transition to the Middle Ages*. Oxford: Oxford University Press, 1959 (3rd edn).

Ghurye, G. S. *Indian Sādhus*. Bombay: Popular Prakashan, 1964 (2nd edn).

Gibb, H. A. R., ed. *Ibn Battuta: Travels in Asia and Africa*. London: Routledge & Kegan Paul, 1957 (2nd edn).

Gode, P. K. "The Aśvamedha performed by Sevai Jayasingh of Amber 1699–1744 A.D." In *Studies in Indian Literary History*. Bombay: Bharatiya Vidya Bhavan, 1954: 292–306.

Godman, D. (ed.). *Be as you are: The Teachings of Ramana Maharsi*. Boston: Arkana, 1985.
Gold, D. *The Lord as Guru: Hindī Saints in the Northern Indian Tradition*. New York: Oxford University Press, 1987.
Golwalkar, M. S. *Bunch of Thoughts*. Bangalore: 1966 (2nd edn).
Gonda, J. *Aspects of Early Viṣṇuism*. Utrecht: 1954. Reprint Delhi: Motilal Banarsidass, 1965.
—— *Vedic Literature (Saṃhitās and Brāhmaṇas)*. (*A History of Indian Literature*, vol. 1. fasc. 1). Wiesbaden: Harrassowitz, 1975.
Gopal, R. *British Rule in India: An Assessment*. New York: Asia Publ. House, 1963.
Gopal, S. *Radhakrishnan. A Biography*. Oxford University Press: Delhi, 1989.
Gordon, D. H. *The Prehistoric Background of Indian Culture*. Bombay: N. M. Tripathi, 1960.
Goudriaan, T. and Sanjukta Gupta. *Hindu Tantric and Śākta Literature*. (*A History of Indian Literature*, vol. II, fasc. 2. ed. Jan Gonda). Wiesbaden: Otto Harrassowitz, 1981.
Griffith, R. T. H. *The Texts of the White Yajurveda*. Reprint Benares: Chowkhamba, 1957 (3rd edn).
—— trans. *Hymns of the Ṛgveda*, 2 vols. Reprint Benares: 1963 (4th edn).
—— trans. *Hymns of the Yajurveda*. Reprint Benares: 1957.
Gṛhyasūtras, H. Oldenberg and F. M. Müller, trans. In *SBE*, vols. 29 and 30.
Griswold, H. D. *Religion of the Rigveda*. Delhi: Motilal Banarsidass, n.d.
Growse, F. S. *Mathurā: A District Memoir*. Reprint New Delhi: Asian Education Services, 1979.
Günther, H. V. *Yuganadha: The Tantric View of Life*. Benares: 1952; reprint Boulder, CO: Shambhala, 1976.
Gupta, S., D. J. Hoens, and T. Goudriaan. *Hindu Tantrism. Handbuch der Orientalistik*. B. Spuler, general ed. Leiden: Brill, 1979.
Haberman, D. L. *Journey Through the Twelve Forests. An Encounter with Krishna*. Oxford University Press: New York and London, 1994.
Halbfass, W. *India and Europe: An Essay in Understanding*. Albany: State University of New York Press, 1988.
—— *On Being and What There Is – Classical Vaiśeṣika and the History of Indian Ontology*. Albany: State University of New York Press, 1992.
Hardgrave, R. L. *The Dravidian Movement*. Bombay: Popular Prakashan, 1965.
Hardy, E. T. *Viraha Bhakti*. Delhi: Oxford University Press, 1983.
—— *The Religious Culture of India: Power, Love and Wisdom*. Cambridge: Cambridge University Press, 1994.
Harle, J. C. *The Art and Architecture of the Indian Subcontinent* Harmondsworth: Penguin, 1987.
Harper, M. H. *Gurus, Swamis, and Avataras: Spiritual Masters and Their American Disciples*. Philadelphia: Westminster Press, 1972.
Havell, E. B. *Benares, The Sacred City: Sketches of Hindu Life and Religion*. London: W. Thacker & Co., 1905.
Hawley, J.S. *Kṛṣṇa, the Butter Thief*. Princeton: Princeton University Press, 1983.

—— *At Play with Krishna: Prilgrimage Dramas from Brindavan*. Princeton: Princeton University Press, 1981.

—— *Sūrdās: Poet, Singer, Saint*. Seattle: University of Washington Press, 1985.

Hawley, J. S., and D. M. Wulff, eds. *The Divine Consort: Rādhā and the Goddesses of India*. Berkeley: University of California Press, 1982.

—— (eds.) *Devī: Goddesses of India*. University of California Press, Berkeley, 1996.

Hazra, R. C. "The Purāṇas." In *CHI*, vol. 2, 240ff.

—— *Studies in the Purāṇic Records of Hindu Rites and Customs*. Dacca: University of Dacca, 1940; reprint Delhi: 1968.

—— *Studies in the Upapurāṇas*, 2 vols. Calcutta: Sanskrit College, 1958–63.

Hedayetullah, M. *Kabir: The Apostle of Hindu–Muslim Unity*. Delhi: Motilal Banarsidass, 1978.

Heimsath, C. H. *Indian Nationalism and Hindu Social Reform*. Princeton: Princeton University Press, 1968.

Hein, N. *The Miracle Plays of Mathurā*. New Haven: Yale University Press, 1972.

Hertel, B. R and C. A. Humes (eds.). *Living Banāras: Hindu Religion in Cultural Context*, Albany: State University of New York Press, 1993.

Hooper, J. S. M. *Hymns of the Āḷvārs*. Calcutta: Association Press, 1929.

Hopkins, E. W. *The Great Epic of India*. New York: 1902; reprint Calcutta: Punthi Pustak, 1969.

Hopkins, T. J. *The Hindu Religious Tradition*. Belmont: Dickenson, 1971.

Hume, R., trans. *Principal Upaniṣads*. Oxford: Oxford University Press, 1921.

Hunashal, S. M. *The Vīraśaiva Social Philosophy*. Raichur: Amaravani Printing Press, 1957.

Inden, R. "Orientalist Constructions of India." In *Modern Asian Studies*, 20, no. 3 (1986): 401–446.

Indradeva, S. "Cultural Interaction Between Ancient India and Iran." *Diogenes* 111 (1980): 83–109.

Ions, V. *Indian Mythology*. London: Paul Hamlyn, 1967.

Isaacs, H. R. *India's Ex-Untouchables*. New York: John Day, 1965.

Israel, B. J. *The Bene Israel of India, Some Studies*. Bombay: Orient Longman, 1984.

Iyengar, N., ed. and trans. *Mumukṣupadi of Lokācārya*. Madras: 1962.

Jaimini's Mīmāṃsāsūtra with Śābara's Commentary and Notes, Ganganatha Jha, trans., 3 vols., Gaekwad Oriental Series, Baroda: 1933–36; reprint Oriental Institute, 1973–74.

Janaki, S. S. *Śiva Temple and Temple Rituals*. Madras: Kuppuswami Sastri Research Institute, 1988.

—— (ed.) *Mm. Professor Kuppuswami Sastri Birth Centenary Commemoration Volume*, 2 vols. Madras: Kuppuswami Sastri Research Institute, 1981 and 1985.

Jarrige, J. F. "Die frühesten Kulturen in Pakistan und ihre Entwicklung." In Ph. von Zabern (ed.), *Vergessene Städte am Indus: Frühe Kulturen in Pakistan vom 8. bis zum 2. Jahrtausend*. Mainz: Verlag Ph. von Zabern, 1987.

Jayakar, P. J. *Krishnamurthi: a Biography*. Delhi: Penguin India, 1987.
Jesudason, C. S. H. *A History of Tamil Literature*, Heritage of India Series. Calcutta: YMCA Publishing House, 1961.
Jha, Ganganatha. *Pūrva Mīmāṃsā in Its Sources*. Benares: Benares Hindu University, 1942: reprint Delhi, 1981.
Jhangiani, M. A. *Jana Sangh and Swatantra: A Profile of the Rightist Parties in India*. Bombay: Manaktalas, 1969.
Jindal, K. B. *A History of Hindī Literature*. Allahabad: Kitab Mahal, 1955.
Kak, Subhash C. "On the Chronology of Ancient India." In *Indian Journal of History of Science* 22/3 (1987): 222–234.
—— "The Indus Tradition and the Indo-Aryans." In *The Mankind Quarterly* 32 (1992), no. 3: 195–213.
—— *The Astronomical Code of the Rigveda*. New Delhi: Aditya Prakashan, 1994.
Kakati, B. K. *The Mother Goddess Kāmākhyā*. Gauhati: Lawyers' Book Stall, 1948.
Kane, P. V. *History of Dharmaśāstra*, 5 vols. (7 parts). Poona: Bhandarkar Oriental Research Institute, 1930–62.
Karmarkar, A. P. "Religion and Philosophy of the Epics." In *CHI*, vol. 2, 80ff.
—— *The Religions of India*. Lonavla: Mira Publ. House, 1950.
Kauṭilīya's Arthaśāstra, R. P. Kangle, ed. and trans., 3 parts. Bombay: University of Bombay, 1960–61.
Keay, F. E. *Hindī Literature*. Calcutta: YMCA Publishing House, 1960 (3rd edn).
Keith, A. B. *The Age of the Ṛgveda*. Cambridge, MA: Harvard University Press, 1922.
—— *A History of Sanskrit Literature*. London: Oxford University Press, 1920.
—— *Indian Logic and Atomism*. Oxford: Clarendon Press, 1921.
—— *The Karma Mīmāṃsā*. Calcutta: Association Press, 1921.
—— *The Religion and Philosophy of the Veda and Upaniṣads*. Cambridge, MA: Harvard University Press, 1925.
—— *The Sāṁkhya System*, Heritage of India Series. Calcutta: YMCA Publishing House, 1949 (3rd edn).
Kennedy, M. T. *The Chaitanya Movement*. Calcutta: Association Press, 1925.
Kenoyer, J. M. *Ancient Cities of the Indus Valley Civilization*. (American Institute of Pakistan Studies). Karachi: Oxford University Press, 1998.
Keyserling, Count Hermann A. *Indian Travel Diary of a Philosopher*, transl. J. Holroyd-Reece. Mumbai and New Delhi: Bharatiya Vidya Bhavan, 1999 (2nd edn).
Kingsbury, F., and G. E. Philips, trans. *Hymns of the Tamil Śaivite Saints*. Calcutta: Association Press, 1921.
Kinsley, D. *Hindu Goddesses*. Berkeley: University of California Press, 1986.
—— *Hinduism: A Cultural Perspective*. Englewood Cliffs: Prentice-Hall, 1982.
—— *The Sword and the Flute: Kālī and Kṛṣṇa, Dark Visions of the Terrible and the Sublime in Hindu Mythology*. Berkeley: University of California Press, 1975.
Klostermaier, K. K. *A Survey of Hinduism*. Albany: State University of New York Press, 1994 (2nd edn).

—— *Hinduism: A Short Introduction*. Oxford: Oneworld, 1998.
—— *A Concise Encyclopedia of Hinduism*. Oxford: Oneworld, 1998.
Kopf, D. *The Brahmo Samāj and the Shaping of the Modern Indian Mind*. Princeton: Princeton University Press, 1979.
Kosambi, D. D. *An Introduction to the Study of Indian History*. Bombay: Popular Book Depot, 1956.
—— *Myth and Reality: A Study in the Foundations of Indian Culture*. Bombay: Popular Prakashan, 1961.
Kramrish, S. *The Art of India: Traditions of Indian Sculpture, Painting and Architecture*. London: Phaidon, 1954.
—— *The Hindu Temple*, 2 vols. Calcutta: University of Calcutta 1946; reprint Delhi: Motilal Banarsidass, 1977.
—— *The Presence of Śiva*. Princeton, NJ: Princeton University Press, 1981.
Krishnamurti, J. *The Awakening of Intelligence*. New York: Avon Books, 1976.
—— *The First and Last Freedom*. London: Victor Gollancz, 1967 [1954].
Kṛṣṇakarṇāmṛta of Līlāsūka. M. A. Acharya, ed. and trans. Madras: V. Ramaswamy Sastrulu, 1958.
Kumari, V., trans. *The Nīlamata Purāṇa*, Srinagar: J & K Academy of Art, Culture and Language, 1968.
Lal, B. B. "The Indus Script: Some Observations Based on Archaeology." In *JRAS*, 1975, no. 2: 173–209.
—— "Reading the Indus Script." In *IFR* (April 15, 1983): 33–36.
Lal, C. *Hindu America*. Bombay: Bharatiya Vidya Bhavan, 1961.
Lal, K. *Holy Cities of India*. Delhi: Asia Press, 1961.
Lamb, B. P. *India: A World in Transition*. New York: Praeger, 1968 (3rd edn).
Lannoy, R. *The Speaking Tree*. Oxford: Oxford University Press, 1971.
Larson, G. J. *Classical Sāṁkhya*. Delhi: Motilal Banarsidass, 1969 (2nd edn).
Latham, R. E., trans. *The Travels of Marco Polo*. Harmondsworth: Penguin, 1958.
Laws of Manu, G. Bühler, trans. In *SBE*, vol. 25.
Legget, T. (trans.). *The Complete Commentary by Śaṅkara on the Yoga Sutras: A Full Translation of the Newly Discovered Text*. London: Kegan Paul, 1990.
Leifer, W. *Indien und die Deutschen: 500 Jahre Begegnung und Partnerschaft*. Tübingen and Basel: Horst Erdmann Verlag, 1969.
Lele, J. (ed.). *Tradition and Modernity in Bhakti Movements*. Leiden: Brill, 1981.
Lipner, J. *The Face of God*. Albany: SUNY Press, 1986.
—— *Hindus. Their Religious Beliefs and Practices*. London: Routledge, 1994.
Lorenzen, D. N. *The Kapālikas and Kālamukhas: Two Lost Śaivite Sects*. Berkeley: University of California Press, 1972.
—— "The Life of Śaṅkarācārya." In *Experiencing Śiva*, F. Clothey and J. B. Long, eds. Columbia, MO: South Asia Books, 1983.
—— (ed.). *Bhakti Religion in North India: Community Identity and Political Action*, Albany: State University of New York Press, 1995.
Lupsa, Michele. *Chants à Kālī de Rāmprasād*. Pondicherry: Institute Français d'Indologie, 1967.
Macdonnell, A. A. *A History of Sanskrit Literature*. Reprint Delhi: Motilal Banarsidass, 1961 (2nd edn).

—— *Vedic Mythology*. Reprint Varanasi: Indological Bookhouse, 1963.
—— "Vedic Religion." In *Encyclopedia of Religion and Ethics*. E. Hastings, ed. 1954 (3rd edn), vol. 12, 601–618.
Macnicol, N. *Indian Theism*. London: Oxford University Press, 1915.
—— *Psalms of the Maratha Saints*, Heritage of India Series. Calcutta: Association Press, 1919.
Madan, T. N., ed. *Way of Life. King, Householder, Renouncer. Essays in honor of Louis Dumont*. Delhi: Vikas Publishing House, 1982.
—— "Secularism in Its Place." In *JAS* 64 (1987), no. 4: 747–759.
Mahābhārata (short summary), C. Rajagopalachari, ed. Bombay: Bharatiya Vidya Bhavan, 1958.
Mahābhārata, P. C. Roy, trans. Calcutta: 1884–96 (several reprints: Calcutta Oriental without date).
Mahābhārata, Books 1–5. J. A. B. van Buitenen, trans. 3 vols. Chicago: Chicago University Press, 1973–78.
Mahadevan, T. M. P. *Outline of Hinduism*. Bombay: Cetana, 1960 (2nd edn).
—— *Ramana Maharsi and His Philosophy of Existence*. Annamalai: 1951.
—— *The Sage of Kanchi*. Secunderabad, 1967.
—— "Śaivism." In *HCIP*, vol. 2, 433ff.
—— *Ten Saints of India*. Bombay: Bharatiya Vidya Bhavan, 1961.
——, ed. and trans. *Hymns of Śaṅkara*. Madras: 1970.
Mahadevananda, Swami, trans. *Devotional Songs of Narsi Mehta*. Delhi: Motilal Banarsidass, 1985.
Maitra, S. *An Introduction to the Philosophy of Sri Aurobindo*. Benares: Benares Hindu University, 1945 (2nd edn).
Majumdar, A. K. *Caitanya: His Life and Doctrine*. Bombay: Bharatiya Vidya Bhavan, 1969.
Majumdar, J. K. *Raja Rammohan Roy and Progressive Movements in India, volume I. A Selection from Records (1774–1845)*. Calcutta: Brahmo Mission Press, n.d.
Majumdar, R. C. *The Classical Accounts of India*. Calcutta: Firma K.L. Mukhopadhyay, 1960.
—— *Hindu Colonies in the Far East*. Calcutta: Firma K.L. Mukhopadhyay, 1963 (2nd edn).
——, general ed. *The History and Culture of the Indian People*. Bombay: Bharatiya Vidya Bhavan, 1945–78.
Majumdar, R. C., H. C. Raychaudhuri, and K. Datta. *An Advanced History of India*. London: Macmillan, 1965 (3rd edn).
Mānameyodaya, C. Kunhan Raja, trans. Adyar: Theosophical Publishing House, 1933.
Mānava Dharma Śāstra, J. Jolly, trans. London: 1887.
Mānava Śrauta Sūtra, J. M. van Gelder, trans. New Delhi: International Academy of Indian Culture, 1963.
Māṇḍukyopaniṣad with Gauḍapāda's Kārikā and Śaṅkara's Commentary, Swami Nihkilananda, trans. Mysore: Ramakrishna Math, 1955 (4th edn).
Maṇikana, A Nāvya-Nyāya Manual, E. R. Sreekrishna Sarma, ed. and trans. Adyar: Adyar Library, 1960.

Marfatia, M. I. *The Philosophy of Vallabhācārya*. Delhi: Munshiram Manoharlal, 1967.

Mārkaṇḍeya Purāṇa. F. E. Pargiter, trans., reprint Delhi: Indological Book House, 1969.

Marshall, J. *Mohenjo Daro and the Indus Civilization*. 3 vols. London: University of Oxford Press, 1931.

Marshall, P. J. ed. *The British Discovery of Hinduism in the Eighteenth Century*, European Understanding of India Series. Cambridge: 1971.

Mate, M. S. *Temples and Legends of Maharastra*. Bombay: Bharatiya Vidya Bhavan, 1962.

McDowall, A., and A. Sharma, eds. *Vignettes of Vrindaban*. New Delhi: Books & Books, 1987.

Meenaksisundaram, T. P. *A History of Tamil Literature*. Annamalainagar: Annamalai University, 1965.

Mehendale, M. A. "Puranas." In *HCIP*, vol. 3: 291–299.

Meister, M. W. "Hindu Temples." In *Encyclopedia of Religion*, M. Eliade, ed., vol. 10: 368–73.

—— (ed.). *Encyclopedia of Indian Temple Architecture*, vol.1: South India. New Delhi: American Institute of Indian Studies, 1983.

—— (ed.). *Discourses on Śiva*. Philadelphia: University of Pennsylvania Press, 1984.

Menon, I. K. K. "Kerala's Early Foreign Contacts." In *IFR* (July 15, 1980): 13f.

Miller, D. M., and Dorothy C. Wertz. *Hindu Monastic Life: The Monks and Monasteries of Bhubaneswar*. Montreal: McGill–Queen's University Press, 1976.

Mīmāṃsāparibhāṣa of Kṛṣṇa Yajvan, Swami Madhavanand, ed. and trans. Belur Math: The Ramakrishna Mission Sarada Pitha, 1948.

Minor Lawbooks, J. Jolly, trans. In *SBE*, vol. 33.

Minor, R., ed. *Modern Indian Interpretations of the Bhagavadgītā*. Albany: State University of New York Press, 1986.

Misra, Om Prakash. *Mother Goddess in Central India*. Delhi: Agam Kala Prakashan, 1985.

Mitra, A. M. *India as Seen in the Bṛhatsaṃhitā of Vārahamīhira*. Delhi: Motilal Banarsidass, n.d.

Mollat, M. "The Importance of Maritime Traffic to Cultural Contacts in the Indian Ocean." In *Diogenes* 3 (1980): 1–18.

Möller, V. *Götter und Mythen des indischen Subkontinents*, vol. 5 of H. W. Haussig (ed.), *Wörterbuch der Mythologie*. Stuttgart: Klett-Cotta, 1972.

Mookerjee, A., and M. Khanna. *The Tantric Way: Art – Science – Ritual*. London: Thames & Hudson, 1977.

Morinis, E.A. *Pilgrimage in the Hindu Tradition: A Case Study of West Bengal*, South Asian Studies Series. New York and New Delhi: Oxford University Press, 1984.

Müller, M. *The Six Systems of Indian Philosophy*. Reprint Varanasi: Chowkhamba, 1962.

Mundaden, A. M. *St. Thomas Christians and the Portuguese*. Bangalore: Dharmaram Studies, 1970.

—— *The Traditions of St. Thomas Christians*. Bangalore: Dharmaram Studies, 1972.
Naiṣkārmyasiddhi, K. K. Venkatachari, ed. and trans. Adyar: Adyar Library, 1982.
Nakamura, H. "Indian Studies in Japan." In *Indian Studies Abroad*. New York: Asia, 1964.
Nālādiyār, G. U. Pope, trans. Oxford: Oxford University Press, 1893.
Nandimath, S. C. *Handbook of Vīraśaivism*. Dharwar: L.E. Association, 1941.
Nārada Bhakti Sūtras: Aphorisms on the Gospel of Divine Love, Swami Tyagisananda, trans. Mylapore: Ramakrishna Math, 1955 (3rd edn).
Narain, A. K. and T. N. Roy, *Excavations at Rājghāt: 1957–58; 1960–65*. Varanasi: Banaras Hindu University, 1976.
Neevel, Walter G., Jr. *Yamuna's Vedānta and Pāñcarātra: Integrating the Classical and the Popular*. Chico: Scholars Press, 1977.
Neill, S. *A History of Christianity in India: The Beginnings to* AD *1707*. Cambridge: Cambridge University Press, 1984.
Neog, M. *Early History of the Vaiṣṇava Faith and Movement in Assam: Śaṅkaradeva and His Time*. Delhi: Motilal Banarsidass, 1985 (2nd edn).
Neuman, E. *An Analysis of the Archetype The Great Mother*, R. Manheim, trans. Princeton: Bollingen, 1955.
Neumayer, E. *Prehistoric India Rock Paintings*. Delhi: Oxford University Press, 1983.
Swami Nikhilananda, trans. *Gospel of Sri Ramakrishna*. Calcutta: 1930.
Nimbārka. Vedānta Parijāta Saurabha and Vedānta Kausthubha of Śrīnivāsa, R. Bose, trans. 3 vols. Calcutta: Royal Asiatic Society of Bengal, 1940–43.
Nooten, B. A. van. *The Mahābhārata*. New York: 1971.
O'Flaherty, W. D. *Śiva: The Erotic Ascetic*. New York: Oxford University Press, 1981.
Olivelle, P., ed. and trans. *Vasudevāśrama's Yātidharmaprakāśa. A Treatise on World Renunciation*, 2 vols. Vienna: De Nobili Library, 1977.
—— *Renunciation in Hinduism: A Mediaeval Debate*, 2 vols. Vienna: Institute of Indology University of Vienna, 1986–7.
O'Malley, L. S. *Popular Hinduism: The Religion of the Masses*. Oxford: Oxford University Press, 1941.
Oman, I. C. *The Mystics, Ascetics and Saints of India*. Reprint Delhi: Oriental Publishers, 1973.
Osborne, A. *Ramana Maharshi and the Path of Self-Knowledge*. Bombay: Jaico, 1962 (2nd edn).
—— ed. *The Collected Works of Ramana Maharshi*. New York: S. Weiser, 1959.
Pañcadaśī of Vidyāraṇya, Swami Swahananda, ed. and trans. Madras: Ramakrishna Math, 1967.
Pañcaviṃśa Brāhmaṇa, W. Caland, trans. Calcutta: Asiatic Society of Bengal, 1931.
Pandeya, L. P. *Sun Worship in Ancient India*. Delhi: Motilal Banarsidass, 1972.
Panikkar, K. M. *Asia and Western Dominance*. London: Allen & Unwin, 1955 (3rd edn).

—— *Geographical Factors in Indian History*. Bombay: Bharatiya Vidya Bhavan, 1955.
—— *Hindu Society at Cross Roads*. Bombay: Asia Publishing House, 1956.
—— *Hinduism and the Modern World*. Bombay: Bharatiya Vidya Bhavan, 1956.
Pāṇini's Aṣṭādhyayī, Srisa Candra Vasu, ed. and trans. 2 vols. Reprint Delhi: Motilal Banarsidass, 1961.
Paranjoti, *Śaiva Siddhānta*. London: Luzac, 1954 (2nd edn).
Parekh, M. C. *Brahmarshi Keshub Chander Sen*. Rajkot: Bhagavat Dharma Mission, 1926.
—— *The Brahma Samāj*. Calcutta: Brahma Samaj, 1922.
—— *Śrī Swāmi Nārāyaṇa*. Rajkot: Bhagavat Dharma Mission, 1936.
—— *Vallabhācārya*. Rajkot: Bhagavat Dharma Mission, 1936.
Pargiter, F. E. *Ancient Indian Historical Tradition*. Reprint Delhi: Motilal Banarsidass, 1962.
—— *The Purāṇa Texts of the Dynasties of the Kali Age*. Oxford: Oxford University Press, 1913.
Parpola, A. *The Sky Garment: A Study of the Harappan Religion and the Relation to the Mesopotamian and later Indian Religions*. Helsinki: Finnish Oriental Society, 1985.
—— *Deciphering the Indus Script*. Cambridge University Press: New York, 1994.
Parry, J. P. *Death in Banāras*. Cambridge University Press: Cambridge, 1994.
Patañjali's Yogasūtra, Swami Vijnana Asrama, ed. and trans. Ajmer: Sri Madanlal Laksminivas Chandak, 1961.
Pathak, P. V. "Tectonic Upheavals in the Indus Region and Some Rgvedic Hymns." In *ABORI* 64 (1983): 227–232.
Payne, A. A. *The Śāktas*. Calcutta: YMCA Publishing House, 1933.
Piggott, S. *Prehistoric India*. Baltimore: Penguin Books, 1961.
Pillai, G. S. *Introduction and History of Śaiva Siddhānta*. Annamalai: Annamalai University, 1948.
Pillai, K. K. *A Social History of the Tamils*, vol. 1. Madras: University of Madras, 1973 (2nd edn).
Pillai, S. Satchidanandam. "The Śaiva Saints of South India." In *CHI* vol. 4, 339ff.
Possehl, G. C. (ed.) *Harappan Civilisation: A Contemporary Perspective*. Warminster: Aris & Philips, 1982.
Powell-Price, J. C. *A History of India*. London: T. Nelson, 1955.
Prabhupada, A. C. Bhaktivedanta Swami. *Sri Caitanya-Caritāmṛta of Kṛṣṇadāsa Kavirāja Gosvāmi*. New York: Bhaktivedanta Book Trust, 1975.
Prasad, Modhi. *Kaka Kalelkar: A Gandhian Patriarch*. Bombay: Popular Prakashan, 1965.
Pratyabhijñāhṛdayam, Jaideva Singh, ed. and trans. Delhi: Motilal Banarsidass, 1963.
Presler, F. A. "The Structure and Consequences of Temple Policy in Tamilnadu, 1967–81." In *Pacific Affairs* (Summer 1983): 232–246.
Pusalker, A. D. "Āryan Settlements in India." In *HCIP*, vol. 1, 245–267.

—— "Historical Traditions." In *HCIP*, vol. 1, 271–336.
—— "Historicity of Kṛṣṇa." In *Studies in Epics and Puranas of India*. Bombay: Bharatiya Vidya Bhavan, 1955, 49–81.
—— "The Indus Valley Civilization." In *HCIP*, vol. 1, 172–202.
—— "The *Mahābhārata*: Its History and Character." In *CHI*, 2, 51ff.
—— "The *Rāmāyaṇa*: Its History and Character." In *CHI*, 2, 14ff.
—— "Traditional History from the Earliest Time to the Accession of Parikshit." In *The Vedic Age, HCIP*, vol. 1, 271–322.
Putnam, John J. "The Ganges, River of Faith" with photography by Raghubir Singh. *National Geographic Magazine* (October 1971): 445–483.
Radhakrishnan, S. *Eastern Religions and Western Thought*. New York: Oxford University Press, 1964.
—— *The Hindu View of Life*. New York: Macmillan, 1962.
—— *Indian Philosophy*, 2 vols. London: Allen & Unwin, 1948 (2nd edn).
—— *My Search for Truth*. Agra: Agrawala, 1946.
Raghavan, V. *The Great Integrators: The Saint Singers of India*. Delhi: Ministry of Information and Broadcasting, 1966.
—— *The Indian Heritage*. Bangalore: Indian Institute of Culture, 1956.
Rai, L. *The Ārya Samāj*. London: Longman, 1915.
Raja, C. Kunhan. "Vedic Culture." In *CHI*, vol. 1, 199–220.
Rajaram, N. S. and D. Frawley. *Vedic Āryans and the Origins of Civilization*, 2nd ed. New Delhi: Voice of India, 1997.
Raju, P. T. *The Philosophical Traditions of India*. London: Allen & Unwin, 1971.
—— *Idealistic Thought of India*. London: Allen & Unwin, 1953.
Ram, S. *Vinoba and his Mission*. Kasi: Akhil Bharata Sarva Seva Sangh, Rajghat, 1962 (3rd edn).
Rāmcaritmānas by Tulsīdās. Gorakhpur, Text and transl. Gita Press, 1968.
Rāmānuja's Vedārthasaṅgraha, S. S. Raghavachar, ed. and trans. Mysore: Ramakrishna Ashrama, 1956.
Rāmānujan, A. K., trans. *Speaking of Śiva*. Harmondsworth: Penguin Books, 1973.
Rāmāyaṇa (brief summary), C. Rajagopalachari, ed. Bombay: Bharatiya Vidya Bhavan, 1962 (4th edn).
The Rāmāyaṇa, M. N. Dutt, trans. 3 vols. Reprint Calcutta: Oriental Publishing Co., 1960.
The Rāmāyaṇa. Engl. transl. Princeton University Press, 1984 ff. Gen. ed. R. Goldmann.
Ramdas, Swami. *God-Experience*. Bombay: Bharatiya Vidya Bhavan, 1963.
Ramesan, R. *Temples and Legends of Andhra Pradesh*. Bombay: Bharatiya Vidya Bhavan, 1962.
Ranade, R. D. *A Constructive Survey of Upaniṣadic Philosophy*. Reprint Bombay: Bharatiya Vidya Bhavan, 1968.
—— *Pathway to God in Hindī Literature*. Bombay: Bharatiya Vidya Bhavan, 1959.
—— *Pathway to God in Kaṇṇada Literature*. Bombay: Bharatiya Vidya Bhavan, 1960.

—— *Pathway to God in Marathi Literature*. Bombay: Bharatiya Vidya Bhavan, 1961.

Rao, H. S. "The Two Babas." In *Illustrated Weekly of India* (November 21, 1965).

Rao, S. R. *The Decipherment of the Indus Script*. Bombay: Asia Publishing House, 1982.

—— "Krishna's Dwarka." In *Indian and Foreign Review* (March 15, 1980): 15–19.

—— *The Lost City of Dwāraka*. Delhi: Motilal Banarsidass, 1999.

Rao, T. A. G. *Elements of Hindu Iconography*, 4 vols. Reprint New York: Paragon, 1968.

Rapson, E. I., general ed. *Cambridge History of India*, 6 vols. Reprint Delhi: S. Chand, 1964.

Renou, L. *Destiny of the Veda in India*. Delhi: Motilal Banarsidass, 1968.

—— *Vedic India*. Calcutta: Sunil Gupta, 1957.

——, and J. Filliozat, eds. *L'Inde Classique*, 2 vols. Paris–Hanoi: Imprimerie Nationale, 1953.

Rice, E. P. *Kanarese Literature*. Calcutta: Association Press, 1921.

Riepe, D. *The Naturalistic Tradition in Indian Thought*. Seattle: University of Washington Press, 1961.

—— *The Philosophy of India and its Impact on American Thought*. Springfield, Il: Charles C. Thomas, 1970.

Robb, Peter. "The Challenge of Gau Mata: British Policy and Religious Change in India, 1880–1916." In *Modern Asian Studies* 20, no. 2 (1986): 285–319.

Rocher, L."The Purāṇas." In *HIL*, vol. 2, 3. Wiesbaden: Harrassowitz, 1982.

Roy, D. K., and J. Devi. *Kumbha: India's Ageless Festival*. Bombay: Bharatiya Vidya Bhavan, 1955.

Roy, S. B. "Chronological Framework of Indian Protohistory – The Lower Limit." In *JBOI* 32, nos. 3–4 (March–June 1983): 254–274.

Rudolph, L. I., and S. H. Rudolph. *The Modernity of Tradition*. Chicago: Chicago University Press, 1967.

Ruhela, S. P., and D. Robinson, eds. *Sai Baba and His Message*. Delhi: Vikas, 1976.

Śābarabhāṣya. Engl. trans. in 3 vols.; G. Jha, Baroda: Oriental Institute, 1981.

Sachau, Edward C., trans. *Alberuni's India* Trübner's Oriental Series. Reprint Delhi, 1964.

Sai Baba (Sri Sathya). *Satya Sai Speaks*, 7 vols. Kadugodi: Sri Sathya Sai Education and Publication Foundation, 1972–76.

Sakare, M. R. *History and Philosophy of the Lingayata Religion*. Belgaum: Publ. by the author, 1942.

Śākta, Vaiṣṇava, Yoga, Śaiva, Samānyavedānta, and Minor Upaniṣads. P. Mahadev Sastri, ed. and trans. Adyar: Adyar Library, 1912–1938 (reprints).

Saletore, B. A. *Ancient Indian Political Thought and Institutions*. Bombay: Asia Publishing House, 1963.

Salomon, R., ed. and trans. *The Bridge to the Three Holy Cities, The Samayana-Praghaittaka of Nārāyaṇa Bhaṭṭ's Tristhalīsetu*. Delhi: Motilal Banarsidass, 1985.

Sāmaveda, R. T. H. Griffith, trans., Varanasi: Chowkhamba, 1963.
Sāṁkhyakārikā, S. S. Suryanarayana Sastri, trans. Madras: University of Madras, 1948 (4th edn).
Sankalia, H. D. *Indian Archeology Today*. New York: Asia Publishing House, 1962.
—— "Paleolithic, Neolithic and Copper Ages." In *HCIP*, vol. 1, 125–142.
—— *Prehistoric Art in India*. Delhi: Vikas Publishing House, 1978.
—— *Prehistory and Protohistory in India and Pakistan*. Bombay: University of Bombay, 1961.
Śaṅkarabhāṣya, Swami Gambhirananda, trans. Calcutta: Advaita Ashrama, 1965.
Śaṅkarananda, Swami. *Hindu States of Sumeria*. Calcutta: Firma K.L. Mukhopadhyay, 1962.
Sankaranarayan, P. *The Call of the Jagadguru*. Madras: Akhila Bharata Sankara Seva Samiti, 1958.
Saṅkhāyana Śrautasūtra, S. W. Caland, trans. Nagpur: The International Academy of Indian Culture, 1953.
Santucci, J. A. *An Outline of Vedic Literature*. Missoula: Scholars Press, 1977.
Saraswati, Dayananda. *Satyārtha Prakāśa*. Allahabad: Kal Press, 1947.
Sarkar, S. *The Aboriginal Races of India*. Calcutta: Bookland, 1954.
Sarma, N. S. *Hindu Renaissance*. Benares: 1944.
Sarvadarśanasaṁgraha of Mādhava, E. B. Cowell and A. E. Gough, trans. (incomplete), 1892; reprint Varanasi: Chowkhamba, 1960.
Sastri, K. A. Nilakantha. *The Colas*, 3 vols. Madras: University of Madras, 1935.
—— *The Culture and History of the Tamils*. Calcutta: Firma K.L. Mukhopadhyay, 1964.
—— *History of South India*. Madras: Oxford University Press, 1955.
Sastri, K. S. Ramaswami. *Sivananda: The Modern World Prophet*. Rishikesh: Divine Light Society, 1953.
Sastry, R. A., trans. *Viṣṇusahasranāma: With the Bhāṣya of Śrī Śaṁkarācārya*. Adyar Library General Series. Adyar: Adyar Library and Research Centre, 1980.
Śatapatha Brāhmaṇa, J. Eggeling, trans., 5 vols. *SBE*, vols. 12, 26, 41, 43 and 44.
Savarkar, V. "Essentials of Hindutva." In *Samagra Savarkar Wangmaya, Hindu Rastra Darshan*, vol. 6. Poona: Maharashtra Prantik Hindusabha, 1964.
Scharfe, H. *The State in Indian Tradition*. Leiden: Brill, 1989.
Schilpp, P. A., ed. *The Philosophy of Sarvepalli Radhakrishnan*. New York: Tudor Publishing Co., 1952.
Schomer, K. and McLeod, W. H. eds. *The Saints: Studies in a Devotional Tradition of India*. Delhi–Varanasi–Patna–Madras: Motilal Banarsidass, 1987.
Schrader, F. O. *Introduction to the Pāñcarātra and the Ahirbudhnya Saṃhitā*. Adyar: Adyar Library and Research Centre, 1916.
Schwab, J. *Europe's Rediscovery of India and the East, 1680–1880*, G. Patterson-Black and V. Reinking, trans. New York: Columbia University Press, 1984.
Schwartzberg, J. E. ed. *Historical Atlas of India*. Chicago: University of Chicago Press, 1978; 1990 (2nd rev. edn).
Seal, A. *The Emergence of Indian Nationalism*. Cambridge, 1968.

Seal, B. N. *Comparative Studies in Vaishnavism and Christianity* Calcutta: Private publication, 1899.
Seidenberg, A. "The Geometry of the Vedic Rituals." In F. Staal (ed.), *Agni: The Vedic Ritual of the Fire Altar.* Berkely: Asian Humanities Press, 1983, 150–171.
Sengupta, P. C. *Ancient Indian Chronology.* Calcutta: University of Calcutta, 1941.
Sharma, Arvind. *The Hindu Gītā: Ancient and Classical Interpretations of the Bhagavadgītā.* Lasalle: Open Court, 1986.
—— *Hinduism for Our Times*, Delhi: Oxford University Press, 1996.
Sharma, B. N. K. *A History of Dvaita School of Vedānta and its Literature*, 2 vols. Bombay: Booksellers Publishing Co., 1960–1961.
—— *Madhva's Teaching in His Own Words.* Bombay: Bhavan's Book University, 1961.
—— *Philosophy of Śrī Madhvācārya.* Bombay: Bharatiya Vidya Bhavan, 1962.
Sharma, R. K., ed. *Indian Archeology. New Perspectives.* Delhi: Agam Kala Prakashan, 1982.
Sharma, R. S. *Śūdras in Ancient India.* Delhi: Motilal Banarsidass, 1958.
Sharma, S. R. *Swami Rama Tirtha.* Bombay: Vidya Bhavan, 1961.
Shastri, A. M. *India as Seen in the Bṛhatsaṃhitā of Varāhamīhira.* Delhi: Motilal Banarsidass, 1969.
Shastri, D. R. *Short History of Indian Materialism.* Calcutta: The Book Company, 1930.
Shendge, M. J. *The Civilized Demons: The Harappans in Ṛgveda.* New Delhi: Abhinav, 1977.
Sheth, Noel. *The Divinity of Krishna.* Delhi: Munshiram Manoharlal Publishers, 1984.
Shinn, L. D. *The Dark Lord: Cult Images and the Hare Krishnas in America.* Philadelphia: Westminster, 1987.
Shulman, D. D. *Tamil Temple Myths: Sacrifice and Divine Marriage in the South Indian Śaiva Tradition.* Princeton: Princeton University Press, 1980.
Singer, M. ed. *Krishna: Myths, Rites and Attitudes.* Chicago: University of Chicago Press, 1969.
Singh, N. K. "Anand Marg." In *Seminar* 151 (March 1972): 21–25.
Singh, S. *Vedāntadeśika.* Varanasi: Chowkhamba, 1958.
Sinha, J. *History of Indian Philosophy*, 2 vols. Calcutta: Sinha Publishing House, 1956–61.
—— *Indian Psychology*, 2 vols. Calcutta: Sinha Publishing House, 1958–60.
—— *Indian Realism.* London: K. Paul, French, Trübner & Co., 1938.
Singhal, D. P. "Naturalism and Science in Ancient India." In *India and World Civilisations*, vol. 1, 1969.
Sinha, P. N. *A Study of the Bhāgavata Purāṇa.* Madras: Theosophical Society, 1950 (2nd edn).
Sirkar, D.C. *The Śākta Pīṭhas*, rev. ed. Delhi: Motilal Banarsidass, 1948.
—— "Viṣṇu." *Quarterly Journal of the Mythological Society* 25 (1935): 120ff.
Sivapadasundaram, S. *The Śaivaschool of Hinduism.* London: Allen & Unwin, 1934.

Śiva-Purāṇa. Benares: Pandit Pustakalaya, 1962; J. L. Shastri, trans. 4 vols. Delhi: Motilal Banarsidass, 1970–71.

Sivaraman, K. *Śaivism in Philosophical Perspective*. Delhi: Motilal Banarsidass, 1973.

—— "Śaiva Siddhānta and Religious Pluralism" in H. G. Coward (ed.) *Modern Indian Responses to Religious Pluralism*, Albany: State University of New York Press, 1987, 151–170.

Śivasaṃhitā, S. C. Vasu, trans. Allahabad: Panini Office, 1923.

Sivaya Subramuniyaswami. *Living with Śiva: Hinduism's Nandinātha Sūtras*. California, Hawaii: Himalayan Academy, 1991.

—— *Dancing with Śiva: A Hindu Catechism*. California, Hawaii: Himalayan Academy, 1990.

Ślokavārtika of Kumārila Bhaṭṭa, trans. Ganganatha Jha. Calcutta: Asiatic Society, 1907.

Smith, D. E. *India as a Secular State*. Princeton: Princeton University Press, 1967.

Smith, V. *History of India*. Oxford: Oxford University Press, 1955.

Smith, W. C. *Modern Islam in India*. Lahore: Mohammed Ashraf, 1963 (3rd edn).

Srinivasacari, P. *The Philosophy of Viśiṣṭādvaita*. Adyar: Theosophical Society, 1946.

Srinivasan, D. "Unhinging Śiva from the Indus Civilization." *JRAS* 1 (1984): 77–89.

Srinivasan, D. M. (ed.) *Mathurā: The Cultural Heritage*. New Delhi: American Institute of Indian Studies, 1989.

Śrī Parameśvara Saṃhitā, Sri Govindacarya, ed. Srirangam: Kodandaramasannidhi, 1953.

Śrīpati's Śrīkara Bhāṣya, Hayavadana Rao, ed. Bangalore: 1936.

Staal, J. F. *AGNI: The Vedic Ritual of the Fire Altar*, 2 vols. Berkeley: University of California Press, 1983.

von Stietencron, H. *Gaṅgā und Yamunā*. Wiesbaden: Harrassowitz, 1972.

—— *Indische Sonnenpriester: Śamba und die Śakasdispiya Brāhmaṇa*. Wiesbaden: Harrassowitz, 1966.

Stoler-Miller, B. *Love Song of the Dark Lord*. New York: Columbia University Press, 1977.

—— "Rādhā: Consort of Kṛṣṇa's Vernal Passion." *JAOS* 95, no. 4 (1975): 655–71.

Strabo. *Geography*, Bilingual edition in the Loeb Classical Library series, English translation by H. L. Jones.

Strickman, M., ed. *Classical Asian Rituals and the Theory of Ritual*. Berlin: Springer, 1986.

Śukra Nītisāra, B. K. Sarkar. trans. Allahabad: Panini Office, 1923 (2nd edn).

Sukthankar, V. S. *On the Meaning of the Mahābhārata*. Bombay: Asiatic Society, 1957.

Sukul, K. S., *Vārāṇasī Down the Ages*. Patna, 1974.

Tagore, R. *Sādhana*. Calcutta: Macmillan, 1950.

—— *Creative Unity*. Calcutta: Macmillan, 1959.

Taimni, I. K. *The Science of Yoga*. Wheaton: Theosophical Publishing House, 1972 (3rd edn).

Talageri. S. G. *The Āryan Invasion Theory and Indian Nationalism*, New Delhi: Voice of India, 1993.

Taposwami Maharaj, Swami. *Wanderings in the Himālayas*. Madras: Ganesh, 1960.

Tarkabhāṣa of Keśava Miśra, G. Jha, ed. and trans. Poona: Oriental Book Agency, 1949 (2nd edn).

Tarn, W. W. *The Greeks in Bactria and India*. Cambridge: Cambridge University Press, 1951; reprint 1966.

Tendulkar, D. G. *Mahatma: Life and Work of M. K. Gandhi*, 8 vols. Bombay: V.K. Jhaveri, 1951–1958.

Thapar, R. *A History of India*. Baltimore: Penguin, 2 vols. 1966.

—— *India in Transition*. Bombay: Asia Publishing House, 1956.

Thompson, E. J. and A. M. Spencer. *Bengali Religious Lyrics, Śākta*. Calcutta: Association Press, 1923.

Thurston, E. and K. Rangachari. *Tribes and Castes of South India*, 4 vols. Madras: Government Press, 1929.

Tilak, B. G. *The Arctic Home in the Vedas*. Reprint Poona: Tilak Bros., 1956.

—— *Gītā Rahasya*, 2 vols. Reprint Poona: Tilak Bros., 1956.

—— *Orion or Researches into the Antiquity of the Veda*. Bombay: Sagoon, 1893. Reprint Poona: Tilak Bros., 1955.

—— *Vedic Chronology*. Poona: 1909.

Timberg, T. A., ed. *Jews in India*. New York: Advent Books, 1986.

Timm, J. R. "Vallabha, Vaiṣṇavism and the Western Hegemony of Indian Thought." *Journal of Dharma* 14 (1989), no. 1:6–36.

Tirtha, Swami Bharati Krishna. *Sanātana Dharma*. Bombay: Bharatiya Vidya Bhavan, 1964.

The Tirukkural. G. U. Pope, W. H. Drew, J. Lazarus and F. W. Ellis, trans. Tinnelvelly: South India Saiva Siddhanta Works Publishing Society, 1962.

Tiruvācagam. G. U. Pope, ed. and trans. 1900; reprint Madras: University of Madras, 1970.

Tod, J. *Annals and Antiquities of Rajasthan*, William Crooke, ed., 3 vols. Delhi: Motilal Banarsidass, n.d.

Tripurā Rahasya. A. U. Vasavada, trans. Varanasi: Chowkhamba, 1965.

Tyagisananda, Swami, ed. *Aphorismms on the Gospel of Divine Love or Nārada Bhaktisūtras*. Madras: Ramakrishna Math, 1972 (5th edn).

Upadeśasahasrī of Śaṅkarācārya, Swami Jagadananda, ed. and trans. Madras: Ramakrishna Math, 1962 (3rd edn).

Vadāvalī of Nāgoji Bhaṭṭa, Nagaraja Rao, ed. and trans. Adyar: Adyar Library, 1943.

Vaidyanathan, K. R. *Sri Krishna, the Lord of Guruvayur*. Bombay: Bharatiya Vidya Bhavan, 1974.

Vaiśeṣikardarśana. Anantalal Thakur, ed. and trans. Darbhanga: Mithila Institute, 1957.

Vaiśesikasūtras of Kaṇāda. N. Sinha, trans. Allahabad: Panini Office, 1911.

Varma, K. C. "The Iron Age, the Veda and the Historical Urbanization." In *Indian Archeology, New Perspectives*, R. K. Sharma, ed. New Delhi: Indian Archeological Survey, 1982, 155–183.

Varma, L. A. Ravi, "Rituals of Worship." In *CHI*, vol. 4, 445–63.
Varma, V. P. *Modern Indian Political Thought*. Agra: Laksmi Narain Agarwala, 1968 (4th edn).
Vasudevāśrama: Yatidharmaprakāśa. A Treatise on World Renunciation. P. Olivelle, ed. and transl., 2 vols. Vienna: De Nobili Research Library, 1977.
Vatsyayan, Kapila. "Prehistoric Paintings," *Sangeet Natak, Journal of the Sangeet Natak Akademi* 66, (October–December): 5–18.
Vedāntakarikāvalī of Venkatācārya. V. Krisnamacarya, ed. and trans. Adyar: Adyar Library, 1950.
Vedāntaparibhāṣa by Dharmaraja. S. S. Suryanarayana Sastri, ed. and trans. Adyar: Adyar Library, 1942.
Vedāntasāra of Sādānanda Yogīndra. Swami Nikhilananda, ed. and trans. Calcutta: Ramakrishna Math, 1959 (4th edn).
Vedāntasūtras with the Commentary of Baladeva. S. C. Vasu Vidyaranava, trans. *SBH*. Allahabad: Panini Office, 1934 (2nd edn).
Vedāntasūtras with the Commentary of Madhva. S. S. Rao, trans. Tirupati: Sri Vyasa Press, 1936 (2nd edn).
Vedāntasutras with Rāmānuja's Commentary. G. Thibaut, trans. In *SBE*, vol. 48.
Vedāntasūtras with Śaṅkarācārya's Commentary. G. Thibaut, trans., 2 vols. In *SBE*, vols. 34 and 38.
Vedārthasaṁgraha of Rāmānuja. S. S. Ragavacar, ed. and trans. Mysore: Ramakrishna Ashrama, 1956.
Vidyabhusana, S. C. *A History of Indian Logic*. Calcutta: University of Calcutta, 1921.
Vidyarthi, L. P. *Aspects of Religion in Indian Society*. Meerut: Vednat Nath Rammath, 1962.
Viṣṇu Purāṇa, H. H. Wilson, trans. Reprint Calcutta: Punthi Pustak, 1961.
Vivekacudāmaṇi of Śaṅkarācārya, Swami Madhavananda, ed. and trans. Calcutta: Ramakrishna Math, 1957 (6th edn).
Vivekananda, Swami. *Complete Works of Swami Vivekananda*, 8 vols. Calcutta: Advaita Ashrama, 1970–1971.
Vyas, S. N. *India in the Rāmāyaṇa Age*. Delhi: Atura Ram & Sons, 1967.
Walker, B. *The Hindu World: An Encyclopedic Survey of Hinduism*, 2 vols. New York: Praeger, 1968.
Waghorne, J. P. (ed.). *Gods of Flesh – Gods of Stone. The Embodiment of Divinity in India*, Chambersburg: Anima, 1985.
Warder, A. K. *Outline of Indian Philosophy*. Delhi: Motilal Banarsidass, 1968.
Welbon, G. R. and G. E. Yocum, eds. *Religious Festivals in South India and Sri Lanka*, Delhi: Manohar, 1985.
Westcott, G. H. *Kabir and the Kabir Panth*. Reprint Calcutta: Susil Gupta, 1953 (2nd edn).
Whaling, F. *The Rise of the Religious Significance of Rāma*. Delhi: Motilal Banarsidass, 1980.
Wheeler, M. *The Indus Civilization*. Cambridge: Cambridge University Press, 1953.
Whicher, I. *The Integrity of the Yoga Darśana. A Reconsideration of Classical Yoga*. Albany: State University of New York Press, 1999.

Whitehead, H. *The Village Gods of South India*, Religious Life of India Series. Calcutta: Association Press, 1921 (2nd edn).

Williams, R. B. *A New Face of Hinduism: The Swaminarayan Religion*. Cambridge: Cambridge University Press, 1984.

Wilson, H. H. *Religious Sects of the Hindus*. 1861; reprint Calcutta: Punthi Pustak, 1958.

Winternitz, M. *A History of Indian Literature*. S. Ketkar and H. Kohn, trans. 3 vols. Reprint Calcutta: University of Calcutta, 1927–67.

Witzel, M. (ed.). *Inside the Texts . . . Beyond the Texts. New Approaches to the Study of the Vedas* (Department of Sanskrit and Indian Studies, Harvard University) Columbia, MO: South Asia Books, 1997.

Woodroffe, J. (Arthur Avalon). *Introduction to Tantra Śāstra*. Madras: Ganesh & Co., 1963 (4th edn).

—— *Mahānirvāṇatantra: The Great Liberation*. Madras: Ganesh & Co., 1963 (4th edn).

—— *Principles of Tantra*. Madras: Ganesh & Co., 1960 (3rd edn).

Woods, J. H., trans. *Patañjali's Yogasūtra, with Vyāsa's Bhāṣya and Vācaspati Miśra's Tattva Vaiśāradī*, Harvard Oriental Series 17. Cambridge, MA: Harvard University Press, 1914.

Yamunacarya, M. *Rāmānuja's Teachings in His Own Words*. Bombay: Bharatiya Vidya Bhavan, 1963.

Yatīndramatadīpikā of Śrīnivāsadāsa. Swami Adidevananda, ed. and trans. Madras: Ramakrishna Math, 1949.

Yocum, G. E. *Hymns to the Dancing Śiva: A Study of Manikkavacakar's Tiruvācakam*. Columbia, Mo.: South Asia Books, 1982.

Yogananda, Paramahamsa. *Autobiography of a Yogi*. Bombay:Jaico, 1960.

Yogavāsiṣṭha Rāmāyaṇa, D. N. Bose, trans. 2 vols. Calcutta: Oriental Publishing Co., 1958.

Young, R. F. *Resistant Hinduism: Sanskrit Sources on Anti-Christian Apologetics in Early Nineteenth-Century India*. Vienna: Indologisches Institut der Universität Wien, 1981.

Zabern, Philipp von, (ed.) *Vergessene Städte am Indus. Frühe Kulturen in Pakistan vom 8.–2. Jahrtausend v. Chr.* Mainz am Rhein: Verlag Philipp von Zabern, 1987.

Zelliot, E. "The Mediaeval Bhakti Movement in History. An Essay on the Literature in English." In *Hinduism: New Essays in the History of Religions*, B. L. Smith, ed. Leiden: Brill, 1976.

Zimmer, H. *The Art of Indian Asia*, 2 vols. New York: Bollingen Foundation, 1955.

—— *Philosophies of India*, J. Campbell, ed. Princeton: Bollingen Foundation, 1951.

Zvelebil, K. *Tiru Murugan*. Madras: International Institute of Tamil Studies, 1982.

—— *The Smile of Murugan: On Tamil Literature of South India*. Leiden: Brill, 1973.

INDEX